# MADNESS IN SOCIETY

# MADNESS IN SOCIETY

Chapters in the Historical Sociology
of Mental Illness

GEORGE ROSEN

*The University of Chicago Press*

*Chicago and London*

The University of Chicago Press, Chicago 60637

ISBN: 0-226-72642-8
LCN: 68-13112

*This volume was prepared for publication
under the editorship of Benjamin Nelson*

# CONTENTS

# ABBREVIATIONS

| | |
|---|---|
| *Allgemeine Zeitschrift für Psychiatrie* | *Allg. Ztschr. Psychiat.* |
| *Archiv für Geschichte der Medizin* | *Arch. Ges. Med.* |
| *Bulletin of the History of Medicine* | *Bull. Hist. Med.* |
| *Virchows Archiv für pathologische Anatomie und Physiologie und für klinische Medizin* | *Virchows Arch. path. Anat.* |

# PREFACE

These studies are concerned with the historical sociology of mental illness, not with the history of psychiatry. Their central focus is not the thought and practice of medical men in dealing with the phenomena of mental disorder as a medical problem, but rather the place of the mentally ill, however defined, in societies at different historical periods and the factors (social, psychological, cultural) that have determined it.

Care of the sick and disabled has been an element of group life throughout recorded history and in all likelihood long before. Moreover, as a social activity such care is interlocked with other elements in the structure of group living of which it is a part, with government, the economy, the family, religion and other elements of life. All human actions must be studied within a framework created by men, and with an understanding of their ideas and their hopes. History derives from challenges experienced by various groups of people, and the ways in which they respond to them. The result is a variety of actions and reactions under different circumstances and in widely divergent ideological climates. Yet those actions and reactions have in one way or another brought us to the present. Institutions, patterns of behaviour, systems of ideas—all have developed from something which was there before. Attitudes towards mental disorders, theories of mental illness, arrangements for the care of the individuals affected—all illustrate this truism which is too often overlooked. Historical analysis makes it possible to penetrate past social structures and their changes so as to illuminate our understanding of the process of development which has led to the present.

The older name of the psychiatrist—the alienist—points to one of the basic aspects of mental disorder, namely, that those designated mentally ill are "foreign," alien to their fellow-men. The recognition of this foreignness, this alienation, its interpretation and the action taken on this basis are the central themes in these studies of mental illness. They approach mental disorder from a broad point of view, considering it basically within a community framework, and taking into account the political, social and administrative patterns and factors that have had some relation to mental illness in different periods of history. These studies examine the recognition of mental illness as a problem in the community, and the circumstances which

A* ix

lead to it; the concepts, ideas and theories which are available for interpreting strange behaviour as mental illness and which provide a basis for community action or inaction; and the development or existence of special institutions and personnel to deal with these matters.

These studies are presented in full awareness that they are not exhaustive, They are examples of a method and a point of view which have not hitherto received the attention they deserve. As such they are simply preparatory to a more comprehensive analysis and understanding of mental disorder as a social phenomenon which in the present still bears a considerable burden from the past.

# CHAPTER ONE

# INTRODUCTION: PSYCHOPATHOLOGY IN THE SOCIAL PROCESS

## THE NATURE OF THE PHENOMENA

On Halloween night, 31 October 1938, the Mercury Theatre and Orson Welles broadcast a radio version of *The War of the Worlds* by H. G. Wells. The purported invasion from Mars was portrayed with such immediacy that a large group of listeners became panic stricken. So urgent was the situation for those most acutely affected that their first thought was to flee or prepare to fight the invading space monsters. It has been estimated that one million people were disturbed by the broadcast. As soon as the responsible authorities became aware of the harrowing reports it did not take long to deal adequately with the Martians.[1]

The story of the "phantom anaesthetist" begins on the first night of September, 1944, when a woman in Mattoon, Illinois, reported to the police that someone had opened her bedroom window and sprayed her with a sickish sweet-smelling gas which partially paralysed her legs and made her ill. Other cases with similar symptoms were reported, and the police undertook to apprehend the elusive "gasser." Some citizens claimed that they heard him pumping his spray gun; others that they had glimpsed him. As the number of cases increased—as many as seven in one night—and the local police began to seem inadequate to cope with the emergency, state police and experts in crime detection were brought in. Before long, the "phantom anaesthetist" was being featured in newspapers all over the United States. After ten days of excitement, however, all the victims had recovered, no substantial clues had been uncovered, the police fell back on "imagination" to explain the reports, and some

---

[1] Hadley Cantril, *The Invasion from Mars: A Study in the Psychology of Panic*, Princeton, Princeton University Press, 1940; Professor Cantril's book has just been reprinted with a new Introduction by the author in the series "Researches in the Social, Cultural, and Behavioural Sciences," ed. by Professor Benjamin Nelson, New York, Harper Torchbooks edition, 1966. A similar situation was created in Quito, Ecuador, by the radio broadcast of a Spanish version of *The War of the Worlds*; see S. H. Britt, ed., *Selected Readings in Social Psychology*, New York, Rinehart, 1950.

newspapers turned up with stories on mass hysteria. The "phantom gasser" was gone and the episode over.[2]

## Phenomena of Interest to Students of Mental Disorder as Related to Social Life

Situations such as the two described above attract attention because they are bizarre and do not occur too frequently. However, to judge by accounts available in the historical, sociological, psychological and psychiatric literature they are common enough to have received attention from a variety of investigators who seek to understand the linkage, or absence of it, between mental disorder and social life.[3] Such episodes have occurred in various settings—in schools, in convents, at revival meetings, in whole towns —and over longer or shorter periods of time. They were described in antiquity, in the Middle Ages, and in succeeding centuries right up to the present.

A variety of terms have been used to designate and to characterize these episodes. Under such labels as psychic epidemics, collective psychoses, mass delusions, crazes, or group psychopathology, have been grouped many different kinds of events and situations. For example, episodes involving groups like those previously mentioned have been lumped together with events and movements involving religious enthusiasts, ascetics and sectarians such as the medieval Flagellants, the Brethren of the Free Spirit, or the Fifth Monarchy Men; with the belief in witchcraft, which took its toll in blood from the waning of the medieval period in Europe to the eighteenth century; with the activities of primitive political groups, the behaviour of mobs, and the occurrence of epidemics of convulsions, dancing and the like. None of the designations is really satisfactory, however, and the same can be said of most descriptive or analytical accounts of such phenomena.

## Difficulty of Conceptualization

While there is a rather extensive literature on such group phenomena, most authors who have endeavoured to comprehend the materials

[2] Douglas M. Johnson, "The 'Phantom Anesthetist' of Mattoon: A Field Study of Mass Hysteria," *Journal of Abnormal and Social Psychology*, 40: 175–186, 1945.

[3] Among recent episodes, see A. S. Schuler and V. J. Parenton, "A Recent Epidemic of Hysteria in a Louisiana High School," *Journal of Social Psychology*, 17: 221–235, 1943; N. H. Medalia and O. N. Larsen, "Diffusion and Belief in a Collective Delusion: The Seattle Windshield Pitting Epidemic," *American Sociological Review*, 23: 180–186, 1958; Leon Festinger, Henry W. Riecken, and Stanley Schachter, *When Prophecy Fails*, Minneapolis, University of Minnesota Press, 1956, New York, Harper Torchbooks edition, 1964.

within some conceptual framework have felt uncomfortable in dealing with them. One of the clearest statements of this kind introduces the chapter by Arieti and Meth on "rare, unclassifiable, collective, and psychotic syndromes" in the *American Handbook of Psychiatry*.[4] "Only after hesitation," they write, "was it decided to include this chapter in the *Handbook*."

> The hesitation stemmed from several factors. First of all, even a preliminary examination of several conditions to be described in this chapter . . . revealed that they cannot be considered psychoses without some reservations and that perhaps they should be more exactly termed "pseudo-psychoses." Other conditions could be included in some already-known categories such as schizophrenia or paranoid states. Original reports of collective psychoses are of historical character and lack clinical standards.[5]

The discomfort and uneasiness arise from the difficulty or inability to conceptualize the phenomena so that they will fit into contemporary categories of mental disorder. From this point of view, the psychiatrist in dealing with such data is often at a loss to determine what is normal and what is abnormal.

Despine, a French psychiatrist of the later nineteenth century, exhibited the same attitude in his discussion of epidemic insanity.

> Epidemics of insanity [he wrote] occur only among healthy people, and they are produced by moral contagion. The neuropathic hysterical state which manifests itself rather frequently in these epidemics is by no means their cause; it is an epiphenomenon which is neither necessary nor constantly present, and which manifests itself only under certain conditions. This hysterical state is the result either of physical, debilitating causes that harm the nervous system, or of an excitation of the system brought about by inflamed feelings and emotions spread by moral contagion. In short, the hysterical state is produced by the influence of the emotions and the mind on the nervous system.[6]

Here, too, there is an uneasy awareness that individual madness and certain deviant forms of group behaviour are somehow not congruent.

A similar situation is found in the article on "mass phenomena"

---

[4] Silvano Arieti and Johannes M. Meth, "Rare, Unclassifiable, Collective, and Exotic Psychotic Syndromes," in *American Handbook of Psychiatry*, ed. by Silvano Arieti, New York, Basic Books, 1959, vol. I, pp. 546–563.

[5] *Op cit.*, p. 546.

[6] Prosper Despine, *De la Folie au point de vue philosophique ou spécialement psychologique étudiée chez le malade et chez l'homme en santé*, Paris, F. Savy, 1875, p. 721.

by Brown in the *Handbook of Social Psychology*.[7] After discussing the primary and secondary dimensions of collectivities, the author states that "Mass phenomena do not ordinarily include group interaction," and that on the next level of size beyond the room-size collectivity "the crowd is a central concept,"[8] The discussion of the crowd deals overwhelmingly with the "active" crowd which is designated the "mob," and various kinds of mobs are considered. This section is followed by one concerned with "collectivities too large to congregate." Here under the heading of "mass contagion" are grouped fads and crazes. The latter are illustrated by the "phantom anaesthetist" of Mattoon (whom we have already met), the Salem witch trials, the tulip mania of seventeenth-century Holland the Florida real estate boom of the 1920s, and the dancing mania of the Middle Ages. According to Brown, such episodes attract the attention of social scientists because of the collective folly exhibited by those who participate in them. It is clear that the author does not quite know what to do with this material, nor does he appear to have investigated any of the illustrative examples. The witch trials, for example, were certainly not mass phenomena that did not include group interaction. As we shall see, this is just what they did include, and it is equally true of the so-called dancing "mania," as well as of other episodes of this kind.

Pathological states of mind have been observed in persons who are participating members of social groups, and episodes have been reported in which disordered behaviour has occurred in larger or smaller groups. The kind of shared psychopathology which has received most attention is that first described by Baillarger in 1857 as *folie communiquée* and later termed *folie à deux* by Lasègue and Falret (1877).[9] Detailed reviews of this problem were given by Carrier in 1903 and Gralnick in 1942.[10] A considered review of the general problem of socially shared psychopathology was made available by Gruenberg in 1957. The value of this paper is based on two principles: (1) to ignore "the issue of determining who is 'really' ill and who only appears to be ill," and "to regard all such episodes [of shared psycho-

[7] Roger W. Brown, "Mass Phenomena," in *Handbook of Social Psychology*, ed. by Gardner Lindzey, Cambridge, Addison-Wesley Publishing Company, 1954, vol. II, pp. 833–873.

[8] *Op cit.*, p. 840.

[9] J. G. F. Baillarger, "Examples de contagion d'un délire monomanique," *Moniteur des Hôpitaux*, 45: 353–354, 1857; C. Lasègue and J. Falret, "La folie à deux ou folie communiqué," *Annales médico-psychologiques*, 38:121–335, 1877.

[10] G. Carrier, "Contribution à l'étude des folies par contagion," *Archives de neurologie*, Série 2, 15, 1903, 129–154; A. Gralnick, "Folie à deux—The Psychosis of Association," *Psychiatric Quarterly*, 16: 230–263, 491–520, 1942; a review of 103 cases.

pathology] as natural phenomena which we wish to understand;" and (2) "to indicate the kinds of psychopathology which occur in situations where the psychopathological is shared by a social group."[11]

The principles stated by Gruenberg can be extended as follows: (1) Most episodes and situations of the kind discussed here are complex phenomena and therefore require examination from multiple viewpoints involving various disciplines (history, sociology, psychology, political science, theology and others); (2) there is a need to examine the data not only in their own terms but also cross-culturally; and (3) it is necessary to specify precisely what is under discussion—the events that transpired, the conditions under which they occurred, and their location in space and time. On this basis, questions such as these can be raised: By what processes do such "epidemics" appear and disappear? What is meant by an epidemic? What is the relationship of individual psychopathology to group behaviour in these situations? Within what social and cultural context did the episode arise? Are there any social values that are being satisfied? How do mass delusions originate? Are there patterns according to which delusions are diffused in a community? And so forth.

### A HISTORICAL APPROACH TO A CONCEPTUAL STRUCTURE

To develop a better understanding of collective psychoses, mass delusions, epidemics of hysteria and related phenomena, and to produce a conceptual structure which will do justice to the complexity of the problem, it is important to investigate such episodes over a span of time ranging from antiquity to the present, and in various parts of the world. In this brief paper, one can only illustrate the approach and point of view through a selected example.

### Witchcraft as an Example

Witchcraft in its relation to mental disorder may serve as the example. Magical beliefs and practices, the existence of spirits, and similar ideas are to be found in every part of the world.[12] Witches and

[11] Ernest M. Gruenberg, "Socially Shared Psychopathology," in *Explorations in Social Psychiatry*, ed. by A. H. Leighton et al., New York, Basic Books, 1957, p. 212.

[12] Some examples of the literature on this subject are: Geoffrey Parrinder, *West African Religion*, London, Epworth Press, 1949, pp. 170–186; S. H. Turney-High, *Chateau-Gérard; The Life and Times of a Walloon Village*, Columbia, University of South Carolina Press, 1953, pp. 224–274; H. W. M. DeJong, *Demonische Ziekten in Babylon en Bijbel*, Leiden, E. F. Brill, 1959.

werewolves were known in pagan antiquity. Sympathetic magic occurs in Theocritus, werewolves are found in Petronius, and anointment and night-flying in Apuleius. Some of the Church fathers such as St. Augustine preserved peasant superstitions such as these, but in general the Church of the Dark Ages tended to regard such matters as old wives' tales, as the rubbish of paganism which the light of the Gospel had dispelled. Demonic possession was acknowledged, but even the Prince of Darkness was dismissible through exorcism.

Consciousness of Satan was not at its height in the Dark Ages. But the twelfth and thirteenth centuries, the period which witnessed the building of the great cathedrals, the rise of the universities, and the flowering of scholastic philosophy, were precisely the years in which awareness of the Devil and his powers was carried to a new and terrifying height.[13] And then towards the end of the medieval period, during the Renaissance and the century of the New Science, all Europe seemed to swarm with witches. By their own confession, thousands of women, mostly old, some men and some children, slipped through windows, chimneys and keyholes and flew off on animals or sticks to worship the Devil at the nocturnal witches' Sabbath. There they worshipped the Devil, sometimes in the form of a man, sometimes as a male animal (most often a goat), to the accompaniment of weird and macabre music, dancing around him, kissing him under the tail, and feasting on such delicacies as suited local and ethnic tastes. Furthermore, those present were alleged to celebrate the Black Mass by practising cannibalism or by parodying and desecrating the Host. Witches were accused of bewitching their neighbours or their neighbours' animals, of causing the death of infants, producing miscarriages, or drying up the milk of cows. They were further accused of producing impotence in a bridegroom, causing blights or raising tempests.[14]

The consequences of such beliefs assumed a dreadful aspect in the waning Middle Ages. For almost three centuries, Europe and its overseas colonies were the scene of organized witch hunts which led to the death of thousands of people by burning, hanging, drowning or other methods. Indeed, it was not until the end of the eighteenth

---

[13] The history of witchcraft, demonology, and related matters is very extensive. Interested readers may turn to: J. Hansen, *Zauberwahn, Inquisition und Hexenprozess im Mittelalter*, München, Oldenbourg, 1900; H. C. Lea, *Materials Toward a History of Witchcraft*, Arranged and ed. by A. C. Howland, 3 vols., Philadelphia University of Pennsylvania Press, 1939.

[14] Henry E. Sigerist, "Impotence as a Result of Witchcraft," in *Essays in Biology: in Honor of Herbert M. Evans*, Berkeley, University of California Press, pp. 541–546; Gerda Hoffmann, "Beiträge zur Lehre von der durch Zauber verursachten Krankheit und ihrer Behandlung in der Medizin des Mittelalters," *Janus*, 37: 129–144, 179–182, 211–220, 1933.

century that the last executions for witchcraft were carried out in Europe. It is worth noting that there were four witch trials in Mexico between 1860 and 1874, and a witch is reported to have been burnt there on 20 August 1877.

## WITCH HUNTING AND THE PLACE OF PSYCHOPATHOLOGY IN THE SOCIAL PROCESS

How had this come about? What made it possible for a large segment of humanity to indulge in the persecution of witches, and then to stop, leaving a rubbish heap of beliefs and practices for dabblers in occultism, black magic, satanism or for simple hinterland practitioners of folk medicine? Numerous contributions to this problem over the past hundred years make it possible to advance an answer, and to indicate the place of psychopathology in the historical and social process.

Witch hunting expresses a dis-ease of society, and is related to a social context. This was as true in Europe over five hundred years ago as it is in Africa of the twentieth century.[15] No explanation of witch hunts can be based on single factors or a simple cause. It is a complex phenomenon, involving political, social, psychological and ideological factors, which appears when a society, or a social group within it, experiences tensions and difficulties under the stress of rapid change. Under such circumstances, fear, uncertainty, suspicion may lead members of the affected group to cast about for some explanation, to find some reason for the situation. Institutions in existence may be altered, or new ones may be created to cope with the new needs, and older ideas may be pulled together in a new form and thus made more powerful and effective to deal with the ills of life.

The consequences of such a process can be seen in Europe from the eleventh into the seventeenth century. There can be no doubt that the Church was largely responsible for the creation of the witchcraft delusion during the later Middle Ages. Although witchcraft and the practice of black magic were punishable during the early Middle Ages, the punishments prescribed by different synods were comparatively light.[16] The Canon Episcopi, which probably dates from

[15] Geoffrey Parrinder, *Witchcraft: A Critical Study of the Belief in Witchcraft from the Records of Witchhunting in Europe Yesterday* and *Africa Today*, Baltimore, Penguin Books, 1958, 123–186. See also E. Evans-Pritchard, *Witchcraft, Oracles and Magic Among the Azande*, Oxford, Clarendon Press, 1937.

[16] J. T. McNeill and H. M. Gamer, *Medieval Handbooks of Penance: A Translation of the Principal Libri Poenitentiales and Selections from Related Documents*, New York, Columbia University Press, 1938, pp. 331–332.

the Carolingian period, considered a belief in night flights by women a delusion brought about by Satan to be fought from the pulpit.[17] However, the practice of witchcraft was prosecuted by the secular authorities because it caused damage to people's persons and property. Cases are recorded of witches condemned to death and executed, but there was no organized campaign.

## The Feeling of Melancholy as a Force

Numerous students of the period have commented on the feeling of melancholy and pessimism which marked the declining Middle Ages. "If one period deserves the name of the 'age of anxiety,' " writes Paul Tillich, "it is the pre-Reformation and Reformation."[18] Stadelmann refers to the "morbid psyche" of the disintegrating medieval period.[19] A general sense of impending doom hung over men and women, aggravated by an obsession that the world was coming to an end.[20] Huizinga describes the "sombre melancholy" that weighed on people's souls. "Whether we read a chronicle," he says, "a poem, a sermon, a legal document even, the same impression of immense sadness is produced by them all. It would sometimes seem as if this period had been particularly unhappy . . ."[21]

Nor was this feeling unjustified. A world was indeed falling apart, and in its midst a new order, of which the outlines could be seen but dimly, was struggling to emerge. The all-absorbing medieval Christian commonwealth, fashioned and guided by the Church of Rome, was wracked by dissension, hatred, violence. The feudal order was giving way to political absolutism and the nation state. Similarly, abuses in the Church led to a desire to return it to its original state, to give it a new birth of life. New social groups of urban origin had arisen. The origins of these developments lie in the changes that feudal Europe experienced in the tenth and succeeding centuries.[22]

---

[17] Joseph Hansen, *Quellen und Untersuchungen zur Geschichte des Hexenwahns, und der Hexenverfolgung in Mittelalter*, Bonn, 1901, pp. 38 ff.

[18] Paul Tillich, *The Courage To Be*, New Haven, Yale University Press, 1952, p. 48.

[19] Rudolph Stadelmann, *Vom Geist des ausgehenden Mittelalters*, Halle-Saale, Max Niemeyer Verlag, 1929, p. 7.

[20] Will-Erich Peuckert, *Die Grosse Wende: Das Apokalyptische Saeculum und Luther*, Hamburg, Classen & Goverts, 1948, pp. 103–106, 148–151, 152–191.

[21] Johan Huizinga, *The Waning of the Middle Ages*, Garden City, Doubleday, 1954, pp. 31 ff.

[22] Friedrich Heer, *Aufgang Europas: Eine Studie zu den Zusammenhängen zwischen politischer Religiosität, Frömmigkeitstil und dem Werden Europas im 12. Jahrhundert*, Wien-Zürich, Europa Verlag, 1949, pp. 384–575.

*The Consequent Wish to Purge the World of Suffering and Sin*

Between the close of the eleventh and the middle of the seventeenth century, it occurred repeatedly in Europe that the desire of the poor, the uprooted and the discontented to improve the conditions of their lives became transfused with expectations of an earthly paradise, a world purged of suffering and sin, a Kingdom of the Saints. The Middle Ages had inherited from Antiquity—from the Jews and the early Christians—a prophetic and apocalyptic tradition which during this period took on a radical and exuberant vitality. There existed an eschatology or body of doctrine concerning the final state of the world. It foretold a millennium, not necessarily limited, in which the world would be inhabited by a humanity at once perfectly good and perfectly happy. Apocalyptic thinkers and propagandists expected that God would destroy the world and substitute a new one for the old.[23]

Generation after generation, apocalyptic expectations and efforts to realize these aims were combined.[24] From time to time these yearnings and expectations, these hopes of some sudden, miraculous event which would bring about a complete transformation of the world were channelled by the rise of a prophet or leader into a more or less co-ordinated and determined attack on existing ecclesiastical and civil institutions. In all these movements, religious, political and economic motives were interwoven. The idea of a final prodigious struggle which would usher in the reign of God also implied that it would lead to the establishment of a new social order.

Achievement of the millennium required the removal of various impediments, the chief of which was Antichrist. The final struggle at Armageddon would be between the hosts of Christ and the hosts of Antichrist. But who was Antichrist? Antichrist was in every way a demonic counterpart of the Son of God, and tended to merge into the figure of Satan. This concept has its roots in the dualism which came into the early Christian church from several sources— heterodox Judaism, Greek philosophy and Gnosticism. The influence of Iranian dualism is evident in the extreme apocalyptic character of

[23] L. Gry, *Le Millénarisme dans ses origines et son développement*, Paris, 1904; E. Wadstein, *Die eschatologische Ideengruppe: Antichrist, Weltsabbat, Weltende und Weltgericht*, Leipzig, 1896; Walter Nigg, *Das ewige Reich*, Zürich, Artemis Verlag, 1954.

[24] Norman Cohn, *The Pursuit of the Millennium*, Fairlawn, Essential Books, 1957, New York, Harper Torchbooks edition, 1961. This erudite study of medieval millennial movements is weakened by several tendencies: to assume that revolutionary chiliasm is due to mental disorder, to underplay the rational core of what may seem odd behaviour, and to equate modern revolutionary movements, particularly their ideas, with those of the medieval movements. If one keeps these caveats in mind, this is a very useful book.

the Qumran community.[25] The prince of demons, Satan, the adversary of God, was the source of evil on Earth. The belief that Jesus had overcome Satan was faced with Paul's teaching about the dual realm of spirits, and Augustine's doctrine of two predestined realms, *civitas Dei* and *civitas Diaboli*. Satan remained powerful with God's permission, and even endeavoured to enlarge his dominion. Heterodox notions and doctrines continued to flourish among the literate and the illiterate. These doctrines could appeal to numerous groups, not necessarily in the lowest strata of society, and they might attract various people for different reasons.[26] The result was the appearance of various heresies and heretical groups, and these mushroomed in the eleventh and twelfth centuries.

Beliefs and acts of this kind were regarded as threatening the fabric of Christian society. Many believed that extermination of the agents of Antichrist was a prerequisite for the attainment of the Kingdom of God. Among these agents at various times and places the clergy were prominent. Small wonder that heretics were considered by theologians and the defenders of orthodoxy as the servants and instruments of the Devil. As heresy began to assume increasingly alarming proportions, belief in the power of the Devil grew and his might appeared capable of overthrowing the Church and all existing order. Heretics were accused of alliance with Satan, and of practices related to witchcraft. The Cathari, for example, were accused of flying to their assemblies on broomsticks or poles anointed with oil, of singing songs to the Devil who appeared in a monstrous form, of cannibalism and of drinking potions made from the bodies of abducted children. Similar accusations were made against the Waldensians, the Knights Templars and others. Little by little, the Church in its struggle against heresy equated it with sorcery and witchcraft.[27] The witch hunt grew out of the hunt for heretics, just as the witch trial evolved out of the trial for heresy. The Scholastics systematized, embellished and condemned the superstitions which had previously been considered with disdain, and thus provided a theological and "scientific" basis for such beliefs. Among the more prominent participants in and supporters of this

[25] See, for example, *The War of the Sons of Light against the Sons of Darkness*, p. 1.1, and the *Manual of Discipline*, p. 1.23–24.

[26] R. M. Grant, *Gnosticism and Early Christianity*, New York, Columbia University Press, 1959, pp. 1–69; Wilhelm Schepelern, *Der Montanismus und die Phrygischen Kulte*, Tübingen, J. C. B. Mohr Verlag, 1929; A. Borst, *Die Katharer* (*Schriften der Monumenta Germaniae Historica*), vol. XII, Stuttgart, 1953; Ernest W. McDonnell, *The Beguines and Beghards in Medieval Culture . . .*, New Brunswick, Rutgers University Press, 1954, pp. 488–504, 505–514.

[27] Joseph Hansen, *Zauberwahn, Inquisition und Hexenprozesse in Mittelalter*, pp. 212–216 (see note 13).

ideology were Alexander of Hales, Bonaventura, Albertus Magnus, and Thomas Aquinas.[28] The latter, for example, asserted the possibility of sexual intercourse between human beings and the Devil.

## The Ideology of the Inquisition

In this way, a grotesque ideology was invented, and later massively confirmed by the Inquisition. At first the Inquisition had been directed expressly against heretics, but by the second half of the thirteenth century inquisitors had begun to arrest magicians and fortune-tellers. Then in 1326, Pope John XXII issued a bull, "Super illius specula," in which he equated magicians and wizards with heretics, thus subjecting them to the procedures and courts of the Inquisition. From the fourteenth century on there are reports of witchcraft trials by the Inquisition. A number of these were already mass trials; thus, in the years around 1330 there were more than 400 accused of witchcraft in Toulouse and Carcassonne. About half of these were executed.[29] At the same time, one must note that the secular authorities were also active in attempting to discover witches and to bring them to justice. In the fourteenth and fifteenth centuries there was an increasing number of such trials before secular tribunals.[30] In this way, the witch trial was slowly separated from the Inquisition, and the way was prepared for the discovery and trial of suspects by other than the ecclesiastical authorities. This was the situation in Switzerland, Germany, the Netherlands, and in the fifteenth century the persecution of witches had assumed the form which it had in the two subsequent centuries.

In 1484, Innocent VIII declared open war on witches with the promulgation of his bull "Summis desiderantes." Interestingly enough, at this time, witches were considered a sect of very recent origin. The belief was prevalent that the crushing impact of the Inquisition on heresy had led the Devil to organize a new group, the witches, to carry out his evil purposes. Bernard of Como, an inquisitor who died in 1510, put the origin of this sect in the first half of the fourteenth century. Five years after the issuance of Innocent's bull, Heinrich Krämer and Jakob Sprenger, the two chief inquisitors for Germany, produced the notorious *Malleus Maleficarum* (Hammer of

---

[28] S. Riezler, *Geschichte der Hexenprozesse in Bayern*, Stuttgart, J. G. Gotta, 1896, p. 42; Charles E. Hopkin, *The Share of Thomas Aquinas in the Growth of Witchcraft Delusion*, Philadelphia, University of Pennsylvania Dissertation, 1940, pp. 174 ff.

[29] Soldan-Heppe, *Geschichte der Hexenprozesse*, 2 vols., Dritte Auflage, München, 1912, vol. I, p. 201.

[30] Hansen, *Quellen* (see note 17), pp. 466 ff.

Witches), a manual of procedure and theory for witchcraft trials. Thenceforth, torture and ideology employed on the basis of accusations derived from sexual antagonisms, family stresses, social conflict, cupidity, suggestion, hallucinations and mental illness created an empire of darkness which spread under its own momentum.

Fear of demonic powers acting directly or through other human beings to cause illness, death, or other kinds of destruction was widely diffused throughout the population in the later Middle Ages—in fact this fear underlies the demonology which was accepted by clergy and laity alike. When a situation arose which was not only menacing, but went altogether outside the usual run of experience, when people were confronted with hazards which were all the more frightening because they were unfamiliar—such times drove masses of people to seek to assuage their anxiety and to find and hold to account those responsible for the situation. "Death and the devil," says Tillich, "were allied in the anxious imagination of the period."[31] The wrath of God could be mollified by various pious acts and practices, and the Devil could be attacked through his representatives, the witches.

The Reformation brought no change in the persecution of witches. If anything, the situation became worse. Protestant clergymen and lay officials could believe in the Devil and be as merciless to witches as Catholics.[32] Gradually, a change in the evaluation of witchraft was brought about by the voice of reason in some areas, by the churches and the Inquisition itself in others, and by the fact that the new social order that had emerged out of the Middle Ages had become sufficiently secure to deal in other ways with social and individual anxiety. For example, in Spain the Inquisition as early as 1537 recognized that alleged witches might be insane, and there are several cases on record where such individuals were transferred to hospitals.[33] Also, by the later seventeenth century, the new scientific attitude had begun to penetrate the study of witchcraft and demonology. Physicians collected detailed case histories of demoniacs, and began to speak of physiology and pathology in connection with these cases. These data were also used by deists and rationalists to explain such beliefs and observations in terms of mental illness.[34] The light of

[31] Tillich, *op. cit.*, p. 59.

[32] Oscar Pfister, *Calvin's Eingreifen in die Hexer und Hexenprozesse von Peney, 1545, nach seiner Bedeutung für Geschichte und Gegenwart*, Zürich, Artemis Verlag, 1947.

[33] H. C. Lea, *A History of the Inquisition of Spain*, New York, Macmillan Company, 1907, vol. III, pp. 58–63.

[34] Frank S. Manuel, *The Eighteenth Century Confronts the Gods*, Cambridge, Harvard University Press, 1959, pp. 70–81.

reason dispelled the darkness of demonology, and the old beliefs and practices went undergound. They remained alive in out-of-the-way places.[35]

Meanwhile, thousands of women, men and children had been tried as witches and many had been executed. From the records of these cases and from the writings on witchcraft, we derive our knowledge of the witches, their accusers, judges and of others connected with them. It is also possible to obtain a picture of the factors involved, and to arrive at a reasoned opinion of the place of psychopathology in the persecution of witches.

### The Hazards of Being a Woman, Old, or Odd

Most of those accused of being witches were women. In the light of official doctrine that the witches were an organized sect, bent on subverting the social order, it is worth noting that many of the accused were old women, ignorant peasants, who could not possibly have performed the evil deeds ascribed to them. Furthermore, the whole campaign against witches is permeated with the spirit of aversion towards women. According to the *Malleus*, crimes of witchcraft are committed predominantly by women, whose primary motive is carnal lust.

One must also keep in mind that the accusation of witchcraft frequently arose because the person was old. Ackerknecht has pointed out that "being different is not yet being psychopathological" and that the psychopathology of the queer and awkward people in society is due "much more to their ambiguous position than to their organic structure."[36] For a long time, women, and especially old women, were undoubtedly among the awkward ones of the social group and occupied an equivocal position. In 1596, for instance, two women were taken into custody in Marburg (Germany) and accused of witchcraft. They had approached another woman for some means by which they could bring back the students who had made them pregnant. In addition they were accused of being whores and of having urged other women to join their misdeeds.[37]

In another case, the accusation arose out of the fact that a woman refused to go to church when ordered to do so by the pastor. Since she was already suspected of being a witch she was arrested and

[35] Herman Alfred Schmid, *Die Entzauberung der Welt in der Schweizer Landeskunde* . . ., Basel, Helbring und Lichtenhahn, 1942, pp. 9–48.

[36] E. H. Ackerknecht, 'Psychopathology, Primitive Medicine, and Primitive Culture," *Bull. Hist. Med.*, 14: 30, 1943.

[37] Karl Heinz Spielmann, *Die Hexenprozesse in Kurhessen, nach den Quellen dargestellt*, 2. Auflage, Marburg, N. G. Elwert, 1932, pp. 57–58.

questioned under torture. Thereupon, she admitted having committed adultery with her brother-in-law, the form in which the Devil had come to her.[38] Here the fact of being different is apparently linked to antagonisms derived from other sources—intrafamilial dissension, gossip, sexual antagonism, enmity arising from economic and other circumstances. For example, Elizabeth Seip, of Kappel near Marburg, was indicted as a witch in 1656. In the course of the proceedings, her husband complained to the authorities that his wife was an honest woman who had reported various crimes, and that the accusations had been invented by her enemies in order to obtain revenge. Furthermore, a peasant who attested to the fact that the wife was a witch, also stated that Seip, the husband, owed him 80 gulden; when he had tried to get his money by putting a lien on the debtor's property his child had thereupon fallen ill. Similarly, in 1581, Johann Klenke, of Rinteln was accused of blasphemy and witchcraft. The accusation stemmed from the mayor of the town because Klenke had lent him money and insisted on having it repaid.[39]

## Growing Awareness of the Social Implications of the Accusations

An awareness of the social situation of women accused of witchcraft, of the social implications of the persecutions and their relation to psychopathology was present in the sixteenth century. As early as 1550, Girolamo Cardano described those called vulgarly *strigae* as miserable, beggarly old women, and he attributed their behaviour to poverty, hunger and hardship. Johann Weyer, in 1563, while maintaining his belief in witchcraft, insisted that the accused witches were only melancholy old women, feeble of intellect and misled by the Devil. In some instances, there are more precise descriptions of senile psychotic behaviour. An account of the last witch-burning in Scotland, in 1772, relates that the accused, who is described as demented and "a fatuous old woman", appeared to be quite unaware of what was going on about her as she was led to the stake. She stretched out her hands to the pyre, pleased with "the bonnie fire".[40]

Other forms of psychopathology have been described and suggested by investigators. Tuke felt that many of the women who were put to death for witchcraft were "victims of cerebral disorder".[41] A more important assessment of the problem was made in 1881 by

---

[38] *Ibid.*, pp. 79–89.

[39] *Ibid.*, pp. 81–83.

[40] C. Rogers, *Scotland, Social and Domestic*, London, 1869, p. 301.

[41] D. Hack Tuke, *Chapters in the History of the Insane in the British Isles*, London, Kegan Paul, Trench & Co., 1882, p. 36.

David Nicolson, Deputy-Superintendent of the Criminal Lunatic Asylum at Broadmoor.[42] After reviewing a number of witchcraft trials, he wrote:

> There are sane as well as insane who believe in witchcraft, just as there are insane as well as sane who do not believe in witchcraft. The belief in witchcraft is not the measure of sanity or of insanity; nor yet is the belief in supernatural agency in any form.
>
> In the study of criminal trials, such as those with which we are at present concerned, we are brought face to face with the social phenomena of the time being in all their bearings, and, in the cases here given, there will always be found something of psychological interest, either as regards the domestic and other concerns of the community, or as regards individuals prosecuted or individuals prosecuting. The evidence, where given, will throw light upon the different ways that people had of looking upon their relationships, and of interpreting the circumstances taking place around them. Sometimes the eccentric or insane appearance or conduct of the individual will be found to have given rise to an accusation founded upon a *bona fide* belief in the individual's actual or potential guilt. Sometimes the insanity will reveal itself in the wild and ecstatic utterances of the individual at whose instigation, or upon whose evidence, a charge is sustained against a reputable and unoffending neighbour. Sometimes the mixture of hysteria or epilepsy with a malicious or criminal disposition will mask the real character of the case, and give, as in any form of criminal charge, grounds for the expression of honest though contradictory opinion on the two sides.[43]

About a decade later, Otto Snell, a German psychiatrist, also studied a number of witchtrials from a psychological point of view, and came to similar conclusions. He pointed out that very few mentally ill individuals were themselves victims of the witch trials. This is borne out in at least one case. In 1669 a Jewish woman was brought to Marburg and incarcerated because she had set fire to her house in order to burn down the village. She admitted freely having sold herself to the Devil, of having had sexual relations with a baker, and demanded that she be put to death by beheading. Recognizing that she was insane, the court did not try her as a witch. A young girl of seventeen who in 1698 set fire to her village at the Devil's command was not so fortunate; she was burnt at the stake.[44] On the other hand, psychoses and neuroses led to numerous trials because the

[42] David Nicolson, "Some Observations on the State of Society, Past and Present in Relation to Criminal Psychology," *Journal of Mental Science*, 27: 359–370, 1881; 28: 6–16, 510–519, 1882.

[43] *Ibid.*, p. 367.

[44] Spielman, *op. cit.*, pp. 91, 142.

sick person was believed to be possessed, and one had to discover and punish the witch who had caused the condition.[45]

Possession by the Devil, actually a very ancient idea, was widely believed to be due to witches. According to the authors of the *Malleus* the possessed behaves wildly, is endowed with unusual strength and qualities, makes noises like an animal, speaks languages he did not learn and has many other unusual characteristics. The Devil must be driven out by exorcism. Numerous cases of demoniacal possession have been recorded, and modern authors have recognized various forms of mental illness under this designation. Snell identified melancholia, paranoia, epilepsy, manic conditions, and hysteria as having figured in the witch trials. Kirchhoff, also a German psychiatrist, names senile dementia and epilepsy as conditions that affected those accused of witchcraft.[46] More recent investigators have seen such cases as forms of mental illness which would be classed among the schizophrenias.[47] Pathological swallowers (nails, needles, and the like), compulsion neurotics, sufferers from chorea—all were seen as affected with supernatural disease and the cure required that the cause be found and removed.[48]

Where such ideas are an integral part of the culture, people can learn to produce such phenomena or to see them where we would not. Charcot, in the presentation of the *grand hystérie* taught his subject to produce the desired phenomena. As one reads the records, it is obvious that within a definite cultural context, namely, the Salpêtrière Clinic, he was training hysterics so that they could put on a finished performance. The same thing occurred in the various outbreaks of possession of the sixteenth, seventeenth and later centuries recorded in the literature. In the case of Urbain Grandier, which has been so well described by Aldous Huxley, a number of nuns in a convent were taught how to enter states of possession. Indirectly, by various cues, they were told what to do, and they performed. Grandier was accused of having bewitched them, and he was burnt at the stake.[49] The Salem witch trials exhibit the same phenomena.

[45] Otto Snell, *Hexenprozesse und Geistesstörung*, München, J. F. Lehmann Verlag, 1891; *idem*, "Ueber die Formen von Geistesstörung welche Hexenprozesse veranlasst haben," *Allg. Ztschr. Psychiat.*, 50: 534–535, 1894.

[46] T. Kirchhoff, "Beziehungen des Dämonen—und Hexenwesens zur deutschen Irrenflege," *Allg. Ztschr. Psychiat.*, 44: 329, 1888.

[47] Sigmund Freud, "A Neurosis of Demoniacal Possession of the Seventeenth Century," *Collected Papers*, 4: 436–472, 1949. First published in *Imago*, Bd. IX, 1923.

[48] Saul Jarcho, ". . . Summary of the Life of Maria Caterina Brondi . . ." *Bull. Hist. Med.*, 15: 400–419, 1944.

[49] Aldous Huxley, *The Devils of Loudun*, New York, Harper & Bros., 1952, Harper Colophon Books, edition, 1965; Gabriel Legué, *Documents pour servir à l'histoire médicale des possédées de Loudun*, Paris, Adrien Delahaye, 1874.

Furthermore it is not surprising that children brought up in such a culture should have accused old women of witchcraft, or that they should have been such ready pupils at learning to be possessed by the Devil.[50]

### Witchcraft Persecution Not a Simple Phenomenon

It should by now be clear that the witchcraft persecution was not a simple phenomenon as seems to be implied by such terms as "mania," "delusion," or "craze". To be sure, some individuals involved in witch trials were mentally and emotionally disordered. Most of those involved were not. In part, their reactions were learned, in part, they conformed because of fear-producing pressures. Opponents of the belief in witches and the Devil were suspected at best of having been duped, or at worst of being witches themselves. Many people were undoubtedly expressing aggressive impulses towards others, but in another context they would have done so differently. They were able to hunt and kill witches—in the form of old women and other queer or disliked individuals—because an ideology and a governmental (ecclesiastical and secular) apparatus had been created and was available. These instruments had been created to eradicate dissent, to establish conformity, and thus to protect the established order.[51] To these elements must be added a state of societal crisis. Similar phenomena have occurred at various times in history, the Popish Plot in the reign of Charles II, the Red Scare of 1919–20, and others.[52]

### RELATION OF WITCHCRAFT PERSECUTION TO OTHER PSYCHOPATHOLOGICAL PHENOMENA

The approach in this sketch of the witchcraft persecutions and their relation to mental disorder is applicable to other phenomena that have been lumped under the headings of crowd delusions, mass hysteria and the like. The "mob" as a social phenomenon has recently been subjected to close study, and it has become clear that some

[50] Sandford Fleming, *Children and Puritanism*, New Haven, Yale University Press, 1933; E. Caulfield, "Psychiatric Aspects of the Salem Witchcraft Tragedy: A Lesson in Mental Health," *American Journal of Diseases of Children*, 65: 788, 1943; M. Tramer, "Kinder im Hexenprozess des Mittelalters: Kind und Aberglaube," *Zeitschrift für Kinderpsychiatrie*, 11: 140–149, 180–187, 1945; Marion L. Starkey, *The Devil in Massachusetts*, New York, Alfred A. Knopf, 1949.

[51] John Morley, *Life of Cornelius Agrippa*, 2 vols, London, Chapman & Hall, 1856, vol. II, p. 71.

[52] John Pollock, *The Popish Plot*, Cambridge, Cambridge University Press, 1944; Robert K. Murray, *Red Scare: A Study in National Hysteria, 1919–1920*, Minneapolis, University of Minnesota Press, 1955.

"mobs" at least were not simply aggregates of individuals out to loot and destroy in an irrational orgy.[53] Similar phenomena that require analysis are the dancing frenzies, the use of trance and ecstasy to achieve social goals, the ways in which cultures make it possible for psychopathological individuals to play certain roles at a particular time. For example, in ancient history prophets and diviners were common. Whether these individuals were mentally ill or not is a moot question. However, there are records of such individuals in more recent periods who, in times of stress, have been able to occupy positions of influence and to exhibit odd behaviour. An interesting case occurred in England in the middle of the seventeenth century. In plague-stricken London of 1665, Solomon Eccles walked about naked with a dish of fire and brimstone on his head prophesying woe. He forecast a universal conflagration for the following year, which occurred, of course, but the world survived, and he vanished.[54] Eccles was accepted because the society of which he was a part was no stranger to prophets of woe exhibiting odd behaviour.

The main point is not to label the behaviour of a group, even though its members may seem odd, by usual criteria. There may well be a rational core behind the apparently irrational. One must first examine the behaviour in its context before judging it. Further studies of this problem will present other group behavioural phenomena and examine their relation to psychopathology.

---

[53] George Rudé, "The Gordon Riots: A Study of the Rioters and Their Victims," *Transactions of the Royal Historical Society*, 5th Series, 6: 93–114, 1956; *idem.*, *The Crowd in the French Revolution*, Oxford, Clarendon Press, 1959; E. J. Hobsbawm, *Primitive Rebels: Studies in Archaic Forms of Social Movements in the 19th and 20th Centuries*, Manchester, Manchester University Press, 1959, pp. 108–125.

[54] Anthony Hunter, *The Last Days*, London, Anthony Blond, 1959.

# THE ANCIENT WORLD

# CHAPTER TWO

# ANCIENT PALESTINE AND NEIGHBOURING ADJACENT AREAS

*David Feigns Madness*

When David broke with Saul after the latter tried to kill him, he first fled south into Judea. Then recognizing his inability to withstand the royal power, David decided to seek refuge elsewhere. As a possible protector he turned to Achish the Philistine, king of Gath, the city from which Goliath had come. According to one version of this event, David, uncertain of the reception which he, a former enemy, might receive, resorted to a ruse and pretended to be mad.

> So he changed his behaviour before them [the Philistines] and feigned himself mad in their hands, and made marks on the doors of the gate, and let his spittle run down his beard. Then said Achish to his servants, "Lo, you see the man is mad; why then have you brought him to me? Do I lack madmen, that you have brought this fellow to play the madman in my presence?"[1]

This episode as well as other passages in the Old Testament show clearly that mental disorders occurred and were recognized as such among the ancient Hebrews and the peoples who were their neighbours. Although the incidence or prevalence of such conditions cannot be known, the available information does permit the delineation of certain forms of psychopathology, of ideas concerning their causes, and of the ways in which those afflicted were regarded and dealt with by the community. In this connection, the story of Saul, the first king of Israel (reigned *c.* 1020–1000 B.C.) is of particular interest, because more detailed information than usual is available about him.

*Is Saul Also Among the Prophets?*

The need for unified leadership felt by the Israelite tribes in meeting the attacks of neighbouring peoples (Ammonites, Philistines,

[1] I Samuel 21: 13–15. All Biblical quotations, unless otherwise stated are from *The Oxford Annotated Bible. The Holy Bible, Revised Standard Version containing the Old and New Testaments* ... Ed. by Herbert G. May and Bruce M. Metzger, New York, Oxford University Press, 1962.

Amalekites) led them to give up their earlier organization as a tribal confederacy and to unite under a centralized monarchy. Samuel, the last of the judges, opposed but could not prevent the appointment of a king. To reign over them, the Israelites called Saul, a tribesman of Benjamin, who first came to the fore as a military and political leader by rallying his countrymen to relieve Jabesh-Gilead, besieged by the Ammonites.

At first, Saul acted energetically and decisively, and his rapid initial successes were undoubtedly the consequence of his military and political ability. Yet, Saul seems to have carried in his personality the seeds of his destruction. The saying "Is Saul also among the prophets?", which became proverbial, hints at a tendency to emotional instability.[2] Two stories are told to explain the origin of the proverb. In the first of these, Samuel tells the newly anointed Saul of a number of signs confirming his new position, which he will encounter on his homeward way, among them a meeting with a company of prophets whom Saul will join in prophesying. And so it happened. "When they came to Gibeah, behold, a band of prophets met him; and the spirit of God came mightily upon him, and he prophesied among them. And when all who knew him before saw how he prophesied with the prophets, the people said to one another, 'what has come over the son of Kish? Is Saul among the prophets?'"[3]

Another version of the origin of the proverb links it with Saul's attempt to kill David after he began to fear him as a potential rival. With the help of Michal, his wife, David escaped and fled to Samuel at Ramah. Saul pursued him and

> came to the great well that is in Secu; and he asked, "Where are Samuel and David?" And one said "Behold, they are at Naioth in Ramah." And he went from there to Naioth in Ramah; and the Spirit of God came upon him also, and as he went he prophesied, until he came to Naioth in Ramah. And he too stripped off his clothes, and he too prophesied before Samuel, and lay naked all that day and all that night. Hence it is said, "Is Saul also among the prophets?"[4]

That there are two versions of the origin of this proverbial saying is immaterial. The very existence of two explanations tends to remove any doubt about the fact itself. Saul was among the prophets because he was susceptible to the psychic contagion of group excitation. Both traditions specifically associate him with the bands of ecstatic prophets who appear prominently in Israel's history at the time of

[2] I Samuel 10: 12; 19: 24.
[3] I Samuel 10: 10–11.
[4] I Samuel 19: 22–24.

Samuel. The behavioural and psychologic aspects of prophecy will be discussed below. Here it is sufficient to point out that by means of music and dancing these groups worked themselves into a frenzy or trance, during which they uttered their prophecies. Experiences of this sort can be induced by a wide range of stimuli, frequently acting at the same time, which produce physiological and psychological stresses.

On both occasions when Saul prophesied he was under strong emotional tension. The oracle communicated by Samuel to Saul, that he had been chosen by the Lord for kingship, and that he would encounter confirmatory signs of this choice, created a state of excitement and expectation in which Saul was prepared to act the prophet, and thus be "turned into another man" qualified to lead Israel. Saul's behaviour was conditioned and coloured by his expectations, but it is also likely that Samuel recognized him as a man who would readily respond to the excitement and elation of group prophesy.[5] Indeed, the story of Saul prophesying before Samuel at Ramah offers a hint that he was found among the prophets more often than on the two occasions reported in I Samuel.

Repeated exposure to situations and stimuli that lead to group arousal phenomena tends to sensitize the participants so that they lose contact with their surroundings more and more readily. Moreover, the state of acute excitement and emotional disruption which develops under such circumstances very often ends with collapse in total exhaustion, a condition in which the individual may remain unconscious for varying periods of time, sometimes for hours.[6]

How often Saul experienced such psychological disturbances, and exhibited their physical manifestations, is not known. None the less, episodes of this kind must have occurred often enough to impress the popular consciousness that this trait was characteristic of Saul. Moreover, the events at Ramah can also be related to changes in Saul's political situation and state of mind that developed earlier. Apparently, the episode at Ramah took place at a time when Saul was already suffering from emotional disturbance. Although the chronology of the Biblical text is somewhat uncertain, the outbreak

---

[5] Alfred Guillaume, *Prophecy and Divination among the Hebrews and other Semites*, London, Hodder & Stoughton, 1938, p. 300.

[6] Maya Deren, *Divine Horsemen. The Living Gods of Haiti*, London and New York, Thames & Hudson, 1953, pp. 250–262, 322–323. The experience of Miss Deren, who in 1949 went to Haiti to study and film Haitian dancing is relevant here. During a Voodoo service she became possessed by Erzulie, the goddess of Love. Subsequently, she experienced seven or eight episodes of possession, and found that she fell into this state with increasing ease. Furthermore, she remained unconscious for varying periods, on one occasion some four hours elapsed before she regained consciousness.

of his illness is brought into direct relationship to a conflict with Samuel.

## Saul's Disobedience and Rejection

The conflict was occasioned by the victory won by Saul in his war (*c.* 1016 B.C.) against the Amalekites, a fierce, nomadic people, traditionally descended from Esau, who had long been enemies of the Israelites.[7] Before the campaign began, Samuel charged Saul in the name of the Lord to extirpate Amalek, to put to the sword "both man and woman, infant and suckling, ox and sheep, camel and ass."[8] Despite these instructions, Saul, perhaps motivated more by political than religious considerations, did not kill Agag, king of the Amalekites, but took him prisoner. Nor did he destroy all the flocks, but allowed his soldiers to keep some animals as spoils of war and for sacrifice at the sanctuary of Gilgal. Aroused by these acts, Samuel confronted Saul, denounced his disobedience, and inspired by prophetic wrath pronounced his doom. Implacable and uncompromising in his anger, Samuel withdrew divine support from Saul, saying "you have rejected the word of the Lord, and the Lord has rejected you from being king over Israel . . . The Lord has torn the kingdom of Israel from you this day, and has given it to a neighbour of yours who is better than you."[9]

Kingship as conceived by the Israelites was an expression of God's favour. The king was elected by God, and appointed to his office by the Lord's messenger, the prophet. Although the bearer of God's grace, the monarch's tenure was conditional upon his submission to the will of God. As long as the king obeyed the word of the Lord, he and his kingdom would flourish; disobedience and rebellion ineluctably evoked retribution and ultimately annihilation.[10]

Samuel's defiance and rejection of Saul for his failure to carry out a divine command was thus both a challenge to the monarchy and a warning of punishment to come. Tradition recalled this dramatic conflict and its consequences by presenting the onset of Saul's mental illness within this context. Following the bitter, irreparable quarrel with Samuel, "the Spirit of the Lord departed from Saul, and an evil spirit from the Lord tormented him."[11]

[7] Exodus 17: 8–16; Deuteronomy 25: 17–19.
[8] I Samuel 15: 1–3.
[9] I Samuel 15: 26–28.
[10] Yehezkel Kaufmann, *The Religion of Israel. From its Beginnings to the Babylonian Exile.* Trans. and abridged by Moshe Greenberg, Chicago and London, University of Chicago Press, 1960, pp. 263–266, 272–273.
[11] I Samuel 16: 14.

*Saul and David: A contest for power*

The breach with Samuel and the prophetic groups who supported him undoubtedly weighed heavily on Saul's mind and temper, bringing to the surface and intensifying his latent emotional instability. In the light of the profound significance of Samuel's action, it is not surprising that Saul responded as he did. Moreover, Saul's religious and political difficulties were further aggravated by problems that arose at his court and within his own family, notably his quarrel with David, his son-in-law, and his disappointment with his son, Jonathan. The Biblical text has retained the essential core of these dramatic relationships and through a number of vivid stories throws a bright light on the personalities involved.

The initial interweaving of the fates of Saul and David apparently occurred at a time when Saul's mental disorder had already become clearly manifest. Saul's attention was first directed to David, a young Judean, member of a prominent family of Bethlehem, when he was advised by his counsellors to secure a skilful musician whose playing would relieve the torments inflicted by the evil spirit from God.[12] David was celebrated by Israelite tradition as a musician and poet, and his talent became evident, no doubt, at an early age.[13] By inviting David to enter his service, Saul was probably also endeavouring to further his policy of establishing a firmer union between the men of Judah and the Israelites of central Palestine.[14]

All the relevant traditions describe David as an attractive, engaging figure, possessed of great personal charm, and at first he found favour with the king. Indeed, according to the oldest account of their relationship, Saul's suspicion of David did not become evident until sometime after he had come to the royal court. During this period, David acquired important posts, as the king's armour-bearer and as a military leader, and he became Saul's son-in-law. At the same time, he also established ties of friendship and blood brotherhood with Jonathan, the king's son and his presumptive successor.

As Saul's illness in itself was obviously no hindrance to David's rise, one can hardly assume that the sudden change in his attitude towards David, the suspicion and hostility which he developed to a pathological degree, occurred without any provocation on David's

[12] I Samuel 16: 15–18.
[13] Kaufmann, *op. cit.*, pp. 110, 267–268; W. F. Albright, *The Biblical Period from Abraham to Ezra*, New York, Harper Torchbooks, 1963, pp. 50–51; *ibid.*, *Archaeology and the Religion of Israel*, Baltimore, Johns Hopkins Press, 1942, pp. 125–129.
[14] Elias Auerbach, *Wüste und Gelobtes Land*, Erster Band. *Geschichte Israels von den Anfängen bis zum Tode Salomos*, Berlin, Schocken Verlag, 1936, p. 196.

part. Later writers, in order to glorify David and his dynasty, felt it necessary to depreciate Saul and to present David's actions in the most favourable light. None the less, there are tantalizing traces in the Biblical text that hint at intrigues and a conspiracy against Saul in which David was involved. Samuel, in pursuing his policy of opposition to Saul, may have entered into relations with David, after he obtained a position of power and influence, thus arousing Saul's suspicion. Certainly, David's flight to Samuel at Ramah after Saul's attempt to assassinate him suggests such a connection.[15] Moreover, there is evidence which also suggests strongly that Jonathan conspired with David to carry out a palace revolution to remove Saul from the throne.[16]

Whatever the precise course of events may have been, Saul began to fear David as a potential rival and determined to kill him. As the conviction grew within him that his former favourite now was his enemy, Saul pursued him with unrelenting obduracy. On one occasion, in an attack of uncontrolled rage he tried unsuccessfully to pierce David with a spear.[17] After another attempted assassination failed, David fled Saul's court.[18] The break between them now became an open struggle for political primacy. Driven by an obsessive hatred of David, Saul repeatedly tried to capture him, devoting to this aim energies and resources which might have been more fruitfully applied to other pressing and crucial problems. For Saul's kingdom was still not firmly established. He had defeated the semi-nomadic Ammonites and Amalekites, but the solidly organized Philistine confederation loomed as a major menace, and it was in his desperate effort to stem the Philistine advance that catastrophe overwhelmed him.

Yet, even if the political need to neutralize or destroy his enemy is taken into account, Saul's behaviour undoubtedly exhibits an increasingly pathological quality. If stress is severe enough, the most stable personality may show evidence of anger, aggressiveness, anxiety, depression, irritability and excitement. Saul began his career as a popular hero, rising over Israel like a shining star. At first confident and determined, he won important military victories over Israel's enemies, but as the problems which he faced became more difficult and increased in number, his latent susceptibility to psychic disturbance turned into increasingly manifest disorder.

Suspecting treachery on the part of those who served him, and unable to brook opposition, Saul vented his fear and hostility in emotional outbursts associated with uncontrollable impulses, as on

[15] I Samuel 19: 18; see also I Samuel 16: 1–13.
[16] Auerbach, *op. cit.*, pp. 198–199; I Samuel 20: 30–31; 22: 7–8.
[17] I Samuel 18: 10–11; 19: 9–10. The same incident appears to be told twice.
[18] I Samuel 19: 11–17.

the occasion when he lost control of himself and hurled a spear at David, or when he acted similarly towards his son Jonathan.[19] At other times, Saul became moody and depressed, a condition which apparently recurred more frequently as he proved increasingly unable to cope with his difficulties. In part, perhaps, the attacks of depression and uncontrolled behaviour were also an adverse result of the ecstatic seizures which he often experienced. Mental depression, impaired judgement and increased suggestibility may ensue after prolonged indulgence in ecstasy.[20]

Saul's meeting with the medium of Endor provides a striking portrayal of his state of mind on the eve of the battle in which he found a tragic death.[21] The man who had been a determined and decisive leader now hesitated, unable to decide what course of action to take and depressed by a foreboding of impending doom. Indeed, Saul's resort to necromancy was an act of desperation, the act of a man at the end of his tether. Certain mantic techniques were prohibited by Israelite religion, among these necromancy, and tradition has it that Saul suppressed wizards and mediums.[22] Yet when the Lord did not answer his inquiries "either by dreams, or by Urim [i.e. by lots] or by prophets," his feeling of abandonment and isolation led him to resort to the extreme measure of raising the ghost of Samuel so as to learn from him what do do. But this last desperate act brought Saul neither counsel nor hope. The shade of his dead opponent only confirmed his own grim apprehension that he was doomed to defeat and death. Thereupon, "Saul fell at once full length upon the ground filled with fear because of the words of Samuel."[23] Finally accepting what was to come, he determined "not to flee from it or, by clinging to life, to betray his people to the enemy and dishonour the dignity of kingship; instead, he thought it noble expose himself, his house and his children to these perils and, along with them, to fall fighting for his subjects."[24] Thus, on the following day, when the Philistines and the Israelites clashed on Mount Gilboa, Saul fought bravely as long as he could, and committed suicide by

[19] I Samuel 18: 10; 20: 32–33.

[20] William Sargant, *Battle for the Mind. A Physiology of Conversion and Brain-Washing*, Baltimore, Penguin Books, 1961, pp. 74, 108–109.

[21] I Samuel 28: 20–21. The traditional English rendering, the witch of Endor, carries with it connotations and associations that make it inappropriate. The woman of Endor was able to raise the ghost of Samuel, so that Saul could consult him, in short, for the purpose of necromancy. From this viewpoint, it appears more suitable to refer to her as a medium.

[22] Deuteronomy 18: 10–11; Kaufmann, *op. cit.*, pp. 78–93; I Samuel 28: 3.

[23] I Samuel 28: 20.

[24] Josephus, with an English translation by H. St. J. Thackeray, Ralph Marcus, and Allen Wikgren, 9 vols., (Loeb Classical Library), Cambridge, Mass., Harvard University Press; London, Wm. Heinemann, vol. 5, 1958, p. 341.

falling on his sword only after three of his sons had been killed and he had been severely wounded.[25]

*An Evil Spirit From the Lord*

For a number of reasons, the story of Saul, king of Israel, is of more than passing interest. Not only does it provide specific detail about an early case of mental and emotional disorder, but in doing so also offers a causal explanation and describes a form of therapy. Moreover, a consideration of the terminology used to describe Saul's behaviour, when taken together with other evidence, enables us to delineate certain social attitudes towards the mentally disordered and to others who appeared to act like them.

The belief that illness was inflicted by a supernatural power or by an angry deity as a punishment for sin was widespread among the peoples of the ancient world. Among the Hebrews, those who presumed to disobey Gods commandments and to violate his ordinances were threatened with dire retiribution, including the curse of madness. Deuteronomy, which dates from the seventh century B.C. but rests on ancient tradition, contains a warning by Moses to his people that if they "will not obey the voice of the Lord your God or be careful to do all his commandments and his statutes ... the Lord will smite you with madness and blindness and confusion of mind ..."[26] Similarly the prophet Zechariah, who lived in the sixth century B.C., foretells that God will punish those who attack Jerusalem. "On that day, says the Lord, I will strike every horse with panic and its rider with madness."[27]

The origin and onset of Saul's illness is a specific instance of such punishment. Israel's king was regarded as the elect of God, as the bearer of divine grace. The rite of anointing, symbolizing his election, was followed by an outpouring of the divine Spirit upon the chosen one. This viewpoint is clearly reflected in the account of Samuel's selection of David to succeed Saul. "Then Samuel took the horn of oil and anointed him in the midst of his brothers and the Spirit of the Lord came mightily upon David from that day forward."[28] However, divine election and the associated special endowment with the Spirit were conditional upon the king's continuing submission to the will of God. Rebellion against the divine command annulled his election,

---

[25] II Samuel 1 offers a different version of Saul's death, according to which he was slain by an Amalekite at his request, because he was too weak from his wounds to kill himself as he wished to do.

[26] Deuteronomy 28: 15, 28.

[27] Zechariah 12: 4.

[28] I Samuel 16: 13; cf. I Samuel 10: 1, 6 ff., 11: 6 ff.

removed from him the favour of God, and made him subject to divine wrath. To walk in the ways of the Lord or to be punished by an angry God were the polar alternatives by which Israel's divinely elected king was to guide his actions.[29] This is the context which gives full meaning to the statement, "the Spirit of the Lord departed from Saul and an evil spirit from the Lord tormented him."

The disorder which befell Saul proceeded from God through a spirit, but beyond this bare statement no details are given in the Biblical text. The nature of the spirit which troubled Saul is not specified nor is it endowed with any psychic attributes. In a large number of instances, the term *ruach* (spirit) is used in the Old Testament to denote a supernatural energy or influence acting on man.[30] In this case the adjective "evil" differentiates this spirit from the Spirit of the Lord (*ruach YHWH*) which occurs in the same sentence.

Furthermore, subjective symptoms are almost entirely absent in the story of Saul's disorder. The instances in which Saul raged and acted in an uncontrolled manner provide information about his observable behaviour, but there is no direct information on his subjective condition when he was tormented. Later writers elaborated on the Biblical text by supplying details not contained in it, but which rested perhaps on early traditions. Thus, the Greek version of the Old Testament, the Septuagint, which dates from the third century B.C., has it that the evil spirit "choked" Saul.[31] About four centuries later, the historian Josephus (A.D. 37–38—*c*. A.D. 100,) in his massive *Jewish Antiquities* (A.D. 93–94), related that Saul "was beset by strange disorders and evil spirits which caused him such suffocation and strangling that the physicians could devise no other remedy save to order search to be made for one with power to charm away spirits . . ."[32] Josephus used Hebrew (or Aramaic) and Greek versions of the Biblical text, adding to his account amplifications derived from traditional lore for which parallels exist in other writings.

A significant instance relating to Saul occurs in a work dating from the same period, written by an unknown Jewish contemporary of Josephus. *The Biblical Antiquities*, as this book is now called, is available only in a Latin translation, made from a Greek version, and that again from a Hebrew original. By accident, the name of

[29] S. H. Hooke, ed., *Myth, Ritual, and Kingship. Essays on the Theory and Practice of Kingship in the Ancient Near East and in Israel*, Oxford, Clarendon Press, 1958, pp. 207–211; Kaufmann, *op. cit.*, pp. 265–272.

[30] H. Wheeler Robinson, *Inspiration and Revelation in the Old Testament*, Oxford, Clarendon Press, 1956, p. 74.

[31] *The Septuagint Version of the Old Testament*, with an English Translation, London, S. Bagster & Sons; New York, James Pott & Co., n.d., p. 378.

[32] Josephus, *op. cit.*, p. 249 (see note 24).

Philo, the Jewish philosopher of the first century, was attached to it when it was first published in 1527.[33] This attribution is wholly unfounded and since the author, possibly a Palestinian Jew, is unknown he has been called Pseudo-Philo for convenience. His work, perhaps modelled on the book of *Chronicles*, tells the Bible story from the creation of the world to the death of Saul. Significantly, Pseudo-Philo in his account of Saul also relates that after his rejection he was choked by an evil spirit.[34]

The versions of Saul's illness presented by Josephus and Pseudo-Philo, and the wording employed in the Septuagint, apparently represent an established tradition which may rest on accounts closer in time to the events described in the Old Testament and transmitted either orally or in writing. Certainly, choking sensations would not be inconsistent with the reported onset of Saul's disorder, particularly in view of the circumstances in which it first appeared. Saul's repudiation by Samuel was undoubtedly a very serious political blow, but the psychological impact on the king was devastating. Saul's behaviour in his dramatic confrontation with Samuel reveals the dismay with which he heard the man who had anointed him now renounce him as unfit to rule Israel. "As Samuel turned to go away, Saul laid hold upon the skirt of his robe ... Then he said, 'I have sinned; yet honour me now before the elders of my people and before Israel and return with me, that I may worship the Lord your God.'"[35] Samuel agreed to this request, but immediately after Saul had worshipped Samuel returned to Ramah and never saw him again.

Saul's harsh treatment of his actual or potential enemies is well documented. His command to slaughter the priests who sheltered David, and to exterminate the inhabitants of Nob where their shrine was located, his repeated attempts to kill David, and his murder of the Gibeonites, all indicate very clearly that Saul did not shrink from bloodshed.[36] It is all the more significant, therefore, that the available sources give no hint of any action taken by Saul against Samuel following their break. Yet it seems implausible to assume that Saul harboured no resentment and hostility towards his erstwhile sponsor. The final breach with Samuel probably left Saul seething with conflicting emotions, overwhelmed with rage and humiliation, but these tensions could not easily be resolved. However much Saul

[33] *Pseudo-Philo's Liber Antiquitatum Biblicarum*, ed. with an introduction by Guido Kirsch, Notre Dame, University of Notre Dame Press, 1950; *The Biblical Antiquities of Philo*, now first translated from the old Latin Version by M. R. James, London-New York, The Macmillan Co., 1917.

[34] *Biblical Antiquities*, p. 232.

[35] I Samuel 15: 27–30.

[36] I Samuel 22: 6–19; II Samuel 21: 1–2.

may have wanted to rid himself of Samuel, the awesome power of his opponent probably compelled him to repress his desires. Perhaps he feared to take up a struggle against the mysterious divine power represented by Samuel, the power from which an outpouring of Spirit had filled his being and which had now departed from him.[37] Such an attitude is suggested by the phrase, "the Lord your God", referring to the God of Samuel, used by Saul in his plea to Samuel to attend his worship and not to humiliate him before the elders of Israel. The king realized the great need not to provoke the religious forces which governed his actions, even though the mouthpiece of this force, the channel of divine-human communication, was a hated enemy whom he might wish to destroy. This ambiguous psychological situation probably did not remain without consequence for Saul. Fear of Samuel's God, guilt at having provoked divine wrath, and his ambition to retain his kingdom very likely led Saul to repress his anger and resentment and to refrain from action against Samuel. However, this repression may unconsciously have led him to express his actual desires in a symbolic, distorted way through somatic symptoms. From this viewpoint it is at least plausible to suggest that the tradition of an evil spirit choking Saul may have been derived from an interpretation in contemporary terms of episodes of hysterical suffocation which he experienced, a condition now regarded as due to an unconscious rejection of aggressive fantasies and desires. Moreover, such somatic symptoms may subsequently be replaced wholly or in part by anxiety and depression associated with the conflict out of which they arose, a development which also appears consistent with Saul's case.

Unfortunately we know nothing certain, and can only speculate and conjecture about the subjective aspect of Saul's condition. Nevertheless, we do know something specific about Saul's treatment, and the way in which his overt behaviour was viewed and described. To these aspects we now turn.

## Music Charms away the Evil Spirit

Music had a prominent place in the life of ancient Israel, and Hebrew musicians because of their skill were highly esteemed not only by their compatriots but apparently also by foreigners. Thus, Sennacherib, the Assyrian king, considered the "male and female musicians" in the tribute sent to Nineveh by Hezekiah of Judah significant enough to mention in his account of the defeat of the

---

[37] Martin Buber, *Werke*, 3 vols., Kösel, Lambert Schneider, 1964, vol. 2, pp. 804–805; R. Brinker, *The Influence of Sanctuaries in Early Israel*, Manchester, Manchester University Press, 1946, pp. 253–255.

Judean king and the capture of Jerusalem in 701 B.C.[38] Moreover, the effect of music on the emotions was well-known, and the use of singing and instrumental music to create or to intensify emotional experiences is fully documented by numerous references in the Old Testament.

Following the Egyptian defeat at the Red Sea, Miriam took a timbrel in her hand to lead the women of Israel in a song and dance of victory.[39] Deborah the prophetess also celebrated the important victory of the Israelites over the Caananite general Sisera with a song.[40] Elisha called for a musician to help induce the prophetic trance in which he delivered the oracular message of the Lord.[41] And when David brought the ark of God to Jerusalem he and the Israelites rejoiced before the Lord "with all their might, with songs and lyres and harps and tambourines and castanets and cymbals."[42] Furthermore, the elaborate musical organization of the Temple described in I Chronicles may be an idealization, but it almost cerrainly rested on a historical basis probably developed by David himself.[43]

This musical tradition undoubtedly provided in part the context for the therapeutic counsel given to Saul when his disorder first became apparent, namely, "to seek out a man who is skilful in playing the lyre; and when the evil spirit from God is upon you, he will play it and you will be well." However, the musical tradition does not explain the choice of this therapy. The version given by Josephus serves as a useful point of departure for discussing this problem. According to his account, Saul's physicians ordered "search to be made for one with power to charm away spirits and to play upon the harp."[44] This statement is based on contemporary ideas and practices. Thus, Pseudo-Philo cites the psalm which David composed and sang to Saul in order to drive away the evil spirit.[45] Josephus refers to Solomon's reputed skill in casting out demons, and mentions that he "left behind forms of exorcisms with which those possessed by

[38] James B. Pritchard, ed., *Ancient Near Eastern Texts Relating to the Old Testament*, 2nd edition, Princeton, Princeton University Press, 1955, p. 288; S. B. Finesinger "Musical Instruments in the Old Testament," *Hebrew Union College Annual* 3: 21–75, 1926; O. R. Sellers, "Musical Instruments of Israel," in, *The Biblical Archaeologist Reader*, ed. by G. Ernest Wright and David Noel Freedman (Anchor Books), New York, Doubleday & Co., 1961, pp. 91–94.

[39] Exodus 15: 20–21.

[40] Judges 5: 1–31.

[41] II Kings 3: 15.

[42] II Samuel 6: 5.

[43] I Chronicles 25: 1, 6–8; Albright, *Archeology and the Religion of Israel*, pp. 125–129 (see note 13).

[44] I Samuel 16: 16; Josephus, *op. cit.*, p. 249.

[45] *Biblical Antiquities of Philo*, pp. 232–233.

demons drive them out, never to return." In this connection, he remarks that "this kind of cure is of very great power among us to this day;" and relates that he had seen "a certain Eleazar, a country-man of mine, in the presence of Vespasian, his sons, tribunes and a number of other soldiers, free men possessed by demons . . ."[46] Possession by unclean or evil spirits and demons is also a frequent cause of illness, especially of madness, in the New Testament, and Jesus performed a number of cures by casting out such spirits.[47]

Belief in intrusive evil spirits is nearly world-wide, and invasion by such forces has been a common explanation of abnormal behaviour of various kinds from the earliest times.[48] Frequent examples of this belief occur in the literatures of Egypt, Babylonia and Assyria, and it was widespread throughout the ancient Mediterranean–Near East area.[49] The popular religion of Israel also included belief in the existence of invasive spirits, even though only a few traces remain in the Old Testament. As the Yahwist religion of the Bible developed, ancient materials were recast in its mould. Thus, the evil spirit from the Lord that tormented Saul was probably originally a separate invasive force, demonic in nature, which came to be regarded as an extension of Yahweh.[50]

The therapeutic use of vocal and instrumental music can be under-stood within this context. Treatment for illness caused by intrusive spirits is basically simple: remove or mollify the cause. For this purpose various means many be employed including the incantatory power of music. From the earliest times to the present primitive healers have used charms and spells that were sung. Homer tells how the sons of Autolycus cared for Odysseus when he was slashed by a boar during a hunt, and how they stilled the bleeding with a chanted spell (*epaiode*).[51] In treating illness, modern shamans like their

[46] Josephus, *op. cit.*, p. 595; Louis Ginzberg, *The Legends of the Jews*, 6 vols., Philadelphia, Jewish Publication Society of America, vol. IV, 1954, pp. 149–153; vol. VI, 1946, p. 291, notes 48 and 49.

[47] Matthew 8: 28–34; Mark 5: 1–13; Luke 8: 2, 26–33.

[48] Edward Norbeck, *Religion in Primitive Society*, New York, Harper and Bros., 1961, p. 215.

[49] "The Legend of the Possessed Princess," in *Ancient Near Eastern Texts* (see note 38), pp. 29–31; Erwin Rohde, *Psyche, Seelencult und Unsterblichkeitsglaube der Griechen*, Fünfte and sechste Auflage, 2 vols., Tübingen, J. C. B. Mohr (Paul Siebeck), 1910, vol. 2, p. 26, note 1; pp. 413–414, New York, Harcourt Brace & Co., 1925, Harper Torchbooks edition, 1966.

[50] Kaufmann, *op. cit.*, pp. 122–149; Robinson, *op. cit.*, p. 179.

[51] Homer, Odyssey XIX, 455–460. See also *The Odyssey of Homer* trans. by Ennis Rees, New York, Random House, 1960, p. 326. Professor Walter Artelt has called my attention to a recent study on this subject by Irmgard Hampp: *Beschwörung, Segen, Gebet. Untersuchungen zum Zauberspruch aus dem Bereich der Volksheilkunde*, Stuttgart, Silberburg Verlag, 1961.

ancient predecessors use vocal and instrumental music to deal with the spirits involved in the case.[52] As Chadwick puts it, music is "the language of spirits" and is employed to summon or to banish them.[53] According to Pseudo-Philo, the psalm which David composed had the power when sung by him to mollify the evil spirit and to make him depart. At present, there is no way of knowing whether David's playing had as its purpose to appease or to expel the evil spirit, but that he played before Saul with one or both of these motives is very likely.

Clearly, the treatment which Saul received must be interpreted from two different viewpoints. From our angle of vision, it is highly probable that whatever relief Saul obtained from David's playing was a psychotherapeutic effect. Indeed, psychic treatment was not unknown in antiquity, and rabbis of the post exilic period occasionally permitted the use of incantations to set a patient's mind at ease.[54] The effect of music on the emotions was also known (a subject which will be discussed below) and was used in cases of mental disorder.[55] For Saul, David and their contemporaries, however, men who lived almost three thousand years ago, treatment by singing and playing an instrument was employed within a very different framework of perception and action. Our view of their thought and behaviour is obscured because of the fragmentary and often ambiguous nature of the evidence, which is therefore difficult to interpret. None the less, it is clear that their behaviour was governed by belief in the reality of supernatural forces which controlled their actions. Thus, the full significance of the mode of treatment proposed by Saul's counsellors can be grasped only by endeavouring to understand it from their point of view. In these terms it seems very likely that David's playing was part of a therapeutic incantation which was repeated from time to time as the need arose.

[52] Owen Lattimore, *Studies in Frontier History. Collected Papers 1929–58* London, Oxford University Press, 1962, pp. 379–292. Julius Berendes, "Musik und Medizin," *Ciba Zeitschrift*, No. 100, Band 9, 1961, pp. 3314–3319.

[53] Nora K. Chadwick, "The Spiritual Ideas and Experiences of the Tatars of Central Asia," *Journal of the Royal Anthropological Institute* 66: 291–329, 1936 (see p. 297).

[54] Joshua Trachtenberg, *Jewish Magic and Superstition. A Study in Folk Religion*, New York, Behrman's Jewish Book House, 1939, p. 196, Meridian Books, 1961.

[55] Beat Boehm, "Heilende Musik im griechischen Altertum," *Zeitschrift für Psychotherapie und Medizinische Psychologie* 7: 132–151, 1957; Joseph Schumacher, "Musik als Heilfaktor bei den Pythagoreern im Licht ihrer naturphilosophischen Anschauungen," in *Musik in der Medizin*. Beiträge zur Musiktherapie, Herausgegeben von Dr. med. H. R. Teirich, Stuttgart, Gustav Fischer Verlag, 1958, pp. 1–16; Eric Werner and Isaiah Sonne, "The Philosophy and Theory of Music in Judaeo-Arabic Literature," *Hebrew Union College Annual* 16: 251–319, 1941; 17: 511–572, 1942–43 (see particularly vol. 16, pp. 262–263, 273–288).

## To Act the Prophet

"And whenever the evil spirit from God was upon Saul, David took the lyre and played it with his hand; so Saul was refreshed, and was well, and the evil spirit departed from him."[56] Apparently, Saul experienced remissions in the course of his disorder; indeed, his actions on the whole were not those of a man who was completely mentally unbalanced. Saul was, in fact, quite aware of the political and military realities of the situation with which he had to deal. He saw that the Philistines would have to be stopped if he was to maintain control of the northern territories of Israel; it was with this objective that he undertook to defend the Esdraelon pass and engaged the enemy in the hopeless battle where he met his death.

However, the musical therapy practised by David does not invariably seem to have been successful. On one or more occasions when David was playing, Saul became extremely agitated, flew into a rage, and hurled his spear at David. According to I *Samuel*, "an evil spirit from God rushed upon Saul, and he raved within his house, while David was playing the lyre, as he did day by day. Saul had his spear in his hand; and Saul cast the spear, for he thought, 'I will pin David to the wall.' But David evaded him twice."[57] On another occasion, when Jonathan attempted to defend David to his father, Saul in a paroxysm of rage "cast his spear at him to smite him."[58] The possible political implications of these episodes and their relation to the development of Saul's state of mind have been examined above. But how did Saul actually behave in these episodes? How did he act when he is described as "raving"? Here an examination of the Hebrew text and of the words used to describe Saul's behaviour may throw some light on the character of his actions, and perhaps help us to understand how they were viewed by those who were closer in time to him.

The Hebrew word which is rendered into the English phrase "and he raved" is *wayithnabbē'*.[59] The verb in this word, *nibbā'*, *hithnabbē'* is almost certainly a denominative from the word *nābhī'*, a prophet and in its simplest sense means to act like a prophet.[60] It is used to describe the behaviour of Saul at Naioth in Ramah, when, yielding

[56] I Samuel 16: 23.
[57] I Samuel 18: 10–11. The same incident appears in I Samuel 19: 9–10 and in all probability is simply a repetition from another source.
[58] I Samuel 20: 30–33.
[59] *Biblia Hebraica*, ed. R. Kittel, 7th edition ed. by Alt, Eissfeldt, Kahle, Stuttgart, Privilegierte Württembergische Bibelanstalt, 1951, p. 434. Unless otherwise specified all further references to the Hebrew text are from this edition.
[60] H. H. Rowley, "The Nature of Prophecy in the Light of Recent Study," *Harvard Theological Review* 38: 1–38, 1945, pp. 6–8.

to the excitation of group prophecy, he stripped off his clothes, rolled about naked on the ground, and prophesied before Samuel. In their contest with Elijah on Mount Carmel, the prophets of Baal danced about their altar, cut themselves with swords and lances so that their blood gushed out upon them, and cried aloud to their god. They are described as raving, and the same verb which was used of Saul's behaviour is employed in this connection.[61] Thus, in a wider sense, "to act like a prophet" is to behave in an uncontrolled manner.

Does this usage throw any light on the views of mental disorder held by the ancient Israelites? Does it mean that uncontrolled, unreasonable behaviour was regarded as evidence of madness, or that prophets were considered mad because of the way in which they acted? Some clarification of these points can be obtained by examining the use of two other words connected with mental disorder, and by analysing the experiences and actions of various prophets.

When Moses, in Deuteronomy, warns that the Lord smites with madness those who disobey his commandments, and when Zechariah predicted that the soldiers who attack Jerusalem will be driven mad, in both passages the word for madness is *shiggayon*.[62] The same word, however, occurs in the superscription of the seventh Psalm, which is entitled "a *shiggayon* of David." Here it obviously does not denote madness; it is used rather to designate a form of impulsive expression.[63] Yet even in this connection, where the word no longer denotes madness, it still carries overtones of overwrought or highly emotional behaviour.

Etymologically related to *shiggayon* is *meshugga*, the Hebrew word for a madman. It occurs in the episode where David attempted to seek refuge with Achish, king of Gath, and then feigned madness to escape from a situation he considered dangerous.[64] However, it is significant that this term is also used of prophets and their actions. Thus, in the ninth century, when Elisha fomented the revolution of Jehu against Jehoram, king of Israel, he sent one of his followers, a young prophet, to Ramoth-Gilead to anoint the Israelite commander

---

[61] I Samuel 19: 24; I Kings 18: 28–29; *Biblia Hebraica*, pp. 437, 545.

[62] See notes 26 and 27; *Biblia Hebraica*, pp. 305, 306, 980.

[63] Robert C. Dentan in his introduction to the Psalms in the Oxford Annotated Bible says that the meaning of the term *shiggayon* is no longer definitely known (see note 1, p. 656). This position seems unduly conservative, however; and I have accepted the translation "impulsive speech," used by William G. Braude in his version of the Midrash on Psalms. See *The Midrash on Psalms*, trans. from the Hebrew and Aramaic by William G. Braude, 2 vols. (Yale Judaica Series vol. XIII), New Haven, Yale University Press, 1959, vol. I, pp. 101 ff.

[64] See note 1, *Biblica Hebraica* p. 441; the word *meshugga* has been treated by D. B. Macdonald, *The Hebrew Literary Genius*, Princeton, 1933, p. 80.

as the new king. Following this act, which was performed secretly in his house, Jehu returned to his officers who inquired, "Why did this mad fellow (*hameshugga*) come to you?" "And he said to them, You know the fellow and his talk."[65] Again, Hosea in the eighth century used the same word in speaking of a prophet as one who is mad and a fool.[66] Finally, there is the episode where Zephaniah ben Maaseiah was blamed for failing to punish Jeremiah. Reminded that he had been put in charge of the Temple "over every madman (*ish meshugga*) who prophesies, to put him in the stocks and collar," he was asked, "Now why have you not rebuked Jeremiah of Anathoth who is prophesying to you?"[67]

Thus, it appears quite clear that among the ancient Israelites a significant objective criterion of mental disorder was the occurrence of impulsive, uncontrolled and unreasonable behaviour. Apparently, this was the basis for characterizing prophets as madmen, since prophets did do strange things and acted peculiarly, inspiring awe and fear in some people and scorn in others. Prophetism and various phenomena associated with it are therefore of considerable importance for an understanding of the limits within which the ancient Israelites viewed peculiar, eccentric behaviour as socially acceptable, and which thus also defined the boundaries of the psychopathological. But before examining this aspect of prophetism, we must devote some attention to its nature and history.

*Prophecy in Israel*

There are no clear traces of a prophetic movement as such in Israel earlier than the end of the eleventh century. Nevertheless, Israelite prophecy already had a long history by this time. The Hebrews very probably brought some form of prophetic activity with them when they entered Canaan, for tradition regarded prophecy as part of the Mosaic heritage and belonging to the most ancient elements of Israelite culture.[68] In fact, one occasion is reported when Moses and a group of seventy elders were seized by the spirit of the Lord and prophesied together.[69] Furthermore, the accounts of the Hebrew tribes during their wanderings and the period of the Judges refer to a number of individuals as prophets, among them Miriam, the sister of Moses; Deborah, who was also one of the judges; and an unknown prophet who came to inspire the Israelites when they were oppressed

[65] II Kings 9: 4–11; *Biblia Hebraica*, p. 572.
[66] Hosea 9: 7; *Biblia Hebraica*, p. 904.
[67] Jeremiah 29: 24–27; *Biblia Hebraica*, p. 759.
[68] Numbers 12: 6; Deuteronomy 18: 15, 18; 34: 10; Hosea 12: 13.
[69] Numbers 11: 16–29.

by Midian.[70] However, so little is known of these early prophets, that except for Moses they must remain shadowy figures.

What is important, though, is that they were followed by a sucession of prophets, culminating in the canonical prophets who were active from the eighth century to the fourth century B.C. It was not until the time of Samuel and the establishment of the monarchy under Saul that the prophets really appeared prominently. Indeed, Samuel himself is described as a prophet, and as specifically associated with prophetic groups and their rites.[71] From that time on, however, prophets were a regular feature of Israelite society. To be sure, an Amos, an Isaiah, or a Jeremiah did not emerge immediately from prophetic groups such as those with which Samuel was connected. The great prophets are the culmination of a long period of development extending over several centuries, a process which was undoubtedly influenced by many factors. As so often occurs in the historical evolution of social roles and functions, there is a marked contrast between the origins and the resultant consequences. The canonical prophets were a remarkable group of religious and moral teachers, but they clearly acted from within a recognized prophetic tradition. The spiritual content of their message was new, but in the form of its delivery, in their behaviour when they announced it, the later prophets exhibited many similarities to their predecessors. It is with the latter element that this study is concerned, not with the theological validity or the moral value of prophetic revelation, but rather with the behavioural and psychological aspects of prophecy.

The phenomenon of prophecy is widely distributed in time and space. Under various circumstances, men have sought to penetrate the inscrutable future and to avert the dark forces of evil by means of oracles. Through them they sought to divine what courses of action to choose, or to avoid. Divination and prophecy were closely linked originally, the latter probably emerging out of the former.[72] Prophecy was a shamanistic activity developed by certain persons with unusual psychological qualities, perhaps with an inner strength which they could communicate. Thus, the prophet was a living oracle, who supplemented and eventually replaced the inanimate oracles of lot

---

[70] Judges 6: 7–8.

[71] I Samuel 3: 20; *Biblia Hebraica*, p. 410; Murray Newman, "The Prophetic Call of Samuel," in *Israel's Prophetic Heritage. Essays in honor of James Muilenberg*, ed. by Bernhard W. Anderson and Walter Harrelson, New York, Harper & Bros., 1962, pp. 90–92; Brinker, *op. cit.*, p. 112.

[72] Gadd considers oracles and prophecy as separate, with the latter generally older; see C. J. Gadd, *Ideas of Divine Rule in the Ancient East* (Sweich Lectures), Oxford University Press, 1948, pp. 20 ff.

and omen divination.[73] Early prophets were not necessarily adherents of a specific cult; rather they were individuals equipped with certain technical skills who were mobile and whose services were available to anyone who wished to employ them. Gordon has pointed out the parallel between the prophet Balaam who was summoned by Balak of Moab to curse Israel, and the prophets included in the Homeric epic among the *demiourgoi*, whose services were sought everywhere.[74] Many such individuals, however, were connected with specific cults and sacred places, and served as members of the cult personnel.[75] These or similar prophets undoubtedly had a significant place in the life of ordinary people, but even more important perhaps were the politico-religious functions they performed by keeping rulers in contact with the supernatural forces which governed their actions, and by advising in various matters of state.

Among the thousands of cuneiform tablets found in the palace of Zimri-Lim (*c.* 1730–1700 B.C.) king of the ancient city-state of Mari on the middle Euphrates, were a number of texts in which oracles or messages from gods were transmitted to the ruler. In some instances, the messenger (*apilu*) responds to a question put to the god by the king; in others the *apilu* was the unbidden and unasked messenger of a deity whose instructions and pronouncements came to him by inspiration, and which he delivered orally to the king.[76] For example, such messengers or prophets[77] urged that offerings be made for a certain Jahdun-lim, possibly an official, who had died, or announced that the king would defeat hostile Benjaminites.[78]

Early in the eighth century, Zakir, king of Hamat and Lu'ath was attacked by an alliance of seven (?) kings led by Barhadad of Damas-

---

[73] Numbers 12: 6–7; Deuteronomy 13: 1–5; I Samuel 28: 6, 15.

[74] Cyrus H. Gordon, *The Common Background of Greek and Hebrew Civilizations*, New York, W. W. Norton, 1965, p. 41.

[75] Alfred Haldar, *Associations of Cult Prophets among the Ancient Semites*, Uppsala, Almquist & Wiksells Boktryckeri, 1945, pp. 21–29, 57–60.

[76] A. Lods, "Une tablette inédite de Mari, intéressante pour l'histoire ancienne du prophétisme sémitique," *Studies in Old Testament Prophecy* . . . ed. by H. H. Rowley, Edinburgh, T & T Clark, 1950, pp. 103–110; M. Noth, "History and the Word of God in the Old Testament," *Bulletin of the John Rylands Library* 32: 194–206, 1950; W. von Soden, "Verkündigung des Gotteswillens durch prophetisches Wort in den altbabylonischen Briefen aus Mari," *Die Welt des Orients* 6: 397–403, 1950.

[77] The English word prophet is derived from the Greek *prophetes*, which means one who speaks for another, that is, a spokesman or interpreter. In this sense it denotes one who reveals, announces or interprets the will of a deity.

[78] A. Parrot and G. Dossin, eds., *Archives Royales de Mari*, vols. I–VI, Paris, 1950–1954, vol. III, No. 40; G. Dossin, "Une Révélation du Dieu Dagon à Terqua," *Revue d'Assyriologie* 42: 125–134, 1948; for the Benjaminites see *Ancient Near Eastern Texts* (note 38), p. 482.

cus, king of Aram. To commemorate his victory, he set up a stela on which he told how he called on his god for help and was answered. "But I lifted up my hand to Be'elshamayn and Be'elshamayn heard me. Be'elshamayn [spoke] to me through seers and through diviners. Be'elshamayn [said to me]: Do not fear, for I made you king, and I shall stand by you and deliver you from all [these kings who] set up a siege against you."[79]

A series of interesting Assyrian oracles dating from the reign of Esarhaddon, in the seventh century B.C., has been preserved. The oracles, delivered in the name of the goddess Ishtar of Arbela, are promises to the king to protect him and to bestow various benefits upon him. Most of those through whom the goddess spoke were women, probably in a trance state. Some of them are identified by name, but there is no indication that they were priestesses.[80]

Prophecy in Israel must be seen in relation to this environment. Various suggestions have been made concerning the outside sources that influenced Hebrew prophecy, but there is no doubt that many of its characteristics were similar to those found among the surrounding peoples.[81] There is a good deal of evidence that Israelite prophets were consulted concerning private as well as public matters. When Saul could not find his father's lost asses, he went to Ramah to inquire of Samuel about them. Jeroboam sent his wife to the prophet Ahijah to find out whether his son would recover. Even more interesting is the story of Ahaziah, king of Israel. Having fallen from the upper story of his palace, the injured ruler sent messengers to inquire of Baal-zebub, god of Ekron, concerning the outcome of his illness. But the angel of the Lord commanded the prophet Elijah to intercept the embassy, and to say to them: "Is it because there is no God in Israel that you are going to inquire of Baal-zebub, the god of Ekron?" Elijah clearly accepted the mantic and healing functions of prophecy, but he stressed the supremacy of Yahweh in this connection, and the obligation of the Israelite to consult his prophets in order to discover the future or to obtain wise guidance for the present.[82]

Prophets also played an active part in the political and military life of Israel. Nathan, one of the prophets at the court of David, supported Solomon in the struggle for the succession to the throne,

---

[79] *Ancient Near Eastern Texts* (note 38), pp. 501–502; Haldar, *op. cit.*, pp. 74–75; M. Noth, "La'asch und Havrak," *Zeitschrift des deutschen Palaestina-Vereins* 52: 124–141, 1929.

[80] *Ancient Near Eastern Texts* (note 38), pp. 449–450; Haldar, *op. cit.*, p. 24; Guillaume, op. cit., pp. 42 ff.

[81] T. J. Meek, *Hebrew Origins* (revised edition), New York, Harper & Bros., 1950, pp. 155–156; Harper Torchbooks edition, 1960; Haldar, *op. cit.*, pp. 21–29, 109–111; Kaufmann, *op. cit.*, p. 95.

[82] I Samuel 9: 6–10; I Kings 14: 1–4; II Kings 2–4.

showing himself well-versed in court intrigue. After Solomon's death, Ahijah of Shiloh instigated Jeroboam to revolt against Rehoboam, his son, thus disrupting the united monarchy and bringing about the establishment of the two kingdoms of Israel, and Judah. The accounts of the prophets in the northern kingdom during the dynasties of Omri and Jehu contain numerous incidents illustrative of such activities. When Ben-hadad of Syria besieged Samaria, the capital of Israel, an unnamed prophet predicted that the Israelites would defeat their attackers: "Have you seen all this great multitude? Behold I will give it into your hand this day; and you shall know that I am the Lord." And when Ahab inquired of the prophet how best to lift the siege, the latter provided military guidance, telling the king what troops to use and when to engage the enemy. Similarly, before the battle at Aphek between the Syrians and the Israelites, a man of God announced the coming victory of Israel, "Because the Syrians have said, 'The Lord is a god of the hills, but he is not a god of the valleys', therefore I will give all this great multitude into your hand, and you shall know that I am the Lord."[83]

When Ahab, king of Israel, quarrelled with Ben-hadad of Damascus, he formed a military alliance with Jehoshaphat, king of Judah, and made plans to attack Ramoth-Gilead, the town over which the dispute began. Before going into battle, the kings of Israel and Judah decided to inquire of their god concerning the outcome, and sent for prophets to forecast the issue of the projected campaign. Led by Zedekiah ben Chenaanah, the prophetic host numbereng several hundred urged Ahab to "Go up to Ramoth-Gilead and triumph; the Lord will give it into the hand of the king."[84]

Not all prophets, however, delivered favourable oracles, approving the plans of those who consulted them or supporting their general policies. Thus, Micaiah ben Imlah who opposed Ahab's plan and forecast his defeat, appears to have announced unfavourable oracles on previous occasions, for Ahab says: "I hate him, for he never prophesies good concerning me, but evil."[85] The reason for Micaiah's opposition to Ahab is not given, just as no basis beyond a general condemnation is provided for the prophecy of Jehu ben Hanani concerning the downfall of Baasha of Israel and his dynasty.[86] These instances may perhaps be regarded as expressing the antagonism and resentment of Yahwist prophets towards the syncretizing religio-political tendencies of the Israelite monarchs, attitudes which found more prominent expression in the opposition of Elijah to Ahab's

[83] I Kings 1: 9–34; 11: 26–40; 12: 1–20; 20: 13–15, 26–29.
[84] I Kings 22: 5–6, 10–12.
[85] I Kings 22: 8.
[86] I Kings 16: 1–4.

policies, and in the agitation of his successor Elisha for the extirpation of the house of Ahab.[87]

## Prophecy, Ecstasy and Madness

While bearing in mind the widely different historical settings in which the prophets appeared, as well as the diverse functions they performed, it is none the less clear that they were deeply concerned with affairs of state and constantly dealt with such matters in their oracles. Moreover, an understanding of diplomatic and military practice in the ancient Near East is well attested in the prophetic oracles. Why then should prophets be called madmen? Why should the verb "to behave like a prophet" also mean "to rave," or "to act like one beside himself?" Was there no way to make any clear distinction in mental experience and outward manifestation between the prophet and the madman?

Somewhat over fifty years ago, the publication of Hölscher's *Die Profeten* brought into prominence the view that Hebrew prophecy was essentially ecstatic in character.[88] According to this view, the prophetic movement in Israel was rooted in group excitation, which gave rise to psychological experiences and behavioural manifestations that were brought together under the term ecstasy. Whether this usage is correct need not detain us here (it will be discussed below), but it is important to note that it has been employed to cover such varied phenomena as auditions, visions and ineffable raptures, inspiration, trance, loss of consciousness, frenzy and violent agitation of the body.

Discussion of the nature of these phenomena has raised the question whether and to what extent the experiences and actions of the Israelite prophets were psychologically abnormal.[89] Certainly, some of them acted in ways which seem strange, if not abnormal to us, but there is no doubt that the prophets also differed in behaviour and appearance from the people of their own time. Prophets went about unshorn, clothed in a hairy mantle of sackcloth held together by a leather girdle.[90] Moreover, some acts performed by prophets

[87] For detailed analysis of the political aspects and relations of Israelite prophecy see Norman K. Gottwald, *All the Kingdoms of the Earth. Israelite Prophecy and International Relations in the Ancient Near East*, New York, Harper and Row, 1964.

[88] Gustav Hölscher, *Die Profeten. Untersuchung zur Religionsgeschichte Israels*, Leipzig, Hinrichs, 1914.

[89] O. Eissfeldt, "The Prophetic Literature," in *The Old Testament and Modern Study. A Generation of Discovery and Research*, by ed. H. H. Rowley, Oxford, Clarendon Press, 1956, pp. 115–161 (see especially pp. 134–145).

[90] II Kings 1: 8; Isaiah 20: 2; Zechariah 13: 4.

were indeed peculiar or dramatic. Thus, after Elijah slaughtered the prophets of Baal, he performed a major feat of physical prowess by running seventeen miles before the chariot of Ahab to the town of Jezreel in order to herald the victory he had won. When the kings of Israel and Judah consulted the prophets on the outcome of the projected attack, on Ramoth Gilead, their leader Zedekiah made horns of iron for himself, placed them on his head and forecast victory for the Israelites. "Thus says the Lord," he announced, "With these you shall push the Syrians until they are destroyed." In the eighth century, Isaiah walked naked and barefoot about the streets of Jerusalem during a period of three years.[91]

In 593 B.C., when the kings of Ammon, Edom, Moab, Sidon and Tyre invited Zedekiah, king of Judah, to join them in a revolt against Nebuchadnezzar of Babylon, Jeremiah put a wooden yoke upon his neck and advised the kings to submit to Babylonian rule. He then continued to go about the streets of Jerusalem wearing his yoke, until one day Hananiah, another prophet, seized his yoke and broke it, predicting that thus the Lord would break the yoke of Babylon. Shortly thereafter, however, Jeremiah received a revelation that Hananiah was a false prophet, and replaced his wooden yoke with one of iron. On another occasion he bought a potter's earthen vessel, called together some of the elders of the people and the priests, and went with them to the Potsherd Gate. There he broke the vessel, and said "Thus says the Lord of hosts: So I will break this people and this city, as one breaks a potter's vessel, so that it can never be mended." After the fall of Jerusalem, Jeremiah was forced to flee with a group of fugitive Israelites to Tahpanes in Egypt. There, at the entrance to the palace of Pharaoh, he buried great stones and prophesied that Nebuchadnezzar would conquer Egypt and erect his throne on them.[92]

Even stranger and more dramatic are the acts of the prophet Ezekiel.[93] On receiving his prophetic call, Ezekiel was commanded by Yahweh to eat a papyrus scroll on which were written words of lamentation and mourning, symbols of the message he was to deliver. When he did so, he had the sensation of eating honey. Subsequently, his prophecies concerning Judah and Jerusalem during the period 593–587 B.C. were frequently accompanied by unusual acts, but sometimes these actions were not commented on verbally. He indicated the fate of Jerusalem by drawing on a sun-dried brick a plan of a besieged city surrounded by engines of war, placing an iron

---

[91] Isaiah 20: 2–3; I Kings 22: 11 (cf. Deuteronomy 33: 17, Zechariah 1: 18–21, Daniel 7: 19–27, Psalms 75: 4–5); I Kings 18: 46.

[92] Jeremiah 27; 28: 10–14; 19: 1–11; 43: 1–11.

[93] Ezekiel 2:8–3:3; 4: 1–3, 9–17, 5: 1–4, 10–12; 12: 1–6; 4: 4–8.

plate between himself and the brick to symbolize the city blockaded by the Chaldeans. Then to forecast the famine and other horrors to which the siege would lead, Ezekiel rationed his food and drink, and prepared it using for fuel human dung, which was considered unclean. As a sign of the calamities that would befall Jerusalem, he cut off his hair and beard using a sword as a razor, then burned one-third, destroyed another third with the sword, and scattered the remainder to the four winds. Ezekiel foretold the approaching exile of Zedekiah, king of Judah, and of the survivors of the siege of Jerusalem, by collecting his belongings and carrying them in the dead of night through a hole, which he had previously pierced in the wall of his house. To indicate the time during which Israel and Judah respectively would be exiled, he was commanded by Yahweh to lie down for two periods, once on his left side for 390 days (190 days in the Septuagint), and once on his right side for forty days.

To understand the behaviour of the prophets, to appreciate the purpose and the impact of their unusual acts, they must be considered in the context of their setting and period. Historically, their actions are functional phenomena related to the needs of a particular situation within a given environment. When the need or the environment cease to exist, the behaviour disappears, or changes in relation to a new situation.

In the nineteenth century, the acts performed by the prophets, which they felt compelled to carry out, were interpreted along rationalistic lines; indeed, this view is still espoused at present.[94] Acts such as those described above were regarded as symbolic gestures, as mimed parables consciously invented and acted out by the prophets in order to enhance the effect upon their auditors of the message they delivered. Thus Kaufmann, who describes the prophets as "for the most part, psychically abnormal," goes on to comment that "this madness had its method; it made an impression ... notwithstanding the prophet's madness, the people believed and feared him."[95]

To be sure, no discussion of the Israelite prophets which neglects the symbolism of their acts can be considered satisfactory, for this element is characteristic of their behaviour. For those who look at such bizarre behaviour from the viewpoint of a more sober culture, it may be attractive to have a rationalistic explanation of these acts. Nevertheless, an interpretation in terms of conscious, rational action

---

[94] Ernest Renan, *Histoire du peuple d'Israel*, Paris, Levy, 1887, vol. 2, p. 485; Hubert Junker, *Prophet und Seher in Israel*, Trier, Paulinus Verlag, 1927, pp. 13–14; I. P. Seierstad, "Erlebnis und Gehorsam beim Propheten Amos," *Zeitschrift fur die alttestamentliche Wissenschaft* 52: 22–41, 1934.

[95] Kaufmann, *op. cit.*, p. 276.

is inadequate and fits only a few of the situations described in the Old Testament. An example where it is appropriate may be seen in Jeremiah's meeting in the Temple with the Rechabites, a fanatical religious sect. He offered them wine, knowing that the founder of the sect had ordered them to abstain from wine; and when they refused to drink, Jeremiah approvingly contrasted their faithfulness to their principles with Judah's lack of faith in the word of the Lord.[96] But there are other situations where a rationalistic explanation is not adequate, because the symbolic behaviour of the prophets is a much more complex phenomenon which requires consideration on several levels.

From the great significance attached by the prophets and their audience to symbolic acts and the verbal messages with which they were frequently associated, it is quite apparent that both were believed to have a definite influence on the future. Thus, the words of the prophets were not merely predictions of future happenings. The prophets spoke not their own words but those of the Lord; consequently, they were words of power, filled with a vital force which would bring about their own fulfilment and mould the future. This belief in the power of the word is part of the magical element present in the Old Testament, a legacy derived from ancient ideas which were transformed to express new conceptions developed by Israelite religion.[97] The magical notion of words as causally efficacious for good or evil is very old, and is perhaps best illustrated by blessings and curses.[98] Linked with this notion is the idea that the power to bless and curse belongs particularly to certain people who can communicate with the godhead, or who have an inner strength which they can pass on to others. For example, when Balak, king of Moab, summoned the diviner Balaam from Pethor on the upper Euphrates to curse Israel, he did so presumably because Balaam had a reputation for pronouncing effective curses and blessings.[99]

However, the effectiveness of curses and blessings, such as those of Balaam, does not depend merely on verbal magic, on the belief that the words uttered are forces let loose in the world for evil or good.

---

[96] Jeremiah 35.

[97] Kaufmann, *op. cit.*, pp. 78–85.

[98] Aubrey R. Johnson, *The Vitality of the Individual in the Thought of Ancient Israel*, University of Wales Press, 1949; S. Mowinckel, "Segen und Fluch in Israels Kult and Psalmdichtung," *Psalmenstudien V*, Oslo, 1924; T. H. Gaster, ed., *The New Golden Bough. A New Abridgment of the Classic Work by Sir James George Frazer*, (Mentor Books), New York, New American Library, 1964, pp. 235–46, 271–72.

[99] W. F. Albright, "The Oracles of Balaam," *Journal of Biblical Literature* 63: 207–233, 1944; S. Daiches, "Balaam—a Babylonian *baru*," *Herman Hilprecht Anniversary Volume*, 1909, pp. 60–70.

Belief in the effectiveness of such utterances is something much more complex. They are regarded as efficacious not only because they are words of power, but because they are held literally to effect what they signify, because they are embodied activity. In short, as Dorothy Emmet has suggested, such verbal acts are in a way "performative utterances," in which saying is doing.[100]

Ahab's reaction to the pessimistic prophecy of Micaiah ben Imlah before the battle of Ramoth-Gilead is clarified further when viewed within this context.[101] When the prophet envisioned Israel as a flock of sheep wandering without a shepherd, he was not merely predicting Ahab's death; by pronouncing his ill-omened prophecy he was acting to bring it about. Because Ahab considered Micaiah's utterance a hostile act which had released an inimical force against himself, he took steps to diminish his peril by imprisoning the prophet, and by attempting to appear inconspicuous in the eyes of the enemy when he engaged them in battle. But Ahab could not avert the judgement of the prophet, for he lost his life in the attack on Ramoth-Gilead.

When Jeremiah prophesied in the court of the Temple in 609 B.C., predicting its destruction, he provoked a similar reaction. The priests and the prophets of the Temple demanded that he be sentenced to death, "because he has prophesied against the city." Jeremiah was saved from execution only by the intervention of some of the officers of the king and by the elders who invoked the precedent of the prophet Micah whose prophecies at the time of Hezekiah, king of Judah, had not led to any repressive action against him. Less fortunate was another prophet, Uriah of Kiriath-jearim, who had prophesied "in words like those of Jeremiah". When King Jehoiakim tried to kill him for having "prophesied against this city and against this land," Uriah fled and escaped to Egypt, but was handed over to the king of Judah, who slew him with the sword.[102]

The magical power of the spoken word is clearly evident in Israelite thought in both causal and performative senses, even though no distinction is drawn between them. Just as Joshua stops the sun with a spell, so Jeremiah extirpates or restores kingdoms simply by predicting their fate. The symbolic acts of the prophets also belong this realm of magical power for they were evidently regarded as having an effective role in the realization of events. This miming of

---

[100] Dorothy Emmet, *Function, Purpose and Powers. Some Concepts in the Study of Individuals and Societies*, London, Macmillan & Co., 1958, pp. 213–215; for the concept of a "performative utterance", see J. L. Austin, *How to do things with Words*, ed. by J. O. Urmson, Cambridge, Mass., Harvard University Press, 1962, pp. 4–7; *idem.*, *Philosophical Papers*, Oxford, Clarendon Press, 1961, pp. 44–48.

[101] I Kings 22: 17, 26–27.

[102] Jeremiah 26: 7–23.

future happenings, a practice familiar in magical rites, has been linked in the Old Testament with the idea of the prophet delivering the word of the Lord.[103] Belief in the reality of magic persisted, however, so that the actions of the prophets, even though performed at the command of Yahweh to carry out the divine will, bore a formidable aura of magical power.

When Zedekiah ben Chenaanah mounted iron horns on his head he intended to bring about, and not merely to foretell, victory of Israel over the enemy. No doubt the summary account in I *Kings* offers only a glimpse of the preparations that preceded the battle of Ramoth-Gilead, but it is highly probable that they included rites of an imitative or sympathetic character, among them a symbolic war dance performed by Zedekiah to encourage the Israelite warriors by enacting on a small scale the fate awaiting the enemy.[104] Similarly, Jeremiah's breaking of an earthen vessel at the Potsherd Gate and the accompanying pronouncement of the destruction of Jerusalem were interpreted not merely as a prediction but as an act to bring about the overthrow of the city. Consequently, when Jeremiah repeated his prophecy in the court of the Temple, he was seized by Pashhur, the priest in charge of the Temple police, beaten and punished publicly by being put in the stocks. Clearly, the acts of the prophet were no trifling matter. Unless counter-measures were taken, the hostile force which he released could lead to catastrophe. Undoubtedly combined with this attitude was the view that Jeremiah was a traitor, for his enemies accused him of discouraging resistance and undermining morale by his prophecies of disaster.

Another example of a prophetic act derived from magical practice is Ezekiel's ill-treatment of his hair to symbolize the fate of the inhabitants of Jerusalem. Almost universal is the use for magical purposes of human exuviae, that is, hair, nail clippings, spittle, teeth, excreta, and other parts or products of the body. These substances are employed in practices intended to bring ill-fortune or harm to some person. Behind such practices seems to be a primitive notion of what may be called an extended self. Thus, to burn the hair or nail clippings of an individual is a means of causing him to suffer.[105] This is precisely what Ezekiel does, at the command of Yahweh, of course, to indicate the suffering of Israel.

Moreover, it should not be forgotten that the Biblical world was dominated by a living oral tradition. Many people could not read,

---

[103] Kaufmann, *op. cit.*, pp. 80–82; Norbeck, *op. cit.*, pp. 54–56.

[104] I Kings 22: 10–12; Dorothee Günther, *Der Tanz als Bewegungsphänomen*, Reinbeck, b. Hamburg, Rowohlt Taschenbuch Verlag, 1962, p. 146.

[105] Norbeck, *op. cit.*, pp. 56–58; Gaster, *The New Golden Bough*, pp. 62–65, 176, 226–229.

so that writing did not play the role that it does now. Emphasis was placed on the oral transmission of significant materials. Indeed, there is little doubt that some of the Biblical manuscripts found among the Qumran discoveries were copied from dictation, and probably also from memory, as indicated by readings clearly due to *hörfehler*.[106] In this environment, teaching was almost entirely oral, and at times exclusively visual. Thus, the prophetic message was often presented not so much in speech as in the language of action and example.[107]

Clearly, the acts of the prophets alone, even though strange to us, offer no basis for judging them psychopathological. Nevertheless, numerous students of the Israelite prophets have regarded them as in some way abnormal. As indicated above, this view is generally linked with the so-called ecstatic character of prophecy.[108] For this reason, it is necessary to examine the nature of prophetic ecstasy, and to endeavour to establish whether such unusual psychological states and the behaviour associated with them are in any way psychopathological. An important difficulty in discussing the character of the prophetic experiences which have been termed ecstatic is the lack of clear definition of the phenomena in question. The word ecstasy has been interpreted in various ways so that its use has brought more confusion than clarity into this aspect of prophecy. Because of the general acceptance of the term, however, we shall continue to use it. But to determine whether and in what sense it may be meaningfully applied to Israelite prophecy, it is necessary to specify the elements that occur most frequently in cases to which it has been applied.

The association of unusual emotional states and psychic experiences with religion is of great antiquity and undoubtedly ante-

---

[106] Harry M. Orlinsky, "Notes on the Present State of the Judean Biblical Cave Scrolls," in E. C. Hobbs, ed., *A Stubborn Faith* (W. A. Irwin Festschrift), Dallas, 1956, pp. 117–131 (see particularly p. 124).

[107] For a somewhat later example of such communication see Jacques Lacarrière, *Men Possessed by God. The Story of the Desert Monks of Ancient Christendom*, Garden City, Doubleday & Co., 1964, pp. 206–207.

[108] H. Gunkel, "The Secret Experiences of the Prophets," *Expositor* (9th series), I: 356–366, 427–435, II: 23–32, 1924; Hölscher, *op. cit.*, (note 88); W. Jacobi, *Die Extase der alttestamentlichen Propheten* (Grenzfragen des Nerven und Seelenlebens), München, Bergmann, 1923; A. S. Kapelrud, *Joel Studies* (Uppsala Universitets Årsskrift: 4), Uppsala, A. B. Lundequistska Bokhandeln, Leipzig, Otto Harrassowitz, 1948; Kaufmann, *op. cit.*, (note 10); A. Lods, *The Prophets and the Rise of Judaism*, London, Routledge & Kegan Paul, 1937; H. W. Robinson, *op. cit.*, (note 30); T. H. Robinson, "The Ecstatic Element in Old Testament Prophecy," *Expositor* (8th Series) 21: 217–238, 1921; *idem*, *Prophecy and the Prophets in Ancient Israel*, London, Duckworth, 1923; H. H. Rowley, *op. cit.*, (note 60); *idem.*, *Prophecy and Religion in Ancient China and Israel*, London, Athlone Press, University of London, 1956. These are only a few representatives examples of an extensive literature on this subject.

dates any documentary evidence. This is an area in which beliefs and ritual practices have been linked in the closest possible way to psychological and physiological mechanisms, which are still obscure, in order to communicate with the supernatural and to obtain revelations considered significant by individuals or groups. The range of experiences, states of being, and observable behaviour involved in such situations can vary widely from vague, ineffable feelings with few associated physical and behavioural phenomena to conditions that seem to lie outside the usual course of events and are characterized by seizures, trances, hallucinations and other forms of behaviour which appear abnormal.[109] The terms most frequently employed to comprehend these phenomena are ecstasy and possession. These terms are not entirely satisfactory, partly owing to a lack of precision, and partly because their use implies the occurrence of two distinct states of being. Possession denotes invasion of the body by some intrusive entity, while ecstasy implies that the psychic element can be separated from the body and is potentially independent of it.[110] Nevertheless, the objective acts and signs and the subjective states to which these terms have been applied do not belong to two separate and distinct conditions, but form a general, typical pattern of which examples abound in history from ancient times to the present.

Possession and ectasy characteristically manifest themselves in the following manner. An extraordinary inner tension seizes the individual, and he experiences irresistible and perhaps incomprehensible emotions. As if under the compulsion of some force acting upon him, the individual feels constrained to speak or to act. In this state, he may also feel fear and resist the apparent invasion of his personality. At the same time he may experience pains and seem to lose his strength and breath. These internal developments are associated with external bodily changes. The individual's features are altered, and he begins to act as if he had lost control of his motor system. Trembling, lassitude and drowsiness may precede the period of convulsive agitation. Then, the limbs become agitated, the gestures wild and excited, the voice changes, and what is uttered seems to be the expression of another personality. Violent trembling, frenzied leaps, spasmodic convulsions and other forms of motor hyperexcitement occur for varying periods, and are followed finally by prostration and unconsciousness. While in trance, the possessed or

---

[109] Marghanita Laski, *Ecstasy. A Study of some Secular and Religious Experiences*, London, Cresset Press, 1961, pp. 40–42; T. K. Oesterreich, *Possession, Demoniacal and other among Primitive Races, in Antiquity, the Middle Ages and Modern Times*, London, Kegan Paul, Trench, Trubner & Co., 1930.

[110] Edwyn Bevan, *Sibyls and Seers. A Survey of Some Ancient Theories of Revelation and Inspiration*, London, George Allen & Unwin, 1928, pp. 134–135; Karl Meuli, Scythica, *Hermes* 70: 121–176, 1935.

ecstatic person has hallucinatory experiences such as visions, auditions (voices), as well as other distortions of sensation. To be sure, these aspects are not all present in every instance. Under various circumstances some individuals show no tendency to violent activity. Furthermore, certain persons learn to produce a state of trance in themselves or in others with little or no strong emotional stimulation. None the less the general pattern is similar, whether in Bali, Haiti, Tibet or the United States.[111]

The occurrence of such a pattern widely distributed in time and space arises from the circumstance that the basic action patterns in man depend on the reactions of the higher nervous system to stimulation. Man can react physiologically only along limited lines to environmental changes, including various physical and psychological stresses to which he may be subjected. Despite their consequent basic similarity, however, all such states do exhibit numerous variations because they are strongly moulded by cultural values and conventions. Motor behaviour associated with possession and ecstasy tends to be conventionalized, and this is also true of the content of the psychological experiences associated with these states as well as of the means employed to achieve them.

The cultural and religious history of Israel did not begin with a *tabula rasa* at the time of Moses. It had behind it traditions which show continuity over a long period of time and give evidence of contact with the high civilizations of Mesopotamia.[112] This point is certainly applicable to Israelite prophetism which, as has been indicated above, was no isolated development, but represents a branch of ancient Near Eastern prophecy. Prophesying in a state of frenzy followed by trance was not confined to Israel, and there is evidence that such behaviour was not uncommon in neighbouring countries.

In a papyrus dating from the eleventh century B.C., Wen-Amon, an official of the Temple of Amon at Karnak, tells how he was sent to the Phoenician city of Byblos to obtain lumber for the barge of the god. The Prince of Byblos refused to receive him and to grant his request until one day when the Prince was sacrificing, "the god seized one of his youths and made him possessed." In a prophetic

---

[111] Jane Belo, *Trance in Bali*, New York, Columbia University Press, 1960, pp. 5–6; Alfred Métraux, "Dramatic Elements in Ritual Possession," *Diogenes*, No. 11, 1955, pp. 18–36; Heinrich Harrer, *Seven Years in Tibet*, New York, Dutton, 1954, pp. 197, 203–206; Amy E. Tanner, *Studies in Spiritism*, New York and London, D. Appleton & Co., 1910, pp. 14–16.

[112] G. E. Mendenhall "Biblical History in Transition," in *The Bible and the Ancient Near East. Essays in Honor of William Foxwell Albright*, ed. by G. Ernest Wright (Anchor Books), Garden City, Doubleday & Co., 1965, pp. 27–58 (see pp. 36–49); Haldar, *op. cit.*, p. 110.

frenzy, he was inspired to deliver an oracle that the Baal of Byblos had granted the desire of Amon, the Egyptian God. J. A. Wilson, in a footnote to his translation of this document, points out that "the determinative of the word '(prophetically) possessed' shows a human figure in violent motion or epileptic convulsion."[113] Furthermore, it should be noted that Wen-Amon's journey is contemporary with the period of Joshua and the Judges.

Other evidence is provided by Sumero-Babylonian texts in which there are references to a type of priest called a *maḫḫū*, who in a state of frenzy delivered or interpreted oracles. *Maḫḫū* means "frenzied," or "one who is out of his senses," and is apparently derived from the verb *maḫū*, "to rave." *Maḫḫūtū* meaning "frenzy" or "derangement', is derived from the same root.[114] These words provide a noteworthy parallel to the Hebrew *nābhi'* and the words related to it which have been discussed above (see pp. 35–37). In both cases, the ideas of frenzy and mental derangement are brought together.[115]

The account of the prophets of Tyrian Baal when they contended with Elijah provides still another example of prophesying in a frenzy, and contains details of the rites which they employed to work themselves into this state. After preparing a bullock for a burnt offering, they called upon Baal from morning until noon. Then they began to perform a kind of dance, in which they moved around the altar with limping steps, bending first one knee, then the other, and hopping from one leg to the other, thus turning the body from side to side. As the dancers circled the altar, the tempo increased until at the climax they attained a state of frenzy, slashed themselves with swords and lances, and prophesied.[116]

---

[113] *Ancient Near Eastern Texts* (note 38); pp. 25–29 (see particularly p. 26 note 13); the text was originally published by W. Golenischeff, *Recueil de travaux relatifs à la philologie et à l'archéologie égyptiennes et assyriennes*, 1899, XXI, pp. 74–102, and is discussed by W. F. Albright, "The Eastern Mediterranean about 1060 B.C.," in *Studies presented to David Moore Robinson*, ed., E. G. Mylonas, St. Louis, Washington, 1951, vol. I, pp. 223–231.

[114] Haldar, *op. cit.*, 21–26: W. F. Albright, *From the Stone Age to Christianity, Monotheism and the Historical Process* (Anchor Books), Garden City, Doubleday & Co., 1957, p. 304.

[115] Haldar (*op. cit.*, pp. 108–109) specifically equates *nābhi'* and *maḫḫū*.

[116] This type of dance and the ritual of which it is a part are well known from other sources. It is noteworthy that the Septuagint version of I Kings 18: 21 renders the Hebrew verb *pisseah*, to limp, which is used to describe the dance of the Baal prophets, by the Greek *oklazein*, to crouch down. The use of the Greek word is illuminated by Heliodorus, whose novel *Aethiopica* dates from the third century A.D. In it he depicts a dance by Phoenician merchants, who give thanks to the god Heracles, the Greek equivalent of Melkart, the Baal of Tyre. They danced "in the Syrian manner to the accompaniment of stringed instruments, and with a rapid tempo. First, they rose in the air with quick leaps, then sank down crouching (*epoklazontes*) on the ground, twisting the whole body as if

The term *ecstatic*, as used by Biblical scholars since Holscher, designates behaviour of the type described above.[117] It is characterized by motor hyperexcitement of varying intensity, followed by a state of trance, an experience of supreme exaltation where thought and volition cease, and concurrent or subsequent behaviour seems to be due to the action of external powers. It is in this last stage that the participants in such activities may have visions, auditions, or other distortions of perception and sensation, and deliver messages from supernatural or divine sources. Various means were employed to induce this condition: music—including singing, chanting and playing of instruments—dance and rhythmic movement, and ultimately self-laceration or mutilation.[118] Clearly, the phenomena characterized as ecstatic in discussions of Near Eastern prophecy are similar to those described above in the analysis of possession.

Behaviour of this kind was known in early Israel. For example, there were the seventy elders who were seized by the spirit and prophesied together as they surrounded the tent in which God spoke with Moses; the band of prophets from Gibeah whom Saul met and with whom he prophesied; and the group prophecy over which Samuel presided at Ramah. Evidence for such practices in later periods from the ninth to the sixth century B.C. is provided by Elisha's demand for music to induce the trance from which he prophesied after having been touched by the hand of the Lord; by Hosea's denunciation of prophets who gash themselves; and by Zechariah's statement that a prophet could be known by the wounds he had inflicted on himself.[119]

There is little doubt that Israelite prophetism originally differed little from the related practices characteristic of the neighbouring peoples.[120] Religious frenzies and trances produced by cult rituals

[117] Haldar, *op. cit.*, pp. 114–115; Kapelrud, *op. cit.*, p. 130, Rowley in Hooke *op. cit.*, (note 29), p. 239, note 3.

[118] André Caquot, "Les danses sacrées en Israel et à l'entour," in *Les Danses Sacrées* (Sources Orientales VI), Paris, Éditions du Seuil, 1963, pp. 121–143 (see particularly pp. 128–133); Haldar, *op. cit.*, pp. 118–119; Kaufmann, *op. cit.*, pp. 95–97.

[119] Numbers 11: 16–17, 24–25; I Samuel 10: 10–11; 19: 18–24; II Kings 3: 14–16; Hosea 7: 14; Zechariah 13: 5–6.

[120] S. Mowinckel, "Ecstatic experience and rational elaboration in Old Testament prophecy," *Acta Orientalia* 13: 264–291, 1935 (see pp. 266 ff.); Kaufmann, *op. cit.*, pp. 96, 100.

possessed." (Heliodore, "Les Éthiopiques ou Histoire de Théagène et Chariclée," in *Romans Grec et Latins*, ed. by Pierre Grimal (Bibliothèque de la Pléiade), Paris, Gallimard, 1958, p. 618. A striking account of the frenzied dance of the priests of the Syrian goddess is presented by Apuleius in his *Metamorphoses* (VIII, 27–28). From this description it was apparently very similar to the rite performed by the priests of Baal.

and intended to achieve communication with the divine provided the soil out of which later Israelite prophetism developed. Since there is an unbroken continuity down to the later pre-exilic prophets, it is not surprising to find aspects characteristic of the earlier period still present in their behaviour. Indeed, it is impossible to draw any sharp lines of division between the great prophets of Israel and the other prophets of their time, because their close adherence to the ways and language of earlier Israelite prophetism indicates that they remained to a large extent within a common tradition. Examples of such elements occur in a number of prophets.

Isaiah was convinced that he was inspired by the hand of the Lord; he had visions and heard Yahweh, his god, speaking to him in his ears. He may also have spoken in tongues.[121] Of the outstanding Israelite prophets, it was Ezekiel who experienced the phenomena of earlier prophetism in their most striking form. He was subject to frenzies in which he clapped his hands, stamped his feet, uttered inarticulate cries, and shook a sword to and fro. Trance experiences in which the spirit or the hand of the Lord came upon him are frequent in his prophecies. On one occasion, as Ezekiel sat among a group of elders, he saw a figure of gleaming light and fire that put forth a hand, picked him up by a lock of hair and brought him to Jerusalem where he saw idolatries practised in the Temple.[122]

The body of evidence concerning such phenomena is too extensive to present here. However, it is clear that not only Isaiah and Ezekiel but other prophets experienced trances, visions, auditions and other sense illusions.[123] To be sure, the great prophets no longer induced inspiration by means of music, dancing or intoxicating drinks; indeed, they condemned their contemporaries who still resorted to such methods.[124] Apparently, they were able to produce a state of trance in themselves by concentrating on deeply-felt feelings or ideas, thus achieving self-hypnosis.[125] But the appearance and behaviour of an Isaiah or a Jeremiah were not sufficiently different to set them apart from other prophets who claimed to be seized by the hand or the spirit of the Lord.

---

[121] A synonym for glossolalia, the term used to designate the unintelligible jabbering, the indistinct words and sounds uttered by persons in a state of possession or trance.

[122] Ezekiel 6: 11; 8: 1–4; 21: 14–17.

[123] Visions, see Amos 7: 1–9, 8: 1 ff., 9: 1 ff; Jeremiah 1, 24; Zechariah 1–6; auditions, see Isaiah 22: 14; 40: 3, 6; compulsions and emotions, Jeremiah 6: 11 ff. 20: 9.

[124] Micah 2: 11; Isaiah 28: 7, 8; 29: 9–10.

[125] J. Lindblom, "Die Gesichte der Propheten," *Studia Theologica* 1: 7–28, 1935; *ibid.*, "Einige Grundfragen der alttestamentlichen Wissenschaft," *Bertholet Festschrift*, pp. 325–337.

Possession, trance and related phenomena were accepted and regarded as socially significant within the cultic and prophetic framework. The question remains whether they are to be considered normal or abnormal. Possession and its associated phenomena are frequently explained in terms of nervous and mental disorder. Physicians are prone to offer such explanations, but this tendency is not restricted to them, and for good reason. The initial stages of possession exhibit symptoms that appear clearly psychopathological, resembling attacks of hysteria or epilepsy. Indeed, possession and epilepsy sometimes show a great resemblance, and, as Temkin pointed out, for a long time they were confused with each other.[126]

Concentration on the symptomatic aspects has led some authors to view these conditions as forms of epilepsy. Based on such evidence, Preuss described Saul's behaviour at Ramah, when he threw off his clothes in a frenzy and rolled naked on the ground, as an example of *status epilepticus*, and claimed that his illness was an epileptoid condition, even though it was impossible to say that he had genuine epilepsy.[127] In this connection we may also recall the story of Wen-Amon, and J. A. Wilson's comment that the hieroglyph referring to the possessed priest showed a man quivering all over as if in an epileptic convulsion.

Other investigators of possession explain it in terms of hysteria or of a psychosis, such as schizophrenia. P. M. van Wulfften Palthe, a Dutch psychiatrist who studied possession and trance experiences in Bali, concluded that the subjects who are possessed and enter into trance exhibited symptoms comparable to those of hysteria, but he does not suggest that such individuals are hysterics. Although van Wulfften Palthe does not regard persons who exhibit such symptoms as pathological, he points out that those who go into a trance differ from their fellows. He says: "Not all persons, however, can enter into a trance or can be made to do so. Only some who differ from their fellow villagers through marked emotionality, a lively imagination, and in general through a somewhat infantile psychic structure are able to attain the level of reduced consciousness required to achieve this transformation . . ."[128] J. C. Dorsainvil, a physician, in his study of Haitian voodoo, goes much further and explicitly designates the state of possession as pathological. He characterizes voodoo as "a religious psychoneurosis, which is racial, characterized

---

[126] Owsei Temkin, *The Falling Sickness. A History of Epilepsy from the Greeks to the Beginnings of Modern Neurology*, Baltimore, John Hopkins Press, 1945, pp. 84 ff.

[127] Julius Preuss, *Biblisch-talmudische Medizin. Beiträge zur Geschichte der Heilkunde und der Kultur überhaupt*, Berlin, S. Karger, 1911, pp. 356–358.

[128] P. M. van Wulfften Palthe, "Over de bezetenheid," *Geneeskundig Tijdschrift voor Nederlandsch-Indie* 80: 2123–2153, 1940, p. 2147.

by a doubling of the self (*moi*), with functional alterations of sensibility, of motility, and predominance of oracular (*pythiatique*) symptoms."[129] A number of anthropologists (Radin, Kroeber, Linton, Devereux, to name but a few), who have studied shamans and their activities, have also been inclined to consider them mentally abnormal, if not actually psychotic, and to, view their behaviour in this light.[130]

There is, however, a body of evidence and opinion which clearly indicates that an explanation of possession, trance and behaviour associated with these states solely in terms of psychopathology is untenable. One approach has been to show that personality types or behaviour that would be considered abnormal, neurotic or psychotic in our culture may be highly valued and regarded as acceptable in other cultures. Ruth Benedict stated this position very clearly in 1934.

> It does not matter what kind of "abnormality" we choose for illustration, those which indicate extreme instability, or those which are more in the nature of character traits like sadism or delusions of grandeur or of persecution, there are well described cultures in which these individuals function at ease and with honour, and apparently without danger of difficulty to the society.
>
> The most notorious of these is trance and catalepsy. Even a very mild mystic is aberrant in our culture. But most peoples have regarded extreme psychic manifestations not only as normal and desirable, but even as characteristic of highly valued and gifted individuals.[131]

The position that mental abnormality is culturally defined was stated even more emphatically by Herskovits in 1937, with specific reference to Haiti. He rejected an explanation of voodoo in terms of psychopathology, stressing the rigidly controlled and stylized aspects of its phenomena.

> One must reject an hypothesis which attempts to explain the *vodun* cult of Haiti in terms of the neuroses, even when, as in the admirable exposition of Dr. Dorsainvil, the approach neglects neither accepted genetic theory in stressing the inheritance of neurotic tendencies in

[129] J. C. Dorsainvil, *Vodou et Névrose*, Port-au-Prince, Haiti, 1931, p. 111, quoted in Belo, *op. cit.*, p. 7.

[130] A. L. Kroeber, *The Nature of Culture*, Chicago, University of Chicago Press, 1952, pp. 310–319; Ralph Linton, *Culture and Mental Disorders*, Springfield, Charles C. Thomas, 1956, pp. 81–86, 118 ff.; George Devereux, "Normal and Abnormal, the Key Problem of Psychiatric Anthropology," in *Some Uses of Anthropology*, Washington, D.C., Anthropological Society of Washington, 1956, pp. 23–48; Paul Radin, *Primitive Religion*, New York, Viking Press, 1937, p. 154.

[131] Ruth Benedict, "Anthropology and the Abnormal," *Journal of General Psychology* 10: 59–80, 1934; see also her *Patterns of Culture*, New York, 1935, pp. 25 ff.

C

voduist family lines nor the important historical forces which have been operative ... In terms of the patterns of Haitian religion, possession is not abnormal but normal, it is set in a cultural mould as are all other phases of conventional living.[132]

Within this framework, possession was a normal means of establishing relations with supernatural powers. Herskovits was also aware that not everyone becomes possessed, and suggested that various individuals may be differentially predisposed or susceptible to such behaviour because of nervous instability, psychic tension and unfulfilled desires.

In 1943, E. H. Ackerknecht made it clear that shamans and other individuals in primitive societies who become possessed or manifest induced trance behaviour cannot therefore be considered abnormal, that being different cannot be equated with being psychopathological. Indeed, as he put it, the psychopathology of those in society who are different, queer or awkward is "due much more to their ambiguous position than to their organic structure."[133]

An important contribution to this problem was made by S. F. Nadel in 1946 in his study of shamanism among the people of the Nuba Mountains south of the Sudan.[134] He noted that there is a dual relationship between psychopathology and shamanistic behaviour. By providing a social function and a social role for individuals with psychopathic tendencies, shamanism makes use of these dispositions and at the same time makes it possible for such individuals to become stabilized. They may be highly unstable personalities, but they need not be neurotics, still less psychotics, because their social role makes it possible for them to act in ways which would be considered pathological under other circumstances. Nadel observed that shamans do not behave abnormally in daily life; if they did they would be considered mad. However, in socially defined situations such as those involving religious rites, possession and trance are acceptable forms of behaviour. The means by which these states are achieved and how they manifest themselves are established by tradition, and their value is sanctioned by the participation of the group.

Her study of trance seizures and impersonations of witches and demons in Bali led Jane Belo, also, to conclude that such practices

[132] Melville J. Herskovits, *Life in a Haitian Valley*, New York, 1939, p. 147.

[133] E. H. Ackerknecht, "Psychopathology, Primitive medicine, and primitive culture," *Bulletin of the History of Medicine* 14: 30–69, 1943.

[134] S. F. Nadel; "A Study of shamanism in the Nuba Mountains," *Journal of the Royal Anthropological Institute* 76: 25–37, 1946; see also Claude Lévi-Strauss, "Introduction à l'oeuvre de Marcel Mauss" in Marcel Mauss, *Sociologie et Anthropologie*, Paris, Presses Universitaires de France, 1950, pp. XVIII–XXIII.

offered a channel for the expression of neurotic tendencies. Nevertheless, she found it "very questionable that a majority of the Balinese trance subjects were abnormal to any appreciable degree. Many of them seemed, outside of their trance behaviour, indistinguishable psychologically from their fellows who did not go into trance." She also points out that at the time these investigations were conducted there were some two hundred hospitalized mental patients as well as a number of individuals who were at liberty but could just as well have been put into the hospital. These individuals were regarded as mad (*boedoeh*). On the other hand, the investigators knew about 150 persons who habitually went into trance, none of whom were considered mentally deranged. Thus, she too concluded

> that in another culture some of them would have been considered to be suffering from hysteria, for many of the patterned symptoms they exhibited would fall under this rubric. The scheduled seizures they experienced, integrated with the religious life, given a meaning and the dignity of socially significant behaviour, may well have served as therapy. Individuals who were inducted into the trance practices, if they were abnormal to begin with, would find their difficulties alleviated by the institutionalization of their trance roles.[135]

Apparently in various human populations, perhaps in all, there are numbers of individuals who are capable of experiences such as possession and trance. These experiences, which may occur under a variety of circumstances, are characterized in current psychiatric terminology as dissociative states, that is, conditions where there is a division of consciousness with a segregation of mental processes and ideas to such an extent that they function as unitary wholes as if belonging to another person. These states and the experiences associated with them are not innately religious in character, but religious interpretations and values may be attributed to them, thus endowing them with special significance for a given group.

Possession and trance in religious ceremonies are ways of approaching the supernatural by reproducing psychopathological states. The techniques for inducing possession and ecstatic trance are intended to produce artificially hallucinations, hysterical crises and similar phenomena. However, the participants in these rites are not all abnormal; some are true neurotics, or afflicted with some other mental disorder, others are normal individuals. Does this mean then that not all possessions and trances are authentic? Does someone who is possessed by a god, or who feels the spirit of the Lord upon him, actually have dissociation of personality, does he actually lose all sense of reality, or is he only playing a part in a traditional cult

[135] Belo, *op. cit.*, pp. 9–10.

ritual? The answer is that there are genuine as well as spurious possessions and trances.[136] In certain cases, such behaviour is part of the stock repertoire of the professional religious practitioner, whether shaman, priest or prophet. Like any other professional group, religious practitioners also have their share of insincere, base members, as well as others who are just ordinary pedestrian individuals; only a minority are highly endowed, outstanding personalities. Representative of the former group are the false prophets of the Old Testament who are condemned as liars, adulterers, gluttons and drunkards.[137] Their insincerity is clearly implied when Jeremiah accuses them of stealing each other's oracles, and when Micah charges them with avarice, prophesying only for money, and telling the populace what it wants to hear—soothing promises of peace and prosperity.[138] On the other hand, there are individuals who must deal with severe inner conflicts and various kinds of psychological distress before they are able to accept the role of shaman or prophet. Such persons experience possession as an actual struggle against the trance which seems to occur in spite of the subject himself.[139] Because of the way in which they deal with their inner conflicts and with the mental and emotional distress occasioned thereby, these individuals may achieve exceptional inner strength, and in an appropriate environment considerable external authority on a moral and religious basis. Not only Israelite prophets such as Jeremiah, Hosea and Ezekiel, but also other religious innovators, among them Muhammad, Martin Luther and George Fox, are instances in point.[140]

What such a person sees and hears in possession and trance is a product of subconscious material and processes, the result of ideas and reflection, of previous religious experiences, and of deeply rooted tendencies of his being worked through to a greater or lesser degree in the unconscious mind, and rising to the level of consciousness so that it seems to him to come from outside himself. A prophetic oracle or a religious revelation comes through the mediation of personal consciousness, but its occurrence and content are related to a specific socio-cultural milieu. In our time we distinguish

[136] Norbeck, *op. cit.*, pp. 113–114.

[137] Isaiah 28: 7–8; Jeremiah 23: 14; 29: 23.

[138] Jeremiah 8: 10–11; 14: 13–15; 23: 17, 30; 27: 14 ff.; 28–29; Micah 3: 5; see also Ezekiel 12: 24; 13: 10.

[139] Norbeck, *op. cit.*, p. 110; Verrier Elwin, *The Religion of an Indian Tribe*, London, Oxford University Press, 1955; Jeremiah 1: 5; 11: 18–12: 6, 7–10; Isaiah 8: 11.

[140] Paul Radin, *The World of Primitive Man*, New York, 1953, p. 175, Anton T. Boisen, *The Exploration of the Inner World*, New York, Harper & Bros., 1936, Harper Torchbooks edition, 1962; Erik H. Erikson, *Young Man Luther*, New York, W. W. Norton, 1958; W. Montgomery Watt, *Muhammed, Prophet and Statesman*, London, Oxford University Press, 1961, Chap. II.

sharply between objective and subjective phenomena. Hearing a voice where there is no visible speaker, or having a vision which is unrelated to the normal environment, is generally attributed to some unusual psychological condition of the individual who has these experiences. For the ancient Israelites such an explanation was not available. Experiences such as visions and auditions were explicable within the traditions of a theocratic community where religious capacities were venerated. God was the source of these experiences, a view consistent with previous beliefs of long standing. Moreover, there was a generally accepted vocabulary to describe the state in which a divine effluence acted to produce phenomena characteristic of prophetic experience. The prophetic spirit was not in the prophet; it was the spirit, the word, or the hand of the Lord that came upon him, or took hold of him.

As has already been implied, the question of the mental normality or abnormality of the Israelite prophets cannot receive a sharp yes-or-no answer. Certain statements about them can be made, however, which do provide a qualified judgement. The available information about the earlier and the later prophets does not indicate that there were psychotics among them. Indeed what we know about them points in an altogether different direction. Jehu's officers called the young prophet, who was Elisha's messenger, a mad fellow, but one should also note that they were eager to learn the content of his message, which was political. As used here, the expression, "mad fellow" was clearly not intended to describe a disoriented lunatic, but rather to voice a feeling of contempt, perhaps mingled with awe, which a soldier, a bluff man of action, might have for a man who stands apart from ordinary people and who from time to time may acquire the spirit of Yahweh, the Lord.[141] Moreover, we may recall that the earlier prophets appeared in bands, sometimes numbering one hundred or more, and were often associated with sanctuaries such as Bethel or Gilgal, with the royal court, and perhaps the Temple at Jerusalem. Since the publication of Hölscher's book on the prophets, these bands or guilds have often been compared to the dervish orders of Islam.[142]

This comparison cannot be pushed too far, but it does illuminate the problem under discussion. Like modern dervishes, the bands of prophets lived in organized communities; they prayed and ate

[141] II Kings 9: 11–12. Such attitudes are expressed in similar fashion at present, for example, when we speak of someone as "nuts" or through the use of such words as "beatnik" or "holy roller" to express contempt for some form of disapproved behaviour.

[142] I Kings 22: 6; II Kings 4: 42–43; J. Lindblom, *Profetismen in Israel*, Stockholm, 1934, pp. 39–42; J. Pedersen, *Israel, Its Life and Culture*, III–IV, London-Copenhagen, Oxford, 1940, pp. 106 ff.

together, and acted under the authority of a leader.[143] Obviously such groups are not composed of psychotics, whatever other psychological deviations individual members exhibit. Nadel observed that certain possessions which initially appear simulated can terminate in schizophrenia, but such an outcome is not common. The principle underlying Alfred Métraux's comment about possession and hysteria in Haiti is applicable here. As he put it, "the number of persons subject to possession is too great for it to be called hysteria unless one considers the entire population of Haiti to be suffering from mental illness."[144] Probably this was also true of the prophetic bands in ancient Israel.

But what of the latter prophets? Here too the answer must be that as far as the available evidence goes, none of them were psychotic. Of the canonical prophets Ezekiel would seem to be the most likely candidate for a diagnosis of this kind. Evidently he was a peculiar person, abrupt and peremptory in his actions. There was something of the fanatic in him, and he was also a poet endowed with a fantastic imagination and intense passion. But he was not mad. Karl Jaspers endeavoured to show that Ezekiel may have been a schizophrenic.[145] However, it cannot be said that the attempt was successful. To establish a diagnosis of schizophrenia for a prophet, such as Ezekiel or Isaiah, it would be necessary to demonstrate a radical difference between the prophet's world and that of his contemporaries. Unless this can be done, the diagnosis cannot be maintained.[146] By the very nature of his vocation, the Biblical prophet occupied a place apart

[143] George Widengren, *Literary and Psychological Aspects of the Hebrew Prophets* (Uppsala Universities Arsskrift: 10) Uppsala, A. B. Lundequistska Bokhandeln: Leipzig: Otto Harrassowitz, 1948, pp. 94–96. This book is a curiosity in that the author attempts to explain the visions, auditions and other manifestations of the spirit of Yahweh on the basis of parapsychology, thus producing a unique example of Biblical science fiction. See also John P. Brown, *The Dervishes or Oriental Spiritualism*, ed. with an introduction and notes by H. A. Rose, London, Oxford University Press, 1927; E. W. Lane, *Manners and Customs of the Modern Egyptians*, London, J. M. Dent, n.d., pp. 437–462. For those who cannot attend a dervish ritual, the next best thing is to listen to a recording. Two recordings that can be recommended are *Islamic Liturgy. Song and Dance at a Meeting of Dervishes* (Folkways Records FR–8943), and *Sufi Ceremony, Rifa' Ceremony*, (Folkways Records FR–8942).

[144] Métraux, *op. cit.*, p. 30.

[145] Karl Jaspers, "Der Prophet Ezechiel. Eine pathographische Studie," in his *Rechenschaft und Ausblick, Reden und Aufsätze*, München, R. Piper & Co., Verlag, 1951, pp. 95–106. This paper was originally published in *Arbeiten zur Psychiatrie. Festschrift für Kurt Schneider zu dessen 60. Geburtstag*, Heidelberg, Scherer Verlag, 1947.

[146] Hans Heimann, "Religion und Psychiatrie," in *Psychiatrie der Gegenwart. Forschung und Praxis. Band III. Soziale und Angewandte Psychiatrie*, herausgegeben von H. W. Gruhle et al., Berlin Springer Verlag, 1961, pp. 470–493 (see pp. 482–484); *idem., Prophetie und Geisteskrankheit*, Bern, Haupt, 1956.

from the rest of the community, but he had a specific position in its social structure, and he maintained close contact with his environment. Thus, when Sennacherib, king of Assyria, attacked Jerusalem, Hezekiah, king of Judah, sent his officials to consult the prophet Isaiah on the outcome.[147] A schizophrenic "prophet," on the other hand, lives in a world of his own, and has no doubts about his mission and message. Indeed, the very fact that he is considered mad proves to him that he was sent by God. Unlike the schizophrenic, however, the antagonism, mockery and isolation which the Old Testament prophets experienced as a consequence of their mission often led them to doubt its authenticity.[148] Jeremiah, for example, in exposing his inner conflicts, his awareness of his own weakness and fear, of his bitter doubts and secret griefs, lays bare the profound spiritual struggle of an exceptional human being, which is as compelling today as it was over two thousand years ago. He cries out, "Woe is me, my mother, that you bore me, a man of strife, and contention to the whole land! I have not lent, nor have I borrowed, yet all of them curse me." And again he laments,

> O Lord, thou has deceived me, and I was deceived . . . I have become a laughing stock all the day; everyone mocks me! For whenever I cry out, I shout, "Violence and destruction!" For the word of the Lord has become for me a reproach and derision all day long. If I say, "I will not mention him, or speak any more in his name," there is in my heart as it were a burning fire shut up in my bones, and I am weary with holding it in, and I cannot . . . Cursed be the day on which I was born! The day when my mother bore me, let it not be blessed! . . . Why did I come forth from the womb to see toil and sorrow, and spend my days in shame?[149]

These are the thoughts and words of a man in the throes of a deep emotional struggle, of a man who is sensitive to his relations with his fellow-men, but who stands firm in his conviction that he can do no other than to hearken to the divine voice which echoes within him.

No one can show that the Israelite prophets were mentally ill in the sense of suffering from psychosis, but there is no doubt that they were different. Several recent writers, such as Hines, Andrae and Heschel, have pointed out that the experiences of the prophets are akin to those of mystics.[150] This comparison is fully justified in the

---

[147] II Kings 19:1–7.

[148] J. Wyrsch, *Die Person des Schizophrenen*, Bern, Haupt, 1949.

[149] Jeremiah 15: 10–21; 20: 7–18; see also 11: 18–12: 6; 17: 14–18; 18: 18–23.

[150] H. W. Hines, "The Prophet as Mystic, His Psychology," *American Journal of Semitic Languages and Literatures* 40: 37–71, 1923; Tor Andrae, *Mystikens psykologi*, Stockholm, 1926; Abraham Heschel, *Die Prophetie*, Krakow, Polish Academy of Sciences, 1936.

sense that the Israelite prophets, like the medieval Jewish, Christian and Muslim mystics, as well as those found among the Brahmans, Buddhists and Taoists of the Middle and Far East, all experienced trance states and the associated phenomena which have been discussed above.[151] Such a comparison, however, can hardly be carried much further. Generally speaking, interpretations of the phenomena vary widely, depending on time and place, on social circumstances and cultural traditions, and on group goals and individual needs. For example, that form of mysticism where the mystic loses all consciousness of selfhood and becomes one with God or with the Universe has no counterpart in the religious experience of the Old Testament prophets. There was no tradition on which to base such an interpretation of trance experiences.

Whether or not the Biblical prophets are regarded as mystics, the significant point is that the prophet's personal experience of God was not merely a private matter. His message was an element in the continuing revelation of the Lord to his people, and he was aware that he was one of a larger company of speakers for God. Thus, the prophetic experience served as the locus where the ancient traditions of Israel the burning issues of the present, and the prophet's intense belief in his call, were fused into powerful accusations of guilt, calls for repentance and righteousness, warnings of judgement, and demands for faith in Yahweh. This continuing oscillation between the heights of communion with the Lord and the need to bring the truth of God to bear on communal traditions and problems, requires a kind of personality that can accept and work through profound spiritual and intellectual travail towards a new understanding and consciousness of the way of the Lord. As W. F. Albright put it, "A certain 'abnormality' is required to divert a man's thoughts and his emotional experiences from the common treadmill of human thinking and feeling."[152] The nature of this difference, this "abnormality" cannot be determined at present. All that can be said is that personality structure, social situation and cultural tradition enabled those whom we know as the prophets to exhibit the kinds of behaviour which have been described as "border-line psychological states."[153]

[151] Henri Maspero, *La Chine Antique* (nouvelle édition), Paris, Imprimerie Nationale, 1955, pp. 409–411; Leon Weiger, *Les Pères du Système Taoïste*, Paris, Cathasia-France, 1950, p. 85 (I wish to thank Professor Arnold Koslow of Brooklyn College for his kindness in calling my attention to the Chinese references); R. J. Z. Werblowsky, *Joseph Karo, Lawyer and Mystic*, Oxford, Clarendon Press, 1962; R. C. Zaehner, *Mysticism, Sacred and Profane*, Oxford, Clarendon Press, 1957; Walter T. Stace, *The Teachings of the Mystics*, New York, New American Library, 1960.

[152] Albright, *From the Stone Age to Christianity*, op. cit., p. 325.

[153] Ruth Benedict, "Religion," in *General Anthropology*, Franz Boas, ed., New York, D. C. Heath & Co., 1938, p. 658.

## The Mentally Ill and the Community

When a society regards highly individuals who are able to produce unusual psychological states, such persons will appear. However, the society also stipulates the boundaries within which it will accept or at least tolerate such behaviour. Cultural values serve not only to encourage or to check the experiences and acts of these individuals; they also provide the criteria by which deviant behaviour of this type is judged and differentiated from other forms. Thus many societies distinguish between the insane, that is, mentally deranged individuals whose condition is chronic, and those whose behaviour appears similar in some respects, but who exhibit it only in socially sanctioned situations such as religious rites, or in roles upon which the society places great value such as that of the prophet.

This differentiation is clearly evident among the Israelites before and after the exile, and is reflected in community attitudes and reactions to such individuals. When Zephaniah ben Maaseiah, the priest charged with maintenance of order within the Temple precinct, is rebuked for failing to punish the "madman" Jeremiah, it is obvious that the accusation of madness brought against the prophet is not directed to his inspiration in ecstatic trance. It is a violent reaction from a nationalist viewpoint to the political advice offered by the prophet to the Israelites in Babylonia, urging them to recognize that they would remain in exile for an indefinite period. From the standpoint of Shemaiah, the prophet's opponent, only a madman could propose such a policy.

It is clear that the prophet's personal experience of inner communion with God served as the powerful organizing centre and criterion for what he said and did. The word of God as he revealed it was intended to give insight and guidance to the king and the people, to insist on the applicability of the ancient tradition in dealing with problems of the present. However, there were limits to the acceptance of his revelation. In the first place, prophets contradicted one another, and there were difficulties in differentiating the true from the false prophets. Secondly, prophetic revelations in numerous instances were opposed to the prevailing views of powerful political or religious groups. Three illustrations of the use of sanctions against prophets when they espoused unpopular positions are the imprisonment of Micaiah ben Imlah, the murder of Uriah of Kiriath-jearim, and the demand for Jeremiah's death which led to his public punishment by being beaten and put in the stocks. In short, the prophet was allowed to act as he wished, even if some mocked him and others considered him mad, as long as what he said and did were not sufficiently threatening. Only when the prophets appeared to present a serious threat to public order were sanctions invoked against him in the name of the community.[154]

It is in these terms, namely, as a threat to the community and a social problem, that the relationship of society to the prophet comes closest to its reaction to the mentally ill. Like other peoples of antiquity, e.g. the Greeks and Romans (see below p. 121 ff.), the Israelites regarded mental illness as a private matter except where public safety and legal questions were involved. The handling of the insane varied according to circumstances. Madmen who were not violent wandered about, roaming the streets in towns and the roads of the countryside. Not infrequently they were followed by children or street loafers who mocked, ridiculed and abused them, and often threw stones at them. The custom of letting madmen wander at large is implied in the account of David's feigned madness before the Philistine king of Gath. More explicit on this point is the later legend of Solomon as a beggar. According to the legend, the demon Asmodeus outwitted Solomon, threw him out of Jerusalem and took his place as king.[155] Deprived of his power, Solomon wandered about begging his daily bread, but insisting that he was the great king of Israel. Naturally, people considered this claim preposterous and looked upon Solomon as demented. Although the legend dates from the Talmudic period, after the destruction of Jerusalem in A.D. 70, the situation which it describes would have been equally characteristic of the centuries before this time. Related to these two instances, is the vignette of an insane person in a Midrash on Psalm 34.[156] According to the commentator, David had asked why God put madness into the world, and in this connection describes a demented man ridiculed by children. "Master of the universe," he said, "what profit is there for the world in madness? When a man goes about the market place and rends his garment, and children run after him and mock him, is this beautiful in Thine eyes?"

However, the practice of allowing the insane who were not violent to roam the streets was followed only by the lower classes and those who had no family. Members of well-to-do, noble families were placed in the care of a personal attendant or were confined at home. This practice is referred to by a commentator on Psalm 34 in explaining the reaction of Achish, king of Gath, to David's feigned madness. When the king said to his servants, "Do I lack madmen that you have

[154] The relation of prophetism to other forms of unusual behaviour and mental disorder to the social environment will not be discussed any further at this point. Under altered conditions ancient Israelite prophetism assumed other forms.

[155] Micha Josef bin Gorion, *Der Born Judas: Märchen und Geschichten* (neue Ausgabe), Berlin, Schocken Verlag, 1934, pp. 80–82; Ginzberg, *The Legends of the Jews*, Vol. IV (note 46), pp. 169–172.

[156] *The Midrash on Psalms* (note 63), p. 409.

brought this fellow to play the madman in my presence?" the commentator explains that "the daughter of Achish and her mother were both mad, and the two were screaming and carrying on in madness within, while David was screaming and playing at madness without."[157] Confinement at home was an accepted way of dealing with the mentally deranged who were disoriented and violent. When there was danger that a mentally ill person would injure himself or those who associated with him, he was not only confined, but he was restrained as well. Such an individual might be bound, or placed in the stocks, as is implied in the demand that Jeremiah the "madman" be treated in this way.

The Mosaic law as presented in the Pentateuch does not cover the complete range of public and private life so as to constitute a complete code. In addition to such a codification, therefore, judges seem to have made law, and empirical precedents appear to have been cited to deal with specific cases. For example, Jeremiah was saved from death because the court was reminded that there was a precedent in the case of the prophet Micah. In this process of legal development, mental derangement and mental defect were considered in relation to various specific problems. The *Mishna*,[158] that is, the oral law which was developed on the basis of the Scriptures over hundreds of years (ca. 500 B.C.—A.D. 200), employs the word *shoteh* for the mentally disordered in general, apparently including under this term both the insane and the mentally defective. The mentally disordered person was regarded as one deprived of his reason and therefore mentally incompetent. For this reason, such individuals are lumped together with minors and deaf-mutes, since none of these groups could be held legally responsible for their actions. In cases, where individuals were judged to be mentally incompetent, the court could appoint a guardian.[159] It is worth noting that the word for guardian in the *Mishna* is "apotropos," obviously derived from the Greek επιτροπος that is, a guardian or administrator. This example is indicative of the deep linguistic impression that Hellenism left among the Jews of Palestine. While

---

[157] *Ibid.*, p. 410.

[158] The Mishna was finally codified and compiled in written form under the aegis of R. Jehuda I, ha-Nasi, at the time of the Emperor Antoninus Pius. See S. Funk, *Die Entstehung des Talmuds*, (Sammlung Göschen 479) Berlin, Walter de Gruyter & Co., 1919; Joseph Yahuda, *Law and Life According to Hebrew Thought*, London, Oxford University Press, 1932; N. N. Glatzer, *Geschichte der talmudischen Zeit*, Berlin, Schocken Verlag, 1937, pp. 123–143.

[159] *Der Babylonische Talmud*, Neu übertragen durch Lazarus Goldschmidt, Siebenter Band, Berlin, Jüdischer Verlag, 1933, pp. 132–133 (Tractate Baba Qamma IV, 4); *Mishnayoth*, vol. IV, Order Nezikin, ed. and trans. by Philip Blackman, London, Mishna Press (L. M. Schoenfeld), 1954. p. 44.

faithful to the ancient religious tradition, the Judeans became to a considerable extent imbued with Hellenism after the second century B.C., a development which is reflected in the use of various technical terms such as that noted above.[160]

Mental incompetence was also taken into account in cases involving personal injury, defamation and insult, and marriage relations. A mentally disordered individual who caused bodily harm to another person could not be held legally responsible.[161] On the other hand, no legal action could be taken against anyone charged with defaming a mentally disordered person.[162] Where either or both partners to a marriage were mentally ill, the marriage was invalid. However, if the man recovered, a marriage into which he had entered could be validated. A letter of divorce given by a man who was mentally disordered to his wife was considered invalid, so that dissolution of a marriage under these circumstances was impossible since generally only the husband could initiate a divorce.[163] It is noteworthy that the mental disorder, to which reference is made in this connection, is called *qurdejaqos* and is apparently a disturbance of the sensorium. The term is undoubtedly derived from the *morbus cardiacus* of the Graeco-Roman authors, but it is impossible to link it with any of our clinical concepts, because its usage varied very widely even in antiquity.[164] A husband could not divorce his wife if she became mentally ill. When a man was mentally ill and his wife was under suspicion of adultery, the court was obliged to initiate the procedure prescribed in the Bible for such cases, because the husband had no clear understanding of the situation.[165] Finally, someone who was mentally ill could not testify in a court of law. However, an individual who suffered from a periodic mental disorder was considered normal in periods of remission, and his acts and statements at such times were therefore legally valid.[166]

Besides dealing with specific situations in which mental disorder had to be taken into account, some Talmudic teachers established

---

[160] S. Lieberman, *Greek in Jewish Palestine*, New York, 1942; J. Fürst, *Glossarium Graeco-Hebraeum oder der griechische Wörterschatz der Jüdischen Midraschwerke. Ein Beitrag zur Kultur-und Altertumskunde*, Strassburg, 1890, p. 69.

[161] *Babylonische Talmud* (note 159), p. 298.

[162] *Ibid.*, pp. 295–296.

[163] *Mishnayoth*, vol. III, 1953 (note 159), pp. 401, 426.

[164] For morbus cardiacus see Celsus, *De Medicina*, with an English trans. by W. G. Spencer, 3 vols., Cambridge, Mass., Harvard University Press, 1945–48, vol. 1 pp. 303–309; Caelius Aurelianus, *On Acute Diseases and On Chronic Diseases*, Ed. and trans. by I. E. Drabkin, Chicago, University of Chicago Press, 1950, pp. 243–297.

[165] *Mishnayoth*, vol. III (notes 159 and 163), p. 354 (Tractate Sotah IV, 5).

[166] *Ibid.*, p. 402 (Tractate Gittin II, 6).

general principles. Some maintained, for instance, that every law-breaker and criminal was mentally ill. As Resh Laqish put it: "No man commits a transgression unless the spirit of madness has entered into him."[167] This principle is exemplified by men who indulge in sexual excesses, women who commit adultery, children who are rebellious towards their parents, and those who worship idols.

However, despite such efforts to establish general principles of behaviour as related to mental disorder, the Talmud does not define mental illness or mental defect. Several attempts were made to define who was mentally ill, but with little success. Nevertheless, the criteria used to establish mental illness are of considerable interest. One case is reported in which permission to remarry was denied by Mar bar R. Ashi to a widow before the termination of the customary two-year nursing period even though her infant had died. This judgement was based on his fear that some other woman might use this precedent to kill her child so as to be able to remarry sooner, a situation which he had once encountered. His colleagues opposed this judgement on the ground that in the case to which he referred the woman was insane. Normal mothers do not strangle their children, it was pointed out, so that the actions of the mentally deranged cannot be used to justify a judgement involving normal individuals.[168] In short, the behaviour of the mentally deranged is to be judged by the behaviour of most individuals whom the community regards as normal.

Other attempts were made to define mental disorder in behavioural terms. It was proposed that a person who wandered about alone at night, who spent the night in a cemetery, or who tore his garments and destroyed what was given to him might be considered deranged —if such behaviour appeared irrational. However, it was pointed, out that otherwise normal persons could also behave in this way, e.g. one who spent the night in a cemetery might have done so to practise magic, or that another who tore his clothes might have done so in a fit of anger, or because he was a cynic philosopher exhibiting his contempt for material things.[169]

Despite the inability of Talmudic scholars to establish adequate criteria for mental illness, they were aware that mental disorder was linked to certain causal factors. They were aware of the connection between ageing and a diminution of mental ability, an observation that had already been made much earlier, as indicated by the exchange between David and Barzillai the Gileadite, when the latter says to the king, "I am this day eighty years old; can I discern what is pleasant and what is not?" Similarly Ecclesiasticus commented,

[167] Preuss, *op. cit.*, p. 365.
[168] *Ibid.*, pp. 364–365.
[169] *Ibid.*, pp. 363–364.

"My son, help thy father in his age, and grieve him not as long as he liveth. And if his understanding fail, have patience with him; and despise him not when thou art in the full strength."[170]

The Talmud also relates a case in which excessive grief led to insanity and eventually to death. When R. Simon b. Laqish (Resh Laqish) died, his brother-in-law and fellow student, R. Jochanan, cried and grieved over him to such an extent that he became deranged. His condition was so harrowing that his students beseeched God to have mercy, and he was released by death from his suffering.[171]

Though the Talmud says little about the treatment of mental illness there are a number of references to physicians and other healers. Such references also occur in the Old Testament.[172] When Asa, king of Judah, was afflicted by a severe disease of the feet, he sought help from physicians instead of from the Lord. The verse which follows this statement reports his death.[173] In the Talmudic period the provision of medical care by physicians was apparently quite common, to judge by the proverb "He who has pain goes to a physician."[174] This view is strengthened by a remark in the Midrash Bemidbar (or Numbers) Rabbah that "when people die in their beds as people ordinarily do," doctors come in and visit "them in the same way as all other sick people are visited."[175] Further support for the availability of physicians is provided by the story in Mark 5: 25–26 about the "woman who had had a flow of blood for twelve years and who had suffered much under many physicians, and had spent all that she had, and was no better . . ."[176]

Given the availability of physicians, it is more than likely that they were called upon to treat mentally disordered patients. This may be assumed from the passage in the *Jewish Antiquities* of Josephus, where he relates that when Saul was attacked by an evil spirit he was attended by physicians.[177] In its account of this episode, the Biblical text refers simply to the servants of Saul, and it is very likely that

[170] II Samuel 19: 35; Ecclesiasticus 3: 12–13 (This quotation is from the King James Version).

[171] *Babylonische Talmud* (note 159), p. 725.

[172] Job 13: 4.

[173] II Chronicles 16: 12–13.

[174] *Babylonische Talmud* (note 159), p. 157 (Tractate Baba qamma V, 1).

[175] *Midrash Rabbah*, trans. under the editorship of Rabbi Dr. H. Freedman and Maurice Simon. *Numbers*, trans. by Judah J. Slotki, 2 vols., London, Soncino Press, 1939, vol. II, p. 724 (XVIII, 12).

[176] Other references indicating that medical care by physicians was available may be found in the *Midrash* on Psalms (note 63), vol. 1, p. 98; *Babylonische Talmud* (note 159), pp. 268–269, 290 (Tractate Baba qamma VII, 7; VIII, 1).

[177] Josephus, *Jewish Antiquities*, with an English translation by H. St. J. Thackeray and Ralph Marcus (Loeb Classical Library), vol. 5, Cambridge, Mass., Harvard Univesity Press, 1958, p. 249.

Josephus projected into the past conditions with which he was acquainted in his own time. Thus, in describing the illness with which Herod the Great was afflicted after murdering his wife Mariamme, and during which he temporarily lost his reason, Josephus speaks of "the physicians who surrounded him."[178] Nevertheless, kings have had healers and medical men at their courts since ancient times and this was also true of the kings of Israel and Judah, as witness Asa to whom we have already referred above. To what extent physicians were used by other social groups and elements of the population for the diagnosis and treatment of mental illness must remain an open question. The data to answer it are not available. All that can be said is that physicians were available in many places and were used.

Aside from confinement and restraint, what kind of treatment was provided for the mentally ill? The evidence on this point is also scanty. Nevertheless, it seems clear that with Hellenism, the Jews of Palestine, Egypt and Italy also came in contact with Graeco-Roman medicine which they accepted in large measure, both in theory and practice. Moreover, such knowledge seems to have become available in non-medical circles as well. Thus, R. Ruben remarked that the word *shoteh* may be equated with the Greek *moria* ($\mu\omega\rho\acute{\iota}\alpha$), and the Midrash, Numbers Rabbah comments that "in the seaport towns they call fools *morim*."[179] This penetration of Greek and Latin terms and ideas is also indicated by the references in the Talmud to *morbus cardiacus* (see above) as well as to other conditions. In so far as Jewish physicians practised Graeco-Roman medicine, their treatment of the mentally ill need not be discussed here; it belongs in a consideration of mental disorder in the Graeco-Roman world which is the subject of the next chapter.

Before turning to Greece and Rome, however, we should note that folk medicine and magical practices continued to play a large part in the treatment of the mentally ill by the Jews and other peoples of ancient Palestine. Nor is this surprising in the light of the dictum in the Talmud, that there is no medicine for the insane.[180] Thus, Josephus, in discussing Solomon's ability to cast out demons and thus heal those possessed by them, describes his own observation of such a practice. "This was the manner of the cure," he says. The exorcist Eleazar

> put to the nose of the possessed man a ring which had under its seal one of the roots prescribed by Solomon, and then, as the man smelled it,

---

[178] *Ibid.*, vol. 8, 1963, p. 115.

[179] $\mu\omega\rho\acute{\iota}\alpha$ = folly in Greek; $\mu\omega\rho\alpha\acute{\iota}\nu\omega$ = to be silly or foolish. Preuss, *op. cit.*, p. 366; *Midrash Rabbah*, Numbers II (note 175), p. 759.

[180] Preuss, *op. cit.*, p. 366.

drew out the demon through his nostrils, and, when the man at once fell down, adjured the demon not to come back into him, speaking Solomon's name and reciting the incantations which he had composed. Then wishing to convince the bystanders and prove to them that he had this power, Eleazar placed a cup or foot-basin full of water a little way off and commanded the demon, as it went out of the man, to overturn it and make known to the spectators that he had left the man.[181]

The root mentioned in this ritual may be the Baaras plant, to which Josephus refers in the *Jewish War*, and which has the capacity to expel demons.[182]

Another practice is described in the Midrash, Numbers Rabbah. R. Jochanan b. Zakkai, who lived in the first century A.D., was asked one day by a pagan whether the purification rite of the Red Heifer was not a kind of witchcraft. Thereupon, R. Jochanan asked him: " 'Has the demon of madness ever possessed you?' 'No,' he replied. 'Have you ever seen a man possessed by this demon of madness?' 'Yes,' said he. 'And what do you do in such a case?' 'We bring roots,' he replied, 'and make them smoke under him, then we sprinkle water upon the demon and it flees.' "[183]

Clearly, certain individuals were regarded as deranged in ancient Israel and among the Jews during the Talmudic period. The ways in which the community reacted to such persons reflected its ideas on the nature and causation of the conditions affecting these individuals, and set the limits within which it could tolerate deviant behaviour. The community's reaction also indicated the prevailing view of the respective responsibilities of the kinship group and of the larger community for those of their members who were unable to care for themselves.

[181] Josephus, *op. cit.*, p. 597.
[182] Josephus, *The Jewish War*, *op. cit.* (note 24), vol. III, pp. 557–559.
[183] *Midrash Rabbah*, Numbers II, p. 757.

# CHAPTER THREE

# GREECE AND ROME

*A Madness of Kings*

Beginning with Homer, Greek writers portrayed a very wide range of human behaviour, including instances so unusual as to be considered abnormal and requiring some special explanation. Several cases of this kind are recorded by Herodotus in his *Histories.* Two of them recounting the acts and experiences of the Persian king Cambyses (530–522 B.C.), and of Cleomenes I, king of Sparta, (ca. 520–490 B.C.), are of particular interest because they throw light on Greek views of mental illness and indicate some of the means used to cope with the mentally deranged.

Herodotus tells many tales of the impieties and outrages committed by Cambyses against the Egyptians whom he had conquered, as well as against members of his family, and his court. He relates how the king suffered a defeat in his campaign against the Ethiopians, and turned back to Memphis where he found the Egyptians celebrating the feast of Apis. Suspecting them of rejoicing at his setback, Cambyses in a rage threatened with death anyone who celebrated the festival, ordered the priests of the god to be whipped, and stabbed a bull sacred to Apis so that the animal died. According to an Egyptian account, the Persian king "who even before had not been quite in his right mind, was forthwith . . . smitten with madness for this crime."[1] On another occasion, allegedly enraged by her reproaches, Cambyses attacked his pregnant wife (who was also his sister), so that she suffered a miscarriage and died.

These and many other arbitrary and irrational acts which he reports led Herodotus to conclude that the Persian king had been mad. Modern historical opinion, though divided, tends to discount these stories of Cambyses' savagery and irrational behaviour, particularly as they relate to Egypt, and therefore to doubt his madness.[2] For the ancient Greeks, however, the problem was not whether Cambyses was mentally deranged; his madness was accepted

---

[1] *The History of Herodotus,* trans. by George Rawlinson, 2 vols. (Everymans Library), London and Toronto, E. P. Dent, 1924, vol. I, p. 224.

[2] A. T. Olmstead, *The History of the Persian Empire,* Chicago, University of Chicago Press, 1948, pp. 89–92; R. Ghirshman, *Iran from the Earliest Times to the Islamic Conquest,* Harmondsworth, Penguin Books, 1954, p. 138.

as a fact supported by a variety of evidence.[3] Contributing very significantly to this acceptance was the king's conduct in making "a mock of holy rites and long-established usages," because, as Herodotus emphasized, unless a man is mad, "it is not likely that he would make sport of such matters."[4]

But what had caused the king's madness? This was the question that stirred the Greeks, and a number of reasons were offered to explain why his wits had become disordered. Some accounts attributed the madness of Cambyses to punishment for his many impieties. Another explanation claimed that his condition was the consequence of a serious disease, "which some people call sacred," with which he was afflicted from birth. The disease in question may be congenital epilepsy, but the reference is inconclusive because in popular usage the term "sacred disease" was sometimes applied to conditions other than epilepsy.[5] Herodotus records both explanations, but inclines to the latter, commenting that when the body suffers from a serious ailment it is not surprising to find the mind affected as well.[6]

In his long account of the reign of Cleomenes of Sparta, Herodotus had another opportunity to consider mental derangement and its possible causes. Fascinated by the provocative personality of the Spartan king, he endeavoured through the collection of various incidents in the career of Cleomenes to ascertain the reasons for his eventual madness and self-destruction. Indeed, as J. L. Myres appropriately suggests, the whole story might well be entitled *Kleomenes mainomenos*, or "Cleomenes losing his wits."[7] The king of Sparta, a brilliant and vigorous but erratic personality, played a leading role in Greek politics at the end of the sixth century. Not overly scrupulous in the choice of measures to achieve his aims, he even went so far as to commit sacrilege: in order to bring about the deposition of Demaratus, his co-king and enemy, Cleomenes did not shrink from bribing the priestess at Delphi to make a statement unfavourable to his rival. Fearing public anger when his corruption of the Pythia became known, he fled to Thessaly, and then to Arcadia where he plotted against his country.[8] Subsequently an altered political situa-

[3] Cf. Plato, *Laws* 695; *The Dialogues of Plato*, trans. by B. Jowett, 2 vols., New York, Random House, 1937, vol. 2, pp. 469–470.

[4] Herodotus, *op. cit.*, p. 229.

[5] O. Temkin, *The Falling Sickness. A History of Epilepsy from the Greeks to the Beginnings of Modern Neurology*, Baltimore, Johns Hopkins Press, 1945, pp. 15–19.

[6] Herodotus, *op. cit.*, p. 226.

[7] J. L. Myres, *Herodotus, Father of History*, Oxford, Clarendon Press, 1953, pp. 77, 175.

[8] Cleomenes is the central figure of Books V and VI of the history of Herodotus; see Myres, *op. cit.*, pp. 173–176, 184–190.

tion enabled Cleomenes to return to Sparta, but soon it became clear that his mind was unhinged. For example, he would strike in the face with his sceptre any Spartan whom he met in a public place. Recognizing that he was out of his mind, his relatives incarcerated Cleomenes and restrained him by putting his feet in stocks.[9] While thus imprisoned, finding himself one day alone with an attendant who was a helot, Cleomenes asked the man for a knife. At first the man refused, but the curses and threats showered upon him by Cleomenes soon frightened the helot who gave him what he wanted. No sooner had Cleomenes obtained the knife than he began to slash himself about the legs, thighs, hips and loins. Finally, he gashed his abdomen, dying of his injuries shortly thereafter.

The Greeks offered various explanations of the madness and death of Cleomenes. According to Herodotus, some held that Cleomenes had never been altogether of sound mind, and that he had "verged upon madness."[10] Most Greeks, however, saw the king's madness as a god-sent punishment for sacrilege,[11] specifically for corrupting the Delphic priestess. The Athenians had another view; they saw the terrible fate of Cleomenes as a punishment for having cut down the sacred grove of the goddesses Ceres and Proserpine at Eleusis. Finally, the Argives claimed that his self-destruction was due to the violation and burning of a grove sacred to Argus, and to a later blasphemy at the famous temple of Hera near Argos. Yet Herodotus also noted the Spartans' opinion that Cleomenes' madness was due not to any supernatural agency, but rather to his heavy drinking of wine undiluted with water.[12] Nevertheless Herodotus preferred not to accept this prosaic explanation, and was inclined to view the death of Cleomenes as a "judgement on him for wronging Demaratus."

## Madness: Natural and Supernatural

Clearly, Herodotus recognized two explanations of mental derangement, one attributing it to supernatural or divine intervention, the other to natural causes which disturb psychic activity. Broadly speaking, these two views represent respectively the popular and the medical attitudes towards mental abnormality prevalent in the Graeco-Roman culture. As the extant texts indicate, Greek medicine very early rejected any supernatural explanation of mental disorder,

---

[9] Cf. above the treatment of the wife and daughter of Achish, King of Gath pp. 64-65 and of Jeremiah, p. 63.

[10] Herodotus, *op. cit.*, pp. 18, 85.

[11] *Ibid.*, pp. 32, 86.

[12] *Ibid.*, p. 89.

viewing it in essentially physiologic terms, a position which was maintained from the time of Hippocrates to that of Galen and his successors. Mental abnormality was considered a disease, or a symptom of one, caused in the same way as disease of the body. This view was based on the theory which was used to explain not only mental disease, but disease in general, namely, the humoral theory. According to this doctrine, the body was composed of four humours, blood, phlegm, yellow bile and black bile, which were produced by physiologic processes in various organs of the body. Furthermore, each humour was endowed with a basic quality, such as heat, cold, dryness, and moistness. Disease developed when internal or external factors produced an excess of one of the humours. The resulting imbalance of these basic qualities acted on organs to produce deleterious effects. Madness, the disease of the mind, was produced in this fashion by excess of a humour. Black bile was a peculiarly potent cause, when present in abundance under certain conditions, of various forms of mental illness, particularly the condition called melancholia.

Reflections of medical attitudes and views occur in the popular conception of mental disorder, but they are found side by side with older, more deep-seated and traditional views. As indicated by Herodotus in the fifth century B.C. and by others in later periods, the popular view throughout Graeco-Roman antiquity was derived from a heterogeneous mass of belief and opinion, in which primitive elements were modified and overlaid by higher elements as Greek and Roman culture developed. A basic element of the popular view, however, was the belief that mental abnormality was due to the action of some supernatural power or being which entered the body or produced its effect by action from without.

Madness considered as possession, or as the consequence of some other action by a supernatural power, is not an isolated phenomenon, but rather an instance of the more general belief among primitive peoples that many ills suffered by men are caused by supernatural agency. To the primitive mind, men are surrounded by a swarm of unknown and unseen forces that affect them for good or ill. These forces are not conceived of as personifications or abstractions, but as actual beings, as demons or spirits that have a real existence. Thus illness is thought of as a maleficent spirit which enters into and takes possession of an afflicted person, that is, the ailment is the possessing spirit.

These ancient, primitive ideas, more or less modified in the course of time, are found throughout Greek and Latin literature. Thus, Hesiod (fl. eighth century B.C.) tells how before the opening of Pandora's box men lived on earth free of the troubles, the grinding toil and catching sicknesses which the *Keres* now bring upon them.[13] A later poet, Semonides of Amorgos (ca. 660 B.C.), reflecting with sardonic pessimism on the vanity of human hopes and desires, ascribes life's uncertainty to the multitudinous *Keres* that hover about men ready to undo them through war, shipwreck, disease, suicide and death.[14] An awareness that all things mortal are exposed to such influences also haunts the mind of Mimnermus (seventh century B.C.).[15] One of his poems laments that the brightness of life is necessarily celebrated in the shadow of the black *Keres* of poverty, disease, old age and death.[16] In a less serious vein, Theognis (sixth century B.C.) complains that the enjoyment of wine exposes man to two evil *Keres*, thirst and drunkenness.[17] Nor are the *Keres* absent when Plato emphasizes how close together good and evil lie in human life. "There are many noble things in human life," he comments, "but to most of them attach evils (*Keres*) which are fated to corrupt and spoil them."[18]

The malign spirits known as the *Keres* were initially the ghosts of the dead. Vague and unelaborated at first, they developed into more differentiated spirits associated with specific evils.[19] They were feared because of their possible harmful action on living men, and therefore as evil influences to be averted. The spirit of a murdered man, for example, was believed to send madness as a punishment for the murderer.[20] Furthermore, there were times of the year when the spirits of the dead returned to the upper world, or were particularly

[13] Hesiod, *Works and Days* 90–92; see *Hesiod, the Homeric Hymns and Homerica*, trans. by H. G. Evelyn-White (Loeb Classical Library), Cambridge, Mass., Harvard University Press, 1950, pp. 8–9.

[14] J. M. Edmonds, ed., *Elegy and Jambus*, 2 vols., (Loeb Classical Library), London, Wm. Heinemann, 1931, vol. II, pp. 212–215. The spelling Semonides appears to be more accurate but is not generally used, so that some still refer to this poet as Simonides of Amorgos to distinguish him from Simonides of Ceos. For example, see R. S. Wright, *The Golden Treasury of Ancient Greek Poetry*, 2nd edition, revised by Evelyn Abbott, Oxford, Clarendon Press, 1889, pp. 154 ff and pp. 206 ff.

[15] Mimnermus was a lyric poet who flourished in the 37th Olympiad, 632–629 B.C.

[16] Edmonds, *Elegy and Jambus*, vol. I, pp. 90–91.

[17] Theognis 837–840; Edmonds, *Elegy and Jambus*, vol. I, pp. 328–329. Theognis flourished about the year 550 B.C.

[18] Plato, *Laws* 937d. For the text see *Platonis Opera*, ed. by John Burnet, Oxford, Clarendon Press, 1937, vol. V, Part II. The translation of the passage is from *The Dialogues of Plato*, trans. by B. Jowett, New York, Random House, 1937, vol. 2, p. 675.

[19] Jane Harrison, *Prolegomena to the Study of Greek Religion*, New York, Meridian Books, 1955, pp. 165–212. See particularly pp. 165–171.

[20] Hippocrates, *Sacred Disease* IV: 36–42. See *Hippocrates*, with an English translation by W. H. S. Jones (Loeb Classical Library), 4 vols., London, Wm. Heinemann, 1923–1931, vol. II, pp. 174–175. Also Plato, *Laws*, 865d.

active. At Athens, this occurred during the Anthesteria, the oldest of the Dionysiac festivals, celebrated on three successive days from the 11th to the 15th of Anthesterion, the month corresponding roughly to February.[21] It was a time for the laying of ghosts and for sacrifices to appease the dark forces of the underworld. People were believed to be especially susceptible at this time to the malign influence of the spirits, which might lead to illness, madness and death. According to some accounts, the spirits of the dead rose on the second day of the festival so that men put pitch on their doors to discourage their visits, and chewed buckthorn to prevent them from invading the body and possessing it. Buckthorn was probably employed because of its purgative effect, since food was considered a significant means by which spirits often entered the body. In this connection, it is worth noting Pliny's comment that beans were forbidden to the Pythagoreans "because the souls of the dead are contained in a bean," and that for this reason "beans are employed in memorial sacrifices to dead relatives."[22] The prophylactic use of buckthorn was probably also related to its magical qualities. Dioscorides reports that branches of this plant were attached to doors or to the outside of houses because it was believed to repel the effects of evil magic.[23] On the last day of the festival, rites were performed to appease the ancestral spirits, and to hasten them on their way. Reverently but firmly, they were expelled with the injunction, "Out of doors, *Keres*, it is no longer Anthesteria."[24]

A mixture of fear and reverence determined the treatment accorded the spirits of the dead, since they were believed to be jealous of the living and therefore touchy and easily offended. Consequently, care was taken not to give offence, for the spirits, as mentioned above, were considered capable of afflicting the living with all kinds of misfortune. An echo of this belief may perhaps occur in modern Greece where the view prevails that a disease such as tuberculosis is a

[21] Jack Finegan, *Handbook of Biblical Chronology*, Princeton, Princeton University Press, 1964, pp. 57–58; see also Benjamin D. Meritt, *The Athenian Year*, 1961.

[22] Pliny, *Natural History*, with an English translation by H. Rackham (Loeb Classical Library), vol. V, Cambridge, Mass., Harvard University Press, 1950, pp. 264–265.

[23] Dioscorides, *De materia medica* I, 119. One may also note Ovid's reference to the use of whitethorn to keep off wandering ghosts, harpies and witches; see his *Fasti* VI, 129–130, 165–166.

[24] Harrison, *op. cit.*, p. 35; John Pollard, *Seers, Shrines and Sirens. The Greek Religious Revolution in the Sixth Century B.C.*, London, George Allen & Unwin, 1965, pp. 79–80. A close parallel to the Anthesteria in this regard is the festival of the Lemuria at Rome. See Ovid, *Fasti*, with an English translation by Sir James George Frazer (Loeb Classical Library), Cambridge, Mass., Harvard University Press, 1951, pp. 290–297.

"jealous" disease which "wilfully and with conscious animation seeks to infect those who are well."[25]

Similar attitudes were also exhibited towards various divinities, spirits and demons who could punish men or prey upon them by causing their minds to go astray. Popular thought in the later fifth century associated a number of deities with mental or psychosomatic disturbances. A passage in the *Hippolytus* of Euripides referring to the love-sick Phaedra lists Pan, Hecate, Cybele the "Mountain Mother," and the Corybantes as deities who cause madness.[26] Another such list occurs in the Hippocratic book on *The Sacred Disease*. While decrying the attribution of the disease to any supernatural powers, the author indicates that its various forms have been blamed on particular gods.

> If the patient imitate a goat, if he roar, or suffer convulsions in the right side, they say that the Mother of the Gods is to blame. If he utter a piercing and loud cry, they liken him to a horse and blame Poseidon. Should he pass some excrement, as often happens under the stress of the disease, the surname Enodia is applied. If it be more frequent and thinner, like that of birds, it is Apollo Nomius. If he foam at the mouth and kick, Ares has the blame. When at night occur fears and terrors, delirium, jumpings from the bed and rushings out of doors they say Hecate is attacking or that heroes are assaulting.[27]

This belief in the power of the gods to cause mental derangement was widespread among the Greeks. The popular conception was that the god inflicted madness as a punishment upon those who incurred his anger by some act of omission or commission. According to the Souidas, it was customary to offer a propitiatory victim to Zeus Meilichios in the month Maimakterion, since raging madness was feared at this time of the year when gusty winds prevailed and the air was frequently and greatly disturbed.[28] This remark is in agreement with the views of Greek medical writers that mental disturbances were more likely to occur at certain seasons than at others.[29] But

[25] Richard and Eva Blum, *Health and Healing in Rural Greece*, Stanford, Calif., Stanford University Press, 1965, p. 136.

[26] Euripides, *Hippolytus* 141–144. See *Euripides* with an English translation by Arthur S. Way (Loeb Classical Library), 4 vols., London, Wm. Heinemann, 1912, vol. IV, pp. 172–173.

[27] Hippocrates, with an English translation by W. H. S. Jones (Loeb Classical Library) 4 vols., London, Wm. Heinemann, 1923–31, vol. II, pp. 146–148.

[28] A. C. Vaughan, *Madness in Greek Thought and Custom*, Baltimore, J. H. Furst Company, 1919, pp. 19–20. The Greek month Maimakterion corresponds approximately to our November–December.

[29] Hippocrates, *Epidemics* I, 18, 22. See Loeb edition, *op. cit.*, vol. I, pp. 172–173, 178–179; Aretaeus, *Extant Works*, ed. and trans. by Francis Adams, London, Sydenham Society, 1856, pp. 58, 301.

while physicians regarded the relation between seasonal influences and mental disorder as a natural phenomenon, the sacrifice in Maimakterion was offered to mollify and appease the raging, panting Zeus, who in his character as an angry god might send madness as a punishment.[30]

The infliction of madness for refusing to accept or actively opposing the worship of Dionysus is a recurrent theme in a group of cult legends concerned with the introduction of the Dionysiac religion in Greece. The diffusion of the worship of Dionysus and any hostility encountered in the process occurred at a very early period so that only traces in myths and cultic rituals remained to be recorded. One legend concerns Lycurgus, king of the Edonians, a Thracian people, who persecuted Dionysus, and for his impiety was driven mad by the god. In his madness Lycurgus killed his son with an axe, imagining he was lopping a branch off a vine.[31] Diodorus the Sicilian recounts the fate of Boutes, a Thracian exile, who settled on Naxos, whence he and his companions raided shipping and settlements. On a raiding expedition to Thessaly, Boutes and his company, upon landing, discovered female worshippers of Dionysus as they were celebrating the rites of the god.

> As Boutes and his companions rushed at the women these threw away the sacred objects and some of them fled for safety to the sea, and others to the mountain called Drius; but Coronis . . . was seized by Boutes and forced to lie with him. And she, in anger at the seizure and at the insolent treatment she had received, called upon Dionysus to lend her his aid. And the god struck Boutes with madness, because of which he lost his mind and, thowing himself into a well, met his death.[32]

Another group of stories deals with women who were maddened by the god. A Theban myth tells how Dionysus, angered by the rejection of his cult, inflicted madness on the woman of Thebes, among them Agave, mother of Pentheus, the Theban king, so that they abandoned their homes and roamed in frenzy on Cithaeron, a mountain range between Attica and Boeotia. Pentheus, bitterly hostile to the new worship, spied on the frenzied women and was torn limb from limb by his mother, to whom in her madness he ap-

---

[30] Harrison, *op. cit.*, pp. 14–21; Vaughan, *op. cit.*, p. 20.

[31] Apollodorus, *The Library*, with an English translation by Sir James George Frazer (Loeb Classical Library), 2 vols., Cambridge, Mass., Harvard University Press, 1961, vol. I, pp. 326–329.

[32] Diodorus of Sicily, *The Library of History*, with an English translation by C. H. Oldfather (Loeb Classical Library), vol. III, Cambridge, Mass., Harvard University Press, 1939, pp. 236–239. See also Homeric Hymn VII, *To Dionysus* in Hesiod, *op. cit.*, note 13, pp. 428–433.

peared to be a wild beast.[33] Closely similar legends were told of the daughters of Proteus and of those of Minyas. The three daughters of Proteus, king of Tiryns, went mad because they would not accept the rites of Dionysus; and after inducing the Argive women to kill their children and follow them, they roamed the mountains until cured by the seer and physician Melampus. Minyas, the legendary ancestor of the people of Orchomenos, had three daughters who were driven mad because they resisted Dionysus. While in this state they were seized with a craving for human flesh, whereupon they killed and devoured Hippasus, the son of Leucippe, one of the three sisters.[34]

Although these legends probably combine both historical and ritual elements, there is evidence to suggest that they reflect in considerable measure the cult ritual of the god. Plutarch, for example, in his account of the daughters of Minyas links the myth with a ritual which was still performed at Orchomenos in his own day. Every year at the festival of Agrionia, women descended from the Minyads, fled from and were pursued by the priest of Dionysus armed with a sword. Plutarch says that "Any one of them that he catches he may kill, and in my time the priest Zoilus killed one of them."[35] Clearly the rite practised at Orchomenos involved a pursuit which could end in a ritual murder. Pausanias relates that at Potniae, near Thebes, there was a temple of Dionysus where a boy used to be sacrificed to the god. Allegedly, this practice was instituted to expiate the murder of the priest who while sacrificing to Dionysus had been killed by the celebrants. Later a goat was permitted as a substitute.[36] Then there is the human sacrifice alleged to have been offered to Dionysus the Devourer by the Greeks before the battle of Salamis.[37]

Recognition of the ritual aspects of these stories illuminates the nature of the mental disturbance inflicted by Dionysus. Accounts of the Dionysiac rites portray the votaries of the god as frenzied or raving, that is, in a state of ecstatic excitement. Diodorus says that in many Greek cities bands of women gathered every third year to

---

[33] The Bacchae of Euripides presents the most powerful and poetic version of this myth. It may be consulted in the edition prepared by E. R. Dodds (2nd edition, Oxford 1960). See also Appollodorus, *Library* III, 2, Loeb edition, *op. cit.*, vol. 1, pp. 330–331.

[34] Plutarch, *Quaestiones graecae* 38, in Plutarch's *Moralia* (Loeb Classical Library), vol. IV, Cambridge, Mass., Harvard University Press, 1962, pp. 220–223; see also Aelian, *Varia Historia* III, 42.

[35] Plutarch, *op. cit.*, p. 223.

[36] Pausanias, *Description of Greece*, with an English translation by W. H. S. Jones (Loeb Classical Library), 5 vols., Cambridge Mass., Harvard University Press, 1960–1964, vol. IV, pp. 206–207.

[37] Plutarch, *The Lives of the Noble Grecians and Romans*, trans. by John Dryden and revised by Arthur Hugh Clough, New York, Modern Library, n.d., p. 142.

worship Dionysus, and that the unmarried girls were allowed to share the frenzied transports of their elders.[38] The existence of such biennial festivals in various parts of the Greek world is attested by both ancient authors and epigraphic evidence. Herodotus refers to a festival in honour of Dionysus held every third year among the half-Hellenized Geloni of Thrace, "at which the natives fall into the Bacchic fury."[39] He also speaks of the worship of Dionysus at Olbia, a Greek settlement on the River Bug, where the celebrants were possessed by the god so that they raved in a frenzy. In this connection, Herodotus reports that the neighbouring Scythians rejected the idea of a god such as Dionysus who leads men to behave madly.[40] Finally, there is the notice by Pausanias of a festival called Sciereia celebrated in honour of Dionysus every other year at Alea in Arcadia, at which women were flogged.[41]

Unusual emotional states and psychic experiences associated with religious rites are found widely distributed in time and space. Violent, frenzied behaviour occurring as part of cultic rituals has already been examined in relation to Israelite prophetism, and the madness manifested in the Dionysiac rites appears to have been of a similar character. The Greeks were aware that unusual behaviour which deviated from the normal in this context differed expressly from madness due to disease. Plato, for example, included telestic or ritual madness among the four types of "divine madness" which he distinguished. Similarly, the physician Aretaeus described a form of frenzied ritual madness, differentiating it from other forms of mental disorder.[42] A more detailed examination of this type of psychopathology will be made below. Here we need only emphasize the belief that a god such as Dionysus could enter into his votaries during the celebration of his cult, so that they become *entheos*, one with the god. In this state when the divine power took possession of them they were mad and powerless in the hands of the god.

Madness was also attributed to various other supernatural causes. Thus, the word *nympholeptos* expresses the belief prevalent among the ancient Greeks that the nymphs were able to possess mortals and

[38] Diodorus of Sicily, *op. cit.*, vol. II, pp. 346–347. The phrase "to share the frenzied transports" is a translation of the Greek word *synenthousiazein* used by Diodorus.

[39] Herodotus, *op. cit.*, p. 329; E. R. Dodds, *The Greeks and the Irrational*, Berkeley, University of California Press, 1959, p. 270.

[40] Herodotus, *op. cit.*, pp. 318–319. For Olbia see John Boardman, *The Greeks Overseas*, Baltimore, Penguin Books, 1964, pp. 259–261.

[41] Pausanias, *op. cit.*, vol. IV, pp. 8–9.

[42] Plato, *Phaedrus* 244–245, 265 B; Aretaeus, *op. cit.*, pp. 62, 304; I. M. Linforth, The Corybantic Rites in Plato, *University of California Publications in Classical Philology*, 13: 121–162, 1946.

madden them.[43] For example, there is the following comment by Socrates in the Platonic dialogue *Phaedrus*. Having withdrawn with Phaedrus to a cool shady spot close to a sanctury of the nymphs, Socrates says to his companion, "There seems to be a divine presence in the spot, so that you must not be surprised if, as my speech proceeds, I become as one possessed (*nympholeptos*)."[44] While Socrates's remark is in a serio-comic vein, the idea which it expressed continued to prevail as an element in Greek folklore and is indeed still current. Early in this century, Lawson reported that the presumed sanctuary of the Pierian muses was shunned as a place where one might be afflicted with madness, and at present various psychophysical ills are still attributed to nymphs and nereids.[45] Possibly related to such beliefs about nymphs are the references to certain springs and streams said to affect the mental faculties and in some instances to cause death. Diodorus, though sceptical, mentions a lake in Ethiopia which had a remarkable quality, "for whoever has drunk of it . . . falls into a frenzy and accuses himself of every sin which he had formerly committed in secret." The architect Vitruvius refers to a spring on the island of Chios alleged to render stupid those who drank of it unawares. Then there is Pliny's remark about the sacred spring in the cave of Apollo at Claros in Asia Minor. Drinking its water inspired the priests of the shrine to prophesy, but shortened the lives of the drinkers.[46] Recently an archaeologist excavating the shrine found the spring, and, undeterred by the ancient warning, tried the water without any ill effects.[47]

Madness could be inflicted not only by spirits and gods, but also through the use of magic spells and rites, sometimes involving the divinities of the underworld, especially Hecate and Hermes. When Talos prevented the Argonauts from touching at Crete, the witch

---

[43] M. P. Nilsson, *Greek Folk Religion*, New York, Columbia University Press, 1940, p. 13, Harper Torchbooks edition, 1961; J. C. Lawson, *Modern Greek Folklore and Ancient Greek Religion*, Cambridge, Cambridge University Press, 1910, pp. 160ff.

[44] Plato, *Phaedrus* 238 D.

[45] Lawson, *op. cit.*, p. 162; Blum and Blum, *op. cit.*, p. 124; Josef Pieper, *Enthusiasm and Divine Madness. On the Platonic Dialogue Phaedrus*, New York, Harcourt, Brace & World, 1964, p. 33.

[46] Diodorus of Sicily, *op. cit.*, vol. I, pp. 396–399; Vitruvius, *On Architecture*, with an English translation by Frank Granger (Loeb Classical Library), 2 vols., London, Wm. Heinemann, 1931–34, vol. II, pp. 170–171; Tacitus, *The Histories*, trans. by C. H. Moore; *The Annals* trans. by J. Jackson (Loeb Classical Library), 4 vols., London, Wm. Heinemann, 1931–1937, vol. II, pp. 470–471; Pliny, *op. cit.*, vol. I, pp. 358–359; for other springs alleged to cause madness see W. R. Halliday, *Greek Divination*, London, Macmillan, 1931, pp. 124 ff.

[47] Paul MacKendrick, *The Greek Stones Speak*, New York, St. Martin's Press, 1962, pp. 344–345.

Medea is said to have caused his death after driving him mad by spells and drugs.[48] Magical means to induce love, to attack enemies, or to counter such actions were common among the Greeks and Romans. The second idyll of Theocritus, in which a Coan girl named Simaetha invokes Hecate and lays a spell on Delphis, the young athlete who no longer loves her, is a poetic account of the fierce and desperate passions that prompted these rites. A story told by Plutarch reflects a belief that such acts might lead to mental derangement. At the time of the Mithradatic War (88–63 B.C.), he writes, Aretaphile, a woman of Cyrene, plotted to kill Nicocrates, the despot of the city, and endeavoured to involve his brother Leander in the plot by making him fall in love with her daughter. To achieve this she is said to have employed charms and other magical means which eventually disordered his mind.[49]

Clearly, madness in the popular conception was basically a condition in which an individual was possessed, controlled or affected by some supernatural power or being. As O'Brien-Moore has demonstrated, further evidence of the imprint of this belief on the Greek mind is to be found in the use of the words *daimonan, kakodaimonan* and *kakodaimonia*.[50] To be sure, in the course of time such words lost to a considerable degree their original connotations of possession by a demon or evil spirit, yet Hesychius, the lexicographer of late antiquity, still defined *daimonan* generally as possession by a demon. At the same time this belief was associated in the popular mind with elements derived from folklore and medicine, such as the baleful qualities of certain plants (mandragora, henbane), drugs, and other materials reputed to cause madness, as well as the prophylactic and curative effects of other substances.[51] There was no attempt at consistency in the association of these ideas and beliefs, and they might be presented with varying emphases in different contexts. Thus, in classical Greece the power of possession was attributed to lunar deities, such as Selenê, Hecate and Artemis. In

[48] Apollodorus, *op. cit.*, vol. I, pp. 118–119.

[49] Dodds, *op. cit.*, pp. 194–195; Nilsson, *op. cit.*, pp. 113–115; Eugene Tavenner, *Studies in Magic from Latin Literature*, New York, Columbia University Press, 1916, pp. 33 ff.; Theocritus, Idyll II. Pharmakeutriai, in the *Greek Bucolic Poets*, with an English translation by J. M. Edmonds (Loeb Classical Library), London, Wm. Heinemann, 1928, pp. 26–39; Plutarch, Bravery of Women (*Mulierum Virtutes*) XIX, in Plutarch's *Moralia*, vol. III, pp. 546–547; Rudolf Egger, *Römische Antike und Frühes Christentum, Ausgewählte Schriften . . .* herausgegben von Arthur Betz und Gotbert Moro, 2 vols., Klagenfurt, Verlag des Geschichtsvereines für Kärnten, 1962, vol. 1., pp. 81–97, 272–311.

[50] Ainsworth O'Brien-Moore, *Madness in Ancient Literature*, Weimar, R. Wagner Sohn, 1924, pp. 14–18.

[51] Vaughan, *op. cit.*, p. 23.

later antiquity, in the Hellenistic and Roman worlds, with the rise of astrology and the acceptance of the belief that the movements of the heavenly bodies influenced the lives and deaths, the fates and fortunes of mankind, the earlier ideas about the gods were incorporated into the complex astral theology in which the heavenly bodies themselves became the divinities. From this viewpoint, human beings were considered more likely to develop mental disorders when various heavenly bodies were in certain positions. For example, according to a Greek astrological poem, composed in the third century A.D., or later, and attributed to Manetho, temple custodians and slaves of the gods are subject to madness when Venus and Saturn are in conjunction.[52]

The beliefs and ideas presented above are significant because they are the stuff in terms of which people in the Graeco-Roman world formed their thoughts and feelings about aberrant behaviour and mental disorders. They supplied the background against which and in reaction from which must be seen various attitudes towards those exhibiting unusual behaviour or regarded as suffering from some form of mental disorder, the way in which mental derangement was defined and established, the social and legal status of persons considered mentally disturbed and the treatment accorded them by the family and the community.

### Graeco-Roman Attitudes to Madness

Where madness is considered for the most part as possession by a divine power or being, it is not surprising to find the mentally disordered linked with the supernatural world and viewed with the awe inspired by the mysterious and the inexplicable. Because of its link with the supernatural, mental derangement set the sufferer apart from his fellows. The mentally afflicted individual might be considered in a sense above ordinary men, even sacred, for under appropriate circumstances he might display extraordinary powers, including the gift of prophecy, denied to the general run of men. Indeed, this attitude still prevails in modern Greece.[53] Plato has such inspired madness in mind when he remarks in the *Timaeus* that no one achieves inspiration and prophetic truth when in his right mind. Divination is possible only for those who have lost consciousness in

---

[52] Manetho, *Apotelesmatica* 4, 214 ff., in A. Koechly, ed., *Poetae bucolici et didactici*, Paris, 1862, pp. 75–84, see particularly p. 78. For Manetho and his poem see Lynn Thorndike, *A History of Magic and Experimental Science*, New York, Macmillan Co., 1929, vol. 1, pp. 292–293; Vaughan, *op. cit.*, p. 19; Temkin, *op. cit.*, p. 91.

[53] Lawson, *op. cit.*, p. 299.

sleep, or when the mind is affected by disease or possession.[54] This association between madness and inspiration receives its most distinctive and positive exposition in the *Phaedrus*, where Socrates affirms the blessings of divine madness. Plato distinguishes two kinds of madness, one resulting from human ailments, the other from a divine disturbance of the accepted norms of social behaviour, anp in the *Phaedrus* Socrates points out that the latter may in reality be a divine boon.

> The greatest blessings come by way of madness, indeed of madness that is heaven sent. It was when they were mad that the prophetess at Delphi and the priestess at Dodona achieved so much for which both states and individuals in Greece are thankful: when sane they did little or nothing. As for the Sibyl and others who by the power of inspired prophecy have so often foretold the future to so many, and guided them aright, I need not dwell on what is obvious to everyone.[55]

After setting forth the virtues of divine madness, Socrates divides it into four types: prophetic, telestic, poetic and erotic. These types will not be discussed here, but some of them will be considered below in examining the nature of madness and the criteria used to determine its presence.

The idea of divine madness (*enthousiasmos*) was not invented or introduced by Plato. Earlier philosophers, perhaps Heraclitus and Empedocles, may have had the idea, but the word *enthousiasmos* was first used by Democritus.[56] In origin, it belongs to a much older period, for it is rooted in magic ritual and orgiastic religion, in primitive purification ceremonies, in ecstatic prophecy, and in Dionysiac or Corybantic possession. The Platonic viewpoint as expressed by Socrates is obviously paradoxical and sophisticated, for in his day madness was considered by many as something discreditable, if not accursed, and certainly to be avoided. Closer to the primitive view is the custom described by Strabo as prevalent among the Albanians, a people who lived in the Caucasus (modern Soviet Azerbaijan) near the Caspian Sea. Their chief divinity was Selenê

---

[54] Plato, Timaeus 71 D–E. For translation of the text see Plato, *Sämtliche Werke*, 3 vols., Heidelberg, Verlag Lambert Schneider, n.d., vol. 3, p. 164; *Dialogues of Plato* trans. by B. Jowett, vol. II, p. 50.

[55] Plato, *Phaedrus* 265 A, 244 A-B; Plato's *Phaedrus* trans. with introduction and commentary by R. Hackforth, Indianapolis–New York, Bobbs-Merrill Co., n.d. p. 56.

[56] A. Delatte, *Les Conceptions de l'enthousiasme chez les philosophes présocratiques*, Paris, Société d'édition "Les Belles Lettres," 1934. The entire monograph deals with Heraclitus, Empedocles and Democritus; the latter's use of *enthousiasmos* is on pp. 28 ff.

the moon goddess, and the office of priest in her temple was

> held by the man who after the king, is held in highest honour; he has
> charge of the sacred land, which is extensive and well-populated, and
> also of the temple slaves, many of whom are subject to religious frenzy
> and utter prophecies. And any one of those who, becoming violently
> possessed, wanders alone in the forests, is by the priest arrested, bound
> with sacred fetters, and sumptuously maintained during that year, and
> then led forth to the sacrifice that is performed in honour of the goddess,
> and, being anointed, is sacrificed along with other victims. The sacrifice
> is performed as follows: Some person holding a sacred lance, with which
> it is the custom to sacrifice human victims, comes forward out of the
> crowd and strikes the victim through the side into the heart, he being
> not without experience in such a task; and when the victim falls, they
> draw auguries from his fall and declare them before the public; and
> when the body is carried to a certain place, they all trample upon it, thus
> using it as a means of purification.[57]

Divine madness in this case was a sign of election. The goddess
designated her choice among the hierodules by taking possession of
the individual, thus rendering him sacred. In the sacrifice the goddess
received her own, but the victim served also as a scapegoat through
whom the people were purified. Analogous ceremonies were performed by the ancient Greeks.[58] Once a year, Abdera, a city in
Thrace, was purified with public rites in which a citizen set aside for
the purpose was stoned to death as a scapegoat. Several days before
the stoning, he was cast out of the community so that he alone would
bear the sins of the people. A similar rite was performed at Athens
every year at the festival of the Thargelia in May.[59] In this rite, which
was also purificatory in character, two men (sometimes a man and a
woman) described by various writers as worthless, degraded outcasts
(*katharmata*), and who may have been criminals, were led about the
streets, expelled from the city and probably stoned to death outside.
The scapegoat on whom the pollution and sins of the people were
loaded was known as a *pharmakos*. Ritual destruction of *pharmakoi*
in time of plague, famine, drought or some other public calamity is
known to have been practised at Athens, Massilia (the present
Marseilles), and among the Greeks of Asia Minor. The essence of the

[57] *The Geography of Strabo* with an English translation by Horace Leonard
Jones (Loeb Classical Library), 8 vols., London, Wm. Heinemann, 1917–1932,
vol. V, pp. 228–231.
[58] Gilbert Murray, *Rise of the Greek Epic*, Oxford, 1907, pp. 253–258; Harrison,
*op. cit.*, pp. 95–111; F. Schwenn, *Menschenopfer bei den Griechen und Römern*,
Giessen, 1915, pp. 36 ff; James George Frazer, *The Golden Bough* (1 volume
edition, originally published 1922), New York, Macmillan, 1958, pp. 670–675.
[59] L. Deubner, *Attische Feste*, Berlin, 1932, pp. 179 ff.

ritual, the transfer of the community's pollution to the scapegoat, is based on a belief in the actuality of evil as an unclean damaging power, and in the possibility of its transmission. In these rites, the infection of pollution was wiped away by transfer to the *pharmakos*, who thus became pollution incarnate, a being both cursed and sacred.[60]

Were deranged individuals ever chosen as ritual scapegoats? Vaughan conjectured that "at certain periods in the history of Greece madmen, by reason of their supposed selection by the gods were at times offered in sacrifice."[61] However, apart from Strabo's report cited above, there seems to be no evidence of mentally disordered *pharmakoi* in Greece. But it is clear from various sources that the madman, even when regarded as in some way touched by the divine, was a person to be shunned. Contact with holiness, like contact with its opposite uncleanness, was perilous and to be avoided. In fifth century Greece, madness was widely considered the consequence of a divine curse, and an insane person was therefore polluted and a thing of evil omen. Meeting a madman exposed one to the damaging power dwelling in such an individual. The ideas underlying this view are undoubtedly not far from the ancient notion of the *Ker*, and the notion of transfer associated with the *pharmakos*. Moreover, they still occur in various cultures at present, for example, among rural Greeks and Yemenite Jews.[62] The latter believe that mental patients may exert an evil influence on others and even make them sick. To ward off such evil or contagion, rituals of aversion or riddance were performed. Spitting, an act of this type, was often practised in antiquity and is still widely prevalent. As a characteristic of the superstitious man, Theophrastus mentions that when he catches sight of a madman or an epileptic, he shudders and spits in his bosom to avert evil. This practice was also common among the Romans. Pliny, for example, comments that in cases of epilepsy spitting repels contagion. Another reference to this custom occurs in the *Captivi*, a play by Plautus. Tyndarus, a slave, charges that Aristophontes is mad, and from time to time suffers attacks of the disease upon which one must spit. Thereupon, Aristophontes angrily asks Hegio, one of those present, if he actually believes him to be afflicted with this

[60] Harrison, *op. cit.*, pp. 107–108. At this point it is worth noting that Isaiah 53 has been interpreted as referring to a ceremony analogous to that of the pharmakos. See T. Henshaw, *The Latter Prophets*, London, George Allen and Unwin, 1958, p. 236.

[61] Vaughan, *op. cit.*, p. 35.

[62] Blum and Blum, *op. cit.*, 136, 187; J. P. Hes, "The Changing Social Role of the Yemenite Moré," in Ari Kiev, ed., *Magic, Faith and Healing*, Glencoe Free Press, 1964, p. 373.

disease, and is assured that spitting has often benefited such cases.[63]

Another means of avoiding contact with the mentally disordered was to drive them away by throwing clods and stones at them. The indignities suffered by the Birds, in the play of Aristophanes, include being pelted as though they were mad. The same practice was current in Rome, to judge from a remark by one of the Advocati in the *Poenulus* by Plautus. He refused to run through the streets because people would pursue him as a madman and throw stones. Indeed, this custom persisted through the centuries and is referred to by Bar-Hebraeus in the Middle Ages.[64]

By the fifth century B.C., although religious fear and awe still influenced attitudes towards the mentally disturbed, other views had become evident. The situation is clearly indicated by Socrates with his comment that "madness was accounted no shame nor disgrace by the men of old," implying that in his day people did consider it shameful and discreditable.[65] With the break-up of the older religious sentiments under the influence of the Greek enlightenment, the earlier beliefs faded but were not extinguished. They continued to exist in the minds of the uneducated, the simple and the credulous. A pertinent example is provided by Archedemos of Thera, a poor immigrant into Attica, who was apparently mentally disturbed, or, as he put it, "seized by the nymphs." Sometime in the fifth century,

---

[63] *The Characters of Theophrastus*, ed. and with an English translation by J. M. Edmonds (Loeb Classical Library), Cambridge, Mass., Harvard University Press, 1946, pp. 82–83; Pliny, *Naturalis historia*, ed. by L. Janus, 6 vols., Leipzig, 1856–1865, vol. 4, p. 162; Plautus, *Captivi* III, 4, 547–555, in *Plautus*, with an English translation by Paul Nixon (Loeb Classical Library), 5 vols., vol. I London, Wm. Heinemann, 1921, pp. 514–515; Tibullus I, II, 53–54, in *Catullus, Tibullus and Pervigilium Veneris* (Loeb Classical Library), London, Wm. Heinemann, 1931, pp. 200–291; F. W. Nicolson, "The Saliva Superstition in Classical Literature," *Harvard Studies in Classical Philolgy* 8: 23–40, 1897; Blum and Blum, *op. cit.*, pp. 40, 130, 136, 186–187; P. Kemp, *Healing Ritual. Studies in the Technique and Tradition of the Southern Slavs*, London, Faber and Faber, 1935, pp. 52, 165, 246.

[64] Aristophanes, *Birds* 524; Plautus, *Poenulus* 527; Gregory John Bar-Hebraeus, *The Laughable Stories*, The Syriac text ed. and trans. by E. A. Wallis Budge, London, Luzac & Co., 1897, p. 162, DCLXV. Stoning was not infrequent as a form of punishment in antiquity. *Pharmakoi* were killed by stoning, and there is the story of the old man who was stoned by the Ephesians when Apollonius of Tyana declared him to be the incarnation of the plague which ravaged the city. See Philostrate, *Vie d'Apollonios de Tyane* IV, 10, in *Romans Grecs et Latin*, Textes presentés ... par Pierre Grimal (Bibliothèque de la Pléiade), Paris, Gallimard, 1958, pp. 1145–1146. Among the Jews theological and sexual offences were punished by stoning. See Leviticus 20: 10 ff; John 8: 7–11; The Mishnah trans. by Herbert Danby, Oxford University Press, 1964, pp. 230, 250, 297 389–392; A. N. Sherwin-White, *Roman Society and Roman Law in the New Testament*, Oxford, Clarendon Press, 1963, pp. 41–43.

[65] Plato, *Phaedrus* 244, A. Hackforth's translation, p. 56.

he created a shrine for the nymphs in a grotto at Vari on Mount Hymettos, planting a garden in front of it, decorating it and carving inscriptions on the walls. Theophrastus provides another example. By including in his sketch of the superstitious man the practice of spitting in one's bosom on seeing a madman or an epileptic, he clearly reflects the survival of the older ideas as well as the more critical approach of the educated public to such matters.[66] The latter viewpoint find its clearest expression in the Hippocratic author of the *Sacred Disease* who denies that any one illness is more divine than another, and affirms that all diseases have natural causes discoverable by the human mind.

Behaviour towards the mentally disordered reflected these attitudes. No effort was made to conceal madmen or mental defectives from public view, so that they were a visible part of everyday experience. By and large, community attitudes towards these individuals were compounded of fear and contempt, mingled to a lesser extent with an element of compassion. Fear of madness persisted, partly as an extension of earlier views, and partly because of possible violence on the part of the deranged.[67] In addition, the view that madness was shameful led many to regard the mentally ill as lacking both the sensibilities and the mental attributes of human beings. Deprived in large measure of a socially acceptable position defined in religious or supernatural terms, the mentally disordered required a role and a position which enabled the social group to tolerate them. To what extent and in what form a society can accept conspicuously abnormal persons is a perennial problem which as been solved in various ways. In antiquity, the mentally disordered became objects of ridicule, scorn or abuse, and remained public butts for the amusement of the populace.

Evidence for such behaviour is to be found scattered throughout Greek and Latin literature from the fifth century B.C. to the decline of the Roman world. In the Platonic dialogue named for him, the soothsayer Euthyphro, for example, complains to Socrates that when he tries to speak in the assembly of divine things and to predict the

[66] Martin P. Nilsson, *A History of Greek Religion*, 2nd edition, Oxford, Clarendon Press, 1949, pp. 263 ff. *idem, Greek Piety*, Oxford, Clarendon Press, 1951, pp. 72–78; Theophrastus, *op. cit.*, pp. 78–83.

[67] Violence as a behavioural characteristic of the mentally disordered will be discussed below in connection with the criteria for establishing the existence of insanity. Fear of the violently insane is indicated in the following: Plato, *Alcibiades* II, 139 C, Jowett translation, vol. II, p. 794; Aristophanes, *Frogs*, 560–566, (Loeb Classical Library), vol. II, pp. 346–347; Plautus, *Casina*, 660–671, (Loeb Classical Library), vol. II, pp. 72–73; Lucian, *The Disinherited*, in the *Works of Lucian of Samosata*, trans. by H. W. and F. G. Fowler, 4 vols., Oxford Clarendon Press, 1905, vol. II, pp. 192 and 193; Plutarch, *op. cit.*, p. 766.

future, the members ridicule him as they would a madman. Some five hundred years later, Phaedrus in one of his fables tells how an Athenian, seeing Aesop in a group of boys playing with nuts, stopped and laughed at him as though he were crazy. The ubiquity of such behaviour is further substantiated by a contemporary of Phaedrus, the philosopher Philo Judaeus, who relates an actual incident which occurred at Alexandria. "There was a certain lunatic named Carabas," he says, "whose madness was not of the fierce and savage kind, which is dangerous both to the madmen themselves and those who approach them, but of the easy-going gentler style. He spent day and night in the streets naked, shunning neither heat nor cold, made game of by the children, and the lads who were idling about." The poor fellow was driven into the gymnasium by a band of rioters who "set him up on high to be seen by all and put on his head a sheet of byblus spread out wide for a diadem, clothed the rest of his body with a rug for a royal robe, while someone who had noticed a piece of the native papyrus thrown away in the road gave it to him for his sceptre." Invested with the mock trappings of royalty, he was made the centre of a mock court. Finally, there is a reference by Artemidorus Daldianus, in the second century A.D., to a madman being followed by children and street idlers who jeered at him and mimicked him.[68]

As one might expect, such treatment was not the lot of all the mentally disordered. Whether they were followed by jeering children or pelted with stones depended on circumstances. Disturbed individuals whose families looked after them would naturally remain unmolested. Generally families of means hired attendants to watch their deranged members and keep them from harm. Consequently, the madmen who wandered at large and roamed the streets belonged mostly to the lower classes.

Yet there is some evidence of compassion for the mentally disordered, perhaps more so in later antiquity. A comment by Philo Judaeus may be considered in this light. "And yet," he says, "why should we not call madness death, seeing that by it mind dies, the noblest part of us? Nay it appears to me that, were a choice offered, a man would be likely to choose without hesitation the death that

[68] Plato, *Euthyphro* 3 C (Burnet's edition cited above, note 18, vol. 1), for translation see *Sämtliche Werke* cited above, note 54, vol. 1, p. 280; Phaedrus III 14, 1–3, in Babrius and Phaedrus, ed. with an English translation by Ben Edwin Perry (Loeb Classical Library), Cambridge, Mass., Harvard University Press, 1965, pp. 280–281; Philo, *In Flaccum* 36–38, in *Philo* with an English translation by F. H. Colson (Loeb Classical Library), 12 vols., vol. IX, Cambridge, Mass., Harvard University Press, 1960, pp. 322–323; Artemidorus Daldianus, *Onirocriticon* Libri V recognovit Roger A. Pack, Leipzig, B. G. Teubner, 1963, p. 222.

separates and dissolves the union of soul and body, in preference to going out of one's senses, feeling that he was choosing the lighter in place of the heavier."[69] In Lucian's monologue, *The Disinherited*, a physician who has been disinherited by his father for not wishing to treat his insane stepmother, declares his inability to cure her and expresses his compassion for her as a worthy person deserving a better fate.[70] Finally, one should note Plato's proposal to impose a heavy fine on anyone who neglected to care for a mad slave.[71]

## What is Madness? Who is Mad?

Whether or not a person is considered mentally ill depends on the degree to which his behaviour is disturbed, and the attitudes of the members of his social group towards deviant behaviour. In this sense, mental disorder is perhaps even more intimately dependent on social factors than is physical illness. This situation may well make it possible to reconcile public opinion to greater tolerance of the mentally ill in one society than in another. A pertinent illustration is provided by the joking exchange between Hamlet and the Clown:[72]

> *Hamlet:* Ay, marry, why was he sent into England?
> *First Clown:* Why, because a' was mad; a' shall recover his wits there; or, if a' do not, 'tis no great matter there.
> *Hamlet:* Why?
> *First Clown:* 'Till not be seen in him there; there the men are as mad as he.

The word madness was used loosely by the ancients, as it is today, to characterize widely varying behavioural phenomena.[73] When a Greek or a Roman spoke of madness, at one extreme the term might be applied to nothing more than queer or unreasonable behaviour, at the other it might well designate undoubted neuroses and psychoses. As in English, a strange or unexpected act might lead a Greek or a Roman to exclaim "He's mad!" without necessarily implying the existence of mental derangement in a strict sense. Certain words might at times be used to express such rhetorical exaggeration and denote little more than great folly and unreasonableness, but they might also be employed with strong connotations of mental aberra-

[69] Philo, *De Plantatione* 36 in *Philo* (Loeb Classical Library), vol. III, pp 288–289.
[70] Lucian, *The Disinherited*, in *The Works of Lucian, op. cit.*, vol. II, p. 187.
[71] Plato, *Laws* XI 934D, Jowett translation, *op. cit.*, vol. II, p. 672.
[72] *Hamlet*, Act V, Scene I.
[73] I am referring to the Greek words *mania, mainesthai* and to the Latin *insania*.

tion. Characteristic examples of such usage are provided by the words *daimonan, kakodaimonan,* and *kakodaimonia.*

In Xenophon's *Memorabilia,* for example, when Socrates discusses the knowledge attainable by man through science and revealed by the gods through divination, he uses the word *daimonan* to characterize as irrational both those who believed that human judgement alone determines success or failure, and those who sought divine guidance in the most trivial matters. Furthermore, speaking of the risks run by adulterers to satisfy their passions. Socrates says, "When such misery and disgrace hang over the adulterer's head, and there are many remedies to relieve him of his carnal desire without risk, is it not sheer lunacy (*kakodaimonontos estin*) to plunge headlong into danger?"[74]

The same word is employed in a somewhat different sense by the orator Dinarchus (ca. 361–ca. 292 B.C.) in his indictment of Demosthenes. Arguing that statesmen are responsible for a city's prosperity or misfortune, he accuses Demosthenes of not ensuring the safety of Athens. If no action is taken against him, the city "may still be plagued by an evil genius (*kakodaimonomen*)."[75] Here the term carries overtones of possession by an evil spirit leading to acts of unreason and folly with disastrous consequences for the city.

Plutarch in his essay on superstition notes the pleasure that men have in mystic rites and initations, as well as in festal days and banquets at the temples of the gods. He goes on to remark that on these occasions the atheist "gives way to insane (*manikon*) and sardonic laughter at such ceremonies, and remarks aside to his cronies that people must cherish a vain and silly (*daimonosin*) conceit to think that these rites are performed in honour of the gods."[76] In this context it is clear that neither of the words referring to mental abberration deals with insanity, but rather with folly, with irrationality that passes all bounds.[77]

A somewhat later instance occurs in the *Ecclesiastical History* of Eusebius (ca. 260–ca. 339–340 A.D.), bishop of Caesarea. Discussing the heretical doctrines of Marcion of Sinope, a Christian Gnostic, in Pontus, and other heresies which developed from them, he mentions

---

[74] Xenophon, *Memorabilia and Oeconomicus,* with an English translation by E. G. Marchant, (Loeb Classical Library), London, Wm. Heinemann, 1923, pp. 6–7, 84–85.

[75] Dinarchus, *Against Demosthenes* 91, in *Minor Attic Orators,* with an English translation by J. O. Burtt (Loeb Classical Library), 2 vols., Cambridge, Mass., Harvard University Press, 1941–1954, vol. II, pp. 240–241.

[76] Plutarch, *De Superstitione* 169D, in Plutarch's *Moralia,* with an English translation by Frank Cole Babbitt (Loeb Classical Library), 14 vols., London, Wm. Heinemann, 1929, vol. II, pp. 480–483.

[77] For other relations of folly and madness at different periods in history see below pp. 151 ff.

a certain Apelles, who was convinced of the correctness of his views "by the utterances of a possessed maiden (*parthenou daimonoses*) named Philoumene."[78] The context gives no immediate basis for linking the young woman's possession with madness. However, a conspicuous phenomenon in later antiquity is the demonizing of religion,[79] a process shared by paganism and Christianity which was to have a significant influence on later views of mental disorder.

In all these usages it is clear that we have to do with a question of mental states. In some instances the words imply more than ordinary folly or stupidity; they are used to convey the idea of madness. Chremylus in the *Plutus* laments the state of the world in which the most undeserving and wicked are rich and powerful while those who are good and righteous suffer poverty and injustice. Such a topsy-turvy world is pure madness (*manion*), perhaps the plaything of an evil, mischievous spirit (*kakodaimonian*).[80] Earlier in the play there is a scene between Chremylus and his neighbour Blepsidemus, in which the former claims the other is mad. Having heard that Chremylus has suddenly become wealthy, Blepsidemus suspects him of robbery, suggesting that he may have taken gold and silver from the temple treasury at Delphi. Chremylus vehemently denies the accusation countering with, "Now by Demeter, friend, you have lost your wits[81] ... Poor chap, you're moody-mad (*melancholas, anthrope*)." But Blepsidemus continues, "His very eye's grown shifty: he can't look you straight in the face: I warrant he's turned rogue." To this Chremylus replies, "I understand, You think I've stolen something ... But 'tis not so: the thing's quite otherwise." "Not stol'n, but robbed outright?" his accuser questions stubbornly. At this point, the inexplicable, unreasonable insistence with which Blepsidemus clings to his idea leads Chremylus to conclude in despair. "The man's possessed (*kakodaimonas*)."[82]

Aristophanes' indiscriminate use of *melancholas* and *kakodaimonas* to express mental aberration or madness is noteworthy. The former

[78] Eusebius, *The Ecclesiastical History*, with an English translation by Kirsopp Lake (Loeb Classical Library), 2 vols., Cambridge, Mass., Harvard University Press, 1959, vol. 1, pp. 466–467. For Marcion and Apelles see Jean Doresse, *Les livres secrets des gnostiques d'Egypte*, Paris, Librairie Plon, 1958, pp. 7, 24–27; Hans Jonas, *The Gnostic Religion*, Boston, Beacon Press, 1958, pp. 137–146.

[79] The phrase—the demonizing of religion—has been borrowed from Nilsson, *Greek Piety*, p. 170.

[80] Aristophanes, *Plutus* 400–504.

[81] *Oǔ toi mà ten Démetr' hugiainein moi dokeĩs*. The term *hugiainein*, to be sane or in one's right mind, also occurs in Aristophanes' *Peace* 95, *Clouds* 1275, and *Plutus* 507.

[82] Aristophanes, *Plutus* 364–373. The translation used here is that by B. B. Rogers in the Loeb edition, vol. III, pp. 394–395.

word is also employed in various other contexts to denote madness. In the *Plutus*, Cario, the slave of Chremylus, characterizes his master as *melancholon*, mad, because he follows "a poor blind old man, just the reverse of what he ought to do. For we who see should go *before* the blind, but he goes *after*." A similar situation occurs in the *Peace*. Describing the onset of Trygaeus's madness, he says "You hear yourselves a sample of his ravings (*manion*). But what he did when first the frenzy (*cholé*) seized him I'll tell you." Clearly, bile is equated with madness and frenzy. Again, in the *Birds*, Euelpides refers to Philocrates, the bird seller, as *melancholon*, just as we might refer to some one as a "nut". Similar usages occur in other Greek writers of the period. Demosthenes in his speech against Olympiodorus characterizes him as one who appears to be not only an offender but a madman (*melancholon*). Then, in the *Phaedrus*, the point is made that one cannot become a physician without any real knowledge of medicine, simply by picking up something out of a book, or by learning something about a common drug. Of such a person, Phaedrus says "I expect they would say 'The man is mad' (*mainetai anthropos*)." Somewhat later in the dialogue, Socrates, in making a similar point about music, remarks that a musician would not rudely dispose of a vain ignoramus by saying "Miserable man, you're crazy (*omochtheré melancholas*)."[83]

Clearly, by the fifth century B.C., a medical view that madness was caused by black bile had become sufficiently current among the people for the words derived from this idea to be used in daily speech and to serve as synonyms for other terms denoting mental derangement. This terminology and the theory underlying it were used in practice, and were presented more systematically in various treatises.[84] Temkin points out, however, that the medical concepts were not uninfluenced by earlier popular views, ideas and terminology. As in our own day, the public adopted medical terms but used them side by side with words derived from older ideas of possession and divine punishment. Such words were used without any attempt at consistency, often interchangeably. A similar usage of analogous terms in Latin is indicated by the indiscriminate way in which Plautus employs *atra bilis*, black bile, and *larvae*, spirits, to denote madness.[85]

[83] Aristophanes, *Plutus*, 10–14, Loeb edition, vol. III, pp. 364–365; *idem, Peace* 65–67, Loeb edition, vol. II, pp. 8–9; *idem, Birds*, 13–14, Loeb edition, vol. II, pp. 130–131; Demosthenes, *Against Olympiodorus*, 56; Plato, *Phaedrus*, 268 C-D.
[84] Hippocrates, *Nature of Man*, Loeb edition, vol. IV, pp. 2–41; *idem, Aphorisms* VI 23, Loeb edition, vol. IV, pp. 184–185; *idem, Epidemics* III, Loeb edition, vol. I, pp. 262–263.
[85] Plautus, *Amphitryon* 727, 777, Loeb edition, vol. I. pp. 74–75, 80–81.

But whatever terms were used to designate mental derangement, their application was based upon the occurrence and observation of some form of inexplicable, unreasonable action or belief. Socrates declared that most men "do not call those mad who err in matters that lie outside the knowledge of ordinary people: madness is the name they give to errors in matters of common knowledge. For instance, if a man imagines himself to be so tall as to stoop when he goes through the gateways in the Wall, or so strong as to try to lift houses or to perform any other feat that everybody knows to be impossible, they say he's mad. They don't think a slight error implies madness, but just as they call strong desire love, so they name a great delusion madness."[86]

Specific cases which illustrate these criteria occur throughout Greek and Latin literature. The stories of Cambyses and Cleomenes have already been presented. Senseless cruelty was one of the symptoms that led to the view that Cambyses was mad, while the insanity of Cleomenes was signalled by his violent, abusive conduct towards his fellow Spartans. Another ruler described as mentally unbalanced was Dionysius, tyrant of Syracuse (ca. 430–376 B.C.). Aware of the hatred he had aroused by his repressive measures, he was harsh and cruel to his enemies, suspecting treachery on all sides. He was so afraid of assassination that no one was permitted in his presence with a weapon. Yet the tyrant of Syracuse was also a dramatic poet, desirous of recognition, who frequently competed in the Athenian theatre and at other appropriate occasions. Diodorus the Sicilian links these two sides of his character to account for the delusions of persecution from which Dionysius is alleged to have suffered. According to this story, Dionysius had presented poems at the Olympic games, where they were received with ridicule. Stung by his reception, which he could not forget, he continued to brood over the fiasco until his mind gave way and he began to accuse his friends of plotting against him out of envy. Eventually, many were executed on false charges, and others were exiled.[87] Very likely the story, as presented by Diodorus, is apocryphal. Yet, *si non è vero, è ben trovato*. Even if his fears were exaggerated, Dionysius had reason enough to be suspicious. This account is significant, however, in emphasizing the psychogenic element in the origin of madness, as well as the assessment of behaviour in terms of its orientation to reality, and of the consequences to which it leads.

Reports of actual or feigned madness in less prominent individuals are also available. Aelian relates that the Athenian astronomer

---

[86] Xenophon, *Memorabilia* III, 9, 6–7, Loeb edition, pp. 226–227.
[87] Diodorus Siculus XV, 7, 2–3; J. B. Bury, *A History of Greece to the Death of Alexander the Great,* New York, Modern Library, 1937, p. 650.

Meton, having doubts about the outcome of the Sicilian expedition of 415 B.C., feigned madness to avoid military service, and burned down his house so that there would be no mistaking his mental condition.[88] A similar story is told about Monimus of Syracuse (fourth century B.C.), a pupil of Diogenes the Cynic philosopher. At one time he was the slave of a Corinthian money-changer, but having heard of Diogenes, for whom he developed a passionate admiration, and desiring to follow him, Monimus pretended to be insane. He "proceeded to fling away the small change and all the money" on his master's table, whereupon he was driven away.[89]

Heraclides of Pontus (388–310 B.C.), an astronomer resident at Athens, described the interesting case of an Athenian named Thrasyllus, who constantly frequented the Piraeus because he believed that all the ships coming into and leaving the port belonged to him. He kept track of them, noting their cargoes and destinations, and when a ship returned safely he rejoiced at the wealth it brought him. After his recovery, Thrasyllus clearly recalled his previous condition asserting that he had never been happier than when he was deluded.[90]

Reminiscent of this case is one related by Horace. "Once at Argos," he says, "there was a man of some rank, who used to fancy that he was listening to wonderful tragic actors, while he sat happy and applauded in the empty theatre—a man who would correctly perform all other duties of life . . ." When he was cured, however, he complained to his friends that he had been deprived of his dearest illusion and pleasure.[91]

---

[88] Aelian, *Varia historia* XIII, 12 ff. For Meton see Benjamin Farrington, *Greek Science*, Baltimore, Penguin Books, 1961, pp. 217, 218, 222, 232; S. Sambursky, *The Physical World of the Greeks*, New York, Collier Books, 1962, p. 69; *Selections Illustrating the History of Greek Mathematics*, with an English translation by Ivor Thomas (Loeb Classical Library), 2 vols., Cambridge, Mass., Harvard University Press, 1939–1941, fol. 1, pp. 308–309. Another version has it that Meton burned down his house so that he might claim the release of his son from military service on grounds of hardship. See Plutarch, *Nicias* 13; *ibid.*, Alcibiades 17 in Plutarch's *Lives, op. cit.*, pp. 244–245, 637 (note 37).

[89] Diogenes Laertius, *Lives of Eminent Philosophers*, with an English translation by R. D. Hicks (Loeb Classical Library), 2 vols., London, Wm. Heinemann, 1925, vol. II, pp. 84–85. Analogous incidents are reported about Solon (Diogenes Laertius, vol. I, pp. 46–49) and Lucius Junius Brutus (Livy, *From the Founding of the City*, with an English translation by B. O. Foster [Loeb Classical Library], 13 vols., London, Wm. Heinemann, 1925, vol. 1, pp. 194–195).

[90] Athenaeus, *The Deipnosophists*, with an English translation by C. B. Gulick (Loeb Classical Library), 7 vols., London, Wm. Heinemann, 1927–1928, vol. V, pp. 520–521; Aelian, *Varia historia* IV, 25.

[91] *Epistles* II, 2, 128–140, in Horace, *Satires, Epistles, Ars Poetica*, with an English translation by H. Rushton Fairclough (Loeb Classical Library), London, Wm. Heinemann, 1926, pp. 424–435.

Accounts of patients afflicted with anxiety states, obsessions, compulsions, phobias, delusions and hallucinations are presented by a number of medical writers. Two curious cases involving flute music have come down to us. One of them reported by Galen concerns a patient, apparently without any other complaint, who saw and heard phantom flute players by day and night. The other, from the Hippocratic Corpus, tells of a young man who for a long time had a fear of the female flute player at banquets, and was terrified when the flute music began on such occasions. If he heard this instrument played during the day, it hardly bothered him; at night he found it unbearable and difficult to control himself. Flute music appears to have had a considerable emotional significance in antiquity, especially in connection with certain cult rituals such as the worship of Cybele, the Phrygian mountain goddess, and the Corbyantic and Dionysiac rites. Hallucinations involving flute music and bizarre visions were particularly prominent in Corybantic frenzy.[92]

Democles, one of his companions, had another problem. Complaining of impaired vision and feeling unable to control his limbs, he could not walk alongside a precipice, pass over a bridge, or even step over the shallowest ditch, though he was able to walk in the ditch itself.[93]

Aretaeus describes the case of an artisan who seems to have been afflicted with agoraphobia. "A certain joiner," he says, "was a skilful artisan while in the house, would measure, chop, plane, mortice, and adjust wood, and finish the work of the house correctly; would associate with the workmen, make a bargain with them, and remunerate their work with suitable pay. While on the spot where the work was performed, he thus possessed his understanding. But if at any time he went away to the market, the bath, or on any other engagement, having laid down his tools, he would first groan, then shrug his shoulders as he went out. But when he had got out of sight of the domestics, or of the work and the place where it was performed, he became completely mad; yet if he returned speedily he recovered his reason again."[94]

Caelius Aurelianus describes still another kind of mental disorder which affected the philologist Artemidorus. The latter was lying on the sand when he was frightened by the sight of an approaching crocodile. His mind was so affected by the sudden shock of seeing the moving reptile that he imagined his left leg and hand had been bitten

---

[92] Galen VII 60f. Kühn; Hippocrates *Epidemics* V, 81 in *Oeuvres complètes d'Hippocrate* . . . ed. E. Littré, 10 vols., Paris, J. B. Baillière, 1839–1861, vol. V, 1846, pp. 250–251; Rohde, *op. cit.*, vol. II, pp. 44–49.

[93] Hippocrates, *Ibid.*, pp. 250–251.

[94] Aretaeus, *op. cit.*, pp. 60, 302–303.

off by the animal, and he lost his memory. The same author also notes obsessive fears and delusions occurring among madmen. Some patients, he says, "will be afraid of caves or will be obsessed by the fear of falling in a ditch or will dread other things which may for some reason inspire fear." Sometimes they are affected by other kinds of aberration: "Thus one victim of madness fancied himself a sparrow, another a cock, another an earthen vessel, another a brick, another a god, another an orator, another a tragic actor, another a comic actor, another a stalk of grain and asserted that he occupied the centre of the universe, and another cried like a baby and begged to be carried in the arms."[95]

Similar delusions are also mentioned by other physicians. Galen refers to depressed melancholics who identified themselves with Atlas bearing the burden of the world on his back. Alexander of Tralles describes one of his patients who bound up her middle finger for fear that the world would collapse if she bent it. Celsus mentions a wealthy man who was in constant fear that he would lose his wealth and starve, to whom pretended legacies were announced from time to time in order to relieve his anxiety. Finally, we may note the reference of Aretaeus to harmless madmen who are "given to extraordinary phantasies; for one is afraid of the fall of the oil cruets . . . and another will not drink, as fancying himself a brick, and fearing lest he should be dissolved by the liquid."[96]

Clearly, the behaviour of the people cited above was regarded as more than merely perplexing or perverse. They were regarded as deranged because their behaviour and, inferentially, their orientation to reality were considered excessively divergent from socially accepted norms. In this sense, mental derangement was defined in terms of a social judgement of the appropriateness of behaviour in a given context. The acceptance and application of this criterion are attested by many sources. The comments of Socrates have already been cited (see above) and to them may be added the remark of Aretaeus that persons who are mad see as others do, "but do not form a correct judgement on what they have seen."[97] Further evidence on this point is to be found in the Greek and Latin comic writers, who employed inexplicable behaviour and unreasonable

---

[95] Caelius Aurelianus, *On Acute Diseases and on Chronic Diseases*, ed. and trans. by I. E. Drabkin, Chicago, University of Chicago Press, 1950, pp. 538–541.

[96] Galen VIII, 190 Kühn; *Alexander von Tralles*, ed. by Theodor Puschmann, 2 vols., Vienna, 1878–79, vol. I, 605, 607; Celsus, *De medicina*, with an English translation by W. G. Spencer (Loeb Classical Library), 3 vols., Cambridge, Mass., Harvard University Press, 1935–38, vol. I, pp. 294–295; Aretaeus, *op. cit.*, pp. 60, 302.

[97] Aretaeus, *op. cit.*, p. 303.

beliefs to create situations in which confusion of meaning readily brought forth accusations of madness.[98]

In addition to the criterion of reality orientation, madness was judged by the style of behaviour. Two forms of behaviour were considered particularly characteristic of the mentally disordered, their habit of wandering about, and their proneness to violence. The practice of permitting harmless madmen to roam the streets and and public places is well attested, and has already been mentioned above in discussing their role as public butts. This is certainly implied in several of the cases previously described, for example, in the instances of Thrasyllus the Athenian who frequented the Piraeus, of the man at Argos who attended an empty theatre, of the joiner described by Aretaeus, and the incident involving the lunatic Carabbas reported by Philo Judaeus. Further support on this point is provided by Artemidorus in his dream book. According to him, for a poor man to dream of singing songs in the streets or market place was a premonitory sign of future madness, because this was how madmen acted when they wandered about.[99] Aretaeus confirms this observation. Discussing the different kinds of deranged people, he notes that those "with whose madness joy is associated, laugh, play, dance night and day, and sometimes go openly to the market crowned, as if victors in some contest of skill; this form is inoffensive to those around." Furthermore, the poor and uneducated in this group were often employed in carrying loads and working as masons or at some other labour.[100]

Other mentally disordered individuals, however, are described as misanthropic, morose, and avoiding their fellow-men. Aretaeus speaks of some madmen who "flee the haunts of men and going to the wilderness, live by themselves." Also, in discussing melancholia, he refers to "avoidance of the haunts of men" as a characteristic of those severely afflicted with this condition.[101] The Gerasene demoniac in the Gospels apparently belonged to this group. According to Luke, the demon who possessed him drove him into the desert after he had broken the bonds used to fetter him.[102] There he lived among tombs wearing no clothes, crying out night and day, and bruising himself with stones. Aretaeus also notes that some madmen roar aloud,

[98] Aristophanes, *Plutus*, 10–15; Plautus, *Aulularia*, 640–643; *ibid.*, *Menaechmi*, 280 ff; Menander, *The Principal Fragments*, with an English translation by Francis G. Allinson (Loeb Classical Library), London, Wm. Heinemann, 1930, pp. 348–349. Terence, with an English translation by John Sargeaunt (Loeb Classical Library), 2 vols., London, Wm. Heinemann, 1926, vol. 1, pp. 122–125.

[99] Artemidorus I, 76, *op. cit.*, pp. 81–83, Aretaeus, *op. cit.*, pp. 59–60, 302.

[100] Aretaeus, *op. cit.*, pp. 59, 302.

[101] *Ibid.*, pp. 300, 304.

[102] Luke 8: 26, 29; Mark 5: 3; also Matthew 8: 28.

bewailing themselves as if they had experienced violence or robbery.[103]

Matthew's account of the meeting with the demoniac differs from the versions in Mark and Luke not only in his reference to two possessed individuals, but even more significantly from our viewpoint in describing them as so fierce that no one could pass near the tombs which they haunted.[104] This remark points to another aspect of behaviour considered characteristic of mental derangement, namely, violence. Aretaeus differentiates the docile, inoffensive madmen from others in whom "madness is attended with anger and these sometimes rend their clothes and kill their keepers, and lay violent hands upon themselves." To which he adds, "This miserable form of disease is not unattended with danger to those around."[105]

A number of references to homicidal mania support these remarks. Situations in two comedies, the *Frogs* of Aristophanes, and the *Casina* by Plautus, indicate public acceptance of the possibility of homicide by a raging madman. In the *Frogs*, Xanthias, a slave, having entered a tavern and consumed an enormous meal, behaves outrageously when the hostess wants to be paid. Bellowing like a bull, a fierce look on his face, and a drawn sword in his hand, he appears to her violently mad and bent on murder. Thereupon she flees to the attic to save her life. An analogous situation is created by Plautus in his play. To terrify her master an old slave woman named Pardalisca describes how the slave girl Casina, sword in hand, was "chasing everyone through the house there, and won't let a soul come near her, they're hiding under chests and couches afraid to breathe a word." "What the deuce has got into her all of a sudden this way?" asks Lysidamus, her master. "She's gone crazy," answers Pardalisca.[106]

The situations created by Aristophanes and Plautus involve imagined or simulated insanity, but cases of murder or suicide by insane persons did occur. The self-destruction of Cleomenes has been described. We may also note the comments in the fragmentary Hippocratic work *On the Diseases of Maidens* (*Peri parthenion*) on the mental symptoms including suicidal tendencies to which young

---

[103] The traits noted by Aretaeus are apparently derived from the lost works of Archigenes of Apamea, who lived and practised in Rome at the time of Trajan. See Max Wellmann, *Die pneumatische Schule, bis auf Archigenes in ihrer Entwickelung dargestellt*, (Philologische Untersuchungen, 14. Heft), Berlin, Weidmannsche Buchhandlung, 1895, see particularly pp. 19–22.

[104] Matthew 8: 28.

[105] Aretaeus, *op. cit.*, p. 302.

[106] Aristophanes, *Frogs*, 555–567, Loeb edition, vol. II, pp. 346–347; Plautus, *Casina* 660–665, Loeb edition, vol. II, pp. 72–73; see also *Menaechmi* 830–861, Loeb edition, vol. II, pp. 448–453.

girls are prone if they have menstrual troubles.[107] Caelius Aurelianus observes that victims of madness have often killed themselves by jumping out of windows.[108] We may recall Aretaeus' observation that violent madmen injure or kill themselves and sometimes their keepers, and in addition there are more specific references to homicides committed by insane individuals. Dealing with cannibalism as a form of human behaviour, Aristotle noted that among savages it occurs as part of a social pattern, but that in other individuals it may be a result of mental derangement or illness. As instances, he cites a man who killed and ate his mother, and another who killed his fellow servant and ate his liver.[109] A rescript of the Emperor Marcus Aurelius deals with the case of a certain Aelius Priscus who in a fit of insanity murdered his mother. A similar case is reported in a rescript of Antoninus Pius. In each instance, the governor of the area is ordered to establish whether the murderer was actually insane when the crime was committed. Finally, we may note the remark in the *Disinherited* of Lucian that the physicians of the insane are in danger from their patients: also the observation by Paul of Aegina that such patients should be secured so that they may not injure themselves or those who approach them.[110]

Other instances of such attacks by madmen undoubtedly occurred, but more common, no doubt, was aggressive behaviour when deranged individuals were teased, chased, pelted with clods or subjected to other indignities. The spurious Platonic dialogue *Alcibiades* II has a remark by Socrates which indicates that madmen were expected to throw stones at people and to beat them. Any who consorted with such individuals might expect to be treated in this fashion. Socrates points out to Alcibiades that if one would have to live in a community dominated by crazy people, "Should we not long since have paid the penalty at their hands, and have been struck and beaten and endured every other form of ill usage which madmen are wont to inflict?"[111] Other writers confirm that this opinion was widespread. In the *Wasps* of Aristophanes, Philocleon, an old man

---

[107] An interpretation of these symptoms, particulary the suicidal behaviour, as an example of psychopathic collective behaviour connected with religious rites is presented by E. D. Baumann,"Die Krankheit der Jungfrauen," *Janus* 43: 189–194 1939.

[108] Caelius Aurelianus, *op. cit.*, pp. 542–543.

[109] Aristole, *Nicomachean Ethics* VII, 6.

[110] Justinian, *Digest* I, 18, 14; Lucian, *The Disinherited*, Fowler translation, *op. cit.*, vol. 2, p. 193; Paulus Aegineta, *The Seven Books*, trans. with commentary by Francis Adams, 3 vols., London, Sydenham Society, 1844–1847, vol. 1, p. 385.

[111] Plato, *Alcibiades* II 139d, Jowett translation, *op. cit.*, vol. II, p. 794. But note the story in Bar-Hebraeus, *op. cit.*, p. 162, indicating that such behaviour was often a response to stones thrown at the mentally deranged (Story DCXLV).

with an obsession for litigation, has been locked up in his house by his son. However, he manages to slip out, emerging singing and dancing, so that his slave Xanthias calls him mad. Philocleon, nevertheless, continues his wild dance, leading Xanthias to shout, "You'll strike by and by," apparently expecting that if the old man became more frenzied, he would beat him or throw stones at him.[112] This point is made even more explicitly in the *Captives* of Plautus. Wishing to discredit Aristophontes, the slave Tyndarus has accused him of being mad. Unable to contain his rage, Aristophontes bursts out, "I positively can't control myself any longer." Thereupon, Tyndarus, wishing to emphasize the alleged insanity, shouts, "Aha! Hear what he's saying? Run, why don't you? He'll be after us with stones in a minute, if you don't have him seized."[113] This behaviour is also mentioned by Plutarch as a characteristic of the mentally deranged when angered or otherwise excited. When Mithridates, king of Pontus, bestowed valuable gifts on the father of Stratonice, his favourite concubine, the old man was so transported with joy that he mounted a horse, and rode through the city crying out "All this is mine." People laughed at him and thought his conduct unseemly, but he said that it was a wonder rather that he did not throw stones at all those he met, as he was so carried away by his joy.[114] Plutarch clearly expected his readers to understand the significance of this remark without any explanation, thus indicating the wide acceptance of the view that those who were mentally deranged were likely to throw stones or exhibit other kinds of aggressive behaviour when agitated.

## From the Wilder Shores of Sanity

Every society recognizes certain extreme forms of aberrant behaviour as mental derangement or insanity. In other words, along the range of human behaviour, from that which a society considers normal to that which it regards as abnormal, there is some point or section at which a social judgement is made and an individual comes to be regarded as mad. Obviously, there will also be individuals whose behaviour is not as extremely aberrant as that of the insane. The assessment of such individuals and their behaviour by members of their society, and their acceptance as merely eccentric within socially tolerable limits, will depend on various factors. One set of factors includes the style and consistency of such behaviour, its orientation to reality, and its consequences. The latter element is particularly

---

[112] Aristophanes, *Wasps* 1482–1491, Loeb edition, vol. I., pp. 544–547.
[113] Plautus, *Captivi* 592–593, Loeb edition, vol. I, pp. 518–519.
[114] Plutarch, *Pompey* 36, Dryden translation, *op. cit.*, p. 766.

significant in legal determinations. A second set of factors involves the extent to which a given society tolerates eccentric behaviour, as well as the existence of social institutions which enable such deviant individuals to function in some acceptable manner.

In practice, the dividing line between sanity and insanity is not always easily established. Graeco-Roman medicine dealt with this problem largely by excluding from consideration those forms of mental disturbance which Plato called the "madness given us by divine gift." Although Aretaeus did describe ritual frenzy as a kind of madness, he clearly differentiated it from other forms of mental disturbance, pointing to its divine origin and noting that the participants were sane in other respects. Caelius Aurelianus was also aware of the Platonic and Stoic distinctions between mental disorders arising from bodily disease, and divine or inspired madness. Thus, his comment that music arouses men to madness is illustrated by noting that "as they chant their prophecies, priests often seem to be possessed by the god." However, he explicitly limited himself only to what he considered a medical problem, madness characterized by "an impairment of reason resulting from a bodily disease or indisposition."[115]

For the non-medical public, however, madness was more inclusive, ranging from ecstatic behaviour as seen in prophetic inspiration, or Dionysiac and Corybantic frenzy, to epilepsy and delusional insanity. An actor, for example, who worked himself into a frenzy and induced a similar reaction in his audience might well be considered mad. In his dialogue on mime, Lucian tells the story of an actor who went temporarily mad through excessive empathy with the character he was enacting. According to Lucian,

> He was acting the madness of Ajax, just after he has been worsted by Odysseus; and so lost control of himself that one might have been excused for thinking his madness was something more than feigned. He tore the clothes from the back of one of the iron-shod time-beaters, snatched a flute from the player's hands, and brought it down in such trenchant sort upon the head of Odysseus, who was standing by enjoying his triumph, that, had not his cap held good, and borne the weight of the blow, poor Odysseus must have fallen a victim to histrionic frenzy. The whole house ran mad for company, leaping, yelling, tearing their clothes. For the illiterate riff-raff, who knew not good from bad, and had no idea of decency, regarded it as a supreme piece of acting; and the more intelligent part of the audience, realizing how things stood, concealed their disgust, and instead of reproaching the actor's folly by silence, smothered it under their plaudits; they saw only too clearly that it was not Ajax but the pantomime who was mad.

[115] Aretaeus, *op. cit.*, p. 304; Caelius Aurelianus, *op. cit.*, pp. 534–535, 556–557.

Later, when he had again come to his senses, he bitterly repented of this exploit, and was quite ill from grief, regarding his conduct as that of a veritable madman."[116]

The subjective aspect of this actor's experience is illuminated by a professional reciter of Homer, who, in a Platonic dialogue, describes how his performances affected himself and his audience. "When I describe something pathetic, my eyes fill with tears; when something frightful and horrid, I am terrified, my hair stands on end and my heart pounds widely . . . And when I look down from my platform at my auditors, they weep and have a fearful look in their eyes, following the words I recite with wonder and amazement, and sharing my emotions."[117] According to Plato, the emotional excitement experienced by the performer occurs in a state of divine possession and madness which comes upon him when he practises his profession, and which is not essentially different from the ecstasy attained by participants in the Dionysiac and Corybantic rites. The similarity is specifically stressed by Socrates.

> All good epic poets do not produce beautiful poems by means of conscious art, but because they are divinely possessed and ecstatic, and this is also the case with good lyric poets. When they compose their songs they are not in their senses any more then the Corybantes when they leap and dance. As soon as they are affected by the power of rhythm and harmony, they become possessed like the Bacchantes who in their frenzy draw milk and honey from rivers.[118]

Underlying the association of poetic inspiration with ritual possession is the concept of divine madness. As previously indicated, this idea rests on the primitive belief that all forms of mental and emotional disturbance are caused by supernatural agency. However, divine madness by no means implied the occurrence of actual mental disease. When dealing with the ideas of the ancients, especially those that concern religion, we must always keep in mind the psychological differences that separate us from them. Generally, the psychological environment in which we live is permeated by the influence of science and technology and is characterized by varying degrees of rationalism. In such an atmosphere, the notion of repeated signals and visits from inhabitants of other planets is more congenial than the idea of habitual communication between divine beings and men.[119] The

---

[116] Lucian, *Of Pantomime*, Fowler translation, *op. cit.*, vol. 2, p. 262.

[117] Plato, *Ion* 535 c, e.

[118] Plato, *Ion* 533 e–534 b.

[119] Leon Festinger, Henry W. Riecken and Stanley Schachter, *When Prophecy Fails*, Minneapolis, University of Minnesota Press, 1956, pp. 33 ff., New York, Harper Torchbooks edition, 1964.

imagination of the ancient Greeks and Romans, on the other hand, was filled with ideas and stories that tended to eliminate the boundaries between men and the gods. To them it seemed entirely possible and likely that gods should come down to earth, mingle with human beings, possess them and endow them with qualities not ordinarily given to mankind. According to a myth prevalent at Lystra, a small town of Lycaonia in Asia Minor, Zeus and Hermes had come down from heaven in the likeness of men and had visited Baucis and Philemon whom they rewarded for their hospitality. Thus, when the apostles Paul and Barnabas came to Lystra and Paul cured a cripple, the people acclaimed them saying "The gods have come down to us in the likeness of men!"[120] To people who held such beliefs the experiences classed as divine madness would not seem unusual or amazing. In this sense, men in the ancient world were much closer to the divine than most people are today. Believing these ideas is a far cry from expecting them to be realized frequently in daily life; nevertheless, in such a setting, an individual who believed himself to be a god incarnate did not stand out quite as sharply in society or appear quite as alien as he would today.

Ancient literature provides several curious accounts of such individuals. One was Menecrates, a Syracusan physician of the fourth century B.C., who claimed to be divine and called himself Zeus.[121] Menecrates "prided himself greatly on being the sole cause of life to mankind through his skill in medicine," and he used

> to compel those whom he cured of the so-called sacred diseases to sign a bond that they would obey him as his slaves if they were restored to health. And one man who became his attendant wore the dress and went by the name of Heracles; he was Nicostratus of Argos who had been cured of a sacred disease. . . . Another attendant with the riding-cloak and herald's staff, "and wings besides," was called Hermes . . . And Hegesander says that Astycreon, who had been cured by him was called Apollo. Still another of his patients who had been restored to health moved about in his company clad in the garb of Asclepius. As for Zeus himself, dressed in purple, with a gold crown on his head and carrying a sceptre, his feet shod with slippers, he walked about attended by this divine choir.[122]

[120] Acts of the Apostles 14: 8–13.

[121] Otto Weinreich, *Menekrates Zeus und Salmoneus. Religionsgeschichtliche Studien zur Psychopathologie des Gottmenschentums in Antike und Neuzeit,* Stuttgart, W. Kohlhammer Verlag, 1933. This brilliant monograph discusses the case of Menekrates in great detail and is recommended to anyone interested in the problem.

[122] Athenaeus, *Deipnosophists,* Loeb edition, vol. III, pp. 296–299. I have followed Temkin in his modification of Gulick's translation of the quoted passage; see Temkin, *op. cit.,* p. 17.

Besides dressing as a god and surrounding himself with a divine court, Menecrates also addressed grandiloquent letters to various kings and other prominent individuals, among them Philip of Macedon and the Spartans Archidamus and Agesilaus. To King Philip he wrote:

Menecrates Zeus to Philip, greeting: You are king of Macedonia, but I am king of Medicine. You can destroy healthy people whensoever you wish, but I can save the ailing, and the robust who follow my prescriptions I can keep alive without sickness until old age comes. Therefore, while you are attended by a bodyguard of Macedonians, I am attended by all posterity. For I, Zeus, give them life'.[123]

His letters to others seem to have been of a similar nature.

There seems to be little doubt that he took himself seriously and that he exerted a strong suggestive influence on the members of his entourage. What then are we to make of Menecrates? Was he a charlatan touting his cures, or was he mad, a victim of megalomania? From the various notices, comments and other extant evidence, it is apparent that even in antiquity the behaviour of Menecrates and his circle was felt to be peculiar and disturbing. It is worth noting that Menecrates seems to be mentioned in only one ancient medical work, the *Menoneia*, where there is a reference to his book on *Medicine* and his views on the four basic elements that compose the body.[124] Does this mean that physicians considered him unworthy of notice? An affirmative answer is impossible simply on the basis of this observation, but the fact is suggestive when taken together with other evidence. Athenaeus characterizes Menecrates as a braggart with an exaggerated sense of his own importance. Then, in his account of Philip's reply to the letter from Menecrates, he says that the king, treating him as crazy (*melancholonta*), wrote: "Philip to Menecrates, come to your senses!"[125] Aelian adds that he also advised the medical Zeus to visit Anticyra. This city was noted throughout antiquity for its hellebore, a plant used as a remedy for madness, so that to send someone to Anticyra became proverbial for a judgement of madness.[126] Extant fragments from plays by Ephippus and Alexis indicate

[123] *Ibid.*, pp. 298–299.

[124] W. H. S. Jones, *The Medical Writings of Anonymous Londinensis*, Cambridge, Cambridge University Press, 1947, pp. 76–77.

[125] Athenaeus, *op. cit.*, Loeb edition, vol. III, pp. 300–301. This reply is actually a pun. Philip substituted for *chairein*, Rejoice!, the usual form of greeting in a letter, the rarer form *hugiainein*, Be of sound health! Plutarch attributes this reply to *Agesilaus*, king of Sparta; see Plutarch, Agesilaus 21. For *hugiainein* see above note 81.

[126] Aelian, *Varia Historia* XII, 51. There were two Greek cities named Anticyra; one was situated in Phocis on the Corinthian Gulf, the other in Thessaly.

that Menecrates was ridiculed by these writers, but whether they considered him mad must be left open.[127]

As for Menecrates's divine following, there is evidence that two of its members were considered at least queer if not mad. Nicostratus the Argive, the Heracles of the group, is also mentioned by the historian Diodorus who refers to his madness.[128] More is known about Alexarchos, a son of Antipater, one of Alexander's generals, and brother of Cassander, who ruled Macedonia from ca. 316–297 B.C. He appears to have had scholarly interests, among them a concern with religious matters. For example, Plutarch cites a letter in which Alexarchos affirmed that Dionysus was the son of Zeus and Isis, and that his Egyptian name Arsaphes denoted virility.[129] More significant, however, is his role as founder and ruler of a new community. In about 316, Cassander gave his brother a small territory on the Athos Peninsula where he established Uranopolis, the city of heaven.[130] The name is strange, but not less so than its founder. With the founding of the city, Alexarchos introduced his own coinage and even created a special language for the citizens. The coins indicate that the inhabitants were styled Uranidai, or sons of heaven. Athenaeus offers samples of this language in a discussion of those who, intentionally or unintentionally, use pompous, pedantic words and phrases with comic and incomprehensible results. "Concerning him," he says, "Heracleides Lembus, in the thirty-seventh book of his *Histories*, narrates the following: 'Alexarchos, founder of Uranopolis, introduced peculiar expressions, calling the cock "dawn crier," the barber "mortal shaver," the drachma "a silver bit," the quart measure "daily feeder," the herald "loud bawler." ' "[131] Furthermore, on one occasion he sent a letter to the authorities of Cassandreia, a city founded by his brother. This strange message, of which a part is extant, reads like double-talk and is so obscure that Athenaeus who cites it is led to remark in despair, "What this letter means, I fancy, not even the Pythian god could

---

[127] Aristophanes, *Sämtliche Komödien*, übertragen von Ludwig Seeger . . ., 2 Bände, Zürich, Artemis Verlag, 1953, Zweiter Band, p. 479.

[128] Diodorus Siculus 16: 44.

[129] Plutarch, *Isis and Osiris* 365 E, in Plutarch's *Moralia*, Loeb Edition, vol. V, pp. 90–91.

[130] Athenaeus, *Deipnosophists*, Loeb edition, vol. I. pp. 424–425; Strabo, *Geography*, Loeb edition, vol. III, pp. 356–357, V. Tscherikower, *Die hellenistischen Städtegründungen von Alexander dem Grossen bis auf die Römerzeit* (Philologus, Supplementband XIX, Heft I), Leipzig, 1927, p. 3, W. W. Tarn, *Alexander the Great*, 2 vols., Cambridge, Cambridge University Press, 1948, vol. II, pp. 429–433; Ernest Barker, *From Alexander to Constantine*, Oxford, Clarendon Press, 1956, p. 19.

[131] Athenaeus, *op. cit.*, pp. 424–425.

make out."[132] Moreover, he is said to have called himself the Sun, *Helios*, and to have characterized the members of his city as "ruled by the sun (*heliokrateis*)."

Clearly, Alexarchos appears to have been an eccentric with pretensions to scholarship; but was he mentally disordered? Weinreich concluded that he was schizophrenic, but the evidence which he adduces is only suggestive. Essentially, this opinion rests on the fact that Alexarchos belonged to the entourage of Menecrates, and on a comparison of the letter quoted by Athenaeus with analogous compositions of modern schizophrenics. Were more information available about Alexarchos, it would probably be illuminating to compare him with others, such as Antonio Conselheiro of Canudos, or George Rapp of Harmony, who undertook to realize Utopia, or the New Jerusalem, or the City of the Sun on this earth.[133] In terms of the extravagant use of language, a parallel may be drawn with the mad Cornishman John Tom, alias Sir William Courtenay.[134] At the age of thirty-three, he suddenly appeared in Canterbury where he soon acquired a following among the poor, and also among some of the more substantial citizens. He was a parliamentary candidate in the 1832 election, but was defeated. Several years later, in 1838, John Tom led a band of deluded peasants into a fight with the military in which he and ten others died. Among other peculiarities, he talked of the months of the year as the First Moon, Second Moon, and so forth, altering a method of referring to the months then current among members of the Society of Friends.

A factor which must not be discounted is the influence that contemporary conditions and personalities may have had on Alexarchos. His actions must be seen within the culturally constituted behavioural and ideational environment in which he moved. Alexarchos may have been a fantastic visionary who on his peninsula played with ideas and words, but the ideas were not foreign to his

[132] *Ibid.*, pp. 424–425. I have replaced Gulick's phrase the "god of Delphi" by the "Pythian god" as a more literal rendering of the text. Gulick's translation of the letter provides the proper tone of pedantic archaizing incomprehensibility: "Alexarchus, to the Primipiles of Brother's Town, Joy: Our sun-fleshed yeans, I wot, and dams thereof which guard the braes whereon they were born, have been visited by the fateful dome of the gods in might, fresheting them hence from the forsaken fields."

[133] Weinreich, *op. cit.*, pp. 14, 76–77; Euclides da Cunha, *Rebellion in the Backlands*, Chicago, University of Chicago Press, 1944, pp. 117–169; Karl J. R. Arndt, *George Rapp's Harmony Society 1785–1847*, Philadelphia, University of Pennsylvania Press, 1965, pp. 15–58; W. H. G. Armytage, *Heavens Below. Utopian Experiments in England 1560–1960*, London, Routledge and Kegan Paul, 1961.

[134] P. G. Rogers, *Battle in Bossenden Wood. The Strange Story of Sir William Courtenay*, London, Oxford University Press, 1961, pp. 1–33, 210.

contemporaries. The Greeks of the fourth century B.C. were obsessed by fear of social revolution, and the disturbances which followed the death of Alexander the Great made visions of peace and happiness particularly attractive. Political and social unrest gave rise to movements, ideas and theories which aimed at abolishing the class war, whose horrors so many Greeks had experienced, by instituting reforms and establishing a more equitable social order. Some of these visions of a better society, influenced in part by Stoic ideas, appeared as Utopias. About 300 B.C., Euhemeros of Messene composed his *Sacred History* in which he described a utopian communist state on the island of Panchaia, located somewhere in the Indian Ocean. Moreover, as Euhemeros claimed to be a friend of Cassander one may suggest that Alexarchos was acquainted with his ideas, even though there is no evidence connecting them.[135] Nor was the idea of a sun-ruler absent. Alexander the Great conceived of himself as Helios, the Sun King, and the theme of a sun state is a recurrent element in the social and political thought of antiquity. The best known example is the utopian Sun State or Heliopolis described by a certain Iambulus about the middle of the third century B.C. Situated upon the islands of the Sun in the Indian Ocean, it exemplified an ideal of brotherly unity and harmonious concord.[136]

Tarn suggested that the Uranopolis of Alexarchos may have been derived from the ideas and goals of Alexander, upon which it throws some light. "It is as near a proof as one is likely to get," he says, ". . . that Alexander did think of all men as brothers, and did put forward ideas which led Alexarchos, as later they led Zeno, to the idea of a world state . . ."[137] Be that as it may, it is clear that if Alexarchos was affected by some mental disorder he was not incapable of participating in the social and intellectual currents of the time. Yet, to judge from the comments of ancient writers, he was considered strange in his behaviour. Did he, then, suffer from some form of mental disorder, and if he did, how are we to comprehend it? Simply to apply a modern diagnostic term, schizophrenia, as Weinreich did, is not very helpful as an explanatory procedure. On the other hand, it may be more illuminating to consider Alexarchos and

[135] Diodorus of Sicily V: 41–46, Loeb edition, vol. III, pp. 210–227; Weinreich, *op. cit.*, p. 14.

[136] Diodorus of Sicily II: 55–60, Loeb Edition, vol. III, pp. 64–83; W. W. Tarn, "Alexander Helios and the Golden Age," *Journal of Roman Studies* 22 (II): 135–160, 1932; *idem, Hellenistic Civilization*, 2nd edition, London, Edward Arnold, 1930, pp. 112–116; R. von Pöhlmann, *Geschichte der sozialen Frage und des Sozialismus in der antiken Welt*, 2nd edition, 2 vols., München, C. H. Beck'sche Verlagsbuchhandlung, 1912, pp. 372–411; Alfred Doren, "Wunschräume und Wunschzeiten," *Vorträge—Bibliothek Warburg*, Leipzig, B. G. Teubner, 1924–25, pp. 158–205.

[137] Tarn, *op. cit.*, vol. II, pp. 429–433.

the other followers of Menecrates Zeus in terms of their relationships to him and to each other.

Characteristic of all human beings is the sharing of mental activity in social situations. This process underlies group formation, a phenomenon which can occur even where ideas and actions are derived from disordered mental activity. Indeed, an integrated social system may be developed on the basis of shared psychopathology. Dewhurst and Todd suggested the term "psychosis of association" to cover all situations of this type, including those which comprise only two or three individuals (*folie à deux, folie à trois*) as well as others which involve many persons, as in certain religious sects.[138] Unfortunately, however, this phrase tends to prejudge the nature of the psychopathology involved, so that it is preferable to employ the broader, more neutral concept of "socially shared psychopathology" used by Gruenberg.[139]

Groups are formed on this basis when a mentally disordered dominating person, most often affected with a psychosis, induces or provokes a delusional condition in one or more individuals who are relatively dependent and submissive. Menecrates appears to have been such a person. Described as haughty and proud, boastful, conceited, presumptuous and officious, it is likely that he had paranoid delusions of grandeur. Such a person may strongly influence others and gather about him a band of followers, especially if their behaviour as viewed by their environment is not grossly inconsistent or in conflict with culturally accepted norms of reality. Menecrates Zeus and his attendant divinities appear to have established for themselves a social situation of this kind, aided no doubt by the circumstance that they belonged to the upper level of society—one was a military commander, another the tyrant of a city, and a third the son of a general and brother to a monarch.

Clearly in Graeco-Roman antiquity it was possible for individuals with mental and emotional disorders to function more or less adequately in society as long as the behavioural environment which they constructed for themselves did not result in undue psychological distortion and socio-cultural impairment. Moreover, culturally constituted systems, particularly religious beliefs and practices provided a means by which such individuals might effectively achieve some form of adjustment to society.

[138] K. Dewhurst and J. Todd, "The Psychosis of Association—folie à deux," *Journal of Nervous and Mental Diseases* 124: 451–459, 1956; L. Bender and Z. Yassell, "Psychoses among followers of Father Divine," *Journal of Nervous and Mental Diseases* 87: 418–449, 1938.

[139] Ernest M. Gruenberg, "Socially Shared Psychopathology," in *Explorations in Social Psychiatry*, ed. by A. H. Leighton, J. A. Clausen and R. N. Wilson, New York, Basic Books, 1957, pp. 201–229.

Pertinent testimony on this point is provided by Aelius Aristides in his *Sacred Discourses*, the only religious autobiography which has come down to us from the pagan world of antiquity.[140] Probably born in 117 A.D. not far from Hadrianutherae, a city of Mysia, in Asia Minor, Aristides was a member of a wealthy family, prominent in the province. His father, Eudaemon, a country gentleman and a priest of Zeus, saw to it that his son received the best available education, and at the age of twelve he was sent to a famous school in Phrygia conducted by Alexander, the tutor of Marcus Aurelius. There he began the study of rhetoric and literature, which he continued at Athens under Herodes Atticus. In his twenties Aristides was already recognized for his wide reading and his ability as an orator. He became the leading sophist, or travelling lecturer, of his time and was greatly admired for his atticizing style. Indeed, his account of the destruction of Smyrna by an earthquake in 178 so impressed Marcus Aurelius that the emperor was persuaded to rebuild the city. The date of the death of Aristides is uncertain. According to Philostratus, "Some writers record that Aristides died at home, others say that it was in Ionia; again some say that he reached the age of sixty, others that he was nearly seventy."[141] From the available data it is probable that his death occurred between 181 and 187 A.D., during the reign of the Emperor Commodus.

In the course of his career, Aristides produced numerous orations among them ceremonial speeches, eulogies of cities, gods, sanctuaries and deceased individuals, declamations on mythical or historical subjects, speeches about the earthquake in Smyrna, several pieces in which he defended himself, and the *Sacred Discourses*, an autobiographical account of his illnesses and his relations with the divine healer Asclepius. The latter work, of which five books and a fragment of a sixth are extant, bears directly on the role of culturally constituted systems, such as religious institutions, in enabling individuals to deal with their mental and emotional conflicts by making it

---

[140] The following sources have been consulted for the life and works of Aristides: Philostratus, "Lives of the Sophists," in *Philostratus and Eunapius* with an English translation by W. C. Wright (Loeb Classical Library), Cambridge, Mass., Harvard University Press, 1952, pp 214–223; André Boulanger *Aelius Aristide et la sophistique dans la province d'Asie au IIe siècle de notre ère*, Paris, E. de Boccard, 1923; F. G. Welcker, "Incubation. Aristides der Rhetor," in his *Kleine Schriften* III, Bonn, Eduard Weber, 1850, pp. 89–156; Otto Weinreich, "Typisches und Individuelles in der Religiosität des Aelius Aristides," *Neue Jahrbücher für das klassische Altertum* 33: 597–606, 1914; Campbell Bonner, "Some Phases of Religious Feeling in Later Paganism," *Harvard Theological Review* 30: 119–140, 1937; André-Jean Festugière, *Personal Religion Among the Greeks*, Berkeley, University of California Press, 1954 (second printing 1960), Chap. VI. "Popular Piety, Aelius Aristides and Asclepius."

[141] Philostratus, *op. cit.*, pp. 222–223.

possible for them to gratify their desires and to reduce their painful fears and anxieties in a socially acceptable manner. The *Sacred Discourses* are based on a diary which Aristides began at the command of Asclepius and which he continued during the years of his illness.[142] In it he recorded all his dreams, conversations and long speeches, the most varied visions, as well as innumerable predictions and oracles by Asclepius on all kinds of subjects, some in prose, others in verse. Aristides adhered scrupulously to the divine command as the years went on, accumulating a formidable total of 300,000 lines. Eventually towards the end of his life, perhaps at the urging of his friends and wishing to glorify the god and the benefits bestowed by him, he compiled his *Hieroi logoi*, the stories of his illness and his religious experience. These *Sacred Discourses* were not put together in any very coherent order, but it is possible to re-constitute from them, with some additions from other writings of Aristides, an account of the various illnesses which for at least twelve to thirteen years turned him into a chronic invalid, and led to the organization of his whole life around his relationship with Asclepius.

Having tried out his talents in Egypt in 142 A.D., Aristides decided to advance his career by going to Rome, the cultural capital to which sophists flocked to present themselves to the cognoscenti and the public, just as musicians come to New York and other centres to give concerts and have their renown acclaimed. Boulanger suggests that he may have been called to Rome by his former teacher Alexander, then a member of the court of the Emperor Marcus Aurelius.[143] Philostratus says that Aristides had been in poor health from boyhood, a report which appears consistent with the fact that when Aristides resolved to go to Rome he had just completed a cure at the hot springs near the Aesepus river in the Troad. His stay at the springs had left him exhausted, and in addition he had caught a cold. But these circumstances did not deter Aristides from his purpose. About December 143, he set out for Rome by way of Thrace and Macedonia to Dyrrachium, where travellers crossed the Adriatic for Brundisium, the point of origin of the Via Appia.[144] It was midwinter, and the cold, wind and rain as well as poor roads and miserable inns combined to make the journey an arduous, exhausting

---

[142] *Aelii Aristidis Smyrnaei quae supersunt omnia*, ed. by Bruno Keil, vol. II Orationes XVII–LIII, Berlin, Weidmann, 1898, pp. 376–467. All references to the *Sacred Discourses* are cited from this edition.

[143] Boulanger, *op. cit.*, p. 124.

[144] Brundisium is the modern Brindisi; Dyrrachium is the ancient Epidamnus and the modern Durazzo. Aristides' journey took him by way of the Via Egnatia, the old Roman road, through present day Turkey, Greece, Albania and Jugoslavia.

ordeal. Nevertheless, despite the illness which befell him en route, Aristides pushed on until he reached Rome about March 144, over three months after he had set out.[145]

The illness of Aristides began en route with earaches and toothaches. Bouts of fever followed, and finally he experienced periods of suffocation, apparently due to asthmatic attacks. As he described his condition, he arrived at Rome half dead, nor did his situation improve despite medical attention. If anything, the treatment prescribed for him aggravated his illness. Aristides describes his terrible sufferings in the second *Sacred Discourse*. "My stomach," he says, "was bloated, my muscles were cramped, shivers ran up and down my body, it was impossible to breathe . . . everything was incurable, there was not the shadow of a hope."[146] Then, when all hope of cure seemed to have disappeared, the affectionate care of his teacher Alexander snatched him from the jaws of death. However, the continuing poor state of his health required him to return to Smyrna, his adopted city, where he arrived after a stormy sea voyage at the beginning of winter, 144 A.D.

Despite the severity of his illness, however, Aristides had not neglected to further his career while at Rome. During this period he produced his panegyric of Rome and declaimed it in public; this performance together with the recommendation of his teacher Alexander brought him to the attention of the Emperor Marcus Aurelius, with whom he maintained cordial relations throughout his career.[147] The tenacity with which Aristides pursued his aims, both in journeying to Rome as well as during his stay there, is illuminated in part by a comment of Philostratus. In his biography of Aristides, he remarks that despite poor health as a boy, he did not fail to work hard.[148] Apparently Aristides was extremely ambitious to achieve great things, and he drove himself compulsively to become a famous orator, an aim which he achieved but at a price both physical and psychological.

Aristides may have harboured unconscious doubts as to his ability, but when illness struck him down and it seemed as if the career that had been opening up for him would be ended before it had even begun, he refused to accept the prospect. Aristides stayed in Smyrna over a year, hoping that he would be cured by the physicians who attended him. The second *Sacred Discourse* depicts vividly the ailments that plagued him.

[145] Aelius Aristides, *op. cit.*, XLVIII, 5–60.

[146] Festugière, *op. cit.*, p. 89 (1960 edition). Unless otherwise indicated all translations from Aristides are taken from this source.

[147] Boulanger, *op. cit.*, pp. 125–126.

[148] Philostratus, *op. cit.*, pp. 214–215.

What man could conceive of the multitude of ills of which I was then a victim? Those who were present on the occasion of each attack know the state of my skin and how sick I was internally. Moreover, my head ran with mucus day after day and night after night; there was fluxion in my chest, my breath would come up to meet the flow of humours in my throat, would be constricted and become inflamed there. So much did I expect death at any moment that I did not have the courage to call a slave; I thought I should be wasting my time, because it would be too late by the time he came. On top of all this, I had every kind of trouble with my ears and my teeth, and tension, round about the veins, and I could neither keep down what I had eaten nor throw it up; for if anything so much as touched my throat or my palate, it closed all the passages and I could not recover myself. I had a burning pain inside my head and every kind of shooting fits. At night I was unable to lie down flat; I had to keep sitting up bent forward my head resting on my knees. In the grip of such ills as these and an infinity of others, I had of course to keep myself wrapped up in woollen blankets and other kinds of covers and be entirely confined with all doors and windows closed, so that the day came to equal the night, and the nights were like days because I could not sleep.[149]

Bronchial asthma was clearly prominent among the ailments with which Aristides was afflicted. Sometimes urticaria precedes the onset of asthma or occurs simultaneously, a condition which seems to be indicated by the reference of Aristides to the state of his skin. An asthmatic attack may last for hours or days (status asthmaticus), and a high state of anxiety is characteristic during the asthmatic paroxysm. In addition, he suffered from headaches, insomnia and gastric disturbances. The significant and often dominant role of emotional factors in the onset and course of bronchial asthma has long been recognized. There is an awareness, however, that psychogenic factors are probably involved in a complex relationship with constitutional autonomic and endocrine lability, allergy, and inherited or acquired proneness of the respiratory tract to dysfunction. Although the exact role of psychological factors in the aetiology of asthma is still under investigation, disturbed mother-child relationships are experienced by some asthmatics. These apparently involve maternal rejection, excessive dependency in childhood, fear of incurring maternal disapproval, and separation anxiety.[150] In this connection it is of interest to note that Aristides refers only once to his mother, without mentioning her name. However, he does mention Philomena, his nurse, for whom he had great affection.[151]

[149] Aelus Aristides, *op. cit.*, XLVIII, 56–58.

[150] E. D. Wittkower and K. L. White, "Psychophysiologic Aspects of Respiratory Disorders," *American Handbook of Psychiatry*, ed. Silvano Arieti, 2 vols., New York, Basic Books, 1959, vol. 1, pp. 690–707 (see pp. 694–698).

[151] Boulanger, *op. cit.*, p. 113.

Whatever may have been the aetiology of his illness, Aristides continued without improvement after his return to Smyrna. The physicians were unable to establish what was wrong with him and abandoned his case as hopeless. To obtain palliative relief, they advised Aristides to visit the hot springs near Smyrna, but even this did not help much. In desperation, he turned to the greatest healer of all, the god Asclepius.[152] For a sick man in such an extremity this was by no means unusual. In the second century the cult of Asclepius was widespread not only in Greece and Asia Minor, but throughout the Roman Empire, and in desperate situations people had recourse to his shrines as their last resort.[153] Apparently, while still under treatment at the springs, Aristides had a dream in which Asclepius appeared to him and which he interpreted as a divine command to go to Pergamum.

> When I had been brought back from Italy having collected in my body many ailments of every sort as a result of the continued hardships and storms which I had had to endure while travelling through Thrace and Macedonia (and I was already ill when I started out), the doctors were at a loss: not only could they think of nothing to help me, but they were not even able to recognize what was wrong with me to begin with ... They thought I should try the hot baths; they might make my condition better, or else I might find the atmosphere more supportable. It was already wintertime, and the baths were not far from the city. That was when the Saviour Asclepius first began to give me revelations. He ordered me to walk barefoot, and I cried out in my dream as if I were wide awake and the vision had been carried out: "Great is Asclepius! the order has been fulfilled!" That was what I dreamed I cried out while walking forward. After this came the God's invitation and my departure from Smyrna to Pergamum to my good fortune.[154]

In the spring of 146 Aristides moved to the shrine of Asclepius in Pergamum, lodging in the sanctuary itself in contact with the temple staff and with other patients, just as if he had gone to a sanatorium or a spa. There he took Asclepius as his physician, placing all his confidence in him and becoming his passionate devotee. At the same time the god took over the treatment of his illness revealing the divine will and prescriptions chiefly through dreams, a number of which are recorded by Aristides. Divine visitation in a dream has

---

[152] For Asclepius and his cult see Emma J. and Ludwig Edelstein, *Asclepius: A Collection and Interpretation of the Testimonies*, 2 vols., Baltimore, Johns Hopkins Press, 1945; R. Herzog, *Die Wunderheilungen von Epidauros* (Philologus, Supplementband XXII, Heft III), Leipzig 1931; Otto Weinreich, *Antike Heilungswunder* (Religionsgeschichtliche Versuche und Vorarbeiten, VIII, Heft I,) 1909.

[153] Edelstein, *op. cit.*, vol. I, pp. 404, 422, 438, 582, 585; vol. II, pp. 251–255.

[154] Aristides, *op. cit.*, XLVIII, 5–7.

been widely accepted by many peoples throughout history, and techniques have been developed to provoke such dreams, as well as rules and methods for their interpretation.[155] Though not entirely for the same overt reasons, dreams and their interpretation were as significant to Aristides and his fellows as they are to our contemporaries. With an unshakeable faith in Asclepius, Aristides believed that every dream must contain a message for him from his divine physician, and he interpreted them in this sense, paying attention to the slightest hint no matter how obscure. If the dream was ambiguous, Aristides did not hesitate to ask Asclepius to clarify his wishes or commands. Each morning he dealt with the dreams of the night before, where necessary consulting the priests of the temple and comparing notes with his friends and fellow patients so as to obtain their advice. After all, the god-sent vision was central to the treatment and legitimized it, thus rendering it effective. As Aristides says, "For the very same regimen and the very same things which, when the god was their author and explicitly commanded them, brought health, strength, agility, comfort, a sense of well-being, all the best things both for the body and for the spirit, had precisely the opposite effect if another recommended them without guessing at the mind of the god."[156] What greater proof of the power of Asclepius could there be?

While awaiting the dreams which revealed the divine therapy, the resident patients, many of whom were men of means, distinction and leisure, passed the time talking about their ailments and comparing the remedies prescribed for them. One day, for example, Aristides encountered another patient named Sedatus, a man of senatorial rank. "We were sitting there in the temple of Hygeia, near the statue of Telesphorus," he says, "and we were asking each other, as usual, if the god had prescribed anything out of the ordinary to either of us; for our illnesses had a good deal in common."[157] Obviously there was a strong sense of fellowship which bound together this community of suffering and faith, for every cure meant renewed hope for others. It is an atmosphere to be found today at religious healing shrines, in certain health resorts and in some measure even in world-famous medical centres. The psychological tone of such a milieu is well presented in Thomas Mann's portrayal of the sanatorium community on the Magic Mountain.

Except for short trips to some other places of healing, Aristides

---

[155] See e.g. J. S. Lincoln, *The Dream in Primitive Cultures*, London, Cresset Press, 1935; Halliday, *op. cit.*, pp. 131ff., Philostratus, *vit. Apoll.* 2, 37; Pausanias I, 34. 5; Strabo XIV, 1, 44; Artemidorus IV, 2.

[156] Aristides, *op. cit.*, XLVIII, 73.

[157] *Ibid.*, L, 16.

remained in the sanatorium at Pergamum for about ten years while Asclepius directed the details of his treatment. Aristides belonged totally to the god, was always at his beck and call, and obeyed him alone. On one occasion, after having been bled to the point of exhaustion, Satyrus, a famous physician, visited him and recommended that the bleedings be stopped. "I answered him," says Aristides, "that I was not master of my blood to do with it as I wished, but that as long as the god ordered me to be bled, I would obey whether I wanted to or not—or rather, it was impossible for me ever not to want to."[158] On another occasion, Aristides developed a swelling of the lower abdomen or the inguinal region, the precise location is not quite clear, and adamantly persisted in following the treatment prescribed by Asclepius. His account of this episode is worth quoting:

> So much for my abdomen. I had a similar experience with a tumour some years previously. The god had forewarned me that I should guard myself with the utmost care against dropsy. . . . He had decided in particular that the flow of humours should be drawn off from beneath. Then I got a tumour from no evident cause, at first such as anyone might get; but then it grew to enormous size. My groin was full of pus, and everything was swollen. There followed terrible pains and a fever for some days. The doctors gave all sorts of opinions. Some would have it removed by incision, others wanted caustic preparations to be applied as the only way to keep me from becoming infected beneath the surface, which would be fatal. But the god gave a contrary opinion, that I should hold out and let it grow. Clearly, between obeying the doctors and obeying the god there was no choice. The tumour grew yet more and I was in much distress. Some of my friends admired my endurance; others accused me of going to excess in placing all my confidence in dreams; some blamed me for a coward, since I would neither allow the thing to be cut off nor take any drug. But the god stood firm to the end, telling me to put up with my present troubles, since it was all with a view to my health. The reason he gave was that the springs of this flow were above, and that these "gardens" did not know which way to divert the streams. Well, the outcome was extraordinary. I went on like this for about four months. . . . I was ordered to do many paradoxical things; among those which I recall there is a race which I had to run barefoot in wintertime, and again horseback riding, the most arduous of undertakings; and I also recall an exercise of the following kind: when the harbour waves were swollen by the south wind and ships were in distress, I had to sail across to the opposite side, eating honey and acorns from an oak tree, and vomit; then complete purgation was achieved. All these things were done when the inflammation was at its peak and had even risen to the navel.[159]

[158] *Ibid.*, XLIX, 8–9.
[159] *Ibid.*, XLVII, 61–65.

As Aristides recognized, the divine prescriptions and remedies were often paradoxical, frequently not so much in the nature of the remedies or the exercises but in the way in which they were employed, for example, when his illness was at its worst. Thus, he says,

> Indeed it is the paradoxical which predominates in the cures of the god; for example, one drinks chalk, another hemlock, another one strips off his clothes and takes cold baths, when it is warmth, and not at all cold, that one would think he is in need of. Now myself he has likewise distinguished in this way, stopping catarrhs and colds by baths in rivers and in the sea, healing me through long walks when I was helplessly bed-ridden, administering terrible purgations on top of continuous abstinence from food, prescribing that I should speak and write when I could hardly breathe, so that if any justification for boasting should fall to those who have been healed in such a way, we certainly have our share in this boast.[160]

Often the dream-prescriptions were indeed extravagant, painful and even cruel, but when taken together with other dreams they appear to be the expression of deep-seated tendencies in the personality of Aristides. Anxiety is a significant element in the piety he professes, so that various acts which he performed were intended to avert some threatening evil or misfortune revealed to him in a dream. Thus he enacted a makebelieve shipwreck to prevent a real one. On another occasion Asclepius demanded that Aristides sacrifice a finger so that he would not have to die, but eventually he was permitted to substitute a finger ring. These and many of the other dreams experienced by Aristides betray an oppressive sense of guilt and an unconscious desire for self-punishment. Nevertheless, this masochistic tendency does not extend to death, so that Aristides accepts the notion that others have to die in his place in order that his valuable life may be spared.[161] Thus, he records without a qualm his belief that two children of his foster-sister, a boy and a girl, had died as substitutes for him.

Such fantasies are not peculiar to Aristides. The sixteenth-century Jewish scholar and mystic, R. Joseph Karo, kept a kabbalistic diary, the *Maggid Mesharim,* in which he recorded the visits of a celestial mentor. More than once his *Maggid* informed him that he owed his life to the vicarious death of others, among them his first wife and three children.[162] In 1543, for example Karo was reminded that "you have thought of improper things, wherefore you have been con-

---

[160] *Ibid., Lalia to Asclepius,* XLII, 8.

[161] *Ibid.,* XLVIII, 44; LI, 19–25.

[162] R. J. Z. Werblowsky, *Joseph Karo, Lawyer and Mystic,* Oxford, Clarendon Press, 1962, pp. 149–150.

demned to death. But I, the *Mishnah*, have interceded for you, as also did Jacob Tur, Moses Maimonides, Rashi . . . and they redeemed you from death. Your sentence was commuted to illness instead, and also many worthy people were substituted for you.''[163]

A similar experience is reported by the psychiatrist Carl Gustav Jung. In 1944, he suffered a cardiac infarction and for a time was gravely ill. During this period he had a number of dreams, as a result of which he was obsessed by the idea that his attending physician would have to die in his place. And indeed, Jung notes, the doctor did die shortly thereafter.[164]

Fantasies such as these are undoubtedly an expression of a deep-seated sense of guilt, and of an underlying severe anxiety, combined with an excessive sentiment of self-regard. Aristides' firm conviction that Asclepius was directly concerned about his health to the minutest detail, including such mundane matters as emetics and purges, blood letting, diet, exercise, baths and clothing, clearly indicates his profoundly self-centred attitude. But it also points to the means by which Aristides was able to deal with the unconscious psychological problems which very probably were at the root of his varied illnesses. Within the religious environment of his time, the cult of Asclepius provided Aristides with a broad, socially accepted pattern of belief and practice. The god was known to help men, ministering to each according to his wants through divine epiphanies, celestial messages, and demonstrations of special election. Within this framework, making use of these channels, Aristides enabled his unconscious to work through in some measure, to assimilate and to fuse in some form the diverse, conflicting elements of his personality and his experience. To judge from his attitudes and behaviour as portrayed in the *Sacred Discourses* and in his other writings, Aristides had an overwhelming need for acceptance and love.[165] Yet he had to face the harsh fact that the illness which he experienced in connection with his trip to Rome, and which had compelled his return to Smyrna, represented failure in his chosen career. This led to self-preoccupation, a not uncommon phenomenon in numerous life situations, as after accidents or in chronic illness. In this situation, Aristides had to reconcile his frustration and sense of guilt at his apparent failure with

[163] *Ibid.*, p. 150.
[164] C. G. Jung, *Erinnerungen, Träume, Gedanken*, aufgezeichnet und herausgegeben von Aniela Jaffé, Zürich, Rascher Verlag, 1962, pp. 296–297.
[165] On the relation of such attitudes to the displacement or redirection of narcissism in the development of the self see Sigmund Freud, "Zur Einführung des Narzissmus," and, "Trauer and Melancholie," in *Gesammelte Werke*, 18 vols., London, Imago Publishing Co., 1940–1952, vol. 10, pp. 138–170 and pp. 428–446 respectively; also "Neurose und Psychose," vol. XIII, pp. 387–391.

his driving ambition and his sense of unique greatness. This he was able to do by finding in Asclepius a divine, inspiring and above all loving mentor who confirmed his most cherished desires and ambitions, and yet enabled him to expiate his unconscious guilt, his internalized aggression, in the extremely painful treatments which the god ordered in his dreams. Asclepius became his perpetual counsellor, directing him in all the details of his existence, and providing the centre around which his ambitions, his repressed self-satisfaction and aggression, his desire for power and success could be organized and who could legitimize them. In this way by clinging to his faith in Asclepius, Aristides was able to achieve and maintain a psychological equilibrium, which permitted him to resume his activities as a lecturer and to achieve the success he so desired.

In his fourth *Sacred Discourse*, Aristides relates how in the tenth year of his illness, his sufferings subsided to the point where he could hope for a complete recovery. At that time he left for the shores of the Aesepus where he was purified by the god. His health was satisfactory enough for him to resume his career as a sophist and even undertake lecture tours. This improvement appears to have lasted about thirteen years until 165 A.D., when Aristides fell ill during a great epidemic which then ravaged Asia Minor. He recovered from this illness but continued to complain about his health until his death.[166]

Aristides was never a healthy man; he was a neurotic with functional symptoms localized most specifically in the respiratory and gastrointestinal tracts. Although he probably had other illnesses such as the plague, one can only agree with Bonner that he must have had the iron constitution of the chronic invalid to survive the effects of Asclepius' various prescriptions. As in similar cases, fundamentally he did not want to be cured. The secondary gains of his illness were too significant to be dissipated for a cure. As Festugière says,

> To be cured would mean no longer to enjoy the presence and companionship of the god; and precisely what the patient needs most is the companionship of the god. The patient must continually have attention paid to him. The god tells him to do things which would soon make an end of an ordinary man. The sick man not only survives these things, but thrives on them. The more unheard-of the treatment, the more patient is convinced that the god is interested in his case, that his case is a special one, and that he is the most privileged being on the face of the earth. Thus he comes to be no longer able to do without the god, and by the same token to be no longer able to do without his sickness.[167]

[166] Boulanger, *op. cit.*, pp. 469–485, 495.
[167] Festugière, *op. cit.*, p. 86.

E           

The case of Aristides has been considered in some detail not alone because of its intrinsic interest, but even more because it illuminates the use of culturally constituted systems as potential means for the resolution of psychological conflicts and for the development of defense mechanisms to satisfy unconscious neurotic needs. The cult of Asclepius was such a system in which faith in the god, the practices of incubation and dream interpretation, the rituals and the therapies, together with the environment created by the priests and the other patients, combined to provide an institutional framework, which enabled patients like Aristides to behave in extravagant but culturally sanctioned ways, thus protecting them from the possibly disruptive consequences of their unconscious needs and private defensive manoeuvres. The god-sent dream was part of this cultural pattern accepted not only by the dreamer but also by those in his environment, thus providing a mechanism by which the patient's self-preoccupation and erotic self-cathexis could be expressed exceedingly well.

Although comprising differing constituent elements, similar culturally constituted patterns employed in analogous ways are to be found in different historical periods. For Joseph Karo in the sixteenth century the socially dominant pattern of Jewish kabbalistic theory and practice, combined with the concept of maggidism provided a means of dealing with his unconscious intrapsychic conflicts and of maintaining an adequate psychological balance. He was able to carry on his considerable intellectual labours and to become the great scholar and codifier of normative rabbinic Judaism.[168] Oriental religious systems apparently perform similar functions for some of our contemporaries. In March, 1966, *The New York Times Magazine* published a story which has numerous parallels with the case of Aristides, that of an American businessman who had become a convert to Zen Buddhism.[169] Here too the conversion was the consequence of a crisis which manifested itself in emotional physical illness. "It was an act prompted by desperation. Plagued with ulcers, allergies, sleeplessness and at forty, with a gnawing sense of the meaninglessness of my life, I grasped at Zen in the hope that it might succeed in helping me where Western medicine and Western religions had not," writes Philip Kapleau.[170] Eventually he became a member of a Zen monastery, where he spent three years as a lay monk, and as with Aristides his physical and mental state improved. "My

[168] Werblowsky, *op. cit.*, pp. 78–83, 265–266, Gershom Scholem, *Sabbatai Zevi*, 2 vols. (Hebrew), Tel-Aviv, 1957 vol. 1, p. 65.
[169] Philip Kapleau, "All is One, One is None, None is All." Report from a Zen Monastery, *The New York Times Magazine*, 6 March, 1966, pp. 27, 78–84
[170] *Ibid.*, p. 27.

allergies completely disappeared," he reports, "my stomach condition considerably improved; my general health has benefited."[171]

Here I must leave the theme of individuals such as Aristides, Karo, and others with similar problems. It is worth noting, however, that such people are apparently more frequent in periods of transition and crisis, when familiar worlds are broken and there is a diffused anxiety in society. These ages of anxiety provide various individuals who reach the wilder shores of sanity where some of them are able to maintain themselves, even if sometimes precariously, while others are submerged in the depths of unreason.[172]

## *Whose Responsibility is the Madman?*

As discussed above, among the ancient Greeks and Romans the mentally disordered were defined as such in terms of their orientation to the accepted idea of reality, in terms of the style and consistency of their behaviour, and its consequences for themselves and those in contact with them. The latter element is particularly significant in considering the legal aspects of madness in the culture of the Greeks and the Romans.

On the whole, Greek and Roman law took account of the madman chiefly in relation to the protection of property, and to insure that he did not harm other members of the community. In Athens, one instrument designed to protect family property was the *dike paranoias*. The following passage in Plato's *Laws* is based on this legal procedure.

And if disease or age or harshness of temper, or all of these together, makes a man to be more out of his mind than the rest of the world are —but this is not observable, except to those who live with him—and he, being master of his property, is the ruin of the house, and his son doubts and hesitates about indicting his father for insanity, let the law in that case ordain that he shall first of all go to the eldest guardians of the law and tell them of his father's misfortune, and they shall duly look into

[171] *Ibid.*, p. 84. In this connection it is of interest to note a cultural and psychological analysis of Buddhist monasticism in Burma by Melford E. Spiro, "Religious Systems as Culturally Constituted Defense Mechanisms," in *Context and Meaning in Cultural Anthropology*, ed. by Melford E. Spiro, New York, Free Press, 1965, pp. 100–113.

[172] E. R. Dodds, *Pagan and Christian in an Age of Anxiety*, Cambridge, Cambridge University Press, 1965, pp. 37–68; Solomon Schechter, "Safed in the 16th century," in his *Studies in Judaism*, 2nd series, 1908, pp. 203–306; Lucian, The Death of Peregrine, *Works*, Fowler ed., vol. 4, pp. 79–95; *The Attic Nights of Aulus Gellius*, with an English translation by John C. Rolfe (Loeb Classical Library), 3 vols., 1927, vol. 2, pp. 392–395; Eduard Zeller, *Vorträge und Abhandlungen*, vol. 2, Leipzig, 1877, pp. 154–188; Scholem, *op. cit.*, vol. I, p. 15.

the matter, and take counsel as to whether he shall indict him or not. And if they advise him to proceed, they shall be both his witnesses and his advocates: and if the father is cast, he shall thenceforth be incapable of ordering the least particular of his life; let him be as a child dwelling in the house for the remainder of his days.[173]

Legal actions by children to deprive their parents of the control of property, as described by Plato, were apparently not uncommon, to judge from comments by other writers. Xenophon relates that Socrates was accused of teaching sons to treat fathers with contempt, persuading them that "he made his companions wiser than their fathers: he said that the law allowed a son to put his father in prison if he convinced a jury that he was insane, and this was a proof that it was lawful for the wiser to keep the more ignorant in jail."[174] Although Xenophon is basically concerned with exculpating Socrates, the accusation implies that such cases were not rare. This inference is strengthened from several sides. One piece of evidence is provided by Aristophanes in the *Clouds*. Reflecting on the apparent mental derangement of his father, Strepsiades, Pheidippides says: "What must I do with my mad father? Shall I indict him for his lunacy, or tell the undertaker of his symptoms."[175] In other words, if there is a prospect of his living long the son is prepared to have his father indicted for mental incompetence in order to protect the family property. On the other hand, if his strange behaviour is evidence of incipient senility, then the thing to do is to alert the coffin makers. Clearly, Aristophanes expected his audience to recognize the situation, an expectation which was apparently well-founded to judge by the experience of Sophocles. As Cicero tells the story,

> Sophocles composed tragedies to extreme old age; and when because of his absorption in literary work, he was thought to be neglecting his business affairs, his sons haled him into court in order to secure a verdict removing him from the control of his property on the ground of imbecility, under a law similar to ours, whereby it is customary to restrain heads of families from wasting their estates. Thereupon, it is said, the old man read to the jury his play, *Oedipus at Colonus*, which he had just written and was revising, and inquired: "Does that poem seem to you to be the work of an imbecile?" When he had finished, he was acquitted by the verdict of the jury.[176]

[173] Plato, *Laws* XI 929 D-E, Jowett translation, p. 668.
[174] Xenophon, *Memorabilia* I, 2. 49, Loeb edition, pp. 36–37.
[175] Aristophanes, *Clouds* 844–846, Loeb edition, vol. I pp. 432–343.
[176] Cicero, *De Senectute. De Amicitia. De Divinatione*, with an English translation by W. A. Falconer (Loeb Classical Library), London, Wm. Heinemann, 1930, pp. 30–31.

The procedure in such cases is mentioned by Aristotle in his account of the Athenian Constitution. Describing the functions of the Archon, he says that criminal and civil law suits "are instituted before him and after a preliminary trial he brings them in before the jury-court." Among such actions are "prosecutions for insanity, when one man accuses another of wasting his property when insane."[177] Apparently the practice of accusing a parent, a relative, or possibly some other person of mental incompetence in order to gain control of property was no rarity, and probably lent itself to abuse. This seems to be indicated by a remark in Aristotle's account of the constitutional changes made by the Thirty when they took power in Athens (404 B.C.).[178] He mentions their action with regard "to the bestowal of one's property on whomsoever one wishes, making the single act of donation valid absolutely, while they removed the tiresome qualifications 'save when in consequence of insanity or of old age, or under the influence of a woman' in order that there might be no opening for blackmailers."[179]

This last point refers to testamentary rights, for which full possession of mental faculties was a prerequisite. As might be expected, attempts were made to have wills declared invalid on the ground that the testator was insane, or that he was unduly influenced by some one while of unsound mind. A case tried by the Athenian orator Isaeus illustrates the point.[180] Cleonymus died leaving his property to certain collateral relatives, and disregarding his nephews, the sons of his sister. After his death the latter attempted to break the will alleging that Cleonymus had been insane. The grounds on which the charge of mental disorder was based were never clearly stated. However, Isaeus who argued the case for the nephews apparently based it on the character of the will, that is, the fact that Cleonymus had passed over his sister's sons, and that he had never revoked the will. Only a man out of his mind would have acted in this way. As Isaeus put it to the jury, "If his mind was so disordered that he continued to care nothing for us his nearest, closest relatives, you will certainly do justice by invalidating such a testament."[181]

To judge from a passage in Plato's *Laws*, an insane person could

[177] Aristotle, *The Athenian Constitution. The Eudemian Ethics on Virtues and Vices*, with an English translation by H. Rackham (Loeb Classical Library), Cambridge, Mass., Harvard University Press, 1952, pp. 154–157.

[178] The Thirty were a group of oligarchs appointed to rule Athens after her defeat by Sparta, 404 B.C., and to frame a new constitution. They ruled from c. September 404 to May 403.

[179] Aristotle, *op. cit.*, pp. 102–103.

[180] Isée, *Discours*, Texte établi et traduit par Pierre Roussel, Paris, "Les Belles Lettres," 1922, pp. 17–32.

[181] *Ibid.*, I, 21, p. 25.

not enter into marriage, an arrangement which parallels Roman and Jewish law in antiquity. In discussing the possibility that the legislator may create hardships for individuals, he says: "And there are cases in which the legislator will be imposing upon him the greatest calamity, and he will be compelled to disobey the law, if he is required, for example, to take a wife who is mad, or has some other terrible malady of soul or body, such as makes life intolerable to the sufferer."[182]

Plato also indicates that the insane were generally not held responsible for criminal actions.[183] Referring to sacrilege, treason and political subversion, he says,

> Laws have been already enacted by us concerning the robbers of the Gods, and concerning traitors, and also concerning those who corrupt the laws for the purpose of subverting the government. A man may very likely commit some of these crimes, either in a state of madness or when affected by disease, or under the influence of extreme old age, or in a fit of childish wantonness, himself no better than a child. And if this be made evident to the judges elected to try the cause on the appeal of the criminal or his advocate, and he be judged to have been in this state when he committed the offence, he shall simply pay for the hurt which he may have done to another; but he shall be exempt from other penalties, unless he have slain some one, and have on his hands the stain of blood. And in that case he shall go to another land and country, and there dwell for a year; and if he return before the expiration of the time which the law appoints, or even set his foot at all on his native land, he shall be bound by the guardians of the law in the public prison for two years, and then go free.[184]

Clearly, in criminal delicts irresponsibility and absence of intention, as in infancy, mental disorder, anger and passion, constituted extenuating circumstances. Under such circumstances, the individual if found guilty had to pay a fine, except for cases involving homicide where exile was the penalty. Just how far these penalties were applied in practice is not quite clear. The story of Solon's feigned madness obviously presupposes that a mentally deranged individual would not be held responsible for his actions and would not be punished. As Diogenes Laertius relates, Megara and Athens had been fighting for possession of Salamis, the birth-place of Solon. "After many defeats the Athenians passed a decree punishing with death any man

[182] Plato, *Laws* 926 A, Jowett translation, vol. II, p. 665.

[183] For Greek judicial practice see G. Glotz, *The Greek City and its Institutions*, London, Kegan Paul, Trench, 1929, pp. 232–262; M. H. E. Meier and G. F. Schoemann, *Der attische Prozess*, 2 vols., 2nd edition revised by J. H. Lipsius, Berlin, 1883–1887.

[184] Plato, *Laws* 864 D, Jowett translation, vol. II, p. 610.

who should propose a renewal of the Salaminian War. Solon, feigning madness, rushed into the Agora with a garland on his head; there he had his poem on Salamis read to the Athenians by the herald and roused them to fury. They renewed the war with the Megarians and, thanks to Solon, were victorious."[185] What might have happened to Solon had the Athenians been defeated is left to our imagination.

Finally, as among other slave-owning peoples of antiquity, the law concerned itself with defects of body and mind in slaves put up for sale. In the fourth century B.C., for example, an Athenian law provided that "when a party sells a slave, he shall declare beforehand if he has any blemish; if he omit to do so, he shall be compelled to make restitution."[186] One example of such a condition was epilepsy.[187] However, to judge from Plato's version of the law mental disorder was probably also included, for he says:

If a man sells a slave who is in a consumption, or who has the disease of the stone, or of strangury, or epilepsy, or some other tedious and incurable disorder of body or mind, which is not discernible to the ordinary man, if the purchaser be a physician or trainer, he shall have no right of restitution; nor shall there be any right of restitution if the seller has told the truth beforehand to the buyer. But if a skilled person sells to another who is not skilled, let the buyer appeal for restitution within six months, except in the case of epilepsy, and then the appeal may be made within a year. The cause shall be determined by such physicians as the parties may agree to choose; and the defendant, if he lose the suit shall pay double the price at which he sold.[188]

But while the buyers and sellers of slaves had some legal protection, what about the slaves? To judge from the story of the Cynic philosopher Monimus (see above p. 95), the answer is that he had little or no protection. A slave who became mentally deranged was probably driven out into the street to wander about and be stoned. That such was the situation is supported by Plato's proposal for a heavy fine on anyone who had a mad slave and neglected to care for him.[189]

Clearly neither the state nor the law felt any obligation to the mentally ill. Where the law was invoked, it was to provide protection against the madman, but little or nothing was done to protect him

[185] Diogenes Laertius, *op. cit.*, vol. I, pp. 46–49; compare also the case of Meton the astonomer mentioned above p. 95.

[186] Hyperides, *The Orations against Athenogenes and Philippides*, ed. and trans. by F. G. Kenyon, London, 1893, p. 19.

[187] Temkin, *op. cit.*, pp. 46–48; Karl Sudhoff, *Ärztliches aus griechischen Papyrus–Urkunden* (Studien zur Geschichte der Medizin, 5–6), Leipzig, Johann Ambrosius Barth, 1909, pp. 142–149.

[188] Plato, *Laws* XI, 916 A, Jowett translation, vol. II p. 672.

[189] *Ibid.*, XI, 934 D, Jowett translation, vol. II, p. 672.

from himself or from others. There is no evidence, for example, to show that a medical examination and judgement was required in a suit to declare a person mentally deranged. No measures were taken by any public agency to provide for his health and welfare. This was left to the family and friends of the madman, if he had any.[190]

In dealing with the mentally disordered, Greek and Roman law exhibit several similarities. The Roman equivalent of the *dike paranoias* was the appointment of a *curator* to take charge of the property of a madman (*furiosus*). The oldest Roman law code, the Law of the Twelve Tables, dating from about the fifth century B.C., provided that "If a man is raving mad, rightful authority over his person and chattels shall belong to his agnates or to his clansmen ... A person who, being insane or a spendthrift, is prohibited from administering his own goods shall be under the trusteeship of agnates."[191] There was no procedure by which a person might be declared officially insane. Originally, the pronouncement of madness probably came from the family or the clan (*gens*). Apparently the lawyers never discussed the basic question, When is a person to be regarded as mad (*furiosus*)? This was considered a question of fact, and was simply left to the magistrates and judges, but was never subjected to any rules by the law. Furthermore, no attention was apparently given by the lawyers to medical concepts and views on mental illness.[192]

This situation derives in part from the origin and purpose of the legal arrangements for the guardianship of the insane (*cura furiosi*). The Law of the Twelve Tables is essentially a codification into statutory law of existing customs, reflecting the preponderantly agricultural character of the Roman community. Apparently, the *gens*, the clan, originally took charge of its members who were legally incapable of acting and provided for their guardianship. These arrangements grew out of the Roman family organization, and the power of the guardian (*curator*) was originally a kind of substitute for the power of the *pater familias* over persons *sui juris*, that is, those not subject to a family head, who because of mental disorder could not act with full legal effect.[193] Individuals who were mentally affected but were under the authority of a family head (*in*

[190] Xenophon, *op. cit.*, pp. 36–37: "That madmen should be kept in prison was expedient, he [Socrates] thought, both for themselves and for their friends ...'

[191] *Remains of Old Latin*, with an English translation by E. H. Warmington, 4 vols. (Loeb Classical Library), Cambridge, Mass., Harvard University Press, 1935–1940, vol. III, pp. 424–515.

[192] Fritz Schulz, *Classical Roman Law*, Oxford, Clarendon Press, 1951, pp. 197–199.

[193] G. J. Sesto, *Guardians of the Mentally Ill in Ecclesiastical Trials*, Washington, Catholic University of America Press, 1956, p. 809.

*potestate patris*) did not fall under the *cura furiosi*. In the development of *curatio*, when the guardianship of the clan disappeared, a person who might have been subject to it fell under the authority of his agnates[194] who had control of his person as well as his property.[195]

In cases where there was no legitimate guardian (*curator legitimus*) or an unsuitable one, the praetor, or the governor in the provinces, could intervene to appoint a guardian, since there was originally no provision for testamentary appointment (*cura furiosi testamentaria*). Later, though there never was any strictly legal basis for appointment of a guardian by will, it became accepted practice for the magistrate to confirm an appointment made in this way by the father of the insane person. In other words, in cases where there were no agnates or clansmen (*gentiles*) to act as guardians, the magistrates acted at their discretion. Thus, it is not at all unlikely that mentally disordered persons who were considered *furiosi* often may have been without a guardian. As far as slaves were concerned, no man could be freed while mentally disordered. If he became mad after emancipation, the magistrate could appoint a *curator*.

Initially guardianship in Roman law was an institution intended to keep property in the agnatic family. As the law developed, however, the guardian's function tended to expand, becoming one of shielding the incapable person from the consequences of his illness, as well as that of administering his property. These were facts of everyday Roman life, and various Latin writers refer to them in passing as something with which the reader is acquainted. Varro says that any man who cannot make a profit out of farming and still wants "to farm has lost his wits, and should be taken in charge by his kinsmen and family."[196] Horace, in the section of his third satire on the follies of mankind, where he assails the madness of ambition, offers this illustration:

[194] Agnates are persons who are related on the agnatic principle, that is, where only relationship through males is recognized. Examples are two brothers, or a brother and a sister, or a man and his brother's son or daughter.

[195] The following account is based on Schulz, *op. cit.*, pp. 197–199; *Leage's Roman Private Law*, 3rd edition by S. M. Prichard, London, Macmillan & Co., 1961, pp. 142–143, 227, 265, 317, 402; H. F. Jolowicz, *Historical Introduction to the Study of Roman Law*, Cambridge, Cambridge University Press, 1954, pp. 120–121, 250–251; F. De Zulueta, *The Institutes of Gaius*, 2 vols., Oxford, Clarendon Press, 1946, vol. I, pp. 62–63; vol. II, pp. 52, 74, 91, 158, 198; J. B. Moyle, ed. *Imperatoris Justiniani Institutionum libri quattuor*, 2nd edition, Oxford, Clarendon Press, 1890, pp. 169–174; *The Theodosian Code ... A Translation with Commentary, Glossary* by Clyde Pharr, Princeton, Princeton University Press, 1952, p. 264.

[196] Marcus Terentius Varro (116–27 B.C.), *vir Romanorum eruditissimus*, began to write his *Res Rusticae* in his eightieth year. See Cato and Varro, *De Re Rustica* (Loeb Classical Library), Cambridge, Mass., Harvard University Press, 1934, pp. 172–173.

Suppose one chose to carry about in a litter a pretty lamb, and treating it as a daughter, provided it with clothes, maids, gold, called it "Goldie" or "Teenie," and planned to have it wed a gallant husband: the praetor by injunction would take from him all control, and the care of him would pass to his sane relations. Well, if a man offers up his daughter, as if she were a dumb lamb, is he sound of mind?[197]

Again in his first Epistle, Horace says to Maecenas that though he notes carelessness in his dress and appearance, he fails to observe more serious discrepancies of thought and action. "You think my madness is the usual thing, and neither laugh at me nor deem that I need a physician or a guardian assigned by the magistrate . . ."[198]

A *furiosus* lacked any capacity to effect a legal act, nor did it make any difference whether he did or did not have a guardian. If he had a remission and became lucid again he automatically recovered his legal capability. In the event that he again became mentally deranged, the curator resumed his powers without any need for action by a magistrate, a principle which was finally established under Justinian.[199] In the later Empire the *cura furiosi* was extended to mental defectives (*mente capti, fatui*), the deaf, the dumb and to those subject to an incurable malady (*cura debilium*). *Debiles*, however, were capable of acquiring and disposing of property, of entering into contracts, and of making wills.[200]

The mentally disordered person could not acquire property or dispose of it. Property could come to him by other means, as through one of his slaves, a method of transferring property which was employed in such situations, or by inheritance *sui heredes* which was automatic.[201] Nor could he make a will or witness one. Any contract into which the *furiosus* entered was void, even if the other party was unaware of his condition.[202] Moreover, a remark by Philo Judaeus seems to imply that the repayment of a loan might be withheld if in the interim the lender had lost his mind. He says: "When you have received something in trust from a man when he was sober, you should not return it to him when he is drunk, or when playing fast and loose with his money, or when mad, for the recipient will not be

---

[197] Horace, *Satires, Epistles and Ars Poetica*, with an English translation by H. R. Fairclough (Loeb Classical Library), London, Wm. Heinemann, 1926, pp. 170–171.

[198] *Ibid.*, pp. 258–259. I have substituted the word "magistrate" for "court" in Fairclough's translation.

[199] Leage, *op. cit.*, p. 143.

[200] Justinian, *Institutiones*, ed. Moyle, I, 23, 3–4, Sesto, *op. cit.*, p. 11.

[201] Schulz, *op. cit.*, p. 281.

[202] Fritz Schulz, *Prinzipien des römischen Rechts*, München and Leipzig, Duncker und Humblot, 1934, p. 170.

in a fit condition to derive any real benefit from recovering it."[203] Delicts committed by him did not render him liable to a fine or damages. Thus, an insane person could not be guilty of theft or of murder (see above p. 124).[204]

Under Justinian a person with an insane descendant was enabled to substitute other persons as heirs to him, an act for which previously special permission from the Emperor was required. However, the substitution had to be made in a given order of priority, first in favour of the sane descendants of the insane person, and only if there were none could other substitutions be made.

Lunatics and idiots were incapable of contracting marriage. Justinian also established the principle that the consent of a madman was not necessary for the marriage of his children. The Theodosian Code indicates that a father who squandered his children's patrimony was treated "as in the case of an insane and demented person" and a guardian could be appointed for the children.[205]

It is clear that the legal protection of the mentally ill and of those who came in contact with them was limited. The Roman jurists were not concerned with the nature and cause of insanity. They were concerned solely to ascertain the fact of unsoundness of mind, and its consequences for the performance of juridical acts. This attitude has characterized the legal approach to mental illness down to the present.

Aside from the aspects previously described, the care of the mentally ill both among the Greeks and the Romans was left to their relatives and friends. Antiquity had no asylums or other institutions for the treatment or custody of the mentally ill. Plato advocated keeping madmen at home by any possible means. "If a man is mad," he said, "he shall not be at large in the city, but his relations shall keep him at home in any way which they can; or if not, let them pay a penalty."[206] From this and other comments it appears that there were two methods of restraining the insane. The mentally deranged individual who was not too disturbed and whose family could afford to do so might be placed in charge of a personal attendant responsible for his conduct. In this situation he might simply be confined at home. If there was danger that the insane person would harm

---

[203] Philo, *op. cit.*, vol. III, pp. 262–264.

[204] Semelaigne, *Études historiques sur l'aliénation mentale dans l'antiquité*, Paris, 1869, pp. 222–223.

[205] Justinian, *Institutiones, op. cit.*, I, 10, pp. 132–134. *Theodosian Code, op. cit.*, p. 264; for guardianship of minors see Schulz, *Classical Roman Law, op. cit.*, pp. 192–193; also *Scriptores Historiae Augustae*, with an English translation by David Magie (Loeb Classical Library), 3 vols., London, Wm. Heinemann, 1921–1932, vol. 1, pp. 158–161.

[206] Plato, *Laws* XI, 934 C-D, Jowett translation, vol. II, p. 672.

himself or those associated with him, he was not only confined to his home but tied up or placed in stocks as well. Aristophanes employs a combination of these methods to achieve a comic effect in the *Wasps*. Old Philocleon, whose obsession is to sit in the court and to judge, is confined within his house which is bolted and barred, where every opening is stuffed, and around which nets are spread. In addition, slaves have been posted to see that he does not escape—which of course he manages to do.[207] However, as the story of Cleomenes, the Spartan king, indicates, there was a stern reality behind the jest. Moreover, from a passage in Xenophon we may infer that where domiciliary confinement was not possible, the violently insane were put in prison.[208]

Similar practices were employed by the Romans under the Republic and the Empire. There is a passage in Cicero's speech against Piso in which he indicates that the friends of a madman, in caring for him, might find it necessary to tie him up in order to keep him from harm.[209] Evidence that this was actually done is to be found in *Leucippe and Clitophon*, a novel by Achilles Tatius, dating from the beginning of the third century A.D. Leucippe, suddenly seized by an attack of frenzy, falls to the ground, and strikes at those who try to help her. Eventually her companions succeed in tying her securely until they can call a physician to treat her.[210] According to Soranus, some physicians prescribed indiscriminately that mental patients be kept in bonds, a practice which he criticizes.[211] Paul of Aegina (625–690 A.D.), however, recommended that patients suffering from mania "must be secured in bed, so that they may not be able to injure themselves, or those who approach them; or swung within a wicker-basket in a small couch suspended from on high."[212]

Although there was no organized effort by the community through government to care for the mentally deranged, it is clear that there were recognized methods of dealing individually with the more violent ones. However, physical restraint was only one element in caring for the mentally ill. Thus, Leucippe, the frenzied young woman mentioned above, was tied up until a physician was summoned. Judging by various references in classical literature, calling

[207] Aristophanes, *Wasps*, Loeb edition, vol. I, pp. 414–419.

[208] Xenophon, *op. cit.*, pp. 36–37.

[209] Cicero, *The Speeches*, with an English translation by N. H. Watts (Loeb Classical Library), Cambridge, Mass., Harvard University Press, 1964, pp. 196–199.

[210] Achille Tatius, "Les Aventures de Leucippé et de Clitophon," in *Romans Grecs et Latins, op. cit.*, pp. 942–944.

[211] Celius Aurelianus, *op. cit.*, pp. 554–555.

[212] Paulus Aegineta, *The Seven Books*, trans. by Francis Adams, 3 vols., London, Sydenham Society, 1844–1847, vol. 1, p. 385.

a physician to diagnose and treat mental illness was not unusual, especially if the patient belonged to a family of means, and had kin to look after him. Catullus, for example, disposes of Ameana, mistress of Mamurra his political enemy, by questioning her sanity and urging that a doctor be called. "Ameana, that worn-out jade asked me for a round ten thousand; that girl with the ugly snub nose, the mistress of the bankrupt of Formiae. You her relations, who have charge of the girl, call together friends and doctors: she is not right in her mind, and never asks the looking glass what she is like."[213] As Horace tells the story of the Argive man of rank, he was cared for by his kin, who saw to it that he was treated with hellebore, presumably by a physician.[214] Also in his first Epistle, Horace refers to the summoning of a physician to a madman together with the appointment of a guardian.[215] Then there is the evidence of Plautus. In the *Menaechmi* (probably third century B.C.), the father of one of the characters calls a doctor to determine whether his son, who has been acting strangely, is mad. Although distorted for comic effect, the underlying reality is clearly recognizable. The physician endeavours first to obtain a history from the father.[216]

> *Doctor:* What did you say was the character of his illness? Tell me, old gentleman, was it madness or demonic possession? Is he lethargic, drowsy, or does he suffer from fluid under the skin?
> *Father:* Why, I brought you here so that you would tell me that and cure him.
> *Doctor:* That is easy, very easy. He will be cured; I promise that on my honour.

Then the doctor approaches Menaechmus, the presumed patient:

> *Doctor:* Good day, Menaechmus, why do you expose your arm? Don't you know how harmful that is to one with your present illness?
> *Menaechmus:* You be hanged!
> *Father:* Do you notice anything?
> *Doctor:* Indeed, I do. Even a wagon-load of hellebore couldn't help in this case. Now see here, Menaechmus.
> *Menaechmus:* What do you want?
> *Doctor:* Answer me this question. Do you drink white or red wine?
> *Menaechmus:* May you end on the gallows!

The function of the physician is evident also from the medical

---

[213] Catullus, *op. cit.*, XLI, pp. 48–49; see also XLIII, pp. 50–51, where he disparaged the charms of Ameana in comparison with those of Lesbia.

[214] Horace, *op. cit.*, pp. 434–435.

[215] *Ibid.*, pp. 258–259.

[216] Plautus, *Menaechmi, op. cit.*, vol. I, pp. 454–457.

literature. The writings of the Hippocratics, of Celsus, Soranus, Arataeus and Galen clearly indicate that they had made clinical observations and treated patients in sufficient numbers so as to acquire a considerable experience.

Generally speaking, medical treatment in the management of cases of mania or melancholia was intended to build up the patient's strength and to alter his constitution as far as possible in order to eliminate the disease or to diminish it as far as possible.[217] Towards these ends both somatic and psychotherapeutic measures were employed, to some degree in terms of the aetiological factors assumed or diagnosed by the physicians. Thus where physical (heat, cold, concussion) or physiological factors (excessive drinking, sexual excesses, suppression of menses, hemorrhoidal bleeding, drugs) were believed to cause the condition, therapeutic measures were taken to remove their action or to moderate it. Rest, limited diet, gentle massage, moderate use of bleeding and cupping and the like were employed. Later, if the patient improved, passive and active exercises, a more varied diet, anointing and massage, rest, as well as non-specific stimulants such as irritant plasters, purges, vomitives, sun bathing and other forms of heating, hot and cold baths, travel and recreation were employed.

In view of the fact that psychological factors, such as grief, excessive anger, anxiety, and straining the mind and the senses through study, business, or other ambitious pursuits, were also regarded as causes of mental illness, the psychotherapeutic approach of a physician such as Soranus is not unexpected. His description of the handling of patients with delusions and hallucinations, the endeavours to avoid any aggravating influences, the use of graduated mental exercises, games and recreation is strongly reminiscent of the milieu therapy employed by Tuke at the York Retreat in the eighteenth century.[218] Even where physical restraint is necessary Soranus insisted on gentleness.

Other physicians, however, advocated violent physical and physiological measures. Severe physical restraint, extremely limited diets, keeping the patient in a dark room, violent purges, excessive bleeding, plunging the patient suddenly into cold water, beating and whipping him—all were employed in antiquity and continued to be used in succeeding centuries. Celsus, for example, suggests in-

---

[217] For medical treatment see Aretaeus, Celsus, and Caelius Aurelianus as cited above. Useful secondary sources are J. L. Heiberg, "Geisteskrankheiten im klassischen Altertum," *Allgememeine Zeitschrift für Psychiatrie* 86: 1–44, 1927; I. E. Drabkin, "Remarks on Ancient Psychopathology," *Isis* 46: 223–234, 1955, also Temkin, *op. cit.*, pp. 27–80.

[218] Caelius Aurelianus, *op. cit.*, pp. 543–553.

dividualizing the treatment and points out that some patients "need to have their violence restrained as is done in the case of those who are controlled even by flogging. In some also untimely laughter has to be put a stop to by reproofs and threats . . ."[219] Whether or not the Greeks employed whipping or beating is an open question, as there seem to be no references to such practices in the extant literature. However, in view of the known propensity to throw stones at the mentally disordered or to pelt them with clods, one may speculate that beatings probably were administered for various reasons, not only to restrain the violently insane but also to drive out the evil spirits. The approach was very probably like that of the mother, in the third mime of Herodes, who admonishes the schoolmaster to beat the very devil out of her errant son "till his last curst breath hangs on his lips."[220] However, it seems likely that physicians did not advocate such practices in Greece.

Celsus also employed various other methods and remedies.

Melancholy thoughts are to be dissipated, for which purpose, music, cymbals, and noises are of use. More often, however, the patient is to be agreed with rather than opposed, and his mind slowly and imperceptibly is to be turned from the irrational talk to something better. At times, also, his interest should be awakened; as may be done in the case of men fond of literature, to whom a book may be read, correctly when they are pleased by it, or incorrectly if that very thing annoys them; for by making corrections they begin to divert their mind. Moreover, they should be pressed to recite anything they can remember. Some who did not want to eat were induced to do so, by being placed on couches between other diners. But certainly for all so affected sleep is both difficult and especially necessary; for under it many get well. Beneficial for this, as also for composing the mind itself, is saffron ointment with orris applied to the head. If in spite of this patients are wakeful, some endeavour to induce sleep by draughts of decoction of poppy or by hyoscyamus; others put mandrake apples under the pillow.[221]

Celsus's reference to medicamentary treatment of mentally deranged patients only begins to touch on the materia medica employed in such cases. A wide variety of animal, vegetable and mineral substances were used for the prevention or the cure of madness. Probably most widely used and best known was hellebore, whose violently purgative effect was employed in the standard

---

[219] Celsus, *op. cit.*, vol. I, pp. 294–295.

[220] Theophrastus et al., *op. cit.*, pp. 102–103.

[221] Celsus, *op. cit.*, vol. I, pp. 294–297. For the use of music in medicine see L. Edelstein, "Greek medicine in its Relation to Religion and Magic," *Bull. Hist. Med.*. 5: 201–246, 1937 (see particularly pp. 234–238).

treatment of insanity in antiquity. The numerous references in the non-medical literature to hellebore indicate that it entered into the popular linguistic usage of antiquity much as aspirin has become a household word today.

The medical handling of mental illness briefly described above makes no pretence at completeness. Owing to several factors the role of medicine in the treatment of mental illness in antiquity was a limited one. Our purpose is to indicate its place and relation to mental illness in Graeco-Roman culture rather than to examine in detail this area of medical theory and practice. Medical practice in Graeco-Roman antiquity was much less standardized than it is today. Moreover, it is not simple or easy to separate rational, scientific approaches to mental illness from popular and magical remedies. As Temkin has shown, many medical preparations and practices had their sources in magic and religion.[222] He notes, for example, that of the forty-five remedies for epilepsy mentioned by Discorides, at least seventeen, more than one-third, have a superstitious connotation. Moreover, a large part of medical practice in antiquity was based on empiricism. Even where physicians sought a rational explanation, the strange character of mental and emotional disorders as well as the lack of adequate means, made it difficult if not impossible to evaluate critically clinical observations and presumed therapeutic results. As an example we may cite Galen's discussion of the therapeutic use of peony root in a case of epilepsy.

> On the whole its effect is very drying, so that I do not entirely relinquish the hope that it may have been reasonable to rely on it to cure epilepsy in children, even if used as an amulet. And I know a child that had not been attacked at all for eight months since wearing the root. When however, somehow the amulet slid off, he was immediately seized. And when another one had been hung around his neck, he again felt perfectly well. But for experiment's sake it seemed better to me to take it off again; and when I had done so, and he was seized by convulsions again, I hung a big fresh part of the root around his neck. And from that time on the boy was absolutely healthy and was no longer seized by convulsions. It was now logical (to assume) either that certain particles of the root fell out, were sucked in by inspiration, and did thus heat the affected part—or that the air itself was tempered and changed by the root.[223]

---

[222] O. Temkin, "Beiträge zur archaischen Medizin," *Kyklos* 3: 90–135, 1930; *idem, Falling Sickness,* pp. 20–26, 77–80; see also Walter Artelt, *Studien zur Geschichte der Begriffe "Heilmittel" und "Gift"* (Studien zur Geschichte der Medizin, Heft 23), Leipzig, Johann Ambrosius Barth, 1937, pp. 89–91.

[223] Temkin, *Falling Sickness,* p. 24.

Finally, it is important to note certain social factors that led many to have recourse to non-medical means of treating mental disorders. For example, relatively few people in Rome could afford the treatment of mania described by Soranus.[224] Patients who could belonged to the upper levels of ancient society. The best kind of care for mental illness required time and favourable circumstances, but very few could afford to submit to medical care under these conditions. Those who had to work for their livelihood required a different kind of treatment; they needed a remedy or a cure that was quick and relatively inexpensive—a drug, a spell, a visit to a religious shrine. This principle, the differential provision of medical care by social class, is to be found in all periods of Graeco-Roman civilization, whether in the fifth century B.C. or the second century A.D.[225] It is no surprise therefore to find it present also in the care of the mentally ill.

At the same time, it is obvious that socio-economic factors were not alone responsible for recourse to religious and magical treatment of mental disorders. The very nature of such conditions, their unpredictable relapses and the fact that they were chronic, as well as other bizarre characteristics, undoubtedly led numerous families and individuals to turn in desperation, as Aristides did, to a religious shrine and to participate in ceremonies of propitiation, purification, and incubation. Various practical non-medical steps to deal with madness are described by Aristophanes in the *Wasps*.[226] Xanthias endeavours to cure his father Philocleon of his obsession, first by rational persuasion, then by subjecting him to purification. When neither of these measures helps, he tries to cure his father by having him participate in the rites of the Corybantic devotees. Finally, Xanthias in desperation took Philocleon to the shrine of Asclepius at Aegina, where he underwent incubation. That such measures continued to be used is indicated in the *Menaechmi* of Plautus. One character says to another: "Tell me, young man, how much do pigs fit for sacrifice cost here? ... Take two shillings from me; get yourself purified at my expense. For its really quite clear that you are insane ..."[227] Among the Greeks and Romans the belief was widely held that an individual who was possessed might be relieved through sacrifices to Dionysos and Cybele. Relief might also be obtained if the possessed one participated in the mysteries of Hecate, or of the

---

[224] Caelius Aurelianus, *op. cit.*, pp. 534–559.

[225] Hippocrates, *Diet* (Littré VI, pp. 594–604); Plato, *Laws*, 720 c, D; *idem*, *Republic* 3, 406c; George Rosen, "The Evolution of Social Medicine," *Handbook of Medical Sociology*, ed. H. E. Freeman, S. Levine, L. G. Reeder, Englewood Cliffs, Prentice-Hall, 1963, pp. 17–61 (see particularly pp. 18–19).

[226] Aristophanes, *Wasps*, *op. cit.*, vol. I, pp. 416–417.

[227] Plautus, *Menaechmi*, *op. cit.*, vol. II, pp. 394–395; Varro, *op. cit.*, pp. 360–361.

Corybantes.[228] Incantations and magical formulas for the expulsion of demonic spirits were also employed.[229] And so we have come full circle. The gods and the spirits cannot only cause madness, they can also cure it.

Our survey of the position of the mentally disordered in the culture of Greece and Rome has clearly revealed that the problem of madness was handled primarily on the basis of custom. The family or friends of the affected person were expected to provide for him. A few measures were taken by the community through its public agencies, but these were primarily concerned with the protection of the community and of property owned by or designated for the affected person. Greek law took little account of the insane, but the Romans went further and created a legal framework, with such institutions as guardianship, that provided a pattern for legal developments concerned with the mentally ill. For the most part, physicians played a relatively small role in dealing with mental derangement as a community problem. There is no evidence to show that medical examination and opinion were required in *dike paranoias* or *cura furiosi*. The insane poor who wandered about received no medical care, and were treated as social butts. Those who had some means could afford treatment by a doctor. Many resorted to religious and magical treatment because of their ideas on the causes of mental disorder, or in desperation because a cure could not be obtained in any other way. The trend intensified in the later centuries of the Roman Empire.[230] This was the legacy of Graeco-Roman culture to medieval Europe out of which the care of the mentally ill developed in cultures and societies far different from those of the Greeks and the Romans.

---

[228] Ivan M. Linforth, "The Corybantic Rites in Plato," *University of California Publications in Classical Philology* 13: 121–172, 1944–1950; Henri Graillot, *Le Culte de Cybèle Mère des dieux à Rome et dans l'empire Romain*, Paris, Fontemoing et Cie, 1912; Franz Cumont, *Die orientalischen Religionen im römischen Heidentum*, Vierte unveränderte Auflage, Stuttgart, B. G. Teubner, 1959; Martin P. Nilsson, *The Dionysiac Mysteries of the Hellenistic and Roman Age*, Lund, C. W. K. Gleerup, 1957.

[229] Campbell Bonner, "The Technique of Exorcism," *Harvard Theological Review* 36: 39–49, 1943; see the account of Josephus, pp. 32-33, 69-70.

[230] S. Eitrem, *Orakel und Mysterien am Ausgang der Antike*, Zurich, Rhein-Verlag, 1947; H. J. Frings, *Medizin und Arzt bei den griechischen Kirchenvätern bis Chrysostomos* (Bonn Dissertation), 1959; O. Temkin, *Byzantine Medicine: Tradition and Empiricism* (Dumbarton Oaks Papers, Number 16), 1962, pp. 97–115.

# FROM THE MIDDLE AGES
## TO THE PRESENT

# CHAPTER FOUR

# WESTERN AND CENTRAL EUROPE DURING THE LATE MIDDLE AGES AND THE RENAISSANCE

All too often the situation of the mentally ill during the later Middle Ages and the Renaissance is passed over with superficial references to medical ignorance, superstitions and brutal treatment, and gruesome witch-hunts. While these aspects were undoubtedly present, they must nevertheless be seen as elements in a much more complex context which also included elements of empirical rationality and humane interest. A balanced view of the subject and the period requires that these diverse elements be seen in perspective and in relation to each other.

During the medieval period, public authorities took only limited responsibility for the mentally deranged. Mentally or emotionally disturbed members of a community were left at liberty as long as they caused no public disturbance. Custody of the mentally ill generally rested with their relatives and friends; only those considered too dangerous to keep at home, or who had no one to care for them, or who were socially disturbing, were dealt with by communal authorities.

Acutely disturbed, agitated patients were admitted to general hospitals in some places, as for example at the Hôtel-Dieu in Paris.[1] Some institutions had either separate rooms or a special facility for such patients. In 1326, a *Dollhaus* (madhouse) was erected as part of the Georgshospital at Elbing, in the domain of the Teutonic Knights. A *Tollkiste* (mad cell), is mentioned in the municipal records of Hamburg in 1375. At Erfurt, the Grosse Hospital, rebuilt in 1385, had a *Tollkoben* (mad hut), where the insane were locked up.[2] Such arrangements also existed in England. In 1403, the Hospital of St. Mary of Bethlem in London had among its nine inmates, six men deprived of reason (*mente capti*). General infirmaries usually received the mentally disordered in other parts of the country. At the end of

---

[1] E. Coyecque, *L'Hôtel-Dieu de Paris au moyen âge. Histoire et documents.* Tome I. *Histoire de l'Hôtel-Dieu. Documents (1316–1552)*, Paris, H. Champion, 1891, p. 109; T. Kirchhoff, *Grundriss einer Geschichte der deutschen Irrenpflege*, Berlin, August Hirschwald, 1890, pp. 17ff.

[2] Alfons Fischer, *Geschichte des deutschen Gesundheitswesens*, 2 vols., Berlin, F. A. Herbig, 1933, vol. I, pp. 78, 109, 268.

the fourteenth century, Holy Trinity (Salisbury) admitted insane patients as well as other sick people.[3] At Paris, mentally deranged patients at the Hôtel-Dieu were placed in beds that were enclosed and had two windows through which the patient could be observed and things handed to him. Patients placed in ordinary beds were attached to them by strong bonds. Mentally disordered persons were also sent to places of detention such as the Châtelet of Melun, south of Paris.[4]

The insane who were native to other communities were frequently expelled and returned to the town from which they had come. This practice appears to have been most common in Germany, but it was not limited to that area. The municipal accounts of Hildesheim from 1384 to 1480 show expenditures for 82 lunatics. Of these, 43 were expelled. At Nürnberg, from 1377 to 1397, 37 insane persons were public charges; 17 of these were transported at public expense to other cities, among them Bamberg, Passau, and Regensburg, even as far away as Vienna and Hungary. Before their expulsion, the mentally ill were confined, generally in the town jail. From 1400 to 1450, 31 insane people out of 62 mentioned in the municipal accounts of Nürnberg were removed to other communities. During the next fifty years, 21 out of 33 were transported. Those who were expelled were kept in prison for only a few days, usually two to six. The insane who were not transported remained incarcerated for longer periods, at at least for two to three weeks and in some cases for months.[5] The latter may have been natives.

Not infrequently, the insane were whipped before being transported. This seems to have been the practice in Basel in the fourteenth century.[6] Instances known from other communities indicate that whipping was a punishment for behaviour considered outrageous, malicious, or sacrilegious. As a rule those who had been expelled and then returned were flogged out of town. In 1451, a madman who had cursed the Host was whipped out of Frankfurt a.M. Flogging for outrageous behaviour in church is also described in Thomas More's *Dialogue of Cumfort* of 1533. A lunatic who often disturbed religious services, especially at the elevation of the Host, by lifting the skirts of praying women, was seized at More's order and

---

[3] John Stow, *A Survey of London*, 2 vols., Oxford, Clarendon Press, 1908, vol. I, pp. 164–165; R. M. Clay, *The Medieval Hospitals of England*, London, Methuen & Co., 1909, pp. 32–34.

[4] Coyecque (note 1), p. 109.

[5] Fischer (note 2), pp. 77, 267; Kirchhoff (note 1), pp. 9–10; Cecil Headlam, *The Story of Nuremberg* (Medieval town series), London, J. Dent & Co., 1900, pp. 158–159.

[6] Karl Baas, *Gesundheitspflege im mittelalterlichen Basel*, Zürich, Orell Füssli, 1926, p. 103.

flogged until the lesson "was beaten home. For he could then very well rehearse his faults himself, and speak and treat very well, and promise to do afterward as well."[7]

The responsibility for conveying the insane to their destination was usually given to a public employee, such as a jailer or an executioner's assistant. Maintenance costs during detention and outlays for transportation were borne by the municipality. Nürnberg records show that from time to time articles of clothing were provided for the unfortunates kept in the subterranean prison under the town hall. Thus, in 1376, a lunatic was given a fur, a pair of shoes, and a cloak; in 1435 a woman received a skirt. A smith's helper, who in 1427 lost his reason at Frankfurt a.M., was twice removed from the city but returned. When this happened a third time, he was taken to Bad Kreuznach, but not before he was newly clothed. Occasionally, instead of transporting mentally disordered persons, they were given some money and sent on their way. Thus, in 1427, a poor woman who was "out of her mind" came with her child to Frankfurt. By order of the town council she was given some money "because it was feared she might kill her child."[8]

References to medical care for insane individuals occur from time to time in town records. In 1386, Master Otten, Nürnberg surgeon, was paid by the municipality for treating a lunatic. From 1437 to 1439, payments to physicians (*aerzt gelts*) are mentioned several times. However, it is not clear whether these instances actually involved the treatment of mental disorder, or of other conditions which affected deranged individuals for whom the community was responsible. A more specific case occurred a hundred years later. In October 1539 Master Peter Maier, physician, arrived in Nürnberg and presented himself to the muncipal authorities offering to treat the mentally deranged. Early in November, he was given an opportunity to demonstrate his skill by treating two patients in the hospital. After a check by the three municipal physicians showed that the patients were indeed improved, they were released to their relatives. The administrator of the hospital was instructed to negotiate with Maier concerning his fee, and early in December 1539 he received 20 gulden. The following year, Maier got into difficulties with patients and colleagues and was compelled to leave Nürnberg.[9]

---

[7] D. Hack Tuke, *Chapters in the History of the Insane in the British Isles*, London, Kegan Paul, Trench & Co., 1882, pp. 56–58; R. Hunter and I. Macalpine *Three Hundred Years of Psychiatry*, London, Oxford University Press, 1963, pp. 5–6.

[8] Kirchhoff (note 1), pp. 10, 18.

[9] Kirchhoff spells the name Mayr; he is described as *artzt* but was probably not a graduate of a medical faculty; Kirchhoff (note 1), pp. 11, 102; Fischer (note 2), pp. 268–269.

Treatment of the mentally ill by exorcism or by pilgrimage to a religious shrine was not infrequently assisted and subsidized by secular and ecclesiastical authorities. During the fourteenth century the chapter of the Hôtel-Dieu of Paris arranged for insane patients to be taken on pilgrimages to the shrine of Saint-Mathurin de Larchant, or to that of Saint-Hildevert de Gournay. There is even a record of payment to a man who was sent to the former shrine to say, a novena for a mentally deranged nun.[10] In the fifteenth century, the municipal authorities of Nürnberg paid for the exorcism of a young woman possessed by the Devil.[11] During the fifteenth and sixteenth centuries, the town council of Basel provided letters of recommendation and safe-conduct, and in some cases financial assistance, to persons who went on pilgrimages to shrines renowned for their healing powers in nervous and mental disorders. Such assistance was given to epileptics in 1452 and 1495 who were going to seek aid at holy shrines, probably at the Benedictine establishment at Rufach in Upper Alsace erected in 1486, where there was a wonder-working relic of St. Vitus.[12] Similar help was given to the insane. On 19 March 1515 a man who wanted to take his wife who had lost her reason to Sankt Anstett, a Benedictine convent in the village of Wittersdorf in Lorraine, received a letter of recommendation. In 1525, an unfortunate man who was possessed was taken to Sankt Anstett by three men who were paid by the municipality for this service.[13]

During the sixteenth century there appears a slowly growing tendency to place the mentally deranged in special institutions. To a considerable degree this tendency was influenced by the social policies of the Protestant reformers and the rise of absolutist government. Although civil authorities had assumed some responsibility for matters of health and welfare before the sixteenth century, the notion existed that there ought to be an effective organization of all agencies of public assistance, and that all facilities and resources (hospitals, domiciliary relief, and the like) be united in the hands of municipal or national authorities. Juan Luis Vives at Bruges in 1526 included the mentally ill in his public assistance scheme, and proposed hospitalization and humane treatment for them. In some parts of Europe, former leper houses were used as institutions for the insane.[14]

[10] Coyecque (note 1), pp. 109–110.

[11] Kirchoff (note 1), p. 13.

[12] Baas (note 6), p. 104; Karl Sudhoff, "Ein spätmittelalterliches Epileptikerheim (Isolier und Pflegespital für Fallsüchtige) zu Rufach im Oberelsass," *Archiv für Geschichte der Medizin*, 6: 449, 1913.

[13] Baas (note 6), p. 103.

[14] F. R. Salter, ed. *Some Early Tracts on Poor Relief*, London, Methuen & Co., 1926, p. 16; Kirchhoff (note 1), pp. 93ff.

Despite numerous local variations, a principle of limited community responsibility was the basis for dealing with the mentally ill during the fifteenth century in Western and Central Europe. Wherever possible, communal authorities tried to avoid what they considered unnecessary burdens. The authorities acted only when there were no relatives, or when the safety of the community appeared involved. At Nürnberg, in 1388, a woman named Klüglin was paid for keeping an insane woman and seeing to it that she did not escape. Presumably she had no relatives. In 1410 the council ordered the relatives of a lunatic to share his maintenance costs and to pay them weekly. A certain E.H. was paid by the council in 1440 for travelling to Eschenbach and Winspach to make inquiries about an insane man who had been imprisoned at Reichelsdorf for mistreating women and other obnoxious acts. He was then brought back to Nürnberg by his relatives. Towards the end of the fifteenth century, the council issued numerous orders enabling the relatives of insane individuals to incarcerate them at their own expense in the town jail or in a tower. Thus in 1481 the widow Tetzel, her trustees and relatives petitioned the council for permission to take her insane son into custody and to put him in a tower of the city wall near St. Catherine's cloister.[15] The petition was granted, the cost to be paid by the family. In 1488 the wife and brother of a man named Fröschel, who was insane, were ordered to keep him in custody to the best of their ability so that he would cause no damage or injury. Should they be unable to comply, the council would do what was necessary and charge the family. In 1493 a mentally deranged man was released from the tower in the custody of his relatives, upon condition that they would confine him themselves should he again become violent. In this event his wife would confine him in her house or arrange to keep him elsewhere at her expense. If required, the council would lend her a jail.[16]

How care provided by relatives and associates worked in practice may be illustrated by the following cases. The first is that of Hugo van der Goes (1435?–1482), the Flemish painter of the Portinari altarpiece. About 1475 he joined the monastic community of the Roode Clooster near Brussels. Five years later while on a journey, "Hugo was struck by a strange disorder of his imagination. He cried out incessantly that he was doomed and condemned to eternal damnation. He would even have injured himself had he not been forcibly prevented by his companions." When they reached Brussels, Father Thomas, the Prior, came to see the

---

[15] The Tetzels were a leading patrician family of Nürnberg.
[16] Kirchhoff (note 1), p. 12.

sick man and learning all that had happened, he presumed that brother Hugo was suffering from the same complaint that had once afflicted King Saul, and reflecting that Saul's disorder had yielded when David plied his harp he immediately gave orders to play music frequently in Hugo's presence. Father Thomas also took care of other entertainments and recreations in order to dispel the phantasmagorias clouding his diseased mind. Yet his condition did not improve; he continued to talk unreasonably, and to consider himself a child of perdition.[17]

Eventually he recovered and seems to have been well until his death in 1482.

Somewhat over one hundred years later the case of Francesco Bassano (1549–1592) ended disastrously. According to Verci, his biographer, Bassano

fell into a fierce hypochondria which often drove him out of his senses. At last, in the grip of a furious fixation, he believed that he was going to be arrested, whereupon he fled without peace from room to room, hiding from his friends even from the servants, and almost losing confidence in his wife, as he suspected that she might deliver him to the police. She, however, who loved him dearly, took care of him, and, at the same time, in order to have him cured by doctors, had him continuously watched by various persons. But every care was in vain, for one day, when by accident he had been left alone, hearing somebody knocking very noisily at the door, he believed that the constable had come for him. Thereupon he fled in terror and, climbing out of a window, precipitously threw himself down hitting his temple on a stone, and lay mortally wounded. [18]

Still another aspect is illustrated by a document published by Hunter and Macalpine. This is a receipt acknowledging the payment of charges for keeping a deranged young man in Bethlem Hospital from 4 February 1588 to 7 May 1589. During this period, "Mr. Fraunces Nycolle of Hardwick in the countye of Northampton gentleman, did paye unto the keeper of Bedlem all such charges and other dueties as grewe and were due unto him by reason of the dyettinge and keeping of the said John Saye in Bedlem . . ."[19] It is not apparent whether Mr. Nycolle was a relative or a guardian acting under the authority of the Court of Wards and Livries, which had been set up in 1540 and dealt with the custody and property of mentally disordered or retarded individuals.

[17] Rudolf and Margot Wittkower, *Born under Saturn*, New York, Random House, 1963, p. 109. See also Joseph Destrée: *Hugo van der Goes*, Bruxelles and Paris, G. Van Oest & Cie., 1914, pp. 214–227.

[18] *Ibid.*, p. 140.

[19] Hunter and Macalpine (note 7), p. 40.

From these and other cases that could be cited, one must conclude that the treatment and care of the mentally ill exhibited a broader gamut of attitude and practice than has usually been presented as characteristic of this period. Obviously one cannot expect fifteenth and sixteenth century attitudes and behaviour towards the mentally ill to transcend radically the limits set by contemporary knowledge, dogmas, and pressures. Few in any age are able in any appreciable degree to move beyond the conventional wisdom of their own time.

Concepts of mental disorder in this period and the treatment of mental illness derived from the ideas of classical antiquity and the modifications which they experienced during the Middle Ages. To these must be added theological dogmas and popular beliefs concerning demonic possession and witchcraft. Gaspar Ofhuys (1456–1523), chronicler of the Roode Clooster, and *infirmarius* of the monastery after 1482, presents a succinct summary of these ideas in his account of the illness of Hugo van der Goes. He explained that

> certain people talked of a peculiar case of *frenesis magna*, the great frenzy of the brain. Others, however, believed him to be possessed of an evil spirit. There were, in fact, symptoms of both unfortunate diseases present in him, although I have always understood that throughout his illness he never once tried to harm anyone but himself. This, however, is not held to be typical of either the frenzied or the possessed. In truth, what it really was that ailed him only God can tell. We may thus have two diverse opinions on the disease of our brother; on the one hand we might say that his was a case of a natural disease. ... There are, of course, several types of the disease depending on its original cause: sometimes the cause is melancholic food;[20] at other times it is the consumption of strong wines which heat the body juices and burn them to ashes. Furthermore, frenzies may occur because of certain sufferings of the soul like restlessness, sadness, excessive study and anxiety. Finally, frenzy may be caused by the virulence of noxious juices, if such abound in the body of a man who inclines to that malady.

However, in addition to this humoral explanation. Ofhuys went on to adduce still another explanation for Hugo's illness, that it was

> God's all-loving providence which had ordained this malady. This brother had been flattered enough in our Order because of his great art —in fact, his name became more famous this way than if he had remained in the world. But since he was, after all, just as human as the rest of us, he had developed a rather high opinion of himself due to the many honours, visits and compliments which were paid to him. But God, not wanting his ruin, in His great mercy sent him this chastening affliction which, indeed, humbled him mightily. For brother Hugo

[20] That is, food which produces black bile.

repented and, as soon as he had recovered he exercised the greatest humility.[21]

The view that mental derangement might be due to natural and/or supernatural causes was also held by physicians. While medical men usually presumed that an illness was due to natural causes and prescribed treatment accordingly, there is no doubt that if the circumstances were too bizarre or too far beyond their past experience physicians would accept supernatural explanations. A case reported by Antonio Benivieni (1443–1502) is an apt illustration.

A new and extraordinary disease [he wrote] is nowadays rife which, though I have seen and treated it, I scarcely dare to describe. A girl in her sixteenth year was seized with pain in the lowest part of her belly and kept on trying to pluck it away with her hands. Then she broke into terrible screaming and her belly swelled up at the spot, so that it looked as if she were eight months' pregnant. When her voice failed she flung herself about from side to side on her bed, and, sometimes touching her neck with the soles of her feet, would spring to her feet, then again falling prostrate and again springing up. She would repeat these actions in exactly the same manner until she gradually came to herself and was somehow restored. When asked, she hardly knew what had happened.

Investigating this disorder, I concluded that it arose from the ascent of the womb, harmful exhalations being thus carried upwards and attacking the heart and brain.

I employed suitable medicines, but found them of no avail. Yet it did not occur to me to turn aside from the beaten track until she grew more frenzied and, glaring round with wild eyes, was at last violently sick and vomited up long bent nails and brass pins together with wax and hair mixed in a ball, and last of all a lump of food so large that no one could have swallowed it whole. As I saw her go through exactly the same procedure many times, I decided she was possessed by an evil spirit who blinded the eyes of the spectators while he was doing all this. She was handed over to physicians of the soul and then gave proof of the matter by plainer signs and tokens. For I have often heard her soothsaying and seen her doing other things besides, which went further than any violent symptoms produced by disease and even passed human power.[22]

Not all physicians, however, were inclined to accept the existence of possession, and some denied it altogether. The elder Riolan (1538–1606) explained enthusiasm, or possession by a deity, as due to the effect of melancholic vapours on phantasy, and went on to

---

[21] Wittkower (note 17), pp. 109–110; Destrée, *op. cit.*

[22] Antonio Benivieni, *The Hidden Causes of Disease*, trans. by Charles Singer, with a biographical appreciation by Esmond R. Long, Springfield, Charles C. Thomas, 1954, pp. 35–37.

point out that "it is not necessary for us to have recourse to a demon as the last refuge of ignorance, since we have a natural cause."[23]

Scepticism and acceptance of possession and its alleged cause, witchcraft, occur also in the case of Mary Glover, a fourteen-year-old girl, who having fallen into fits exhibited increasingly bizarre symptoms, not unlike those of Benivieni's patient.[24] She was treated by Drs. Robert Sherdman and Thomas Moundeford for almost three months, "but all being prooved in vaine, [they] pronounced . . . that som cause beyond naturall was in it." An old charwoman, Elizabeth Jackson, was indicted and brought to trial in 1602 for having bewitched the girl. Although she was convicted, the case is of interest because two physicians, Drs. John Argent and Edward Jorden, testified on behalf of Elizabeth Jackson that the fits allegedly caused by bewitchment were natural. Moreover, in 1603, Jorden published the first English book on hysteria, *A Briefe Discourse of a Disease Called the Suffocation of the Mother*, in which he endeavoured to explain the alleged supernatural effects of witchcraft in terms of a nervous disorder linked to the uterus.

Of equal interest in this case are the grounds on which the presiding judge refused to accept the medical opinion in favour of Elizabeth Jackson. Having elicited from Jorden an opinion that Mary Glover was not simulating her fits, as well as his admission that there was no certain remedy for her condition, the judge commented, "Divines, Phisitions, I know they are learned and wise, but to say this is naturall, and tell me neither the cause, nor the cure of it, I care not for your judgement: give me a naturall reason and a naturall remedy, or a rash for your Phisicke."[25] Obviously the situation of the expert medical witness in the sixteenth century was not too dissimilar from that of his modern counterpart.

Significant also is the nature of the criteria employed to define what was and was not to be recognized as mental illness. These criteria were culturally determined, grounded in the cultural environment from which people of high and low station, the educated elite and the common people, drew the reasons on which they accepted or rejected certain forms of mental and emotional disorder as natural occurrences or supernatural marvels. Phenomena described as possession appear to have been relatively common in the sixteenth and early seventeenth centuries.

Joachim du Bellay, the French poet, was in Rome from 1553 to 1557. While there, he apparently observed quite a number of

---

[23] O. Temkin, *The Falling Sickness. A History of Epilepsy from the Greeks to the Beginnings of Modern Neurology*, Baltimore, Johns Hopkins Press, 1945, p. 138.

[24] Hunter and Macalpine (note 7), pp. 68–75.

[25] *Ibid.*, p. 75.

possessed women, a frequent phenomenon at places of pilgrimage. In one of his sonnets included in *Regrets*, du Bellay gives his friend Remy Doulcin, cleric and physician, an exact description of such a fit and his reaction to it.

> Doulcin, quand quelquefois je voy ces pauvres filles
> Qui ont le diable au corps, ou le semblent avoir,
> D'une horrible façon corps et testes mouvoir,
> Et faire ce qu'on dit ces vieilles Sibylles:
> Quand je voy les plus forts se retrouver debiles,
> Voulant forcer en vain leur forcené pouvoir,
> Et quand mesme j'y voy perdre tout leur sçavoir
> Ceux qui sont en vostre art tenuz des plus habiles:
> Quand effroyablement escrier je les oy,
> Et quand le blanc des yeux renverser je leur voy,
> Tout le poil me herisse, et ne sçay plus que dire.
> Mais quand je voy un moyne avesque son Latin
> Leur taster hault et bas le ventre et le tetin,
> Ceste frayeur se passe, et suis contraint de rire.[26]

Some fifty years later, when *Volpone* was produced in 1605, Ben Jonson offered his audience an interpretation of demonic possession. The lawyer Voltore, who wanted to become Volpone's heir, finds himself caught in a trap at the end of Act V. On the advice of Volpone, he simulates an attack of possession.[27]

*Volpone* ... They said, you were possest: fall down, and seem so:
I'll help to make it good. (Voltore falls.)—God bless the man!—
Stop your wind hard, and swell—See, see, see, see!
He vomits crooked pins! his eys are set,
Like a dead hare's hung in a poulter's shop!
His mouth's running away! Do you see, signior?
Now it is in his belly.
*Corvino.*     Ay, the devil!
*Volpone.*     Now in his throat.

[26] Doulcin, when I sometimes see those poor girls, who have, or seem to have the devil in them, move head and body in a horrible manner and act as we are told of the ancient Sybils;
When I see the strongest become weak trying in vain to master their frenzy; and even those who are most skilled in your art [medicine] lose their knowledge;
When I hear their frightful cries and see the upturned white of their eyes, my hair stands on end and words fail me.
But when I see a monk spouting Latin, fondling them belly and breast, this fright passes and I must laugh. (*translation by George Rosen*)
*Poètes du XVIe Siècle, Texte établi et présenté par Albert-Marie Schmidt* (Bibliothèque de la Pléiade), Paris, Gallimard, 1953, p. 484.
[27] Ben Jonson, *Complete Plays* (Everyman's Library), 2 vols., London, J. M. Dent, New York, E. P. Dutton, 1910, vol. 1, p. 484.

| | |
|---|---|
| *Corvino.* | Ay, I perceive it plain. |
| *Volpone.* | 'Twill out, 'twill out! stand clear. See where it flies, |
| | In shape of a blue toad, with a bat's wings! |
| | Do you not see it, sir? |
| *Corbaccio.* | What? I think I do. |
| *Corvino.* | 'Tis too manifest. |
| *Volpone.* | Look! he comes to himself! |
| *Voltore.* | Where am I? |
| *Volpone.* | Take good heart, the worst is past, sir. |
| | You are dispossest. |
| *1 Magistrate* | What accident is this! |
| *2 Magistrate* | Sudden, and full of wonder! |
| *3 Magistrate* | If he were possest, as it appears, all this is nothing. |
| *Corvino.* | He has been often subject to these fits. |

Both du Bellay and Jonson exhibit the critical attitude which would eventually lead to a thoroughly naturalistic view of mental disorder. Jonson, moreover, indicates that in England at least by the beginning of the seventeenth century there was already some erosion of belief in demonic manifestations. Yet, Jonson's vignette of group reaction to such a fit highlights the elements of credulity and auto-suggestibility that were widespread in the populace and which could easily provide a basis for panic irrationality under stressful conditions. Jonson and his audience might ridicule Voltore, but under conditions of social unrest, personal and group frustrations, where there was a psychological need for scapegoats, where the naive faith, the superstitious fears, or the messianic hopes of groups of people were brought to the surface of awareness and raised to fever pitch, the fantastic powers attributed to Satan and his helpers might lead to phenomena of possession or to other forms of mental and emotional disturbance, and to suspicion of bewitchment.

A situation of this kind occurred several years before Jonson's play was produced. In 1599, Samuel Harsnet vividly described the psychological state of Nottingham during a witchcraft scare.

The pulpets also rang of nothing but Divels, and witches wherewith men, women, and children were so affrighted, as many of them durst not stir in the night, nor so much as a servant almost go into his maysters celler about his businesse without company. Fewe grewe to be sicke or evil at ease, but straight way they were deemed to be possessed.[28]

Under such circumstances in this community and others, it is small wonder that there were numerous trials, convictions, and executions of witches at this time.

[28] P. H. Kocher, *Science and Religion in Elizabethan England*, San Marino, The Huntington Library, 1953, p. 134.

The period of the sixteenth and the first half of the seventeenth centuries was one of intense spiritual and psychological stress and strain derived from the alterations that were taking place in the political, social, religious, and intellectual structure of Europe. As frequently happens, such periods know no dearth of demonic possessions, trances, visionary mystics, and projections of group and individual fears and frustrations on individuals or groups that are social deviants or outcasts. The witchhunts of this period must be seen in this light, and it is undoubtedly no accident that the struggles between the Protestants and Catholics from 1560 to 1590 in Eastern France (Lorraine to Franche Comté) were followed by an epidemic of witch trials.[29] Within this context belong as well the psychopathology of sectarianism and fanaticism. These aspects of the period cannot be discussed here, but attention may be drawn to the perceptive contribution to this subject by Paracelsus.[30]

Within the bounds of this chapter it has not been possible to do more than to indicate and to sketch some themes and topics that are relevant for an understanding of the historical problem of mental illness in the Renaissance. The historical study of the mentally ill must be carried on with a constant awareness of the emotional and intellectual climates prevailing in different periods, of the social, political, and ideological factors that have influenced psychiatric theory and practice, and the degree to which crucial problems, such as defining insanity and separating it from the sane mind, have been formulated in contexts organized along moral, theological, legislative, and social dimensions, rather than in medical terms. Adequate handling of these problems, which in considerable measure are still with us, requires a much deeper and broader analysis than can be presented here.

---

[29] Robert Mandrou, *Introduction à la France moderne. Essai de psychologie historique 1500–1640*, Paris, Editions Albin Michel, 1961, pp. 362–364; see also Francis Bavoux, *Hantises et diableries dans la terre abbatiale de Luxeuil. D'un procès de l'Inquisition (1529) à l'épidémie démonique de 1628–1630*, Monaco, Editions du Rocher, 1956; see also Chapter 1 above.

[30] K. Goldammer, "Der cholerische Kriegsman und der melancholische Ketzer" in *Psychiatrie und Gesellschaft. Ergebnisse und Probleme der Sozial-psychiatrie, herausgegeben von H. Eberhardt, D. Ploog, H. Stutte*, Bern und Stuttgart, Verlag Hans Uber, 1958, pp. 90–101.

# CHAPTER FIVE

# IRRATIONALITY AND MADNESS IN SEVENTEENTH AND EIGHTEENTH CENTURY EUROPE

## I

In 1785 Jean Colombier, inspector-general of French hospitals and prisons, summed up the situation of the mentally ill in a succinct, devastating statement.

> Thousands of lunatics are locked up in prisons without anyone even thinking of administering the slightest remedy. The half-mad are mingled with those who are totally deranged, those who rage with those who are quiet; some are in chains, while others are free in their prison. Finally, unless nature comes to their aid by curing them, the duration of their misery is life-long, for unfortunately the illness does not improve but only grows worse.[1]

The validity of this picture is generally supported by other contemporary evidence.[2] Indeed, one historian of psychiatry was led to conclude from such evidence that up to the end of the eighteenth century there were no real hospitals for the care and treatment of the mentally ill, only "places where they were *kept* . . ."[3] Moreover, he attributed the sad lot of the mentally ill to a psychological factor, to the view that they were "step-children of life," a social attitude which survived in the community as an atavistic inheritance from the primitive past.[4]

Yet the situation was not so simple, nor can it be explained solely in terms of an atavistic but potent psychological factor which has

---

[1] René Semelaigne, *Les pionniers de la psychiatrie française avant et après Pinel*, 2 vols., Paris, J. B. Baillière et Fils, 1930, vol. I, p. 85.

[2] *Procès-Verbaux et rapports du Comité de Mendicité de la Constituante 1790–1791*, publiés et annotés par Camille Bloch et Alexandre Tuetey, Paris, Imprimerie Nationale, 1911, pp. 604–605, 624–626, 762; Alexandre Tuetey, *L'assistance publique à Paris pendant la rèvolution*, 4 vols., Paris, 1895, vol. I, *Les hôpitaux et hospices, 1789–1791*, p. 261.

[3] Gregory Zilboorg, *A History of Medical Psychology*, New York, W. W. Norton, 1941, pp. 312–313.

[4] *Ibid.*, p. 312.

operated through the ages. Various sources clearly indicate that not all those who were mentally or emotionally disturbed were treated in the manner described by Colombier. At the very same time there were to be found in Paris, on the street or in cafés, individuals whose peculiarities of dress or behaviour did not attract undue notice. Without much astonishment, Sebastien Mercier encountered a crack-brained maker of projects in a coffee-house, simply remarking that there were others like him who had the public weal at heart "but who unfortunately were addlepated."[5] Diderot's brilliant portrayal of Rameau's nephew presents another social deviant who is a strange mixture of good sense and folly. Delineated with great acuteness and intelligence, he was, according to Diderot, "one of the most bizarre fellows in a country where God has seen to it that there is no lack of them."[6]

Mentally disturbed individuals occur as social personages, as distinctive characters on the social landscape not only in the later eighteenth century but in earlier periods as well. Consciousness of public responsibility for the mentally deranged was limited in the medieval period. Custody of the mentally ill generally rested with their relatives and friends; only those who were considered dangerous or socially disturbing were dealt with by the community. In some places it was customary to receive persons who were acutely disturbed and agitated into general hospitals.[7] Harmless lunatics were permitted to roam the streets and roads; others were whipped out of town.

William Langland described the "lunatick lollers" wandering over the countryside and referred compassionately to their sad state.[8] Another instance in point was depicted by Thomas More in 1533. Writing of a poor lunatic, he stated that he was

one which after that he had fallen into these frantick heresies, fell soon after into plaine open franzye beside. And all beit that he had therefore bene put up in Bedelem, and afterward by beating and correccion gathered his remembraance to him and beganne to come again to himselfe, being thereupon set at liberty, and walkinge aboute abrode, his old fransies beganne to fall againe in his heade. I was fro dyvers good

[5] Sebastien Mercier, *Tableau de Paris*, Hamburg and Neuchatel, 1781, pp. 103–104.

[6] Diderot, *Oeuvres*, Texte établi et annoté par Andre Billy, Paris, Bibliothèque de la Pléiade, 1951, p. 425.

[7] E. Coyecque, *L'Hôtel-Dieu de Paris au moyen age. Histoire et documents.* Tome I. *Histoire de l'Hôtel-Dieu. Documents (1316–1552)*, Paris, H. Champion, 1891, p. 109; R. M. Clay, *The Medieval Hospitals of England*, London, Methuen & Co., 1909, pp. 33–24; Alfons Fischer, *Geschichte des deutschen Gesundheitswesens*, 2 vols., Berlin, F. A. Herbig, 1933, vol. I, pp. 77–78.

[8] William Langland, *The Vision of William Concerning Piers the Plowman*, ed. by Walter W. Skeat, 2 vols., Oxford University Press, 1954, vol. I, pp. 235–237.

holy places advertised, that he used in his wandering about to come into the churche, and there make many mad toies and trifles, to the trouble of good people in the divine service, and especially woulde he be most busye in the time of most silence, while the priest was at the secrets of the masse aboute the levacion ... whereupon I beinge advertised of these pageauntes, and beinge sent unto and required by very devout relygious folke, to take some other order with him, caused him, as he came wanderinge by my doore, to be taken by the counstables and bounden to a tree in the streets before the whole towne, and ther they stripped [striped] him with roddes therefore till he waxed weary and somewhat lenger. And it appeared well that hys remembraunce was goode ineoughe save that it went about in grazing [wool-gathering!] til it was beaten home. For he coulde then verye wel reherse his fautes himselfe, and speake and treate very well, and promise to doe afterward as well. And verylye God be thanked I heare none harme of him now.[9]

A characteristic group among the vagrants and wandering beggars of Tudor England were the Abram-men or Toms o' Bedlam. They were patients discharged from Bethlem Hospital, sometimes not entirely recovered, who were licensed to beg. As a means of quickly identifying those allowed to solicit alms, they wore a metal plate as a badge on the left arm.[10] The Bedlam beggars were a familiar sight throughout England until well into the later seventeenth century. According to John Aubrey,

Till the breaking out of the Civil Warres, Tom o' Bedlams did travell about the countrey. They had been poore distracted men that had been putt into Bedlam, where, recovering to some sobernesse, they were licentiated to goe a-begging . . . they wore about their necks a great horn of an oxe in a string or bawdric, which, when they came to an house for almes, they did wind, and they did put the drink given to them into their horn, where they did put a stopple.[11]

Some of these beggars were undoubtedly impostors, and by 1675 the license to beg had been revoked. The ubiquitous presence of these vagrant mental patients is fully reflected in the literature of the Elizabethan and early Stuart periods. Illustrative are the close of the third scene in the second act of *King Lear* when Edgar announces his

[9] D. Hack Tuke, *Chapters in the History of the Insane in the British Isles*, London, Kegan Paul, Trench & Co., 1882, pp. 56–58.

[10] A badge for beggars was introduced by Gloucester in 1504. See J. H. Thomas, *Town Government in the Sixteenth Century*, London, George Allen & Unwin, 1933, pp. 115–116.

[11] J. Aubrey, *Natural History of Wiltshire*, ed. Britton, Wiltshire Topographical Society, 1848, p. 93.

intention of becoming a Bedlam beggar, and the mad songs,"Loving Mad Tom,'' and "Old Tom of Bedlam.''[12]

## II

Social attitudes towards the mentally and emotionally disturbed have clearly not been uniform at all times but have exhibited modulations and nuances. During the medieval period and the Renaissance, forms of unreason were considered fundamental elements in the fabric of the universe and of man. Medieval men believed that there were compelling forces making for righteousness and perfection, not only within the individual but as well in nature. Moreover, there were norms in nature which should not be violated, for their transgression led to vice. The later Middle Ages, particularly from the thirteenth century onwards, placed madness in the hierarchy of the vices. Another view of mental derangement is implied by the passage in the Prologue of *Piers Plowman* where a lunatic speaks up to praise the ideal king, while an angel speaks from heaven.[13] The implication that only madmen and angels can speak the truth is related to the idea of holy madness, the idea that the ultimate of Christian truth is revealed to Christ's fools, to those who throw themselves utterly on God.[14] Actually this view is very old and is based on the *New Testament* (I Corinthians 1: 18ff.).

Numerous students of the waning Middle Ages have commented on the feeling of melancholy and pessimism which marked the period.[15] A sense of impending doom hung over men and women, intensified by a belief that the end of time was approaching and that the last days were at hand. Nor was this apocalyptic sense of anxiety and urgency unjustified. A world was indeed disintegrating, and in its midst a new order, the shape of which could be seen only dimly, was agonizing towards birth. The feudal order was yielding to absolute monarchy and the early nation state. The all-embracing Christian commonwealth, fashioned and guided by the Church of Rome, was wracked by dissension, hatred, and violence. Abuses in

---

[12] Robert Graves, *The Crowning Privilege*, Harmondsworth, Penguin Books, 1959, pp. 247–266; Percy's *Reliques of Ancient English Poetry*, (Everymans Library), 2 vols., New York, E. P. Dutton, 1906, vol. II, pp. 148–150.

[13] Langland, *op. cit.*, p. 12.

[14] Natalino Sapegno, "La 'santa pazzia' di Frate Jacopone e le dottrine dei mistici medievali," *Archivum Romanicum* 7: 349–372, 1923.

[15] Rudolph Stadelmann, *Vom Geist des ausgehenden Mittelalters*, Halle a S., Max Niemeyer Verlag, 1929, p. 7; Johan Huizinga, *The Waning of the Middle Ages*, Garden City, Doubleday, 1954, pp. 31ff.; W. E. Peuckert, *Die grosse Wende: Das apokalyptische Saeculum und Luther*, Hamburg, Claasen & Goverts, 1948, pp. 103–106, 148–191.

the Church brought forth a desire to return it to its pristine state, to a new birth of life.[16] The need for renewal was felt by many, and to perceptive men the troubles of the time were evidence that the age was at hand which would usher in the Last Judgement. The prevalence and spread of heresy, popular mysticism and personal piety in the later fourteenth and fifteenth centuries were hardly an accident. History was moving towards renewal and divine fulfilment, and men looked for signs and interpretations that warned sinners and encouraged the just.[17]

Within this context madness through its linkage with the revelation of religious truth became a means of achieving knowledge. Madness was a primitive force of revelation, revealing the depths of menace, destruction, and evil that lurked beneath the illusory surface of reality. Unreason revealed the unbearable, the things in the world upon which one could not otherwise bear to look. Madness was on the increase, clearly a sign that the end of the world was at hand. But it was also a cause, for human folly had unleashed forces of disorganization and destruction that could end only in ultimate catastrophe. These forces were loose in a world that had succumbed to self-delusion, a world grown callous, hard-hearted, and rotten with selfishness, where people maddened with fear were pressed to the very brink of existence, a world which must therefore inevitably end in frenzied self-destruction. This theme of cosmic madness is a major element in the art and literature of the fifteenth and sixteenth centuries. Grünewald's Temptation of St. Anthony, the Lisbon painting by Bosch on the same subject, as well as his Millennium, provide evidence on this point. Writers as diverse as Pierre Ronsard and Sebastian Brant dealt with madness as a cosmic phenomenon, as a cause of the troubles which seemed to herald the end of the world. Ronsard combined these ideas in his *Discours des misères de ce temps,* denouncing the senseless errors of belief that turned the world upside down so that reason and justice were replaced by violence,

[16] Friederich Herr, *Aufang Europas: Eine Studie zu den Zusammenhängen zwischen politischer Religiosität, Frömmigkeitstil und dem Werden Europas im 12. Jahrhundert*, Wien-Zürich, Europa Verlag, 1949, pp. 384–575; Herbert Grundmann, *Religiöse Bewegungen im Mittelalter*, 2. verbesserte und ergänzte Auflage, Hildesheim, Georg Olms Verlagsbuchhandlung, 1961; Morton W. Bloomfield, *Piers Plowman as a Fourteenth Century Apocalypse*, New Brunswick, N. J., Rutgers University Press, 1961.

[17] Rupert Taylor, *The Political Prophecy in England*, New York, 1911; Jeanne Bignami-Odier, *Etudes sur Jean de Roquetaillade (Johannes de Rupescissa)*, Paris, 1952; Morton W. Bloomfield, "Joachim of Flora: a critical survey of his canon, teachings, sources, biography and influence," *Traditio 12*: 247–311, 1957; Henry Bett, *Joachim of Flora*, London, Methuen & Co., 1931; Morton W. Bloomfield and Marjorie Reeves, "The penetration of Joachimism into northern Europe," *Speculum* 29: 772–793 (778ff), 1954.

hate, and death, and even God was no longer secure in his own dwelling. Similarly, the episode in Brant's *Narrenschiff*, where a furious storm drives the ship off its course and wrecks it, symbolized a world driven mad and its coming catastrophic end.[18]

Irrationality personified in the figure of Folly loomed large in the Renaissance, but there was little discrimination between species of folly. Erasmus speaks of foolish persons and of the insane without clearly differentiating between them. He has Stultitia remark that the latter are the happiest of all; perhaps he was referring to harmless deranged folk, perhaps to mental defectives. In large measure this identification of stupidity with irrationality reflects an attitudinal shift from the idea of madness as a cosmic phenomenon to the view that madness is born in the hearts of men. Sebastian Brant published his highly popular satire, *Das Narrenschiff*, in 1494. In it he pilloried the follies connected with a whole gamut of human activities. Irrational desires and behaviour become objects of ridicule in this context and are exposed to the laughter and scorn of the world. Folly is no longer a vice and a punishment, but only a defect of human nature appropriate for castigation by the moralist. For Erasmus, irrationality is no longer a menace but a necessity to make the wheels of the world go round. In the *Moriae encomium*, which appeared in 1511, Folly wearing a fool's cap and bells points out how prosaic is her rule in the affairs of mankind.

Even religion seems to have some affinity with a certain kind of folly. Did not Paul say, "The foolishness of God is wiser than men?" This touches on the old Christian theme that the world is folly in the eyes of God, a theme that was revived in the sixteenth century and explored by thinkers as different as Calvin and Sebastian Franck. According to Calvin,

> as long as our views are bounded by the earth, perfectly content with our own righteousness, wisdom and strength, we fondly flatter ourselves, and fancy we are little less than demigods. But, if we once elevate our thoughts to God, and consider his nature, and the consummate perfection of his righteousness, wisdom, and strength, to which we ought to be conformed—what before charmed us in ourselves under the false pretext of righteousness, will soon be loathed as the greatest inequity; what strangely deceived us under the title of wisdom, will be despised as

[18] Nikolaus Pevsner and Michael Meier, *Grünewald*, New York, Harry N. Abrams, 1958, pp. 108, 116–122; Jacques Combe, *Hieronimus Bosch*, Paris, Pierre Tisné, 1946, pp. 44–67; Wilhelm Fraenger, *Hieronymus Bosch. Das Tausendjährige Reich. Grundzüge einer Auslegung*, Coburg, Winkler Verlag, 1947; Sebastian Brant, *Narrenschiff*, herausgegeben von Friederich Zarncke, Hildesheim, Georg Olmsverlagsbuchhandlung, 1961, pp. 98–100; Pierre Ronsard, *Oeuvres complètes* (Bibliothèque de Pléiade), 2 vols., Paris, Gallimard, 1950, vol. 2, p. 548.

extreme folly; and what more the appearance of strength, will be proved to be most wretched impotence.[19]

When compared to the limitless reason of God, human reason is fallacious and irrational. Man can endeavour to reach God by breaking the chains which bind his spirit and thus escaping into the liberty of other-worldliness. However, in so doing he fathoms the depths of unreason and enjoys the highest wisdom. Heavenly bliss is the greatest madness, and is achieved when man transcends the gap between the things of this world and their divine essence, when he reconciles the cruel contradictions which God created.[20]

Thus, in the sixteenth century, from the humanistic as well as from the Christian viewpoint, irrationality is not regarded as having any absolute existence in the world. Folly exists only in relation to some form of reason, whether it be that of God or of man. Indeed, folly itself becomes a form of reason, even though distorted. "... Reason has taught me," wrote Montaigne, "that to firmly condemn something as false and impossible is to assume that one knows the bounds and limits of God's will and of the power of our Mother Nature; and that there is no more notable folly than to reduce these things to the measure of our capacity, and self-conceit."[21]

> Men fail to recognize the malady of their mind. It does nothing but pry and seek, and keeps spinning about incessantly, constructing and becoming enmeshed in its own work, like our silkworms, and is suffocated in it. *A mouse in pitch.* It thinks that it sees from afar some apparent gleam of imaginary light and truth; but while it is running to it, so many difficulties, obstacles, and new quests cross its path that they mislead and intoxicate it.[22]

Folly and madness had become integral elements of the world of people and things. It is certainly no coincidence that the literature of the late sixteenth and early seventeenth centuries is so rich in the portrayal of distraught and insane characters. Quixote, Lear, Ophelia are simply among the best known in a gallery of characters to be found in such diverse sources as the plays of Fletcher, Dekker, Webster, Ford, Jonson, and other Elizabethan and Jacobean writers,

[19] John Calvin, *Institutes of the Christian religion*, 2 vols., Grand Rapids, Michigan, William B. Erdmans Co., 1949, vol. I, pp. 48–49.

[20] Sebastian Franck, *Paradoxa*, eingeleitet von W. Lehmann, herausgegeben von Heinrich Ziegler, Jena, Eugen Diederichs, 1909, pp. 87–88, 121–125; Johannes Tauler, *Predigten*, übertragen und herausgegeben von Dr. Georg Hofmann, Freiburg, Herder, 1961, pp. 309–310, 313.

[21] Montaigne, *Essais* (Bibliothèque de la Pléiade), Paris, Gallimard, 1950, p. 214.

[22] *Ibid.*, p. 1198.

the novels of Rabelais and Scudéry, or the folk-book recounting the exploits of Tyll Ulenspiegel.[23] All of them are in some way an endeavour to understand human nature and behaviour, to answer the question "What is man and what is wrong with him?" In this effort various writers developed comprehensive analyses of the defects and perversities that were felt to underlie and to determine human behaviour. The Jacobean stage is particularly illuminating in this respect. Not only did the interpretations of the Jacobean playwrights reflect their psychological attitudes to the world in which they moved, but as well the views, the attitudes of this world to folly and madness. They were close to the emotional pulse beat of their contemporaries, and the theatrical presentation of individual and group madness was not solely a popular spectacle to attract the crowd. The presentation of Bedlam and its inmates on the stage indicates acceptance of madness within a socially admissible framework, one which combined the elements of the real hospital known to the London audience with the literary theme of the fools' hospital which appeared hardly more than a century after the arrival of the ship of fools.[24]

While Garzoni's hospital of incurable lunatics of 1586 still has some affinity with the ship of fools, it is symbolic of a social environment which was coming into being and which was to prevail until well into the eighteenth century. Fools bound for Narragonia were to be brought into port and after debarkation lodged in accommodations regarded as appropriate for them. Folly and madness were no longer to roam aimlessly. Order was necessary, and the mentally and emotionally deranged were to be subjected to discipline in institutions created for this purpose. For the seventeenth and eighteenth centuries, mental illness was to be exiled from the social scene in both thought and practice.

## III

The shift in social attitudes towards mental illness which took place in Europe at this time can be analysed and explained in terms of socioeconomic, philosophical, and moral factors. Furthermore, this attitudinal change is closely linked with the character of the institutions developed and used during the seventeenth and eighteenth

[23] Monkemöller, *Geisteskrankheit und Geistesschwäche in Satire, Sprichwort und Humor*, Halle a S., Carl Marhold, 1906, pp. 141-162; Robert Rentoul Reed, *Bedlam on the Jacobean Stage*, Cambridge, Mass., Harvard University Press, 1952; Lawrence Babb, *The Elizabethan Malady. A Study of Melancholia in English Literature from 1580 to 1640*, East Lansing, Michigan State College Press, 1951.

[24] Tomaso Garzoni, *L'Hospidale de 'Pazzi incurabili* ... Ferrara, 1586. I have used the Venice reprint of 1617.

centuries for the mentally and emotionally deranged. These institutions must be seen first in relation to the evolution of the hospital. At various periods in history the need to care for the needy and the dependent, the sick and the disabled, has crystallized sufficiently in terms of attitude, theory, and practice so that one may speak of characteristic institutional models. In this sense, the history of the hospital may be seen in terms of certain types that have predominated in given historical periods.[25] While knowledge concerning the healing shrines and the secular healing institutions of antiquity is not complete enough to be generalized, this is not the case for the medieval period. The medieval hospital in all its varied forms was essentially an ecclesiastical institution, not primarily concerned with medical care. This type was eventually replaced in the sixteenth century by another kind of hospital whose goals were not religious but primarily social. That is, the hospital from the sixteenth into the nineteenth century was intended chiefly to help maintain social order while providing for the sick and the needy. To achieve this aim the medieval hospital was to a large extent secularized, placed under governmental control, and its activities were accepted as a community responsibility.

From the thirteenth century onwards the hospital had begun to come increasingly under secular jurisdiction. As cities in Europe prospered, and the bourgeoisie grew wealthy and powerful, municipal authorities tended to take over or to supplement the activities of the Church. In part this was politically motivated, a desire of the civil authorities to be independent of clerical domination or to render the ecclesiastical power subordinate to themselves. This does not mean that the clergy were eliminated. Monks and nuns continued to provide nursing care as they had done before. Administratively, the municipal authorities were responsible for the hospital facilities, but the Church might participate in some way.[26]

Secondly, hospitals and related establishments were considered increasingly inadequate to deal with situations in which problems of health and welfare were considered from a new viewpoint. From the

[25] George Rosen, "The Hospital: Historical Sociology of a Community Institution" in *The Hospital in Modern Society*, ed. Eliot Freidson, Glencoe, Free Press, 1963, pp. 1–36.

[26] Martha Goldberg, *Das Armen- und Krankenkassenwesen des mittelalterlichen Strassburg* (Freiburg Dissertation), Strassburg, 1909, p. 2; E. Becker, "Geschichte der Medizin in Hildesheim," *Archiv klin. Med.* 38: 317, 1899; Sigfried Reicke, *Das deutsche Spital und sein Recht im Mittelalter* (Kirchenrechtliche Abhandlungen), Stuttgart, 1932, pp. 93–97; Wilhelm Liese, Geschichte der Caritas, 2 vols., Freiburg i. B., 1922, vol. I, pp. 231ff; A. de Calonne, *La vie municipale au XV<sup>e</sup> siècle dans le nord de France*, Paris, 1880, p. 126; D. P. Oosterbaan, *Zeven Eeuwen. Geschiednis von het oude en nieuwe Gasthuis te Delft*, Delft, 1954, pp. 86–133.

medieval standpoint the poor, the sick and the infirm might almost be considered necessary for the salvation of the donor of charity. They did the almsgiver a service. Such an attitude, however, accepted the beggar as a necessary part of society and tended to encourage begging. Small consideration was given to bettering the condition of the poor and the infirm. During the late Middle Ages, and especially following the Reformation, the whole approach to this problem changed.[27]

Though the causes of poverty changed but little from the thirteenth to the sixteenth century, economic and social circumstances altered their significance and intensified their impact. As a result the condition of the poor, which was bad in the earlier period, had become worse by the early sixteenth century. Increased unemployment, higher prices, enclosures of peasant lands and related factors brought into being the problems of unemployment, vagrancy, and beggary which confronted governments from the fourteenth to the eighteenth centuries. Vagrancy appeared in the Netherlands and Germany even earlier than in England and France and then assumed increasingly large dimensions in all countries. In their endeavours to eke out a livelihood many vagrants pretended to be crippled or diseased so as to be able to beg with impunity and to obtain admission to a hospital. Some were professional beggars, frequently organized in gangs, such as those that frequented the *Cours des miracles* in Paris.[28] There is little doubt that the large number of poor and sick wanderers over-taxed the facilities available in various communities. Furthermore, whether or not these vagrants were sick, there was a great deal of economic and social distress by the sixteenth century, and the problem was what to do about it. As Simon Fish put the case in 1529 in his famous *Supplicacyon for the Beggars*: "But whate remedy to releve us your poor sike lame and sore bedemen? To make many hospitals for the relief of the poore people? Nay truely; The moo the worse, for ever the fatte of the hole foundacion hangeth on the prestes berdes."[29] Fish also proposed a solution—that the clergy be expropriated and the hospitals and related facilities taken in hand by the king.

In fact, this was the course followed, a course influenced essentially by the Reformation, mercantilist thought, and the rise of absolute monarchy. While the intervention of the civil authorities in matters of

[27] Charlotte Koch, *Wandlungen der Wohlfahrtspflege im Zeitalter der Aufklärung* (Erlangen Dissertation), Erlangen, 1933, pp. 11–29.

[28] Paul Bru, *Histoire de Bicêtre (hospice-prison-asile) après des documents historiques* . . . Paris, 1890, pp. 15–17, 351–353.

[29] Simon Fish, "A supplicacyon for the beggars" (1529), in *A Miscellany of Tracts and Pamphlets*, ed. A. C. Ward, London, Oxford University Press, 1927, p. 16.

welfare and health before the sixteenth century has been noted, the notion that poor relief including medical care was a community, not a Church, responsibility was definitely established during the Reformation period. Those who wished to bring some order into the area of welfare and health, whether Vives in Bruges or Zwingli in Zürich, were guided by the same principles and oriented to the same goals: elimination of beggary, organization of effective agencies of public assistance, and unification of all facilities and resources (hospitals, domiciliary relief, and the like) in the hands of local or national authorities. With variations, the process and its consequences can be seen in England and on the continent.[30]

This desire to bring some kind of order into the field of assistance went hand in hand with an equally great enthusiasm for the repression of idleness. Condemnation of idleness was, of course, not new; indolence and lassitude had been condemned in ancient and medieval thought. The main difference was that the concerns of the seventeenth century were chiefly political and economic, rather than moral. Most seventeenth-century thinkers accepted the idea that governments should use their power to compel all persons capable of engaging in production to do some work. As a result of this view, the economic literature of this period, in England and on the continent, teems with proposals for dealing with idleness. In general, the proposed remedies fall into two groups: the repression of idleness by corrective or punitive legislation, and the creation of institutions which would provide work for the poor and punishment for those who refused to work. From this viewpoint, charity in the medieval sense was to be discouraged, for it led to idleness and beggary. On the other hand, the idle poor, properly employed, would help to make the nation rich and strong.[31]

Economic motivations were reinforced by those arising out of problems of public order. A pamphlet attributed to Dekker, published in 1622 and entitled *Grievous Groans for the Poor*, stated that

> though the number of the poor do daily increase, all things yet worketh for the worst in their behalf; for there hath been no collection for them, no, not these seven years, in many parishes of this land, especially in the country towns; but many of these parishes turneth forth their poor, yea and their lusty labourers that will not work, or for any misdemeanour want work, to beg, filch, and steal for their maintenance, so that the country is pitifully pestered with them.[32]

[30] F. R. Salter, ed., *Some Early Tracts on Poor Relief*, London, Methuen & Co., 1926, pp. 1–31, 97–103.

[31] E. A. J. Johnson, *Predecessors of Adam Smith. The Growth of British Economic Thought*, New York, Prentice-Hall, 1937, pp. 281–297.

[32] George Nicholls, *A History of the English Poor Law. . . .* 2 vols., London, John Murray, 1854, vol. I, p. 253.

Fears were prevalent that such demoralized, rootless groups, bereft of resources, could endanger public order. In the middle of the seventeenth century the London streets were beset by beggars. Vagrants hung on coaches and begged vociferously at the doors of churches and private houses. There are also reports that "under colour of begging in the day time" many "loose and vagrant persons" pilfered and stole, and at night "did break into houses and shops to the scandall of the governmente of this City."[33] Economic crises tended to intensify these conditions and at various times and places led to riots and conspiracies,[34] in France for example at Paris in 1621, at Rouen in 1639, and at Lyon in 1652.

To deal with the problems of the poor, the dependent, and the vagrant, a policy of internment and indoor relief was generally adopted, and institutions developed to put it into practice.[35] Thus there were workhouses and houses of correction in England, *Zuchthäuser* in Germany, and *hôpitaux généraux* in France. Many of these institutions were not new creations; they evolved out of pre-existing facilities and in response to problems that occurred at various times. However, it was in the later seventeenth century and in the eighteenth century that they achieved their fullest development.

The course of events in France is illuminating in this respect. From the sixteenth century on, royal action to deal with welfare and health problems occurred along two lines, one concerned with finances, the other, with administrative discipline and efficiency. A series of reform regulations from 1544 on turned over the administration of each hospital to a commission composed of merchants, burghers, and artisans who had to give an annual accounting to the local representatives of the king. In addition to endowments and other sources of income, the king authorized or imposed a communal tax. The first of these measures was issued by Henri II in 1551. Moreover, to insure financial stability, institutions were merged or were put under a general administrative board. As early as the reign of Henri IV plans had been made to establish such institutions for the relief of the poor and needy, but little was achieved. Finally, in 1656 a royal decree was issued founding the *Hôpital Général* of Paris. (It had been preceded by the welfare bureau of Lyon and its affiliated hospital, which dated from 1613–1614.) The purposes of the institution were threefold. In part they were economic: to increase manufactures, provide pro-

[33] E. M. Leonard, *The Early History of English Poor Relief*, Cambridge, Cambridge University Press, 1900, p. 270.
[34] Germain Martin, *La grande industrie sous le règne de Louis XIV*, Paris, Arthur Rousseau, 1899, pp. 88–90.
[35] Leon Lallemand, *Histoire de la charité*, Paris, Alphonse Picard, 1910, vol. 4, pt. 1, pp. 214–272.

ductive work for the able-bodied, and to end unemployment; in part, social: to punish wilful idleness, restore public order, and rid Paris of beggars; and in part, religious and moral: to relieve the needy, the ill and suffering, to deal with immorality and antisocial behaviour, and to provide Christian instruction.

The creation of such institutions was not limited to Paris. It was a solution to the problem of poor relief which was tried all through France. Indeed, developments at Paris had been anticipated in the provinces. The *Hôpital Général* at Toulouse dated from 1647, that at Béziers from 1654, and that at Caen from 1655. Most of the provincial general hospitals were established under royal authorization. At Le Mans in 1658 all the hospitals, hostels, and *maisons-Dieu* were united into a general hospital by royal letters patent. This trend was carried further by Colbert, and slowly but steadily general hospitals came into existence throughout France.[36]

## IV

The very nature of the functions which these institutions were intended to perform required some kind of involvement with health problems. Though the *Hôtel-Dieu* was supposed to take care of the sick, the *Hôpital Général* took care of old people, people with venereal diseases, epileptics, and the mentally ill. Thus, in the course of time the general hospital combined the characteristics of a penal institution, an asylum, a workshop, and a hospital.

An important purpose was to deal with immorality and antisocial behaviour. All individuals who were defined as asocial or socially deviant were segregated by internment. This prodecure is analogous to the manner in which the leper was treated in the medieval period. By separating such individuals from society, by exiling them to the *Hôpital Général*, they were consigned to a social and psychological situation of which the dominant character is alienation. A separate socio-psychological lifespace was created for those who removed themselves from or transgressed the moral order considered appropriate to their social position, occupation, or family relationship. Thus, on 20 April 1690 regulations were instituted, providing

that children of artisans and other poor inhabitants of Paris up to the age of twenty-five, who used their parents badly, or who refused to work through laziness, or, in the case of girls who were debauched or in evident danger of being debauched, should be shut up, the boys in the Bicêtre, the girls in the Salpêtrière. This action was to be taken on the

[36] Christian Paultre, *De la répression de la mendicité et du vagabondage en France sous l'ancien régime*, Paris, 1906, pp. 155, 209.

complaint of the parents, or, if these were dead, of near relatives, or the parish priest. The wayward children were to be kept as long as the directors deemed wise and were to be released only on a written order signed by four directors.[37]

At the same time arrangements were made to incarcerate prostitutes and women who ran bawdy houses; they were to be kept in a special section of the Salpêtrière.

The consequence of this policy was described by Tenon in his account of the Salpêtrière in 1788.

> The Salpêtrière [he wrote] is the largest hospital in Paris and possibly in Europe: this hospital is both a house for women and a prison. It receives pregnant women and girls, wet nurses and their nurselings; male children from the age of seven or eight months to four and five years of age; young girls of all ages; aged married men and women; raving lunatics, imbeciles, epileptics, paralytics, blind persons, cripples, people suffering from ringworm, incurables of all sorts, children afflicted with scrofula, and so on and so forth.
>
> At the centre of this hospital is a house of detention for women, comprising four different prisons; *le commun*, for the most dissolute girls; *la correction*, for those who are not considered hopelessly depraved; *la prison*, reserved for persons held by order of the king; and *la grande force*, for women branded by order of the courts.[38]

In short, what had happened by the later seventeenth century was not only or simply an evolution of institutions; it was more than that. It was a change in the social perception of irrationality and madness based on criteria derived from a new view of human nature. Today, the idea of a personal self appears as an indispensable assumption of existence. Actually, like other views of human nature, it is in large measure a cultural idea, a fact within history, the product of a given era. At any given period certain criteria are employed to establish normal human nature, as well as any deviation from it.

## V

For the seventeenth and eighteenth centuries, the touchstone was reason and its right use. Reason provided the norm; any divergence from the norm was irrational. Pascal said that he could conceive of a man without hands, feet, or head, but he added, "I cannot conceive of a man without thought; that would be a stone or a brute."[39]

---

[37] Charles W. Cole, *Colbert and a Century of French Mercantilism*, 2 vols., New York, Columbia University Press, 1939, vol. II, p. 480.

[38] Tenon, *Mémoires sur les hôpitaux de Paris*, Paris, 1788, p. 85.

[39] Pascal, *Oeuvres complètes* (Bilbiothèque de la Pléiade), Paris, Gallimard, 1954, p. 1156.

Moreover, from the context in which this statement is made, it is clear that Pascal has rational thought in mind. Montaigne had still been able to accept and to discuss reason and unreason as related, interwoven facets of human behaviour.[40] By the fourth decade of the seventeenth century, however, a sharp line of separation was being drawn between reason and unreason. Descartes, for example, recognized that reason and irrationality are encountered together, that dreams and errors of various kinds are associated with madness, but he decided to rely upon reason and to avoid the irrational.[41] Thus, unreason and madness were exiled in thought on the basis of a conscious decision.

From this viewpoint, irrationality took on a new aspect; it could be regarded as a matter of choice, as a matter of volition. Unreason, and with it insanity, were related primarily to the quality of volition and not to the integrity of the rational mind. Endowed with reason, man was expected to behave rationally, that is, according to accepted social standards. Rational choice was his to make by virtue of his nature. Eccentric or irrational behaviour, actions which diverged from accepted norms, were considered as rooted in error or as derangements of the will and therefore subject to correction.

This view was not limited to France. It is implied in Thomas More's treatment of the lunatic who made a nuisance of himself and is clearly stated in the comments made in 1812 by Mr. Dunstan, the superintendent of St. Luke's Hospital, London. In an interview with William Tuke, Dunstan held that "confinement or restraint may be imposed as a punishment with some advantage, and on the whole, [he considered] fear the most effectual principle by which to reduce the insane to orderly conduct."[42] It was in France, however, that this view received its sharpest expression and its most consequent application.

The comedy of Molière depends on the presentation of the incongruous, the absurd, and the scandalous against an assumption of the normal and the reasonable.[43] According to the *Lettre sur l'imposteur,*

> The ridiculous is the external, perceptible form which the providence of nature has attached to all that is irrational, so as to make us perceive it and compel us to flee it. To understand the ridiculous one must know

[40] Montaigne, *op. cit.,* (note 21), pp. 189–192.

[41] Descartes, *Oeuvres et lettres* (Bibliothèque de la Pléiade), Paris, Gallimard, 1953, pp. 268–273.

[42] Tuke, *op. cit.,* p. 99.

[43] Will G. Moore, "The French notion of the comic," *Yale French Studies No. 23,* 47–53, 1962.

the rationality whose absence it indicates, and envisage its nature . . . we consider ridiculous that which is entirely unreasonable.[44]

This notion of the comic is meaningful because it is closely linked to certain values that were generally accepted by the social and intellectual leaders of the age of Louis XIV.[45]

Highly important in this connection are the concepts of *honnêteté* and *bienséance*. A major characteristic of a person who was considered an *honnête homme* was that he knew himself (*il se connaît*), which meant knowing his position in society and being able to be everywhere at his ease. By recognizing and observing social distances, and thus conforming to one's station in society, one could be accepted as an equal in the company of *honnêtes hommes*. Saint-Simon's praise of Racine on his death in 1699—"*rien du poète dans son commerce, et tout de l'honnête homme*"—is a clear expression of this view.[46] Racine, a man of bourgeois origin—his father was an administrative official of the salt monopoly—adapted himself to society, knew his place in it, and was therefore able to move in it as an equal among equals.

Involved in the notion *honnêteté* is a sense of tact, a sense of what is appropriate and fitting. This component is also influential in the concept of *bienséance*, which was not only a significant esthetic criterion but also an important social value. Rules of social conduct mingled with axioms of morality and notions of social prudery to provide a standard by which all unseemly depths of emotion were concealed and extravagances of behaviour avoided. In these terms, when accepted values and desires are carried to extremes, they appear in an illegitimate and utterly repellent form. A person who acts in this way cuts the lines of communication between himself and other men, thus becoming less than human. Molière's characters—Harpagon the miser, Alceste the misanthrope, and Monsieur Jourdain the parvenu—show what happens when people break loose from rationality, common sense, and moderation. Thus, in his passion for nobility, Monsieur Jourdain forgets his limits and in his folly is a caricature of the bourgeois striving at any price to achieve a higher social rank. Madame Jourdain with her sturdy common sense says plainly: "You are mad, my husband, with all your fancies, and this

[44] Cited by Moore, *op. cit.*, p. 49.

[45] Erich Auerbach, "La cour et la ville," in *Vier Untersuchungen zur Geschichte der französichen Bildung*, Bern, 1951, pp. 12–50; English translation in *Scenes from the Drama of European Literature. Six Essays*, New York, Meridian Books, 1959, pp. 133–179, (particularly pp. 159–167).

[46] Saint-Simon, *Mémoires* (Bibliothèque de la Pléiade), Paris, Gallimard, 1953, vol. I, p. 623.

has happened to you since you began to mingle with the nobility."[47]

The emergence and acceptance of these values and the attitudes accompanying them are aspects of the cultural unity which was achieved in France in the 1660s and which provided the basis for the "splendid century" of Louis XIV, the classical age. At the death of Louis XIII in 1643 the political, social, and intellectual atmosphere of France was shot through with discord, conflict, and partisanship. This unstable situation is reflected in the Fronde, the last vain and muddled attempt of the nobility to resist the centralizing tendencies of the monarchy, as well as in the competitive co-existence of such intellectual and social currents as rationalism, preciosity, romantic heroism, and *tendresse*. The turning point came in 1661 when the young, handsome, exceedingly popular young king finally found himself in the saddle. These currents were now mastered and synthesized to form that homogeneous culture which provided the backdrop for and the environment of the *Grand Siècle*. This synthesis resulted from an alliance between Louis XIV and his court, on the one hand, and the urban bourgeoisie, particularly of Paris, on the other. The strengthening of the royal authority went hand in hand with support of those values which the king shared with his subjects, especially those which would tend to preserve and to maintain the political and social organization of the realm.

The theory of absolute monarchy conceived of the relation between a ruler and his subjects like that of a father to his children. The ruler knew what was best for his people and by means of laws and administrative measures ordered what they should or should not do. As authority personified, it was his duty to guard and protect the purity of his subjects' religion, just as a father should act towards his children. Similarly, the family itself had to be sustained, both the large family of the nation, and the small immediate family, and it was the king's responsibility to see that order prevailed and that all were protected.

Among the measures taken were those dealing with persons considered socially disruptive. Within this portmanteau category were included a motley group, the members of which were characterized by the fact that they had overstepped the limits set by family, social position, religious institutions, the political order, property relations, and the like. These were the people who were sent to houses of correction where they might be brought to their senses. In this way the insane in late seventeenth and eighteenth century France were put into institutions with others who exhibited socially unacceptable or irrational behaviour. The emphasis in this practice was on the

[47] Molière, *Oeuvres complètes* (Bibliothèque de la Pléiade), Paris, Gallimard, 1962, vol. II, p. 541.

social, not the medical aspect. The purpose of internment in a correctional institution was to preserve paternal authority and family honour, to protect the Catholic religion, and to defend the royal power and preserve public order and security.

This does not mean that mental derangement was overlooked by public officials concerned with these matters. It does mean, however, that even when mental or emotional illness was clearly evident, the individual was committed not primarily to receive medical care but rather to protect society and to prevent the disintegration of its institutions. An example is the comment, made in 1703 about the Sieur de clos Bossard, priest and canon of Vannes, who was recognized as mentally ill, "A cleric like that cannot be hidden carefully enough for the honour of religion and the priesthood."[48] The lesser importance attached to the individual's medical condition is perhaps nowhere better expressed than in the record of Marius, a priest from the Trier diocese, who was admitted to an institution in 1701 because of hallucinations and was finally declared insane in 1706. D'Argenson, lieutenant-general of police, wrote of him in 1711: "I also think and rightly fear that when the interest of Religion no longer compels us to hide him from public view, the derangement of his mind might not impose this obligation."[49]

There were variations among the correctional institutions, so that the Bastille, for instance, harboured more serious offenders than the maison de Saint Lazare. Among the inmates of the latter establishment there was a predominance of the middle clergy, members of the lesser nobility, and of the bourgeoisie. All of them are characterized, however, by that apparently indiscriminate mingling of inmates which our own day finds distasteful, inhuman, and even immoral. Saint Lazare, for example, contained not only psychotics and mental defectives, but debauched individuals who offended public morals, abortionists, sorcerers, pornographers, and others who cannot be described more specifically but who today would probably be categorized as psychopaths. There were still others detained for religious reasons (priests, Jansenists, and Protestants), for family reasons, or in a few cases, for reasons of state.[50]

The bond that linked this mixed company was transgression of the social and moral order with the consequence that they were subject to punishment, correction, and incarceration. For example, in 1737 the Sénéchal de Brest addressed a petition to the lieutenant of police requesting that his son be interned. He justified the request on the

---

[48] Jacques Vié, *Les aliénés et les correctionnaires à Saint-Lazare au XVII⁰ et au XVIII⁰ siècles*, Paris, Presses Universitaires de France, 1940, pp. 92–93.

[49] *Ibid.*, pp. 92–93.

[50] *Ibid.*, pp. 237–239.

ground that his son, who was heavily in debt and had been dismissed from the army, threatened by his ignominious conduct to disgrace his family and himself. The facts presented by the father were considered as justifying his request, and the son was committed to the Charité de Château-Thierry.[51] In 1697 a woman named Loriot was incarcerated in the *Hôpital Général* because she was the mistress of a certain Chartier who had "practically abandoned his wife, his family and his duty to devote himself entirely to this miserable creature who has already cost him the better part of his fortune." Furthermore, as he was a customs official, it was feared that public funds might be misappropriated.[52] Here the basis for internment is the desire to maintain the social structure of the family and the moral obligations entailed by marital relations. Molière had already stated this position explicitly with the assertion by Gorgibus that "marriage is a holy and sacred thing, and it's for decent people to begin with it," and Madame Jourdain's claim that she was defending her rights by endeavouring to prevent her husband from squandering his means.[53] The bourgeois family, its property relations and moral obligations, provided the standard of rationality, and those who overstepped the limits were judged accordingly. Had not such a person lost his senses?[54]

Blasphemy, religious profanation, and witchcraft fell into the same category because they disturbed the religious and public order. Not infrequently individuals accused of such offences were also mentally and emotionally disturbed. It is noteworthy that as general hospitals and houses of correction were established, the severity with which these offences were punished diminished. In 1621 Jean Fontanier, who was in turn Protestant, Catholic, Jew, and finally perhaps a Moslem, was burned alive for heresy.[55] A hundred years later, internment in a house of correction would probably have been his fate. In 1700 a certain De Valmont, "who had scandalized all the spectators at the Comédie, not only by his drunkenness, but also by singing psalms and by accompanying this profanation by the most infamous

[51] René Tardif, *Une Maison d'aliénés et de correctionnaires sous l'ancien régime au XVIII<sup>e</sup> siècle. (Histoire de la Charité de Chateau-Thierry)* (Paris Thesis), Paris, Librairie Le Franzoic, 1939, pp. 16–17; Paul Sérieux et Leucien Libert, "Notice historique sur la Charité de Chateau-Thierry, maison d'aliénés et de correctionnaires (d'après des documents inédits)," *Bull. Soc. hist. Soissons*, 11 Feb. 1932, 182–212 (see pp. 191–192).

[52] *Notes de René d'Argenson, Lieutenant Général de Police. Intéressantes pour l'histoire des moeurs et de la police de Paris à la fin du règne de Louis XIV*, Paris, Emile Voitelain et Cie., 1866, pp. 1–3.

[53] Molière, *op. cit.*, (note 47), vol. I, p. 224; vol. II, p. 568.

[54] See for example "L'interdiction," in Balzac, *La comédie humaine* (Bibliothèque de la Pléiade), Paris, Gallimard, 1958, vol. III, pp. 11–81.

[55] Frederic Lachèvre, *Mélanges*, Paris, Honoré Champion, 1920, pp. 60–81.

harangues, was taken to Fort-l'Évêque by order of the King, and
. . . his Majesty will find it satisfactory to keep him there for an entire
month."[56] Even more striking is the case of a woman named
Bertrand.

> Yesterday [wrote d'Argenson] the wife of a lawyer named Bertrand was
> brought to the Châtelet. This woman, having become possessed of the
> idea that she was holy, took communion every day for more than six
> months without any preparation, and even after having eaten. This
> behaviour deserved the most extreme punishment according to the law,
> but as it was rather a case of madness than evil intent, and besides as
> one cannot punish these crimes publicly without doing harm to religion,
> and providing occasion for the evil talk of free thinkers and dissembling
> protestants, it seemed more discreet to have the husband pay for the
> support of this woman in a convent such as it may please the King to
> choose. For I have no doubt that the good example of a regular com-
> munity, associated with kind attention, will restore her deranged mind
> in a few months.[57]

The attitude of the later seventeenth and eighteenth centuries are
summed up in these remarks.

## VI

When Tuke, Pinel, and the other reformers undertook at the end of
the eighteenth century to alter and improve the situation of the
mentally ill, their actions derived from ideas and attitudes that were
different from those prevailing at the beginning of the century.
Irrationality and madness were now the consequences of historical
development and a changing social environment. As civilization
developed and spread through the inexorable march of progress,
irrationality and insanity were conceived as due to a separation of
man from nature, to a deranged sensibility arising from a loss of
immediacy in his relations with nature. Madness was the obverse
of progress.[58]

From this angle of vision, the seventeenth century view that madness was essentially the loss of rational truth, an error to be rectified
by disciplinary measures, could appear only as a gross distortion, a
form of tyranny depriving such individuals of their natural liberties.
Thus the law of 26 March 1790, which suppressed the *lettres de cachet*

---

[56] D'Argenson, *op. cit.* (note 52), p. 29.

[57] *Ibid.*, p. 7; see also pp. 60, 88, 103. For changing attitudes towards witchcraft, suicide, and insanity see Edmond Locard, *Le XVIIᵉ siècle médico-judiciaire*,
Lyon, A. Storck & Cie., 1902, pp. 160–179, 260–271, 428–466.

[58] See Chapter 6 below.

and revoked the *ordres arbitraires,* and the law of 18 August 1792, which dissolved the congregations and orders, led to the disappearance of the correctional institutions. Most of the inmates, except those who were manifestly deranged, were released. The seventeenth century had created institutions to deal with irrational and disturbed behaviour in its own image. Their creation was the product of a social order, characterized by certain dominant attitudes. As the society underwent change, these institutions came to be seen in another light and were ultimately changed into something considered more appropriate. Yet that which was new bore tell-tale characteristics of its ancestry. It was within this context that the concept of mental illness began to be defined at the end of the eighteenth century and in the earlier nineteenth century.

# CHAPTER SIX

# SOME ORIGINS OF SOCIAL PSYCHIATRY
## SOCIAL STRESS AND MENTAL DISEASE FROM THE EIGHTEENTH CENTURY TO THE PRESENT

There is a widespread conviction today that a close interdependence exists between the social environment in which individuals live and the development of mental illness. The nature of this interplay is not yet fully explained, but it is felt that an important factor, possibly the most important single element leading to mental disorder is the failure of society to make adequate provision for conditions essential to the mental health of its members. By its failure to create and to maintain such conditions, society is responsible for stresses resulting from rapid social change or cultural lag which produce mental conflicts and breakdowns.[1]

According to Rennie and Woodward, "mental health cannot be developed in a social vacuum. Powerful factors operate against it as our present society is constituted. ... Mental health can only be achieved in an environment which provides opportunities for self-expression, social usefulness, and the attainment of human satisfactions."[2] From this position it is not far to the standpoint that individual breakdowns are actually indices of a sick society, that society is actually the patient.

> There is a growing realization among thoughtful persons [wrote Lawrence K. Frank in 1936] that our culture is sick, mentally disordered, and in need of treatment.... The disintegration of our traditional culture, with the decay of those ideas, concepts, and beliefs upon which our social and individual lives were organized, brings us face to face

[1] T. A. C. Rennie, "The Psychosocial Position—A Preparatory Statement," in *Integrating the Approaches to Mental Disease*, ed. by H. D. Kruse, New York, Hoeber-Harper, 1957, pp. 147–154; W. A. Harvey, "Changing Syndrome and Culture: Recent Studies in Comparative Psychiatry," *International Journal of Social Psychiatry* 2: 165–171, 1956.

[2] T. A. C. Rennie and L. E. Woodward, *Mental Health in Modern Society*, New York, Commonwealth Fund, 1948, p. 385.

with the problem of treating society, since individual therapy or punishment no longer has any value beyond mere alleviation of our symptoms.[3]

Confronted by this challenge, workers in the medical and social sciences have endeavoured to get to the roots of this problem. If cultural processes and factors are in some way responsible for the occurrence of mental disease, it should be possible to demonstrate them by comparative examination of differing societies and cultural groups of varying complexity. Virtual absence of certain mental disorders in some preliterate groups has been reported by anthropologists, sociologists and psychiatrists. Moloney reported a strikingly low incidence of psychosis among native Okinawans, and attributed it to their mothering methods, especially breast-feeding.[4] A study of Okinawan immigrants to Hawaii, however, has shown they have a rate of psychosis significantly higher than other groups there, even though the same mothering methods are used.[5] What is different is that the Okinawan in Hawaii has to cope with a depreciated social situation; and the stress and trauma attendant upon this change have been incriminated as the responsible elements. Similar observations have been made by Carothers in Kenya,[6] while additional reports bearing on this problem have come from Laubscher, Kardiner, and several others.[7] Related to such reports is the study of the Hutteries, an Anabaptist sect living in the northwestern United States and Canada, which was undertaken because "of their reputation of being virtually free of psychotic breakdowns and antisocial activities. . . ."[8] As it turned out, this belief did not hold up under closer scrutiny.

Another way of studying the relation of factors such as social change and cultural disintegration to mental illness is to study incidence trends, that is, to see whether there is an increase or

[3] L. K. Frank, "Society as the Patient," *American Journal of Sociology* 42: 335–344, 1936; see similar views in S. Schmalhausen, *Our Neurotic Age*, New York, Farrar and Rinehart, 1932; T. D. Eliot, "The Social Philosophy of Trigant Burrow," *Mental Hygiene* 12: 530–548, 1928.

[4] J. C. Moloney, "Psychiatric Observations in Okinawa Shima," *Psychiatry* 8: 391, 1945; *idem, The Battle for Mental Health*, New York, Philosophical Library, 1952, pp. 36–57.

[5] B. M. Wedge, "Occurrence of Psychosis among Okinawans in Hawaii," *Psychiatric Quarterly* 28: 255, 1954.

[6] J. C. Carothers, *The African Mind in Health and Diseases. A Study in Ethnopsychiatry*, Geneva, World Health Organization, 1953.

[7] B. F. G. Laubscher, *Sex, Custom and Psychopathology in a Bantu Tribe*, London, Routledge and Sons, 1937; see also S. Kirson Weinberg, *Society and Personality Disorders*, New York, Prentice-Hall, 1952, pp. 228–232, 255–258.

[8] J. W. Eaton and R. J. Weil, *Culture and Mental Disorders*, Glencoe, Free Press, 1955, p. 22.

decrease of various mental disorders over a period of time. A number of provocative and partly illuminating studies on this theme have recently appeared. Two of these are of interest as representing types of work in this field. In 1948, Halliday brought out his *Psychosocial Medicine,* which offers the thesis that cultural changes over the past seventy-five years have improved the physical health of the population, but have led to a deterioration of mental health as judged by the rising incidence of psychosomatic disorders.[9] Halliday advances the view that in the 1870s the physical atmosphere of infancy was poor, but psychologically it had much to commend it; the reverse is true today. Five years later, in 1953, Goldhamer and Marshall came to a contrary conclusion with regard to the psychoses.[10] Based on an analysis of admissions to Massachusetts institutions for the insane from 1840 to 1950, they concluded that there has been no long-term increase in the incidence of psychoses in early and middle life. Up to the age of fifty, the rates a hundred years ago and today are roughly the same. Whatever differences do exist are due entirely to the large number of admissions today for psychoses of those over fifty. In short, there seems to be no reason to believe that there has been any great change in the conditions causing psychosis at least in the United States, for a period of a hundred years. Goldhamer and Marshall also suggest the possibility that psychosis is a condition, independent of environmental conditions, and due to some physiological or hereditary aberration.

The same year that saw the publication of the study by Goldhamer and Marshall also saw the appearance of a report by the Expert Committee on Mental Health of the World Health Organization.[11] According to this group

> Certain workers who have attempted a study of this matter in economically under-developed countries have the strong impression that psychiatric disorders are much less prevalent in some of these areas. The view has been put forward, for instance, that incidence of psychiatric disorders in tribal Africans is one-tenth of that usually found in Western Europe and North America.

At the same time the report points out that other workers "hold the view that . . . psychiatric disorders have a rather constant frequency in all societies."[12]

[9] J. L. Halliday, *Psychosocial Medicine. A Study of the Sick Society,* London, Wm. Heinemann, 1949.

[10] H. Goldhamer and A. Marshall, *Psychosis and Civilization,* Glencoe, Free Press, 1953.

[11] W. H. O. *Technical Report Series,* no. 73, 1953.

[12] *Ibid.,* p. 73.

The fact is that adequate data on which to form even a relatively valid judgement on these matters are not available in most parts of the world. Without a population census, the frequency of mental disorders cannot be determined. Studies of incidence and prevalence are difficult enough to carry out in countries like England or the United States where institutional facilities and trained personnel are available. Among primitive groups, accurately recorded observations and impressions are the most one can expect. Statistics in such studies must therefore be treated with great caution. Furthermore, judgements expressed and positions taken by various workers concerned with mental disease may be determined by social values of which they themselves may not even be aware.[13]

Nonetheless, one cannot overlook the fact that from the eighteenth century right down to the present day students of mental illness have been preoccupied with the problems sketched above. Two questions appear over and over in writings on the subject. One is "Is the number of the insane increasing?" And an answer to this question is at the same time also an answer to the question "Does civilization cause more mental illness than simpler stages of cultural development?" These questions imply a causal theory, namely, that social relationships and developments are deeply and significantly involved in the causal nexus which produces mental disease. Examination of this theory in historical perspective may therefore illuminate the current situation by enabling us to see its sources and how these may have determined our approach to the problem of mental illness and its causation.

### Social Order and Mental Health

The Enlightenment and the French Revolution dominate the thought of the eighteenth century on the connections between social relationships, social change, and mental disorder. In the intellectual climate of the Enlightenment, Design, Nature, Natural Law, Reason, and Happiness were key ideas. It was accepted as a basic premise that the world had been established by the Creator according to a definite plan, within which there were ordered ways of behaving. These ordered ways were the laws of nature, which redounded to the glory of the Creator and the greater good of man. Indeed, the Creator had so designed the human body that it would flourish when it lived in harmony with its political and social environment, and conversely

[13] Kingsley Davis, "Mental Hygiene and the Class Structure," *Psychiatry* 1: 55–65, 1938; J. R. Seeley, "Social Values, the Mental Health Movement, and Mental Health," *Annals of the American Academy of Political and Social Science*, March 1953, 15–24.

He had so framed the political order that human health was fostered by good social institutions. These views were sharply formulated and applied by Benjamin Rush, that remarkable exponent of the Enlightenment in America. In his "Inquiry into the Natural History of Medicine among the Indians of North America," which was read before the American Philosophical Society in 1774, Rush observed that disease, political institutions, and economic organization were so interrelated that any general social change produced accompanying changes in health.[14] Twenty-five years later, in 1799, Rush published *Three Lectures on Animal Life* in which he reiterated this view.

> In no part of the human species [he said] is animal life in a more perfect state than in the inhabitants of Great Britain, and the United States of America. With all the natural stimuli that have been mentioned, they are constantly under the invigorating influence of liberty. There is an indissoluble union between moral, political, and physical happiness; and if it be true, that elective and representative governments are most favourable to individual as well as national prosperity, it follows of course, that they are most favourable to animal life. . . .[15]

Rush applied this idea to a concrete case in his "Account of the Influence of the Military and Political Events of the American Revolution upon the Human Body."[16] Ostensibly this inquiry was intended to determine how conditions during the Revolution affected its friends or enemies. Actually, the findings were predetermined by Rush's conviction that individual and social health depended on correct political principles.

In general, good health fell to the lot of the revolutionists. "An uncommon cheerfulness prevailed everywhere among the friends of the Revolution. Defeats, and even the loss of relations and property, were soon forgotten in the great objects of the war."[17] More specifically, Rush observed among other findings that hysterical women who favoured the Revolution were cured of their condition. Furthermore, "marriages were more fruitful than in former years and . . . a considerable number of unfruitful marriages became fruitful during the war."[18] Finally, many persons who had been sickly

[14] B. Rush, "An Inquiry into the Natural History of Medicine among the Indians of North America, and a comparative view of their diseases and remedies with those of civilized nations," in *Medical Inquiries and Observations* . . . (second American edition), Philadelphia, Thomas Dobson, 1794, pp. 24–25.

[15] *The Selected Writings of Benjamin Rush*, ed. by Dagobert D. Runes, New York, Philosophical Library, 1947, pp. 167–168.

[16] B. Rush, *Medical Inquiries and Observations . . . op. cit.*, vol. I, pp. 263–278.

[17] *Ibid.*, p. 273.

[18] *Ibid.*, pp. 273–274.

176

were restored to perfect health owing to change of occupation or location as a result of war conditions.

Sharply contrasted with the good health of the patriots was the mental and physical breakdown experienced by those Americans who remained loyal to England. In many instances, they tended to suffer from a hypochondriasis, which was popularly called the "protection fever" and which Rush termed *Revolutiana*. It was called "protection fever" because it appeared to rise from the excessive concern of the Loyalists for the protection of their persons and possessions. This basic cause was accentuated by such other factors as loss of power and influence, the suspension of the Established Church, changes in manners and diet as a result of inflation, and lastly the legal and extra-legal oppression to which the Loyalists were subjected.

These effects upon the human body were produced through the medium of the mind. Thus, the patriots themselves were not necessarily immune to such conditions, and Rush observed that following the peace in 1783, the Americans, unprepared for their new situation, were affected by an excess of liberty.

> The excess of the passion for liberty, inflamed by the successful issue of the war, produced, in many people, opinions and conduct which could not be removed by reason nor restrained by government. For a while, they threatened to render abortive the goodness of heaven to the United States, in delivering them from the evils of slavery and war. The extensive influence which these opinions had upon the understandings, passion and morals of many of the citizens of the United States, constituted a species of insanity, which I shall take the liberty of distinguishing by the name of *Anarchia*.[19]

In short, proper political stimuli, and a stable and ordered society were required for health. Mental health implied a society which would provide the proper stimuli and necessary conditions for well-being, and this was to be found in an agricultural economy such as existed in the young American Republic.[20]

### Revolution, War and Mental Illness

The views of Benjamin Rush are worthy of consideration for two reasons. For one thing, he called attention to the effects on mental health of acute social changes, and secondly he placed such phenomena in a theoretical context, derived partly from his medical, and

[19] *Ibid.*, p. 277
[20] For a more extended discussion of Rush and the context of his ideas see G. Rosen, "Political Order and Human Health in Jeffersonian Thought," *Bulletin of the History of Medicine* 26: 32–44, 1952.

partly from his social views. The impact of wars, revolutions, and similar phenomena as productive of mental illness is reported by other writers, some of whom cite Rush.

Pinel attributed to the French Revolution an increase in the number of persons affected by psychoses. Marc-Antoine Petit of Montpellier reviewed the effect of the Revolution on public health, and considered mental illness in this context.[21] While aware of the views of Rush, he is more circumspect in uncovering a causal connection between various morbid states and the social tensions and stresses created by the Revolution. Nonetheless, Petit likewise agreed that mental aberrations had apparently appeared in the wake of the revolutionary turmoil. The revolutions of 1848 in turn produced similar observations. Brierre de Boismont reported that immediately after the February events and the bloody June battles in Paris, a large number of patients were admitted to the two institutions for which he was responsible.[22] Similarly, Hospital, physician to the Asylum at Clermont-Ferrand, claimed in 1875 that the Franco-Prussian War and the civil war that followed it in 1871 increased the number of cases of psychosis in France.[23]

Another observation of this type was reported by Belgrave in 1867 from Denmark.

> It appears that the evident decadence of Danish power of late years has so afflicted the national sentiment as to induce a general gloom and melancholy. The traveller may walk through Copenhagen without meeting a smiling countenance. A conviction pervades the Danish nation that it is doomed to absorption by Germany; and this feeling has induced a settled melancholy, which the universal wellbeing of the people and the excellence of their government only contribute to make more conspicuous. In social intercourse the destiny of the nation is constantly discussed and lamented. One result of this painful feeling is an increase in the proportion of lunatics to the general population. The predominating form of mental disease is melancholia, characterized in the majority of instances by a distressingly strong tendency to suicide.[24]

The interest of this observation resides as well in the implication that the entire group is mentally ill, and that the psychotics are a product of a widely prevalent pathological condition. In turn, the

---

[21] Marc-Antoine Petit, "Discours sur l'influence de la Revolution française sur la santé publique," in *Essai sur la Médicine du Coeur* . . . Lyon, 1806, pp. 116–157.

[22] Brierre de Boismont, *Des Hallucinations*, Paris, Baillière, 1862.

[23] Hospital, "Souvenirs Retrospectifs de 1871 (Observation Interessante de Lypemanies), *Annales médico-psychologiques* (5 ser.), 3, 11–18, 1875.

[24] T. B. Belgrave, "The Asylums for the Insane in St. Petersburg and Copenhagen," *Journal of Mental Science* 13: 7–19, 1867 (see p. 17).

conditions and the factors which lead to disease arise from or have been intensified by political developments, such as the decline of national power. Clearly, there is also an implication in Belgrave's observation that one approach to a possible understanding of the social etiology of mental disorders would be to consider the occurrence of psychoses in time and space. Actually, efforts of this type had already been undertaken earlier in the nineteenth century. One general line of development was the discussion of the connection between civilization and psychosis; the other was the endeavour to establish a theory of epidemic disease on a historical basis, which would also take account of psychic epidemics.

## Psychic Epidemics and Historical Process

The latter position was most fully developed by Rudolf Virchow, in conjunction with his co-workers R. Leubuscher and S. Neumann. As an extension of his views on the relation of medicine to society, Virchow developed a theory of epidemic disease as a manifestation of social and cultural maladjustment.[25] Reasoning by analogy, he drew a parallel between the individual and the body politic: "If disease is an expression of individual life under unfavourable conditions then epidemics must be indicative of major disturbances of mass life."[26] The disturbances are socio-economic, for example, business depressions, unemployment, and the like. "Don't we see that epidemics everywhere point to deficiencies of society?" Virchow asked. "One may point to atmospheric conditions, general cosmic changes and the like, but in and of themselves these never cause epidemics. They always produce them only where, because of poor social circumstances, people have lived for a long time under abnormal conditions."[27] Virchow differentiated natural and artificial epidemics, basing the distinction on the degree to which cultural factors are interposed between nature and man.

Artificial epidemics he considered as attributes of society which occur not only as a result of social contradictions, but also as significant manifestations of historical trends and development.

[25] For more extensive discussion of Virchow, his co-workers, and the situation within which their ideas were developed see E. H. Ackerknecht, "Beiträge zur Geschichte der Medizinalreform von 1848," *Sudhoffs Archiv* 25: 61–109, 113–189, 1932; *idem, Rudolf Virchow*, Madison, University of Wisconsin Press, 1953; G. Rosen, "What is Social Medicine? A genetic analysis of the concept," *Bull. Hist. Med.* 674–733, 1947.

[26] R. Virchow, *Die Einheitsbestrebungen in der wissenschaftlichen Medizin*, Berlin, G. Reimer, 1849, p. 46.

[27] R. Virchow, "Die Epidemien von 1848," *Archiv für pathologische Anatomie u. Physiologie* 3: 3–12, 1851 (see p. 10).

Nodal points in history, periods of political and intellectual revolution, are marked by such outbreaks of disease.

> History has shown more than once [Virchow declared in August 1848] how the fates of the greatest empires were decided by the health of their peoples or of their armies, and there is no longer any doubt that the history of epidemic disease must form an inseparable part of the cultural history of mankind. Epidemics correspond to large signs of warning which tell the true statesman that a disturbance has occurred in the development of his people which even a policy of unconcern can no longer overlook.[28]

This train of thought was carried to its logical conclusion in 1849.

> Epidemic diseases exhibiting an hitherto unknown character appear and disappear, after new culture periods have begun, often without leaving a trace. As cases in point take leprosy and the English sweat. The history of artificial epidemics is therefore the history of disturbances which the civilization of mankind has experienced. Its changes show us with powerful strokes the turning points at which civilization moves off in new directions. Every true cultural revolution is followed by epidemics, because a large part of the people only gradually enter into the new cultural movement and begin to enjoy its blessings.[29]

Within his socio-historical theory of epidemic disease, Virchow included the psychic epidemics, a phenomenon and a concept in which interest declined and almost disappeared during the later nineteenth century under the influence of bacteriology and biological determinism, but in which interest has again been aroused in the present century.[30] Virchow pointed out that

> The artificial epidemics are physical or mental, for mental diseases also occur epidemically and tear entire peoples into a mad psychotic movement. Psychiatry alone enables the historian to survey and understand the major fluctuations of public opinion and popular feeling, which on the whole resemble the picture of individual mental illnesses.[31]

While Virchow examined the relations of psychosis to contemporary emotional states, other physicians who shared his views to a greater or lesser degree investigated the same problem historically. Neumann refers approvingly to a work by Ideler on religious madness, and to Leubuscher's adaptation of Calmeil's study of psychosis over a period

---

[28] *Medizinische Reform*, p. 45.
[29] Virchow, *Einheitsbestrebungen*, p. 47.
[30] R. Virchow, *Wissenschaftliche Abhand.*, Bd. I, p. 56.
[31] *Ibid.*

of four hundred years. "Both have demonstrated," he wrote, "how the various forms of lunacy are essentially determined by the contemporary state of civilization of a society."[32]

This discussion of psychic epidemics was stimulated by the appearance in Berlin at the time of a child who performed miracles.[33] It was alleged that this child could cure illness, and it was reported to have been visited by some 10,000 people daily among whom 3,000 to 4,000 "cures" were effected. Occurrences of this type are not uncommon in history in the wake of military defeats or as a reaction to suppressed revolutions. Similar phenomena can be observed in Germany after the First World War, in England under Cromwell's regime, or in Czarist Russia after the defeat of the 1905 Revolution.[34] Virchow explained this event as an abnormal expression of suppressed revolutionary energies that had not been discharged. His interpretation must be seen in terms of a concept of an "organic" historical process, clearly a concept with Hegelian overtones. Virchow tended in general to view the psychological reactions observed during and after the 1848 revolution as a psychic epidemic caused by interference with the historical process.[35]

Unfortunately, this theory of psychic epidemics and its implications have never been explored in any systematic fashion. In our own time a few authors, among them Hellpach, Scheunert and Sigerist, have touched several limited aspects of the problem.[36] There is no doubt that such studies are beset with great difficutlies; nevertheless, a thorough systematic study would be fruitful for an understanding of mental disease in time.

Parenthetically, it is interesting and amusing to note at least one contemporary instance where an attempt was made to pin the label of mental disease on the 1848 democrats. The *Athenaeum* of 23 March 1850 carried the following note:

[32] S. Neumann, "Zur medizinischen Statistik des preussischen Staates nach den Acten des statistischen Bureaus für das Jahr 1846," *Archiv für pathologische Anatomie u. Physiologie* 3: 13–141, 1851 (see p. 89).

[33] R. Leubuscher, *Medizinische Reform*, pp. 207–208; see also Abarbanell, *Medizinische Reform*, p. 216, who denies the character of a psychic epidemic to these events.

[34] See, for example, N. Cohn, *The Pursuit of the Millennium*, Fairlawn, Essential Books, 1957, pp. 315–372, New York, Harper Torchbooks edition, 1961. This section deals with the "Free Spirit" in Cromwell's England, the Ranters and their literature.

[35] R. Virchow, "Die Epidemien von 1848," *Archiv für pathologische Anatomie u. Physiologie* 3: 1–12, 1851 (see p. 5).

[36] W. Hellpach, *Nervenleben und Weltanschauung. Ihre Wechselbeziehungen im Deutschen Leben von Heute*, Wiesbaden, J. F. Bergmann, 1906; G. Scheunert, "Kultur und Neurose am Ausgang des 19. Jahrhunderts," *Kyklos* 3: 258–272, 1930.

In Berlin, a curious subject for a thesis has been found by a student in medicine, the son of M. Groddeck, the deputy, seeking his degree. M. Groddeck has discovered a new form of epidemic, whose virus has of late circulated throughout the Continental Nations with a rapidity contrasting strongly with the solemn and stately march of cholera. Its development, indeed, has been all but simultaneous in the great European Capitals, but we know not that it has before occurred to anyone to treat it medically. M. Groddeck's thesis publicly maintained, is entitled "De morbo democratico, nova insaniae forma" (On the democratic disease, a new form of insanity). The Faculty of Medicine, with the usual dislike of Faculties of Medicine to new discoveries, refused admission, it appears to this dissertation, but the Senate of the University, on M. Groddeck's appeal, reversed their decision.[37]

## Madness and Civilization

The element of bias is only too obvious in the designation of democratic beliefs as a form of mental disease. This is not unlike the practice of designating as mad those who do not agree with one, or who say or advocate things that seem bizarre or obscure. This judgemental aspect, while perhaps not so evident, has also been present in the discussion of the relation between civilization and mental illness carried on for more than a century and a half. Despite such an element of bias, it has been the investigation of this problem which in a large sense has led to current studies on the epidemiology of mental disease, and the concern with social stress in the causation of such illness.

Broadly speaking mental illness emerged as a proper subject for objective medical investigation in the eighteenth century. As asylums were created and data collected on the patients in them, the question was raised: Is insanity on the increase? The problem derived from a number of sources. For one, there was the nature cult of the eighteenth century which viewed the present as a degenerate retrogression from a golden age of natural virtue. Any further development of civilization was found to increase manifestations of degeneracy. Then, this was also the period of the early Industrial Revolution with its attendant evidences of social maladjustment. The alleged increase in the incidence of insanity was viewed as another aspect of this situation, and physicians, philosophers, and others speculated on the question whether man would be able to adapt successfully to the increasing complexities of society. Current viewers with alarm and prophets of impending doom are simply the most recent in a long line. The literature on the question of mental illness and civilization is large, and it will not be possible to consider every writer on the

[37] "A New Form of Insanity," *American Journal of Insanity* 8: 195, 1851.

subject. Several have been chosen for discussion to illustrate the main lines of development.

The situation in the early nineteenth century is well illustrated by two British authors, both of whom published works on mental illness in 1828. According to Sir Andrew Halliday,

> The finer the organs of the mind have become by their greater develop-
> ment, or their better cultivation, if health is not made a part of the
> process, the more easily are they disordered. We seldom meet with
> insanity among the savage tribes of men; not one of our African
> travellers remark their having seen a single madman. Among the slaves
> in the West Indies it very rarely occurs; and, as we have elsewhere shown
> from actual returns, the contented peasantry of the Welsh mountains,
> the western Hebrides, and the wilds of Ireland are almost free from this
> complaint. It is by the over-exertion of the mind, in overworking its
> instruments so as to weaken them, while the healthy functions of the
> body are, by a kind of reaction, interfered with, that insanity may be
> said to take place in a great number of instances; while, in others, it is
> the over-exertion of the bodily powers, and the derangement of the vital
> functions, that react upon the brain, and derange its operations.[38]

A different view was taken by George Burrows, who accepted the social causation of mental disease. He pointed out that

> many of the causes inducing intellectual derangement, and which are
> called moral, have their origin not in individual passions or feelings, but
> in the state of society at large; and the more artificial, i.e., civilized,
> society is, the more do these causes multiply and extensively operate.
> The vices of civilization, of course, most conduce to their increase; but
> even the moral virtues, religion, politics, nay philosophy itself, and all
> the best feelings of our nature, if too enthusiastically incited, class among
> the causes producing intellectual disorders. The circumstances in-
> fluencing their occurrence are to be sought in all the various relations of
> life, in constitutional propensities, and, above all, perhaps in education.[39]

Among the social causes, he also calls special attention to situations of rapid change such as revolutions.

> Insanity bears always a striking relation to public events. Great political
> or civil revolutions in states are always productive of great enthusiasms
> in the people, and correspondent vicissitudes in their moral condition;

[38] A. Halliday, *A General View of the Present State of Lunatics and Lunatic Asylums, in Great Britain and Ireland, and in some other Kingdoms*, London, Thomas and George Underwood, 1828, pp. 79–80.

[39] G. M. Burrows, *Commentaries on the Causes, Forms, Symptoms and Treatment, Moral and Medical, of Insanity*, London, Thomas and George Underwood, 1828, p. 18.

and as all extremes in society are exciting causes, it will occur, that in proportion as the feelings are acted upon, so will insanity be more or less frequent.[40]

In this connection he refers to Pinel, Halloran, and comments on the writings of Benjamin Rush.

Of considerable interest are his sharp remarks on the alleged absence of mental disease among uncivilized and primitive peoples. Repudiating this belief, he pointed out that the noble savage, who "no rule but uncorrupted reason knew," was actually no more than a fiction. Furthermore, the reason why mentally ill people were not found among primitive groups was that they were destroyed without hesitation. Men everywhere, Burrows concluded, were "liable, among other ills, to insanity." But he was also aware that the evidence on many of the points which he considered was too vague to afford any conclusion.

Not quite a decade later however, statistical data were becoming available, so that W. A. F. Browne, medical superintendent of the Montrose Asylum, was able to cite them in support of his belief that insanity was on the increase due to the development of mechanical civilization.[41]

By the calculations of Sir A. Halliday which, although perhaps merely approximations to the truth, have the merit of being the only data we possess, it appears that the proportion of the insane to the sane population of Europe, is 1 to 1,000. In Wales, the proportion is 1 to 800, in Scotland 1 to 574. The Americans, so closely allied to us by descent, language, national character, and customs, it is computed by Dr. Brigham, present 1 lunatic in every 262 inhabitants. This disparity probably depends on the rapid acquisition of wealth, and the luxurious social habits to which the good fortune of our transatlantic brethren has exposed them. With luxury, indeed, insanity appears to keep equal pace. Nay the opinion has been hazarded, that as we recede, step by step, from the simple, that is savage manners of our ancestors, and advance in industry and knowledge and happiness, this malignant persecutor strides onward, signalizing every era in the social progress by an increase, a new hecatomb, of victims. ... With civilization ... come sudden and agitating changes and vicissitudes of fortune; vicious effeminacy of manners; complicated transactions; misdirected views of the objects of life; ambition, and hopes, and fears, which man in his primitive state does not and cannot know. But these neither constitute, nor are they necessarily connected with civilization. They are defects, obstacles which

[40] *Ibid.*, p. 20.

[41] For the development of statistics as applied to health problems in general see G. Rosen, "Problems in the Application of Statistical Analysis to Questions of Health: 1700–1880," *Bull. Hist. Med.* 29: 27–45, 1955.

retard the advancement of that amelioration of condition towards which every discovery in arts, or ethics, must ultimately tend. To these defects, and not to the amount of improvement, or refinement of a people is insanity to be traced.[42]

The question may be raised then, does insanity increase in consequence? To this problem, Browne addressed himself pointing out that it is one of the most interesting questions to be decided by statistics. While he believed that mental illnesses had increased, Browne admitted that "more careful examination is, without doubt required to establish the proposition."[43] Furthermore, he considered the incidence and prevalence of insanity by social class (rich—poor) and by occupation. While he inclines to the view that the wealthy and better educated groups were more likely to have more mental illness, here too he had to admit that "We do not possess sufficient data to determine the relative proportions of the insane rich and the insane poor."[44] At the same time, Browne discussed the available statistical data, especially that of Esquirol, Georget, and other French psychiatrists. He raised questions concerning the validity of the data, the manner in which they were obtained and a number of other problems which still concern those who study the incidence and prevalence of mental disease. Finally, he dealt with the relation of political systems, social commotions, and the like to insanity. Observing that it was not the form of government which caused mental illness he went on to point out that it was rather

the mode in which it is administered, the social relations, the tranquillity or the fluctuations in the habits, value of property and rank, the degree of prosperity, and the moral and religious condition which arise out of it, must obviously do so. In that state, then, be it monarchical or republican, in which the sources of moral agitation and excitement are most abundant, will the proportion of insanity be the highest.[45]

While the baneful effects of civilization were generally accepted on faith or supported by statistics of dubious validity, observations were recorded which tended to contradict this view. When P. L. Panum made his observations on measles during an epidemic in 1846, he also recorded some observations on the mental health of the population.

[42] W. A. F. Browne, *What Asylums Were, Are, and Ought To Be: being the substance of five lectures delivered before the managers of the Montrose Royal Lunatic Asylum*, Edinburgh, Adam and Charles Black, 1837, pp. 52–53.
[43] *Ibid.*, pp. 54–55.
[44] *Ibid.*, p. 59.
[45] *Ibid.*, p. 63.

Since it has been proved that the frequence of mental diseases is generally in direct proportion to civilization and its accompanying social collisions, it might be surmised that these diseases are extremely rare on the Faroes, inasmuch as civilization has certainly not attained a high degree there, and the social collisions so agitating to the mind, under the patriarchal conditions which prevail, are proportionately very few. But on the contrary, there is hardly any other country or indeed any metropolis, in which mental diseases are so frequent in proportion to the number of people as the Faroes.[46]

Despite such discrepant observations, however, the view persisted that insanity must be increasing because society was becoming more complex. Even where there was a clear awareness that the data necessary for a valid judgement were lacking, confirmation was sought by reasoning. Edward Jarvis, an American physician, who was very active in the reform of mental institutions as well as in related matters, wrote in 1851 that

it is impossible to demonstrate, whether lunacy is increasing, stationary, or diminishing, in proportion to the advancement of the population, for want of definite and reliable facts, to show, how many lunatics there are now, and still less to show, how many there have been at any previous period. Wanting these two facts, we cannot mathematically compare the numbers of insane or their proportions to the whole people at any two distinct periods of time, and thus determine whether lunacy increases or retrogrades.[47]

But since the facts were not available or adequate to answer the question, he turned to an examination of the causes of mental illness to see "whether the causes are more or less abundant, and act with more or less efficiency now than formerly, and are likely to produce more or less lunacy."[48] Since the causes derived from mental over-exertion, insecurity, social maladjustments, and the like, Jarvis was able to support his belief. Thus, he concluded:

Insanity is then a part of the price we pay for civilization. The causes of the one increase with the developments and results of the other. This is not necessarily the case but it is so now. The increase of knowledge, the improvements in the arts, the multiplication of comforts, the amelioration of manners, the growth of refinement, and the elevation of morals, do not of themselves disturb men's cerebral organs and create mental

---

[46] P. L. Panum, *Observations Made during the Epidemic of Measles on the Faroe Islands, in the Year 1846*, New York, Delta Omega Society, 1940, p. 13.

[47] E. Jarvis, "On the Supposed Increase of Insanity," *American Journal of Insanity* 8: 333–364, 1851–52 (see p. 333).

[48] *Ibid.*, p. 349.

disorder. But with them come more opportunities and rewards for great and excessive mental action, more uncertain and hazardous employments, and consequently more disappointments, more means and provocations for sensual indulgence, more dangers of accidents and injuries, more groundless hopes, and more painful struggle to obtain that which is beyond reach, or to effect that which is impossible.

The deductions, then, drawn from the prevalence and effects of causes, corroborate the opinion of nearly all writers, whether founded on positive and known facts, on analogy, on computations or on conjecture, that insanity is an increasing disease. In this opinion all agree.[49]

Similar views are to be found in England, Germany, and other countries. For example, John Hawkes, assistant medical officer to the Wilts. County Asylum wrote in 1857:

I doubt if ever the history of the world, or the experience of past ages, could show a larger amount of insanity than that of the present day. It seems, indeed, as if the world was moving at an advanced rate of speed proportionate to its approaching end; as though, in this rapid race of time, increasing with each revolving century, a higher pressure is engendered on the minds of men and with this; there appears a tendency among all classes constantly to demand higher standards of intellectual attainment, a faster speed of intellectual travelling, greater fancies, greater forces, larger means than are commensurate with health.[50]

These in turn are linked to other causes such as ill health, financial embarrassments, over-anxiety, excessive application to business and the like, causes that are not restricted to the upper classes of society. Indeed, Hawkes stresses the need for a wider field of study which would embrace as well "the middle and the lower walks of life."[51]

This belief in the rising tide of madness is a theme that is played with numerous variations. In Germany, Wilhelm Griesinger asserted that different nations were variously predisposed to mental ill health. Yet, he too felt that overall mental illnesses had actually increased. Griesinger did not accept political influences as a cause of insanity, but considered them as a factor in providing the symptom content manifested by patients. But while he accepted the position that the advance of civilization had brought about an increase of insanity, he was equally a product of his time in his belief that this adverse result was balanced by progressive consequences of civilization.[52]

[49] *Ibid.*, pp. 363–364.
[50] J. Hawkes, "On the Increase of Insanity," *Journal of Psychological Medicine and Mental Pathology* 10: 508–521, 1857 (see p. 509).
[51] *Ibid.*, p. 511.
[52] W. Griesinger, *Pathologie und Therapie der Psychischen Krankheiten,* second edition, 1861, p. 144.

Ackerknecht has made the provocative suggestion that the belies in a progressive increase of insanity during the nineteenth century if an aspect of the belief in progress, that the belief was firmly held even when there was no firm basis in fact because the greater prevalence of mental illness was evidence of more advanced civilization, since civilization was considered a basic element in its causation. As Jarvis put it, insanity was the price paid for the high level of civilization attained by nineteenth century Western European culture as a consequence of the Industrial Revolution. In this sense, the problem of mental illness was no different than the contemporary problems of physical disease.

The consequences of this position were recognized by Hawkes when he proposed a preventive programme for community mental health. Mental hospitals, though necessary, he pointed out, will not check the spread of mental disorders. To achieve this aim prevention is required. Just as "we appoint officers of public health," he continued, "whose business it is to hunt out fever and contagious maladies, the offspring of ignorance and neglect, and to trace them to their lair, and to strangle them at birth, . . . let us think . . . how the same principles of prevention may be applied to diseases of the mind."[53] Action towards this end must be organized on a community basis, making use of "resources among all classes of society." The basis of a preventive programme must be a social structure devoid of stresses and maladjustments, in which all classes receive their proper due, and where it is recognized that the basis of society is "formed by the stout hearts and strong arms of the mass of labouring poor."[54] The consequences which follow from these premises provide the specifics of an action programme. "Let us . . . endeavour to promote mental sanitary reform," Hawkes proposed, by

> combining to introduce those changes in the social condition, more especially of the working classes, by which that high pressure system, so prejudicial to the health of the mind, shall be slackened, and the strain which it occasions relaxed. Let these people have those proper periods for repose and recreation, without which man becomes a mere machine. Let the hours of labour be abridged, and let childhood no longer share the curse of the fall. Let the multitudes who have not the means or opportunities of learning from books, be instructed by public teachers the first principles of mental as well as physical hygiene.[55]

Clearly, by the middle of the nineteenth century the problem of mental disease, in terms of incidence, prevalence, trend, causation,

[53] Hawkes, *op. cit.*, pp. 519–520.
[54] *Ibid.*, p. 520.
[55] *Ibid.*, p. 520.

prevention, and community action, had been broached, and various aspects with which we are today concerned had been examined in some respects. Many of these questions clearly could not be settled due to inadequate knowledge and techniques. Yet the theories and points of view which were put forth are still with us, are still being discussed and examined. One widely accepted theory was that mental disorder was in some way related to social instability and maladjustment. Within this broad theoretical framework, attention was focused on the element of rapid social change as an important, possibly basic causal factor. In a period of rapid industrialization, this is hardly surprising. And while the alleged increase of insanity was considered an almost inevitable concomitant, there were voices raised to question whether the price was actually necessary or worthwhile. Finally, the problem of differential social incidence and prevalence was formulated, and thought was given to ways of investigating it so as to throw light on the causation of mental disorder.

Considering whether or not insanity was on the increase, Edgar Sheppard, in 1873, wrote that

> Apart from statistical evidence (which is often very untrustworthy), our inclination to one side or the other will be much coloured by the meaning which we attach to that conventional term "civilization." If it implies all that our optimists say it implies—the practice of all the virtues and a greater capacity for all that is good and noble—then you will be disposed to hold to the opinion that insanity *cannot* be on the increase. But there is another side to the picture. To me . . . "civilization" may but express wear and tear, and high pressure. And the product of these is deterioration of nerve-tissue, and general impairment of our material organizations . . . civilization is really a term singularly inexact and indefinite, and admitting of great latitude of interpretation. It involves an improvement, no doubt, of the social wheat; but there is to be considered also its inevitable correlative—a frightful multiplication of the social tares. If our schools and seminaries, and hospitals and churches have multiplied, so also have our casinos and gin-palaces, and betting-rings; the whole area of speculation is a hundred-fold enlarged; all the energies of life are multiplied and intensified; and men shriek at each other on the Stock Exchange who used to converse in quieter and less "civilized" times.[56]

Sheppard then proceeded to discuss the problem of differential prevalence.

> There has been a great difference of opinion as to whether insanity is more frequent in the male or in the female, and the large aggregation of

[56] E. Sheppard, *Lectures on Madness in its Medical, Legal, and Social Aspects*, London, J. & A. Churchill, 1873, pp. 3–5.

women in our different asylums has led to a belief that they are more obnoxious to mental alienation than ourselves. But a source of fallacy is obvious; *existing* cases do not represent *occurring* cases. Women do not die, and do not recover as we do; hence they accumulate. It is pretty certain that the *occurring* cases in the two sexes are about equal; perhaps an excess slightly obtains in the males. Insanity occurs more frequently between the ages of 30 and 40 than any other decade. It is more frequent in the summer than in the winter months, and among the agricultural than the town populations. Regarded superficially this somewhat circumstance is somewhat puzzling, and in contradiction to what one would naturally expect. The vices and wear and tear of great cities, with all the attendant evils of dense gregariousness, would seem to invite disease in a larger ratio than in the country.[57]

Furthermore, he pointed out, the agricultural population was worse fed than the urban inhabitants, their occupation did not provide adequate intellectual stimulation, and that the children were starved and stunted. Consequently, they tended to suffer from dementia and imbecility. Here was a clear hint that an approach to a possible understanding of the relation of social factors to mental disorders would be to consider the distributions of various mental illnesses in time and space, and to see how they were connected with the characteristics of various population groups.

Studies of this kind began to make their appearance towards the end of the nineteenth century in the United States and in England. The transitional character of these analyses is evident in the review, in 1887, by Judson B. Andrews of the distribution of the insane in the United States.

In the northern belt the New England states take the lead with one insane person to every 359 of the inhabitants. This decreases till we reach the newer States and Territories, with one insane person to every 1,263 inhabitants. ... These figures emphasize the statement that the pioneers of our newer settlements are the more hardy and vigorous citizens, and that the feeble and dependent are left in their former homes, to enjoy the comforts of the hospitals and asylums, which are the special growth of the older civilization.

In this connection he also discussed the occurrence of mental disease among Negroes.

In the Negro race the proportionate increase of insanity is far greater than in any other division of the population. From 1870 to 1880 there was an increase in the census of the coloured race of 34·85 per cent, while for the same period there was an increase of 285 per cent of the

[57] *Ibid.*, p. 13.

insane. This large multiplication has occurred since emancipation from slavery and the consequent changes in conditions and life. The causes are briefly told: enlarged freedom, too often ending in licence; excessive use of stimulants; excitement of the emotions, already unduly developed; the unaccustomed strife for means of subsistence; educational strain and poverty. The total census of the other coloured races is 172,000, with 105 insane, or one insane person to every 1,638. The small percentage of insane among the aborigines and Chinese is fully in accord with the observations of writers upon the causes productive of mental disease. There is much less of the refinement of civilization; less competition and struggle for place, power or wealth, and as a consequence, less tendency to mental deterioration.[58]

Andrews' discussion contains in essence the elements of the ecological study of mental disorder, which in our own time has been and is being vigorously pursued. His theory of a gradient from the frontier to the older settlements is derived from studies carried out by A. O. Wright in 1881 in Wisconsin. Presenting the result to the National Conference of Charities and Correction in 1884, Wright had said

Having made a census of the insane under public care in Wisconsin, the writer, on reducing the number by counties to the ratio to the population of the several counties, was astonished to find here a general law: That the older settled counties had the largest ratio of insane to the population, and that the ratio steadily decreased and reached the smallest ratio in the pioneer counties on the north. This seemed to show that a new country has a smaller proportion of insanity than an old country.[59]

Wright believed that this law is due to the circumstance that new settlements are made by a selected population, mostly young and middle-aged people sound in mind and body. However, in the second generation, all the varied and complex causes that produce mental disorders are at work. At the same time, he also said: "It is often claimed that insanity is a disease of civilization, and that it is increasing because civilization is increasing. This I think to be a mistake."[60]

The differential approach to the study of mental illness was carried further in the twentieth century along the lines previously indicated. In 1902, Daniel G. Brinton, professor of American archaeology and

---

[58] J. B. Andrews, "The Distribution and Care of the Insane in the United States," *Transactions of the International Medical Congress*, Ninth session, 1887, V, pp. 226–237.
[59] A. O. Wright, *Proceedings of the National Conference of Charities and Correction*, 1884.
[60] *Ibid.*

linguistics at the University of Pennsylvania, in a study of ethnic psychology, differentiated certain mental disorders as characteristic of the lowest stages of culture, while others belonged to civilized groups.

> It is a popular error in scientific circles that diseases of the nervous system increase with civilization. The opposite is true. The lowest stages of culture are far more pathological than the higher, in this, as well as in most respects. True that certain neuroses belong to cultured peoples; but morbid emotional states are especially prevalent in lower conditions.[61]

On the other hand, "Diseases of nervous and mental exhaustion belong exclusively among nations of advanced culture."[62]

Basing himself upon the studies of Wright, William A. White, in 1903, contended that "insanity increases in proportion as the stresses incident to the struggle for existence become mental stresses. . . ."[63] He illustrated this view by the statistics obtained from the newly-settled American states. As the crucial point he cited the mining states of the West, such as California, where the prevalence of mental diseases was higher. In this connection, it is worth noting a study of insanity and suicide published by Pilgrim in 1906. This author found that, for the years 1900–04 the suicide rate in 50 large American cities varied from 16 to 20 per 100,000. During the same period, in San Francisco suicides occurred at the rate of 50 to 72 per 100,000. San Francisco at that time differed from other cities through its excess of males, its high percentage of foreign-born, and its general social character which was still close to the frontier.[64]

During this period, a number of studies with similar approaches appeared in Great Britain. Among these may be mentioned those by J. F. Sutherland (1901), W. R. MacDermott (1908), and W. R. Dawson (1911).[65] Illustrative is MacDermott's article. He raised the pertinent question whether the variation in rates in different districts

[61] D. G. Brinton, *The Basis of Social Relations. A Study in Ethnic Psychology*, New York and London, G. P. Putnam's Sons, 1902, p. 112.

[62] *Ibid.*, p. 118.

[63] W. A. White, "The Geographic Distribution of Insanity in the United States," *Journal of Nervous and Mental Disease* 30: 257–279, 1903 (see p. 267).

[64] C. W. Pilgrim, "Insanity and Suicide," *American Journal of Insanity* 63: 349, 1906–07.

[65] J. F. Sutherland, "Geographical Distribution of Lunacy in Scotland," *British Association for the Advancement of Science*, Glasgow, 1901; W. R. MacDermott, "The Topographical Distribution of Insanity," *British Medical Journal*, Sept. 26, 1908, 950; W. R. Dawson, "The Relation between the Geographical Distribution of Insanity and that of Certain Social and other Conditions in Ireland," *Journal of Mental Science* 57: 571–597, 1911.

of Ireland does not undermine the commonly held opinion that insanity is inherited. He compared the rates for districts of Ireland in which the same families had resided for several generations. Thus he had a constant population factor, and was able to turn attention to other elements in the situation.

Contemporaneously, in Germany, Hellpach endeavoured to link social class with certain forms of mental illness.[66] He differentiated the psyche of the proletariat and the bourgeoisie, and endeavoured to show what forms of mental illness were to be observed in each social class. Thus, he considered certain neuroses as characteristic of the middle class and attributed them to changes in middle class culture. Hellpach laid special emphasis on materialism as a value which led to degenerative consequences, as well as on the insecurity in the bourgeoisie which derived from the militancy of the proletariat. One must recall that this was a period (1906) when the German Social Democratic Party had almost reached the apogee of its power, and even dreamed of achieving power on an elective basis. Again, it is evident how non-scientific elements intertwine with scientific problems. Yet, at the same time, such a study points to an aspect of the problem of stress and mental illness which apparently has not received as much attention as it deserves.

## Conclusion

This brings us to a summation of the subject which has been presented in a broad overview. From the eighteenth century to the present there has existed the concept that social stress is in some way related to the causation of mental illness. The whole problem of civilization and insanity revolves around this concept. It is also clear that approaches to the elucidation of the problem have been coloured by various non-scientific views and considerations. In short the analysis of this problem must be considered in terms of the sociology of knowledge as well as an aspect of the history of psychiatry. Furthermore, let us remember that this applies as well to current work in this area. At the same time, within this social context there has gradually emerged a more sharply focused approach based on the ability to distinguish and to define apparently relevant variables. For example, it is certainly true that in broad outline cultures vary widely in their responses to such stressful conditions as epidemics, wars, techno-logical and economic upheavals, and psychological deprivations. Whatever ways men use to defend themselves against stress will in general reflect the answers favoured by their culture to certain

[66] See note 35.

193

human problems.[67] Cultural influences on physiology can be demonstrated in several ways, e.g. variations in nutrition and body manipulation, through attitudes towards injury and disease, and through the effects produced in the internal milieu of the organism by stress applied to it through cultural channels. Fischer and Agnew have suggested the concept of a hierarchy of stresses, and this may be illustrated by Groen's work with Jewish patients with ulcers before, during and after the Second World War. The patients lost their symptoms in concentration camps where the new stresses were objectively far greater, but had them back after their release and return to their more normal life.[68] What this means is that the development of further research requires the linking of epidemiological studies with studies of the physiological and psychological relations of the variables isolated by the former. Studies on one level are not enough. Research is needed on several levels and along various axes including that of time. The historian may be able to contribute perhaps in a small way by clarifying some of the contemporary issues in terms of their background and by suggestion of certain linkages that may not otherwise be apparent.

[67] M. M. Ames, "Reaction to Stress. A Comparative Study of Nativism," *Davidson Journal of Anthropology* 3: 17–30, 1957; A. F. C. Wallace, "Revitalization Movements," *American Anthropologist* 58: 264–281, 1956.

[68] R. Fischer and N. Agnew, "A Hierarchy of Stresses," *Journal of Mental Science* 101: 383–386, 1955; J. Groen, "Psychogenesis and Psychotherapy of Ulcerative Colitis," *Psychosomatic Medicine* 9: 151–174, 1947.

# CHAPTER SEVEN

# PSYCHIC EPIDEMICS IN EUROPE AND THE UNITED STATES

## DANCE FRENZIES, DEMONIC POSSESSION, REVIVAL MOVEMENTS AND RELATED PHENOMENA, FOURTEENTH TO TWENTIETH CENTURIES

Within the framework of his ideas about the relations between health and society, Rudolf Virchow developed a theory that epidemic disease was a consequence of social and cultural maladjustment. Drawing a parallel between the individual and the body politic, he said, "If disease is an expression of individual life under unfavourable conditions, then epidemics must be indicative of major disturbances of mass life."[1] Virchow differentiated natural and artificial epidemics, basing the distinction on the degree to which cultural factors are interposed between nature and man. Moreover, he considered artificial epidemics not only as arising out of social contradictions, but also as significant indicators of historical trends and developments. Such outbreaks of disease, according to Virchow, marked nodal points in history and characterized periods of political and intellectual revolution.

In illustration of his socio-historical theory of epidemic disease, Virchow referred to psychic epidemics, pointing out that "The artificial epidemics are physical or mental, for mental diseases also occur epidemically and tear entire peoples into a mad psychotic movement."[2] Virchow was not alone in his views. While he examined the relations between contemporary emotional states and psychosis, other physicians, who to a greater or lesser degree shared his ideas, investigated the same problem historically. Ideler published a study of religious madness in 1848; in the same year Leubuscher, the co-worker of Virchow, adapted the important study of mental illness over a period of four hundred years by Calmeil, the French psychiatrist. Salomon Neumann referred approvingly to these works, emphasizing that "Both have demonstrated how the various forms

---

[1] R. Virchow, *Die Einheitsbestrebungen in der wissenschaftlichen Medizin*, Berlin, G. Reimer, 1849, p. 46.

[2] R. Virchow, *Wissenschaftliche Abhandlungen*, Bd. I, p. 36.

of lunacy are essentially determined by the contemporary state of civilization of a society."[3]

Interest in psychic epidemics was stimulated by the appearance in Berlin at the time of a child who performed miracles, and attracted a great many people.[4] Virchow explained this event as an abnormal expression of suppressed revolutionary energies that had not been discharged. He tended generally to consider the psychological reactions during and after the 1848 revolution as a psychic epidemic caused by interference with the historical process.[5]

A wide variety of phenomena have been grouped under the rubric, psychic epidemics. For the most part investigators of these episodes have, like Virchow, endeavoured to understand them in terms of collective psychopathology.[6] Essentially, however, such an approach begs the question, assuming in advance what remains to be determined. The main point is not to label the behaviour *a priori* as psychotic, or psychopathological, even though its members may act oddly by ordinary criteria. There may well be a rational core in apparently irrational behaviour. One must first examine the behaviour in its context before judging it.

One of the more bizarre episodes in the history of medieval Europe, and one which is often cited as an instance of an epidemic collective psychosis or of a mass hysteria, is the dance frenzy (more commonly called the dancing mania) of 1374. According to Peter of Herental, a monk, who was apparently an eyewitness,

At that time ... a strange sect, comprising men and women, from various parts of Germany, came to Aachen, and they went as far as Hennegau and France. This was their condition. Both men and women were abused by the devil to such a degree that they danced in their homes, in the churches and in the streets, holding each other's hands and leaping in the air. While they danced they called out the names of demons, such as Friskes and others, but they were unaware of this nor did they pay attention to modesty even though people watched them. At the end of the dance, they felt such pains in the chest, that if their

---

[3] S. Neumann, "Zur medicinischen Statistik des preussischen Staates nach den Acten des statistischen Bureaus für das Jahr 1846," *Virchows Archiv für pathologische Anatomie und Physiologie und für klinische medizin* 3: 13–141, 1851 (see p. 89).

[4] R. Leubuscher, *Medizinische Reform*, pp. 207–208. See also Abarbanell in the same journal (p. 216) who denied that these events constituted a psychic epidemic.

[5] R. Virchow, "Die Epidemien von 1848," *Virchows Arch. path. Anat.* 3: 1–2, 1851 (see p. 5).

[6] For example, Henry E. Sigerist, *Civilization and Disease*, Ithaca, Cornell University Press, 1943, pp. 186, 200; J. A. MacCulloch: *Medieval Faith and Fable*, Boston, Marshall Jones Co., 1932(?), pp. 256ff.

friends did not tie linen clothes tightly around their waists, they cried out like madmen that they were dying. In Liège they were freed of their demons by means of exorcisms such as those employed before baptism. Those who were cured said that they seemed to have been dancing in a river of blood, which is why they jumped into the air. However, the people of Liège said that they had been attacked in this way because they were not truly baptized, inasmuch as most of the priests kept concubines. For this reason the populace proposed that they rise against the priests, kill them and take their property, which would have happened had not God provided a remedy through the aforesaid exorcisms. When the people saw this their anger subsided to such an extent that the clergy were held in even greater reverence than before.[7]

A rhymed account cited by Peter of Herental, as well as a number of contemporary and later chronicles, provides further information and makes it possible to obtain a useful basis for an interpretation of the dance frenzy.[8] For the most part, lower social groups were involved. While people of all social classes and occupations were among the dancers, wealthy individuals and clerics were few. The majority comprised peasants, artisans such as tailors and shoemakers, servants, housewives, unmarried women, young people of both sexes, beggars, and idlers. The dancers are described as setting wreaths on their heads, being bound around with cloths and towels, and carrying staves. Moreover, various chronicles describe them as half-naked or stark naked, except possibly for a loin cloth. Not only did they hold hands, but sometimes they clapped their hands above their heads. When the dancers achieved a state of ecstasy, they exhibited a variety of other motor phenomena. Some suddenly threw themselves on the ground and began to move around on their backs; others lost consciousness and fell down foaming at the mouth; still others described ecstatic visions in which the heavens opened to reveal the enthroned Saviour with the Holy Mother at his side. Most characteristic of all, perhaps, were the paroxysmal convulsive movements and twitchings. It is furthermore reported that the dancer could not abide the sight of anything red or of the long pointed shoes in style at the time, and reacted violently. The paroxysmal twitching and convulsive movements which occurred in the ecstatic state were frequently followed by a swelling up of the abdomen.

The numbers involved apparently varied, but little reliance can be placed in them. Hecker reports 500 persons in Köln, and 1,100 in

[7] J. F. C. Hecker, *Die grossen Volkskrankheiten des Mittelalters. Historisch-pathologische Untersuchungen* . . . ed. August Hirsch, Berlin, Th. Chr. Fr. Enslin, 1865, p. 186.

[8] *Ibid.*, pp. 147, 159, 162, 186–187; E. Louis Backman, *Religious Dances in the Christian Church and in Popular Medicine*, London, George Allen and Unwin, 1952, pp. 190–216.

Metz. From the various accounts it is clear that in no town was the entire population involved, since mention is made of bystanders who provided an audience for the dancers. Indeed, a fifteenth-century chronicle from Flanders reports that the dancers struck bystanders who refused to join them in the dance.[9] Moreover, many of the dancers were apparently not native to the towns and localities in which the dance frenzy occurred. Peter of Herental speaks of people from various regions of Germany; Radulphus de Rivo of Tongeren refers to people from the upper regions of Germany; still others mention that the dancers came to Maastricht, Tongeren, and Liège. Hecker states specifically that the dancers wandered from town to town.[10]

The major outbreaks of dancing occurred over a period of some four months. Beginning at Aachen around 15 July, the dancers moved to Köln (15 August–8 September); Maastricht, Tongeren, Harstal, Liège, Trier (September 11–14) and Ghent (October 22–23). Metz in France, Gelderland (Southwest Holland), and Jülich (Northwest Germany) were also reached during this period. The chronology and the associated geographic distribution show clearly that the dance frenzy moved from east to west, spreading then in northerly and southerly directions. Liebscher's cartographic analysis led to the same conclusion.[11] Furthermore, Backman's conclusion "that the dancing epidemic of 1374 comprised a large number of Hungarian pilgrims who according to ancient custom, proceeded to Aachen and Cologne, to NW. Germany, to Flanders and to the southern Rhine provinces and Trier"[12] reinforces this picture of developments and begins to provide a basis for a reinterpretation of the dance frenzy. The German tribes had already begun to move eastwards into central Europe during the early Middle Ages. Migration in large waves occurred during the twelfth century with the development of mining, and many Germans moved into Bohemia and southward into Hungary.[13] They retained their connections with their old homes and in many cases returned to the Rhineland and Westphalia as pilgrims. The earliest known Hungarian pilgrimage to the Rhine province occurred in 1221, the last in 1769.[14] Generally, the pilgrimages took place

---

[9] Backman, *op. cit.*, p. 147.

[10] Hecker, *op. cit.*, p. 201.

[11] Helmuth Liebscher, *Ein kartographischer Beitrag zur Geschichte der Tanzwut* (Leipzig thesis), Leipzig, 1931, p. 16.

[12] Backman, *op. cit.*, p. 230.

[13] George Rosen, *The History of Miners' Diseases. A Medical and Social Interpretation*, New York, Schuman's, 1943, pp. 40–42.

[14] S. Beissel, "Die Verehrung der Heiligen und ihrer Reliquien in Deutschland zum Beginne des 13. Jahrhunderst," *Stimmen aus Maria-Laach*, XII. Ergänzungs-Bd., Heft 47, Freiburg i. Br., 1890; *idem*, "Die Verehrung der Heiligen und ihrer

annually, but some shrines such as those of the Magi at Köln were visited every seventh year. At the shrine the pilgrims offered thanks by dancing to musical accompaniment.[15] This fact may be coupled with the observations that many danced in churches, churchyards, monasteries, and other holy places. For example, on 18 November 1374, the magistrates of Maastricht issued an edict prohibiting anyone suffering from the dance frenzy from dancing in churches or streets. Such people were permitted, however, to dance in their own homes.[16]

An important fact emerges from the study of the events of 1374, namely, that the dance frenzy was closely linked with religious ritual and institutions. This fact achieves enhanced significance when seen in relation to earlier and later accounts of dance epidemics. Hecker, who made the first attempt to deal systematically and coherently with the dance frenzy, was aware that the events of 1374 were not without precedent. Commenting that such phenomena were well known in the Middle Ages, he referred to the dance at Kölbigk in 1021, the children's dance from Erfurt to Arnstadt in 1237, and the dance at the Maastricht bridge in 1278.[17] Hecker characterized the dance at Kölbigk as a legend, but there probably was a nucleus of fact involving a group of poor, sick peasants who came to pray for help and danced in the churchyard. This event was converted into an edifying legend replete with miracles. Because they committed sacrilege by disturbing the mass and disobeying the priest who ordered them to stop, the dancers were punished by being compelled to dance uninterruptedly for an entire year. Furthermore, even when the year ended, the legend has it that the dancers continued to twitch and have tremors of their limbs for the rest of their lives. Despite the legendary character of the story, a few details are relevant to our study. Several accounts refer to the dancers as epileptics, madmen, and beggars. One version cites a song which was sung during the dance under the direction of one member of the group. Furthermore,

---

[15] Elizabeth Thoemmes, "Die Wallfahrten der Ungarn an den Rhein," *Veröffentlichungen d. Bischöflichen Diozesenarch. Aachen*, 4, Aachen, 1937.

[16] Backman, *op. cit.*, p. 201.

[17] Hecker, *op. cit.*, pp. 153–154. While Hecker located the dance of 1278 at the Mosel bridge in Utrecht, Liebscher and others have shown that the bridge over the Maas River was meant in the source used by Hecker. See Liebscher, *op. cit.*, p. 9.

---

Reliquien in Deutschland während der zweiten Hälfte des Mittelalters," *ibid.*, XIV. Erg.-Bd., Heft 54, 1892; *idem*, "Die Aachenfahrt. Verehrung der Aachener Heiligtümer seit den Tagen Karls des Grossen bis in unsere Zeit," *ibid.*, Ergänzungs-Heft 82, 1902.

a contemporary chronicle mentions certain background circumstances that should be kept in mind. The year 1017 was noteworthy for a virulent plague with high mortality; the following year (1018) was marked by the appearance of a comet which foretold further pestilence and death; and then in 1020 there were a number of calamities that ravaged Eastern Saxony in particular: an unusually long and cold winter which caused many deaths, an unexpectedly severe epidemic in the spring, and finally in the latter part of the year there were widespread floods along the Weser and the Elbe in which many drowned. The events at Kölbigk are supposed to have occurred at the end of this year of terror. Situations of stress such as these are relevant to the occurrence of dance frenzies and similar forms of behaviour, and we shall return to this aspect of the problem.[18]

Much more important is the eyewitness account of a dance frenzy reported by Gerald de Barri (Giraldus Cambrensis), the Welsh churchman and historian, in his *Itinerary throughout Wales* written after he went to Wales in 1188 with the primate Baldwin to preach the third crusade. At the church of St. Almedha in Brecknockshire, he says,

> ... a solemn feast is annually held in the beginning of August, and attended by many people from a considerable distance, when those who labour under various diseases, received the health they desire through the merits of the Blessed Virgin. The circumstances which occur at every anniversary appear to me remarkable. You may see men or girls, now in the church, now in the churchyard, now in the dance which is led round the churchyard with a song, suddenly falling to the ground as in a trance, then jumping up as in a frenzy, and representing with their hands and feet, before the people, whatever work they have unlawfully done on feast days; you may see one man put his hand to the plough, and another, as it were, goad on the oxen, mitigating the animal's sense of labour by the usual rude song; one man imitating the occupation of a shoemaker, another that of a tanner. Now you may see a girl with a distaff drawing out the thread and winding it again on the spindle; another walking and arranging the threads for the web; another as it were, throwing the shuttle and seeming to weave. On being brought into the church and led up to the altar with their oblations, you will be astonished to see them suddenly awakened, and coming to themselves. Thus, by the divine mercy, which rejoices in the conversion, not in the death, of sinners, many persons from the conviction of their senses are corrected and amended on these feast days.[19]

[18] Edward Schröder, "Die Tänzer von Kölbigk. Ein Mirakel des 11. Jahrhunderts," *Zeitschrift für Kirchengeschichte* 18: 94–164, 1897.

[19] Giraldus Cambrensis, *Opera*, ed. James F. Dimock, London, Longmans Green, Reader, and Dyer, 1868, vol. VI, p. 32.

Gerald's account clearly relates the dance to religious rites. Pilgrims came to the shrine of St. Almedha to be cured of various ills, or to purge themselves of sin. Obviously desires, beliefs, and rites were allied to satisfy moral demands and frustrated aspirations. To satisfy these needs, song and dance were employed to achieve a state of ritual trance or possession. In this situation it was possible to reduce emotional tensions and to achieve some degree of relief. That this occurred as a part of accepted religious tradition is indicated by Gerald's description of the symbolic behaviour through which individuals designated their sins. These acts call to mind the way in which the flagellants of 1348–49 symbolized their transgressions by assuming certain positions during the ceremony of absolution. An adulterer lay flat on his belly, a perjurer held his hand up high showing only three fingers, and so forth.[20]

The occurrence of compulsive or continued dancing is also reported after the fourteenth century. In 1428 some women danced in the Water Church at Zürich.[21] Another instance is reported as having occurred between 15 June and 23 June, during the feast of St. Vitus, in the cloister of St. Agnes at Schaffhausen. Here a monk danced himself to death.[22] A third report comes from the records of the Zürich council. In 1452 a man danced in the vestibule of the Water Church.[23]

In 1518 a large epidemic of continued dancing occurred in Strassburg.[24] Eight days before the feast of Mary Magdalene a woman began to dance, and after this went on for some four to six days she was sent to the chapel of St. Vitus at Hohlenstein, near Zabern. Soon thereafter more dancers appeared and the number grew until more than a hundred danced at a time. Eventually the municipal council forbade all public gatherings and music, restricted the dancers to two guild halls, and then sent them off to the chapel of St. Vitus. According to one account, more than four hundred people were affected within four weeks. Various chroniclers point out that this

[20] Arthur Hübner, *Die deutschen Geisslerlieder. Studien zum geistlichen Volksliede des Mittelalters*, Berlin-Leipzig, Walter De Gruyter & Co., 1931, pp. 13–14; Norman Cohn, *The Pursuit of the Millennium*, Fairlawn, N. J., Essential Books, Inc., 1957, pp. 132–133, New York, Harper Torchbooks edition, 1961, pp. 135–136; Ingmar Bergman's film "The Seventh Seal" presents this pattern of behaviour visually. Those who have not seen the film can obtain an impression from *Four Screenplays of Ingmar Bergman*, trans. Lars Malmstrom and David Kushner, New York, Simon and Schuster, 1960, pp. 123–125.

[21] Alfred Martin, "Die Tanzkrankheit in der Schweiz," *Schwiezerische Medizinische Wochenschrift* 4: 470–471, 1923.

[22] Backman, *op. cit.*, p. 232.

[23] Martin, *op. cit.*, p. 470.

[24] L. Witkowski, "Einige Bemerkungen über den Veitstanz des Mittelalters und über psychische Infection," *Allg. Ztschr. Psychiat.* 35: 591–598, 1879.

was a period of ruined harvests, severe famine, general want, and widespread disease. This was also the time of the early Reformation and thus of religious unrest.

Two other instances involving a single person and a small group of children occurred in 1536 at Basel and in 1551 in Anhalt, respectively. Far more interesting is a drawing by Pieter Breughel of a dance epidemic in 1564 at Moelenbeek Sint Jans, a locality which is now a section of Brussels. To the drawing he appended a note that "These are pilgrims who were to dance on St. John's day at Muelebeek outside Brussels, and when they have danced over a bridge and hopped a great deal they will be cleansed for a whole year of St. John's disease."[25] Breughel was probably an eyewitness, for he depicts the participants marching and dancing in groups of three, a woman in the middle flanked by two men. The arrangement is that of the two and one dance, a form of folk dance common at the time. The appearance and behaviour of the women are clearly those of persons in ecstatic trance. Confirmation can easily be obtained by comparing their expression and posture with modern photographs of persons in trance in a wide variety of religious settings in quite different parts of the world, such as Haiti, Bali, and some southern sections of the United States.[26]

The occurrence of dance epidemics during this period is further confirmed by various comments and discussions in the writings of Paracelsus. In his book on invisible diseases, written about 1531–32, he discussed the so-called St. Vitus' dance, attributing it to the irrational power of imagination and belief. Of considerable interest is his comparison between participants in dance frenzies and the fanatical Anabaptists, a point to which we shall return.[27] The same condition is also considered in his treatise on diseases that deprive man of reason, where St. Vitus' dance is described as "nothing but an imaginative sickness" arising more frequently in women from a voluptuous urge to dance.[28]

By the early seventeenth century, however, accounts of dance

[25] *Jahrbuch der Kunsthistorischen Sammlungen des allerhöchsten Kaiserhauses*, Bd. 25, Heft 3, Vienna, 1904, Plate 21; Backman, *op cit.*, pp. 244–247.

[26] P. Verger, *Dieux d'Afrique*, Paris, Paul Hartmann, 1954; William Sargant, "Some cultural group abreactive techniques and their relation to modern treatments," *Proceedings of the Royal Society of Medicine* 42: 367–384, 1949; Jane Belo, *Trance in Bali*, New York, Columbia University Press, 1960; Maya Deren, *Divine Horsemen. The Living Gods of Haiti*, London–New York, Thames & Hudson, 1953, particularly plates 20 and 21.

[27] Theophrastus Paracelsus, *Volumen paramirum und Opus paramirum*, ed. Franz Strunz, Jena, Eugen Diederichs, 1904, pp. 321–328.

[28] *Four Treatises of Theophrastus von Hohenheim called Paracelsus . . .* ed. Henry E. Sigerist, Baltimore, Johns Hopkins Press, 1941, pp. 158, 180–182.

frenzies become infrequent. Towards the end of his life, Johann Schenck von Grafenberg (died 1598), municipal physician of Freiburg i. Br., brought out a remarkable collection of medical observations based on wide reading and his own broad experience. He refers to the dance frenzy as having been common in earlier times, describing in detail the events of 1374. While such situations still occurred in his day, the pattern of behaviour was somewhat different; indeed, it appears to have become institutionalized. (One is strongly reminded here of the development of the revival meeting in the United States during the nineteenth century). Schenck related that in Breisgau and the neighbouring districts those affected by this condition came every year on the festival of St. John to two chapels: one dedicated to St. Vitus at Biessen near Breisach, the other near Wasenweiler dedicated to John the Baptist. People came to these shrines to fulfil vows they had made or to implore the saints for help against the dance frenzy. For the entire month of June preceding the festival of St. John these people felt ill at ease; they were sad, fearful and anxious, wandered about restlessly, driven by drawing pains that appeared suddenly in various parts of the body, awaiting with anticipation the eve of St. John's day. They were convinced that their misery would be relieved by dancing before the chapel altar. Generally, after dancing wildly for three hours, they considered themselves protected for the entire ensuing year.[29]

A similar account is given by Gregor Horst in the early seventeenth century.[30] In 1623 he saw a number of women who made a pilgrimage annually to the chapel of St. Vitus in Drefelhausen near Weissenstein in the Ulm district. There they danced ecstatically until they collapsed from exhaustion. For several weeks before the pilgrimage they suffered from feelings of restlessness and a feeling of painful heaviness, but after the dance they were freed of these attacks and could anticipate a year of well-being. One woman was reputed to have made such annual pilgrimages for twenty years and another for thirty years. The dancing was stimulated by music, eventually producing the desired ecstatic condition. Music is mentioned in many accounts of dance frenzies. Among the instruments used were drums, trumpets, and above all bagpipes. Breughel shows two bagpipes in his drawing of the Moelenbeek dancers.

The medieval dance frenzy cannot be discussed without at least some mention of tarantism, a condition localized mainly in Apulia although cases apparently occurred in other parts of Italy and in Spain. As the history of tarantism has been well presented by Sigerist

[29] Hecker, *op. cit.*, 160–161.
[30] *Ibid.*, pp. 161–162.

and Katner. I shall not discuss it in detail.[31] Characteristic are the following features. Attacks occurred at the height of the summer in July and August. People would suddenly feel an acute pain, which they attributed to the bite of a tarantula; thereupon they would jump up and run into the street where they hopped, jumped, and danced wildly. While all ages and both sexes were affected, the majority of the dancers were young, and more women than men were affected. Most of the dancers were peasants, but members of the gentry and the clergy were involved. By contrast with some of the dancers of northern Europe who abhorred anything red, the Italian *tarantati* could not endure the sight of black. Some bound reeds or vines around their necks; others tore their clothes, immodestly revealing their nakedness; still others beat each other with whips. The physician Baglivi who described tarantism in 1695 reported that women exhibited particularly strange behaviour. Some women dug holes in the earth and rolled about the ground; others liked to be tossed in the air; while still others uttered sighs and howls and made obscene signs. All this took place to the accompaniment of music. Dancing was considered the sovereign remedy for the tarantula bite, and the dancers continued for days until exhausted. Then, like the dancers described by Schenck and Horst, they were relieved until the following year. In many instances the music alone was sufficient to revive the frenzy, and this happened every summer. Tarantism is believed to have been present in Italy in the fourteenth century or even earlier, but did not become prominent until the seventeenth century, and by the middle of the following century had apparently become a subject for historical study.

Hecker introduced his studies of the medieval dance frenzies and tarantism with the statement that these "phenomena provide a deep insight into the psychological nature of human society. They belong to history and will never recur in their original form, but they point to a vulnerable aspect of man, the drive to imitate, and are therefore very closely related to human group life." What does this mean? Does it mean that such phenomena could not arise elsewhere and in other periods of history because the causes which produced the dance frenzies were purely local and had disappeared? Or does it mean that phenomena of a similar kind could appear again, but that they would be perceived and interpreted differently? Actually Hecker was ambiguous on this point. He attributed these phenomena to the existence of an element in human nature which he termed sympathy or

---

[31] Henry E. Sigerist, *Civilization and Disease*, Ithaca, Cornell University Press, 1943, pp. 216–226; Wilhelm Katner, *Das Rätsel des Tarentismus. Eine Ätiologie der italienischen Tanzkrankheit* (*Nova Acta Leopoldina*, N. F., Bd. 18, Nr. 124), Leipzig, Johann Ambrosius Barth, 1956.

imitation. "Imitation, compassion, sympathy" he declared, ". . . are imperfect designations for a bond common to all human beings, for an instinct which binds the individual to the group, which embraces with equal force reason and folly, good and evil, and diminishes the praise of virtue as much as the culpability of vice."[32] But if this instinct or quality is common to all men, then its excitation by like stimuli or in similar contexts should produce comparable phenomena. Furthermore, under conditions of violent excitement, the instinct of imitation may acquire a morbid character, thus providing the basis for group involvement in such events as the dance frenzies. To illustrate his thesis, Hecker described a number of contemporary instances, among them the dances of the convulsionaries of St. Médard at the grave of the Jansenist Deacon Pâris beginning in 1728, an epidemic of convulsions among women workers in a Lancashire cotton mill in 1787, an outbreak of fainting and convulsions in a Berlin hospital in 1801, and another outbreak connected with a Methodist revival at Redruth, Cornwall, in 1814. Indeed, Hecker closes with a statement that psychological aberrations which occur on the basis of religious enthusiasm, such as those produced by the Methodist Revival in England and by the frontier camp meetings in the United States, were for the nineteenth century what the dance frenzies had been for the Middle Ages.

As Hecker intimated, the medieval dance frenzies appear unique only when considered as group psychopathies characteristic of the Middle Ages. He was aware, however, that there were points of resemblance to situation and events in more recent periods. Witkowski in 1879 emphasized even more strongly that the dance frenzies must be studied from a comparative cultural viewpoint rather than as unique disease entities.[33] In fact, bizarre forms of group behaviour similar to the dance frenzies have occurred widely separated in time and space. Transmission of ideas and practices can be proven for some cases; others clearly originated independently.

Behavioural phenomena of the kind exhibited in the dance frenzies continued to appear in Europe in various contexts and under different names. During the sixteenth and seventeenth centuries numerous cases of alleged demonic possession occurred in closed communities, especially in convents.[34] These outbreaks were interpreted in terms of

[32] Hecker, *op. cit.*, p. 121.

[33] Witkowski, *op. cit.*, p. 595.

[34] L.-F. Calmeil, *De la folie . . .*, Paris, J.-B. Baillière, 1845, vol. 1, pp. 254ff.; vol. 2, pp. 1ff.; Th. de Cauzons, *La magie et la sorcellerie en France*, Paris, Librairie Dorbon-Aîné, n. d., vol. III, pp. 176–233; Jean Lorédan, *Un grand procès de sorcellerie au XVIIe siècle. L'Abbé Gaufridy et Madeleine de Demandolx (1600–1670)*, Paris, Perrin et Cie, 1912; Samuel Garnier, *Barbe Buvée, en religion, soeur Sainte-Colombe et la prétendue possession des Ursulines d'Auxonne (1658–*

the widespread belief that the Devil could enter into human beings and alter their behaviour in various ways. Possession by the Devil was attributed to the practice of witchcraft.[35] Cure required exorcism of the Devil and detection of the witch responsible for the situation.

Where such ideas and beliefs are a part of the culture, many people will see demonic possession in cases of bizarre behaviour, and some will produce the required phenomena. A possessed person was believed to be endowed with unusual strength; to behave wildly, writhing, twitching, and producing convulsive states; to make noises like an animal, and to vomit up strange objects and foreign bodies. For example, in 1609 a nun in the Ursuline convent at Aix-en-Provence began to have visions of devils and exhibit severe shaking and convulsive fits. In the course of the year a number of other nuns became involved. Madeleine de Demandolx, the nun who had started the affair, was sixteen or seventeen at the time and in love with Louis Gaufridi, a parish priest in Marseilles. Under exorcism, Madeleine accused the priest of having bewitched her. Despite all attempts to drive the devils out, she became worse. Confined in the grotto at Ste. Baume where there was a celebrated shrine of St. Mary Magdalene, she had visions, danced and laughed, neighed like a horse, and had paroxysms in which she thrashed about. Among the other possessed nuns, one named Louise Capeau exhibited almost equally bizarre behaviour. Eventually, in 1611, the case of the two nuns came before the Parlement at Aix. During the trial, the nuns went into fits and acted very much like the girls in the Salem witch trials. Furthermore, in court Madeleine was seized with trembling and twitching, during which the sexual act was represented with violent movements of the lower abdomen. The accusations made by the girls against Gaufridi at the trial were overwhelming, and he was imprisoned, interrogated under extreme torture, and condemned to be burnt alive. The execution took place on 30 April 1611.[36]

The events at Aix soon became known at the convent of Ste. Brigitte at Lille, which belonged to the same order. Three nuns accused another of having bewitched them so that they became servants of the Devil. Here too the behavioural phenomena were paroxysmal convulsions, speech in strange tongues, and immodest or obscene acts. Upon investigation, Marie de Sains, the nun accused

---

[35] *Malleus maleficarum*, trans. and ed., Rev. Montague Summers, London, Pushkin Press, 1951, pp. 122–140.

[36] Lorédan, *op. cit.*

---

*1663*), Paris, Félix Alcan, 1895; Tallement des Réaux, *Historiettes* (Bibliothèque de la Pléiade), Paris, Gallimard, 1960, vol. 1, pp. 295–297; Sainte-Beuve, *Port-Royal*, Paris, Gallimard, 1952, vol. 1, p. 325.

as a witch, was declared guilty and imprisoned at Tournai. Other flare-ups of demonic possession in convents occurred at Loudun in 1634, leading to the death at the stake of the priest Urbain Grandier, and at Louviers in Normandy, where Thomas Boullé, chaplain to the bewitched nuns, was burned alive in 1647.[37]

These episodes and others which I shall not mention were clearly related to a belief in the power of the Devil, acting through the witches who were his servants and instruments, to injure those who opposed him and in general to subvert the social order. Fear of demonic powers acting directly or through other human beings to cause illness, death, or other kinds of damage was widely diffused throughout the population in the Middle Ages and continued to exist in this fashion in Europe well into the eighteenth century. When a situation arose which was not only menacing, but went altogether outside the usual run of experience, when people were confronted with hazards which were all the more frightening because they were unfamiliar, when the individual or the group faced a situation which could not be openly accepted, as in family stresses or sexual antagonisms—at such times the Devil and his servants were held responsible, and attacks of demonic possession were useful means for detecting the guilty.[38]

Religious movements frequently endeavour to mobilize the emotions in order to intensify the fervour of their adherents or to convert non-believers. This has been true of many religions from ancient times to the present. States of possession or trance accompanied by physical activity have been used to demonstrate the truth of the relevant doctrines. The phenomena of group excitation and the means employed to produce them are very similar to those described in the medieval dance frenzies. These phenomena have been associated with a variety of heterodox movements and have not necessarily been limited to a particular religion. Ronald Knox, whose book *Enthusiasm* is a study of Christian sects that have used group excitation, emphasized the range of religious viewpoints that can be associated with such methods.[39] Moreover, comparable observations are available for certain Jewish sects, cult movements among American Indians, Moslem sects, and various other religious

[37] Cauzons, *op. cit.*, pp. 194–228; Gabriel Legué, *Documents pour servir à l'histoire médicale des possédées de Loudun*, Paris, Adrien Delahaye, 1874; Aldous Huxley, *The Devils of Loudun*, New York, Harper & Bros., 1952, Harper Colophon Books edition, 1965.

[38] For a broader discussion of the problem of witchcraft in relation to this subject, see Chapter 1 above.

[39] R. A. Knox, *Enthusiasm. A Chapter in the History of Religion with Special Reference to the Seventeenth and Eighteenth Centuries*, New York–Oxford, Oxford University Press, 1950.

movements developed in South America and the Caribbean area, in Africa, and in Melanesia.

The enthusiasm of the early Quakers produced strange physical effects which were considered religious "convincements" and evidence of divine inspiration. According to one account, the followers of George Fox were called Quakers from the trembling which they exhibited under the powerful working of the Holy Ghost.[40] According to Fox himself, "Justice Bennet of Derby . . . first called us Quakers because we bid them tremble at the work of God, and this was in the year 1650."[41] However, the term Quakers was used as early as 1647, not of the Friends, but to designate "a sect of women (they are at Southwark) come from beyond the sea, called Quakers, and these swell, shiver and shake, and, when they come to themselves . . . they begin to preach what hath been delivered to them by the Spirit."[42] In 1653, a number of Lancashire justices and ministers prepared a petition to the Council of State against Fox and James Nayler, another Quaker leader. Among the charges against them was that "they have drawn much people after them: many whereof (men, women and little children) at their meetings are strangely wrought upon in their bodies, and brought to fall, foam at the mouth, roar and swell in their bellies."[43] Further testimony is provided in a letter addressed to Fox in 1652 by Thomas Aldam, while imprisoned in York Castle. Describing how he had admonished Major General Harrison, he says, "I was taken with the power in a great trembling in my head and all of the one side all the while I was speaking to them which was a great amazement to the people, and they was silent."[44] George Fox did not refute the charge in the Lancashire petition about this strange behaviour of the Quakers. In fact, he accepted it, for in his work *The Great Mistery*, pointing out that "the mighty power of the Lord God had been known years before," he wrote, "quaking and trembling we own, though they in scorn call us so."[45]

Another disconcerting feature of early Quaker enthusiasm was to walk or to run through the streets completely naked. As early as 1652, Fox justified this form of testifying to the truth when he addressed the people of Ulverston, saying ". . . the Lord made one to go naked among you, a figure of thy nakedness, and of your nakedness, and as a sign amongst you before your destruction cometh, that you

[40] William C. Braithwaite, *The Beginnings of Quakerism*, ed. Henry C. Cadbury, Cambridge, Cambridge University Press, 1955, p. 57.

[41] *The Journal of George Fox*, ed. John L. Nickalls, Cambridge, Cambridge University Press, 1952, p. 58.

[42] Braithwaite, *op. cit.*, p. 57.

[43] *Ibid.*, p. 108.

[44] *Ibid.*, p. 73.

[45] *Ibid.*, p. 57, note 2.

might see that you were naked and not covered with the truth."[46] Going naked as a sign is related to the prophetic character of early Quakerism. By proclaiming the Day of the Lord and calling down woe upon their persecutors, they were acting like the prophets of the Old Testament. They were the servants of a moral demand and of a vision which demanded expression. Furthermore, many millennial visionaries and religious enthusiasts have felt that by breaking with traditional values and taboos it may be possible to return to the pristine past, to the beginning of things. In this sense the Quakers, although not millenarians themselves, still show their relationship to the world of obscure heresies and sects out of which they emerged. For example, the Adamites of Bohemia in the fifteenth century and the Anabaptists in the following century similarly went naked as a sign, and in Canada the modern Doukhobors follow the same practice.[47] Yet the use of nakedness as a sign appears somewhat less extravagant when we remember that the Quakers belonged to a period which was still close to the Middle Ages, when the practice of going naked as a sign of penance or of having divested oneself of all earthly goods was not uncommon.[48] By 1664, however, it was possible for a contemporary to write that "At first they did use to fall into violent tremblings and sometimes vomitings in their meetings, and pretended to be violently acted by the Spirit; but now that is ceased, they only meet, and he that pretendeth to be moved by the Spirit speaketh; and sometimes they say nothing, but sit an hour or more in silence, and then depart."[49]

The eighteenth century, like most other periods of history, is difficult if not impossible to characterize with a few limited phrases. It was not all enlightenment, rationalism, urbanity, and good sense. At the very time when religious enthusiasm was considered with suspicion and reproach, there appeared in several parts of Europe and America religious groups and movements which found a characteristic expression not only in their doctrines but equally in strange bodily agitations and extravagant behaviour. These include the Camisard prophets of the Cévennes in Southern France; the

[46] *Ibid.*, p. 148.

[47] Theodora Büttner–Ernst Werner, *Circumcellionen und Adamiten. Zwei Formen mittelalterlicher Haeresie*, Berlin, Akademie Verlag, 1959, pp. 129–134; Knox, *op. cit.*, p. 136.

[48] Friedrich Zoepfl, "Nacktwallfahrten," in *Wallfahrt und Volkstum in Geschichte und Leben*, herausgegeben von Georg Schreiber (*Forschungen zur Volkskunde*, Heft 16/17), Düsseldorf, L. Schwann, n. d., pp. 266–272; Büttner–Werner, *op. cit.*, pp. 140–141; E. Perroy, *Le moyen âge. L'expansion de l'orient et la naissance de la civilization occidentale* (*Histoire générale des civilizations*, vol. III), Paris, Presses Universitaires de France, 1957, p. 618.

[49] Knox, *op. cit.*, p. 150.

Jansenist convulsionaries at the cemetery of St. Médard in Paris; the sect called Shakers; the Great Awakening initiated by Jonathan Edwards in New England; the early Methodist movement; the mystical, enthusiastic Russian sects, particularly the group known as the Chlysti; and the Jewish sects, specifically the Frankist group and the Hasidism of the Baal-Shem Tov, that developed in the wake of the messianic movement of Sabbatai Zevi. To discuss these developments in detail would exceed the bounds of this presentation, and I shall limit myself to the essential features of some of them.

At the very time when the worship of the Quakers began to be imbued with more decorum, and the inevitable discipline of institutionalism developed, the Huguenots of Southern France brought forth a movement and eventually a revolt characterized by religious exaltation, prophetic utterances, and bizarre physical acts. The revocation of the Edict of Nantes in 1685 and the severe persecutions that followed the obstinate refusal of the French Protestants to abandon their religion evoked among them passionate resentment, dark despair, and, as an almost inevitable concomitant, a burning desire to change the intolerable present as rapidly as possible into a better future.[50] Moreover, as Calvinists, as the chosen people of God, they found in the Bible the inspiration which coloured their thought and anticipations and led them to believe that the end of the existing order was at hand, to be succeeded by a reign of the saints. Armed revolt by the Camisards, as the Huguenots were called, did not occur on any sizable scale until 1702, but the preceding years were filled with emotional turmoil, prophecies, and signs. Chiefly involved were the provinces of Languedoc, Vivarais, and Dauphiné.

Many Protestants fled to England and Holland, but the majority remained in France and attempted to carry on their religion. Meetings for religious observance were held in remote spots in the mountains, not unlike the practice of the Dissenters in England and the Covenanters in Scotland after the Stuart restoration. Often they were held at dead of night and in caves, circumstances which undoubtedly contributed to the emotional eruption experienced by many of the faithful. Furthermore, feelings of remorse and guilt were very probably involved in the production of the state of emotional readiness for the wonderful and the miraculous. At first large numbers had deserted the Calvinist religion and had become *nouveaux convertis*. As time went on, however, despite continued persecution, a number of crypto-Protestants, feeling that they had

---

[50] This account is based on the following sources: George B. Cutten, *Speaking with Tongues Historically and Psychologically Considered*, New Haven, Yale University Press, 1927, pp. 48–66; Charles Almeras, *La révolte des camisards*, (n. p.), Arthaud, 1960, pp. 41–59; Knox, *op. cit.*, pp. 356–371.

abandoned their brethren, returned to their original faith. Under these circumstances, beginning in 1688 in the Dauphiné, individuals achieved states of religious exaltation in which they uttered prophecies for the support, guidance, and incitement of their co-religionists. Among the prophets were many young children, some of whom were trained by a zealous Huguenot named du Serre. In addition to the little prophets, ecstatic phenomena were also common among the preachers at religious meetings.

The prophetic trance was usually preceded and accompanied by a variety of physical manifestations, differing in various areas and among different groups. There were four degrees of ecstasy, namely, the warning (*l'avertissement*), the whisper of inspiration (*le souffle*), the prophecy (*la prophétie*), and finally the gift (*le don*), the highest grade of inspiration. During these stages, the individual shivered and twitched convulsively, fell foaming at the mouth, leaped up again sometimes whirling like a dervish, then fell in a stupor. The abdomen and neck swelled up, and as the spirit came on the inspired one broke out into various kinds of speech. Speaking with tongues (glossolalia) was common, as was the utterance of things to come. Sermons were also preached in this condition. While inspired, the ecstatic was quite unaware of what he did or said. Such experiences were undoubtedly needed to encourage the Camisards in the unequal contest in which they were engaged. With all reserve removed, it was possible to promise things that were highly exaggerated. Gabriel Astier, for example, assured his followers, just before the Royal troops cut them to pieces, that they would not be touched. So, too, the Sioux warriors were assured by their prophets that no bullet could penetrate their ghost shirts, only to discover the true value of this prophecy at Wounded Knee Creek.[51] Nor did the Anabaptists of Münster look any less fervently to the heavens in expectation of the Second Coming, but alas, in vain. Groups that wish to arrest a process of disintegration which they know will lead to their disappearance, groups that wish to revitalize their societies and to create a more satisfactory world in which to live, groups that are fighting against overwhelming odds—all require a belief and conviction that they are under some sovereign guidance and protection which will enable them to attain their hearts' desire.[52]

When the Camisard Revolt came to an end in 1704, the leaders dispersed. A group of these refugees fled to England where they attracted a good deal of attention and even found some followers,

[51] George E. Hyde, *A Sioux Chronicle*, Norman, University of Oklahoma Press, 1956, p. 312.

[52] The psychological character of such groups is well rendered in the play of Jean-Paul Sartre, *Le diable et le bon dieu*, Paris, Gallimard, 1951.

among whom Sir Richard Bulkeley and John Lacy were most prominent. Indeed, the Earl of Shaftesbury relates that in 1707 the prophets of the Cévennes were represented in a puppet show at Bartholomew Fair.[53] Moreover, they did not allow the tradition of ecstatic trance and violent transports to die out. According to Benjamin Franklin, his first employer, the Philadelphia printer Keimer, "had been one of the French Prophets and could act their enthusiastic agitations."[54] Among the adherents whom the Camisards gained in England were James and Jane Wardley, Quakers who lived near Manchester. They adopted the more extreme beliefs and practices of the Camisards, the ecstatic trances, the agitations of the body, the millennial prophecies, the signs of supernatural assistance in times of trouble. While they still adhered to some aspects of Quaker worship, such as sitting in silent meditation, participants would then exhibit

> a mighty trembling, under which they would express the indignation of God against all sin. At other times they were affected, under the power of God, with a mighty shaking; and were occasionally exercised in singing, shouting, or walking the floor, under the influence of spiritual signs, shoving each other about,—or swiftly passing and repassing each other, like clouds agitated by a mighty wind.[55]

In September 1758 this group known as Shaking Quakers or Shakers was joined by Ann Lees, a young woman of twenty-two, the daughter of a blacksmith. After a number of tragic experiences following her marriage, including the loss of four children in infancy, she experienced a complete conversion, arriving at the conviction that her soul could be purified only by abstaining from every kind of carnal gratification. Her experiences undoubtedly influenced her views on sex and marriage. Ann Lees became a zealous member of the Wardley sect, and eventually the head of the group. Except for a few members, the Shakers at this time were poor labourers, mill hands, mechanics, servants, and housewives. Their exuberant, strange mode of worship led to conflicts with the authorities, to imprisonment, and ultimately in 1774 to migration to America. Several years after Ann Lees established a permanent centre at Niskeyuna, about eight miles northwest of Albany, New York, the Shakers were joined by members of the New Light Congregational group and a number of Baptists. They profited in part from the backwash of the Great

[53] Cutten, *op. cit.*, pp. 55–56.

[54] Benjamin Franklin, *The Complete Works of Benjamin Franklin*, ed. J. Bigelow, New York–London, G. P. Putnam, 1887–1888, vol. I, p. 66.

[55] Edward D. Andrews, *The People Called Shakers. A Search for the Perfect Society*, New York, Oxford University Press, 1953, p. 6.

Awakening of 1745, for Western New York drew its population in large measure from the hill country of New England, where between 1740 and 1800 wave upon wave of religious enthusiasm rose and broke at frequent intervals. Many of these people were potential converts to Shakerism, and eleven Shaker settlements were organized from 1787 to 1794.

The Shaker sect evolved as a celibate, communistic order in which, as "mother" Ann Lees put it, people put their hands to work and gave their hearts to God. While the work of God became more decorous during the eighteenth century as the rites of worship were institutionalized and rationalized, the earlier religious exercises of the group were often extravagant and highly emotional, exhibiting many of the mystical experiences and physical phenomena of charismatic or pentecostal sects.[56] Singing and dancing were combined. One witness described a meeting as beginning with singing and then turning to a dance. The performance was characterized

> by a perpetual springing from the house floor, about four inches up and down, both in the men's and women's apartment, moving about as thick as they can crowd, with extraordinary transport, singing sometimes one at a time, and sometimes more than one, making a perfect charm . . . This elevation draws upon the nerves so as that they have intervals of shuddering as if they were in a strong fit of the ague. They sometimes clap hands and leap so as to strike the joyce above their heads. They throw off their outside garments in these exercises and spread their strength very cheerfully this way . . .[57]

Sometimes as the religious worship became more frenetic, the ecstatic state manifested itself in signs. According to Valentine Rathbun, Sr., founder and minister of the Baptist church at Pittsfield, who had originally been attracted to Shakerism and then opposed the sect,

> the power will take their hand, stretch it up, pull the other down, they interpret it—the hand up, is a sign of mercy, the hand down, of judgement: Sometimes their hand is stretched out forward, then away they run after it; if it leads to some other person, they lay their hand on his head,—then cross their arms, one across the other,—then say he must

[56] David M. Ludlum, *Social Ferment in Vermont, 1791–1850*, New York, Columbia University Press, 1939, pp. 12–15, 42; Whitney R. Cross, *The Burned-Over District, The Social and Intellectual History of Enthusiastic Religion in Western New York, 1800–1850*, Ithaca, N.Y., Cornell University Press, 1950, pp. 6–9, New York, Harper Torchbooks edition, 1965, pp.6–9; Elmer T. Clark, *The Smaller Sects in America. An Authentic Study of Almost 300 Little-Known Religious Groups*, Rev. ed., New York, Abingdon Press, 1949, pp. 85–132.

[57] Andrews, *op. cit.*, p. 29.

take up his cross, and renounce the works of the flesh,— then they stretch both hands behind them, and say he must leave the world behind him.[58]

This description is confirmed by other references to signs which were interpreted as gifts of God. Inevitably one recalls the Welsh pilgrims of St. Almedha, the flagellants, the Anabaptists, the Quakers, the Camisards, and all the other enthusiasts who sought help, forgiveness, or inspiration from on high and were only too ready to interpret as a sign from God the bizarre behaviour in which their subconscious impulses and conscious anticipations expressed themselves.

Comparison of the religious behaviour of the Shakers with that of participants in various religious revivals reveals many similarities. The Great Awakening initiated by Jonathan Edwards in New England produced the screaming, trembling, physical collapse, protracted stupor, speaking with tongues, and the other phenomena attendant upon religious frenzy and excessive rapture. It made little difference that Edwards rejected the physical manifestations as of no spiritual significance.[59] John Wesley and the movement known as the Methodist Revival produced comparable phenomena.

The end of the eighteenth century witnessed the rise of another great religious revival. Beginning in Kentucky in 1797, it spread through the adjoining states in the next few years. While the Great Revival in the West was only one of the many religious awakenings which from time to time have stirred the United States, it was most significant for several reasons. First, it brought into being the camp meeting, a social device which was extremely useful in creating an institutional pattern for religion in a frontier environment. Secondly, despite some of the marked emotionalism which characterized its beginnings, the camp meeting played a part in taming the baser aspects of frontier life. Thirdly, the Great Revival brought forth forms of emotional religiosity more grotesque than anything yet experienced in the religious history of the United States.[60]

The movement was started by James McGready, an itinerant Presbyterian who preached a modified form of Calvinism emphasizing the necessity of a new birth, that is a spiritual experience which would convert sinners into repentant Christians.[61] In 1797, this fiery

[58] Andrews, *op. cit.*, p. 30.

[59] Jonathan Edwards, *Religious Affections*, ed. John E. Smith, New Haven, Yale University Press, 1959, pp. 142, 285–288.

[60] Catharine C. Cleveland, *The Great Revival in the West, 1797–1805*, Chicago, University of Chicago Press, 1916, pp. 128–158.

[61] This account of the Great Revival is based on the following sources: Richard M'Nemar, *The Kentucky Revival; or a Short History of the Late Extraordinary Out-Pouring of the Spirit of God in the Western States of America*, New York,

preacher began to hold "sacramental solemnities" in Kentucky, painting with florid, impassioned oratory the horrors of hell and calling on impenitent sinners to reform. Other preachers soon joined him and various denominations—Methodists, Baptists, Presbyterians—combined to promote the religious awakening. During the summer of 1800, the revival movement reached such proportions that McGready described this earlier evangelical work as "a few scattering drops before a mighty rain" when compared with the later "overflowing floods of salvation." Meetings were held in various localities, and the revival spread over Kentucky and Tennessee, into North and South Carolina, western Virginia, and western Pennsylvania. These meetings were attended by thousands of people from distant places, who were exhorted by numbers of frontier preachers. According to Peter Cartwright, the number might reach ten, twenty, and sometimes thirty; and at times six or seven preached, prayed, or harangued, the people simultaneously. This went on night and day, for four or five days, and sometimes a week or even longer. Largely unplanned, the services were frequently spontaneous. The congregation was excited, and many were thrown into a frenzy by lurid sermons depicting the wages of sin and the fate of the damned. Sinners were stricken with a sense of guilt and be- moaned their state. Weeping, breast beating, and shouting were common. Spirituals were sung to remind sinners of the Judgement Day.[62] Under such circumstances, emotionalism had free reign, and numerous bizarre forms of behaviour, called "bodily exercises," appeared.

The "falling exercise" was most common. Individuals uttered a piercing shriek and fell to the ground, losing consciousness. Others fell, but thrashed about violently. Some fallers had auditory and visual hallucinations. The number of the fallen was so great at some meetings that they were removed, collected in one spot, and laid out

---

[62] Songs of the kind used at these camp meetings are still sung in the South and have been recorded by Alan Lomax in the Southern Folk Heritage Series, e.g., "Antioch" and "Calvary" (White Spirituals, Atlantic No. 1349) and "Power" (Negro Church Music, Atlantic No. 1351).

---

Edward O. Jenkins, 1846; W. L. Sutton, "Reports on the medical topography and the epidemic diseases of Kentucky," *Tr. Am. M.A.* 11: 77–123, 1858 (especially pp. 110–123); David W. Yandell, "Epidemic convulsions," *Brain* 4: 339–350, 1881–1882; Catherine C. Cleveland, *The Great Revival in the West*, 1797–1805, Chicago, University of Chicago Press, 1916; Peter Cartwright, *Autobiography of Peter Cartwright, the Backwoods Preacher*, ed. W. P. Strickland, New York, Carlton & Porter, 1857; Charles A. Johnson, *The Frontier Camp Meeting. Religion's Harvest Time*, Dallas, Southern Methodist University Press, 1955.

side by side in orderly fashion. Other "exercises" were rolling, jerking, barking, running, dancing, and singing. The rolling exercise consisted in doubling the head and feet together and rolling over and over like a hoop or wheel. The "jerking exercise" was common in Kentucky and Tennessee. It began as a violent twitching of some part of the body, then increased in violence until the entire individual was contorted. M'Nemar's description is vivid:

> By this strange operation the human frame was commonly so transformed and disfigured, as to lose every trace of its natural appearance. Sometimes the head would be twitched right and left, to a half round, with such velocity, that not a feature could be discovered, but the face appeared as much behind as before, and in the quick progressive jerk, it would seem as if the person was transmuted into some other species of creature.[63]

The barking exercise frequently accompanied the jerking. Men and women would get down on all fours, growl, snap, and bark like dogs. Sometimes they gathered around a tree, barking, yelping, "treeing the devil." Actually, these were regarded as forms of chastisement for sin, and it is worth mentioning that the Shakers engaged in similar behaviour when they stamped, jumped, and whirled about, "saying 'hiss, hiss, hiss!' and crying 'hate the devil, hate the devil, chain the devil, chain the devil.' "[64] Voluntary dancing was used as a means of avoiding some of the more disagreeable exercises. The dance was also used to praise God. Thus, M'Nemar relates that "At the spring sacrament at Turtle Creek in 1804 br. Thompson had been constrained just at the close of the meeting to go dancing and for an hour or more to dance in a regular manner round the stand, all the while repeating in a low tone of voice—'This is the Holy Ghost—Glory!' "[65]

How to explain these phenomena is a question to be answered on several levels—social, cultural, psychological, and physiological. Ronald Knox made the significant observation that they are all part of "a definite type of spirituality, one which cannot be happy unless it is seeing results. Heart-work, Wesley called it; the emotions must be stirred to their depths, at frequent intervals, by unaccountable feelings of compunction, joy, peace, and so on, or how could you be certain that the Divine touch was working on your soul? . . . grace must be something felt, or how could you be sure that it had any existence at all?"[66] Thus, Wesley's energumens writhing on the floor

[63] M'Nemar, *op. cit.*, pp. 64–65.
[64] Andrews, *op. cit.*, p. 138.
[65] M'Nemar, *op. cit.*, p. 60.
[66] Knox, *op. cit.*, pp. 588–589.

and crying for mercy, the Indian Shakers of Puget Sound, the ecstatic Hasidim, the Voodoo votaries who are mounted by divine horsemen, or the Guarani Indians of Brazil seeking to save the world, are in Knox's sense kinsmen.[67]

Common to these groups and to numerous others are the general conditions under which they live, and the consequent attitudes, goals, and behavioural forms which they develop. To paraphrase Hobbes, life for the members of such groups is poor, miserable, nasty, short, and above all insecure. Fear and insecurity tend to be pervasive elements of the psychological climate. There are a variety of factors capable of producing such an atmosphere, and their importance will vary from group to group, time to time, and place to place. The Kentucky Revival illustrates many of the elements involved in similar manifestations elsewhere, but in making comparisons, it is important also to recognize diverse historical traditions and differing levels of culture. With these cautions in mind, however, useful comparisons can be made.

One factor is the effect of a primitive environment. The brute struggle for existence against unfriendly natural forces creates an atmosphere of danger and uncertainty. To this may be added the threat of violence, disability, and death proceeding from hostile human beings or from sickness. The first settlers in Kentucky were constantly exposed to border warfare with hostile Indians; disease, particularly ague, was prevalent, and medical care was lacking; and social control was at a minimum. Under such circumstances, "toughness," a value necessary to survival, was highly prized, while fighting, gambling, drinking, and sexual promiscuity, as the behavioural correlates of this quality, were widespread. Moreover, the newness of the country and its geographical location behind the Appalachians meant that the population was sparse and that settlements were few. An important consequence was the social isolation to which so many of the settlers were subjected. Under such conditions, there were few sources of recreation to relieve the monotony of daily life. Finally, most of the settlers did not come from the professional or educated elements in the older settled areas and were consequently often illiterate and unconcerned with intellectual issues. The need for ways of supporting and dealing with such conditions brings forth attitudes and behaviour patterns which derive from the historical

[67] H. G. Barnett, *Indian Shakers. A Messianic Cult of the Pacific Northwest*, Carbondale, Southern Illinois University Press, 1957; Alfred Métraux, *Le vaudou haïtien*, Paris, Gallimard, 1958; Curt Nimuendaju, "Die Sagen von der Erschaffung und Vernichtung der Welt als Grundlagen der Religion der Apapocuva-Guarani," *Zeitschrift für Ethnologie* 46: 284–403, 1914 (see pp. 287, 318–320, 327).

experience of the group and from the internal and external cultural influences to which it is exposed. Religion is frequently the means by which such groups endeavour to achieve their purpose. An apt comparison in this sense can be made with the inhabitants of the interior of Northern Brazil and with the early factory workers in England and the American South.

Northeastern Brazil, the bulge that points towards Africa, consists of two areas, a coastal agricultural belt which is well-watered and fertile, and the backlands where the rainfall is scarce and undependable, so that the land is arid and covered with scrawny brush. The inhabitants of the *sertão*, as this hinterland is called, are mostly ranchers and herders, whose outstanding characteristics are their toughness, their exaggerated individualism, their superstition, and fanaticism. Graciliano Ramos has compared the social system prevalent in this area to the Biblical patriarchy.[68] From time to time this area has produced religious movements whose avowed aim was to establish a New Jerusalem and to wipe out the degradation and misery afflicting their followers.[69] These movements, religions of the poor and disinherited, are marked by distinctive psychological and ethical traits, similar to those found in the revivalistic religion of the American frontiersman and of the early factory worker. Euclides da Cunha, in his classic account of the movement led by Antonio Conselheiro and of its suppression in 1896–97 at Canudos, provides appropriate evidence on this point.[70]

The frontiersmen, according to H. Richard Niebuhr, "accepted or produced the characteristics of the faith of the disinherited."[71] Above all it is marked by emotional fervour and personalized religious experiences. Accepting the levelling influence of poverty and wishing to cast off social barriers, there is an exclusive emphasis on passion and morality as criteria of faith and salvation. It is in these terms that the lowest and most ignorant can compete on an equal basis. The corollaries to these traits are the rejection of abstract creeds and rituals, as well as an aversion to intellectual matters. Theological notions may be chosen and welded together without regard to consistency. At the same time the followers of such faiths want to be

[68] Graciliano Ramos, *Memórias do cárcere*, Rio de Janiero, J. Olympio, 1953, vol. I, p. 71.

[69] M. L. Pereira de Queiroz, "L'influence du milieu social interne sur les mouvements messianiques brésiliens," *Archives de Sociologie des Religions* 3: 3–30, 1958.

[70] Euclides da Cunha, *Os sertões*, 1902, trans. as *Rebellion in the Backlands* by Samuel Putnam, Chicago, University of Chicago Press, 1944.

[71] H. Richard Niebuhr, *The Social Sources of Denominationalism*, New York, Henry Holt, 1929.

assured that they will ultimately triumph over their oppressors or enemies; they want to know the New Jerusalem as a vision of splendour and to feel that the evil-doers will receive their just punishment.

Liston Pope in his study of religion and industrialism in Gastonia, North Carolina, during the period from 1890 to 1939, emphasized that such faiths and the groups that adhere to them

> thrive wherever a considerable portion of the population exists on the periphery of culture as organized, whether the index used be that of education, economic status, possibilities for psychological satisfaction, or religious organization. Members of the newer religions do not belong anywhere and so they belong, and wholeheartedly, to the one type of institution which deigns to notice them. A considerable percentage of mill workers stand on the outer fringes of their communities, and they provide the invariable starting point of sect movements. The rapidity of growth of the sects is a rough indication of the degree to which mill workers recognize their cultural alienation.[72]

The factor of cultural alienation is characteristic of the Brazilian *sertanejo*, the frontier Kentuckian, and the North Carolina millworker, as well as of other groups that have already been mentioned. Where such situations exist, desires and aspirations of various kinds can be blocked by the absence of suitable channels and means for expression, by deliberate policies of repression and segregation, or by natural events that lead to famine, disease and death. Economic conditions are undoubtedly important. During the depression of the thirties the rate of growth of the sects known popularly as the Holy Rollers was phenomenal.[73] Alienation may be a consequence of repression on grounds of religion, race, ethnic origin, or sex. Thus, the feeling among the Jansenists after 1730 that "the Church had unchurched herself" was at the same time a recognition that the movement of Port-Royal had met defeat. The desire to transcend this situation betrayed these enthusiasts into fantasy, produced an apocalyptic atmosphere, and led to the ecstasies, convulsions, and other phenomena at the tomb of François de Paris in the cemetery of St. Médard.[74] The pentecostal, holiness, and other sects and cults among American Negroes have developed out of an analogous situation to transcend and to provide an otherwordly compensation

[72] Liston Pope, *Millhands and Preachers*, New Haven, Yale University Press, 1942, pp. 136–137.

[73] Anton T. Boisen, "Economic distress and religious experience. A study of the Holy Rollers," *Psychiatry* 2: 185–194, 1939.

[74] Knox, *op. cit.*, pp. 374–385; Sainte-Beuve, *op. cit.*, vol. III, pp. 526, 531; [Ph. Hecquet], *Le naturalisme des convulsions*, Soleure, 1733.

for the current low estate of the participants.[75] Similarly, Hasidism, the ecstatic religious movement which appeared among the Polish Jews in the eighteenth century, was a product of prolonged experience of stress and an endeavour to find an alternative way of supporting the conditions of life other than the unsatisfactory one provided by the official religious authorities.[76]

Moreover, the frenetic behaviour which is a part of the religion of such groups provides a source of excitement and diversion. Life may be monotonous, dull, and without any channels for emotional release and self-expression. Pope quotes a Gastonia worker who explained that "These prayer meetings are about the only entertainment we have."[77] A similar observation was made by an Englishwoman who described the Courtauld mills in Essex in the 1840s. She observed that the women workers needed some excitement and commented that "When no other is provided, religious enthusiasm would occasionally take its place."[78]

But religion was only one channel by which such workers obtained the emotional release which they craved. Hecker had already described an outbreak of convulsive fits which appeared among the workers in a Lancashire cotton mill in 1877. A woman put a mouse down the dress of a fellow worker, who immediately threw a prolonged fit of convulsions. The next day three other women developed fits, and by the fourth day twenty-four workers were affected. The rumour spread that the condition was due to some poison derived from the cotton. Soon neighbouring factories were attacked. The affected workers were treated by means of electric stimulation from a portable electrical machine and by reassurance that the attacks were nervous and not due to any occupational poison. Similar episodes have been reported since then among groups of factory workers as well as other small groups living under similar or related conditions. During the nineteenth and twentieth centuries outbreaks of group twitching, convulsions, ecstatic trances, and the

[75] Raymond J. Jones, *A Comparative Study of Religious Cult Behaviour among Negroes with Special References to Emotional Group Conditioning Factors* (*Howard University Studies in the Social Sciences*, vol. II, no. 2), Washington, D.C., Howard University, 1939.

[76] Gershom-Gerhard Scholem, "Le mouvement sabbataïste en Pologne," *Revue de l'histoire des religions* 143: 30–90, 209–232, 42–77, 1953–54; Torsten Ysander, *Studien zum B'estschen Hasidismus in seiner religionsgeschichtlichen Sonderart* (*Uppsala Universitets Arsskrift*, Bd. I, Teologi 2), Uppsala, 1933, pp. 17–61.

[77] Pope, *op. cit.*, p. 89.

[78] Mary Merryweather, *Experience of Factory Life*, 3rd ed., London, 1862, quoted by E. J. Hobsbawm, *Social Bandits and Primitive Rebels*, Glencoe, Free Press, 1959, pp. 131–132.

like have occurred in schools, hospitals, convents, and remote rural or mountain communities.[79]

In all these episodes the factors already mentioned are operative to a greater or lesser degree, and there is little doubt that they are involved as well in movements derived from the clash of peoples and cultures, particularly in colonial settings. No matter whether in North or South America, in Africa, Asia, or Oceania, where one people has a vastly superior technology and is able to dominate another, deliverers appear who promise to right the wrongs and remove the hardships suffered by the native or aboriginal population, to prevent impending calamities, and to restore the past age of gold. Such messiahs promulgate prescriptions, establish certain usages, and prohibit others. Typical of these movements in many respects is the ghost-dance religion of the Plains Indians of the United States.[80] Derived from ideas and practices that had originated in the area of Washington and British Columbia, the ghost-dance religion began to be preached in Nevada in 1889 by Wovoka, a Paviotso Indian, after visions experienced about 1888. From this point it spread rapidly across the Plains and far to the east. The central doctrine of his preaching was the imminent rejuvenation and renovation of the world, which would restore the conditions and way of life of the Indians to their state before the arrival of the whites. He stressed an ethic by which the individual Indian could reorganize his disorganized personality and prescribed a collective rite which emphasized social solidarity. The Indians were to dance in a manner revealed to the prophet in his vision. This would enable them to commune with the spirits of the deceased and to acquire supernatural power. The

[79] F. Bricheteau, "Relation d'une épidémie de chorée observée a l'Hôpital Necker," *Archives générales de médecine* 1: 433–447, 532–549, 1863; A. Constans, *Relation sur une épidémie d'hystéro-démonopathie en 1861*, 2nd ed., Paris, Delahaye, 1863; M. Bouzol, "Relation d'une épidémie à phénomènes hystéro-choréiques observée à Albon (Ardèche), en 1882," *Lyon medical*, pp. 142–148, 174–183, 211–217, 1884; G. Kirchgaesser, *Ueber epidemisch auftretende Krämpfe*, Bonn, Bach, 1892; Fritz Aemmer, *Eine Schulepidemie von Tremor hystericus (sogennante Chorea-Epidemie)*, Basel, Kreis, 1893; E. A. Schuler and V. J. Parenton, "A recent epidemic of hysteria in a Louisiana high school," *Journal of Social Psychology* 17: 221–235, 1943.

[80] James Mooney, "The ghost dance religion and the Sioux outbreak of 1890," *14th Annual Report ... 1892–93, U.S. Bureau of American Ethnology*, Pt. II, Washington, D.C., 1896; A. L. Kroeber, *Handbook of the Indians of California*, Washington, D.C., Gov't. Print. Off., 1925, pp. 868–873; Leslie Spier, "The ghost dance of 1870 among the Klamath of Oregon," *University of Washington Publications in Anthropology*, vol. 2, no. 2, Seattle, University of Washington Press, 1927, pp. 39–56; idem, *The Prophet Dance of the Northwest and its Derivatives: The Source of the Ghost Dance (General Series in Anthropology*, no. 1), Menasha, Wis., Banta, 1935; Cora DuBois, *The 1870 Ghost Dance (Anthropological Records*, vol. III, no. 1), Berkeley, University of California Press, 1939.

sacred dance, the circumstances under which it occurred, and the ensuing phenomena resemble in many respects the early pioneer camp-meeting of Kentucky. Excitement was high, and as the dance continued it became even more intense. "When the dancers were worn out mentally and physically," writes Mooney, "the medicine men would shout that they could see the faces of departed friends, and relatives moving about the circle. No pen can describe the result. All shouted in chorus and then danced and sang until they fell into a confused and exhausted mass on the ground."[81] Another observer reports that in the ecstatic state

> Some would appear conscious but with every muscle twitching and quivering; some appeared to be perfectly unconscious; some would run, stepping high and pawing the air in a frightful manner. Those who fell were never disturbed, and no notice was taken of them save to keep the crowd away. . . . The dance was kept up until fully one hundred persons out of the three or four hundred who took part were lying absolutely unconscious.[82]

Eventually the Sioux turned the ghost religion into a nativistic political cult determined to overthrow the dominant position of the whites, and this led to its suppression.

Parallels have been found in other areas where, as Andreas Lommel puts it, "The natives wish henceforth to live like whites—but without them."[83] Thus, the Cargo cults of Melanesia centre in the belief that ships laden with the goods, and particularly with the technologic devices, of the whites will arrive and deliver their cargo to the natives, who will then have the benefits. The initiators of these cults have each had a revelation which requires the performance of certain rites including special dances and songs.[84] These dances give rise to the *jipari* or shaking fit, which consists of uncontrolled bodily movements, like convulsions, and which occurs collectively as well as individually. The *jipari* is differentiated by the natives from madness and is considered a mechanism by which instructions concerning the cult are transmitted.

Students of these movements have realized that they cannot be

[81] Mooney, *op. cit.*, p. 806.

[82] F. M. Davenport, *Primitive Traits in Religious Revivals*, New York, Macmillan, 1905, p. 39.

[83] Andreas Lommel, "Der Cargo Kult in Melanesien," *Ztschr. f. Ethnologie*, 78: 17–63, 1953.

[84] F. E. Williams, *The Vailala Madness and the Destruction of Native Ceremonies in the Gulf Division (Territory of Papua, Anthropology Report No. 4)*, Port Moresby 1923; *idem*, *Orokaiva Magic*, London, Oxford University Press, 1928; Peter Worsley, *The Trumpet Shall Sound. A Study of Cargo Cults in Melanesia*, London, MacGibbon & Kee, 1957.

understood when considered in terms of abnormal psychology. Firth has commented that

> the movements are part of a process of imperfect social and economic adjustment to the conditions arising directly or indirectly from contact with the West. They are not mere passive responses, the blind stirrings of a people who feel that they are being pushed around. Absurd as they may seem when considered as rational solutions, they are creative attempts of the people to reform their own institutions, to meet *new* demands or withstand *new* pressures. In the broadest sense their aims are to secure a fuller life.[85]

They are "revitalization movements," as Wallace, an American anthropologist, has termed them.[86]

Moreover, the phenomena of group dancing, possession, trances, twitching, convulsions and so on, that have led observers to discuss such occurrences as forms of delusion and mass psychopathology must be seen within the context outlined by Firth. They are not accidental. They occur within emotionally charged and explosive situations, in situations where there is dissatisfaction with existing conditions, for example, social relations or health conditions in general, with what Merton describes as a contradiction between cultural goals and the institutional means to attain them. Under the stimulus of intense yearnings and of the tensions which build up, there is a need for emotional expression and action. Liston Pope pointed out that the millworkers of Gastonia wanted a religion that "works" and "changes things," and this is equally true of groups subject to strains in different cultural situations.[87] A psychological atmosphere of this kind was often present when mass epidemics occurred, a situation vividly described by Manzoni for seventeenth century Milan, when the populace sought relief in hunting down so-called anointers, who were believed to have caused the plague.[88] Firth has pointed out that action in the form of work is an emotional outlet for people in such groups. At another level of action relief is obtained through motor behaviour of a less controlled kind. Furthermore, these forms of action may be combined with an iconoclastic repudiation of customs, traditions, and values of the past. The excruciating spiritual sacrifice involved in such acts is closely bound

[85] R. Firth, "Social change in the Western Pacific," *J. Roy. Soc. Arts* 101: 803–819, 1953 (see p. 815).

[86] A. F. C. Wallace, "Revitalization movements," *American Anthropologist*, 58: 264–281, 1956.

[87] Pope, *op. cit.*, p. 86.

[88] Alessandro Manzoni, *I promessi sposi. Storia milanese del secolo XVII*, Arnoldo Mondadori Editore, 1954, Ch. XXXI-XXXII.

H*                                    223

up with feelings of guilt. Here are to be found the sources of powerful emotional energies connected with such groups as we have discussed. These energies can be employed to bind people together and have been used to create movements in pursuit of political, social, and religious goals. Within this context the comparison which Paracelsus made between the participants in dance frenzies and fanatical Anabaptists becomes even more meaningful. Indeed, as the Dead Sea scrolls appear to indicate, the original elan of Christianity came out of a milieu derived in large measure from the eschatological beliefs and millenarist traditions of the Essenes and similar Jewish sectaries. A more recent instance in point is the cultural transformation of the Manus islanders since the Second World War.[89]

While this account of the dance frenzies and related occurrences is necessarily sketchy and tentative, it is clear that they represent reactions to stress and are attempts to manage stressful situations. The consequences may be a re-establishment of a pre-existing equilibrium, failure to adapt in some way, or the achievement of fresh potentials for action. An understanding of the stress situation and its consequences must rest on a close analysis of the historical and sociological circumstances within which it occurs. But man needs in some way to satisfy his various emotional needs and to derive moral and spiritual satisfaction from his activities and from the things that happen to him. Therefore, it is equally essential to investigate the psychological and social in relation to each other. Furthermore, it is clear that the bizarre behaviour exhibited in dance frenzies and similar phenomena is instrumental. Such behaviour may represent a critique of existing conditions, magical efforts to change these circumstances, symbolic validation or expression of frustrated goals and repressed guilt, or transcendental compensation—in short, the student of these phenomena must try to understand what moves the participants and not beg the problem by interpreting the behaviour as wholly irrational, pathological, or instinctive. Finally, the physical states so often encountered and the means by which they are achieved require analysis on their own level. While this is largely an unexplored area, recent physiological research and other types of investigation can perhaps throw some light on this aspect. I intend to deal with the psychological and physiological aspects of this problem in another context, but I can say here that mental illness as represented by the psychoses is hardly an important element in most of these group occurrences. On the other hand, the singing, drumming, dancing, and other means employed to achieve states of dissociation, trance, or hypnosis do involve psychopathology in a broad sense.

[89] Margaret Mead, *New Lives for Old. Cultural Transformation—Manus. 1928–1953*, New York, Morrow, 1956.

These complexities indicate that we are dealing here not with esoteric or bizarre phenomena, but with problems that touch on the core of individual and group existence. This is not the place to carry this point further, but its existence cannot be denied. Recognition that we are dealing with great surges of human hope and despair may perhaps help us to have a little more understanding of our own time and its bizarre features.

# CONTEMPORARY PROBLEMS

# CHAPTER EIGHT

# PSYCHOPATHOLOGY OF AGEING
## CROSS-CULTURAL AND
## HISTORICAL APPROACHES

Shifts in the proportion of older people in the population are occurring throughout the world. Increasingly, the consequences of this demographic development have thrust themselves into the community's field of vision, and ageing has become one of the more urgent contemporary concerns. The growing proportion of older people in the community has aroused increased interest in the problems of the aged, problems that are manifold and complex. Involved are political, economic, sociological and medical questions, which in turn raise perplexing and difficult decisions of public policy.

Because of the attention which these questions have received, there is today a heightened awareness that health problems are significantly greater in the later years than at any other time. As the President's Commission on the Health Needs of the Nation noted in 1952, "Our ageing population reflects health progress and yet, paradoxically, manifests some of the greatest health needs . . . [Furthermore] health services are woefully inadequate in quantity and quality for the ageing, wherever they may live."[1] Within this context, mental ill health is recognized as one of the more important hazards of old age, and concern has been expressed over the progressively increasing magnitude of this problem. While there is a large body of knowledge on the biological aspects of mental ill health among the aged, the pathological data do not at present suffice to explain and completely clarify the clinical manifestations found in some old people but not in others. In this situation, increasing emphasis has been put on personality organization and life experience. Studies of these factors point to the social and psychological disorientation by which the vulnerable ageing individual is threatened in unwholesome environments. Mental ill health among the aged is attributed in considerable measure to social conditions in the community.

Yet, old age is not new, and problems of adjustment to ageing are as old as mankind. Other societies have dealt with these problems,

---

[1] *Building America's Health*, Report of the President's Commission on the Health Needs of the Nation, Washington, D.C., U.S. Government Printing Office, 1952, vol. 1, pp. 71–72.

and it seems reasonable to ask: What are the possible adjustments for old people to different physical and social environments? What kinds of mental disorder do different societies recognize as occurring among older people? Is the recognition of mental illness related to the characteristics of the aged that are singled out for attention and emphasis? What about the role or roles of the aged in relation to other people in the society and the occurrence or recognition of mental illness in old people? Are there any uniformities or regularities to be observed in terms of the above questions from a comparison of various societies?

The limitations of this presentation do not permit exhaustive answers to any of the questions that have been raised. For one thing, few comparative studies have been undertaken. Secondly, there are wide gaps in time and space in our knowledge of various societies. Observers of other peoples may not have been interested in the aged, or the records have disappeared. Nevertheless, enough information is available to permit us at least to sketch a cross-cultural and historical view of the psychopathology of old people, and perhaps to throw some light on our current concerns.

While few studies of the aged have been made on a comparative basis, several authors have collected information on preliterate and protohistoric cultures which is at least suggestive for the psychopathology of the aged. While there are noteworthy examples of longevity in primitive groups, the general rule is probably a rather early onset of old age.[2] Recognizing that the statistical data are inadequate, Simmons estimates generally "that the number of persons reaching 65, for instance, is quite low and perhaps rarely ever exceeds 3 per cent."[3]

Under such circumstances it is not surprising to find few references to mentally ill old people in the ethnographic literature. However, Koty's comprehensive review of the treatment of the old and the sick in primitive groups does contain a few relevant reports.[4] In one instance observed among the Australian aborigines of the River Darling, an old man suffered from sudden attacks of mental disorder, accompanied by severe headaches. In this condition he wandered through the woods. The young people of the tribe followed him and urged him to come back with them. When they saw that he paid no heed, they remained near him to see that the old man was not

[2] Ludwik Krzywicki, *Primitive Society and Its Vital Statistics*, London, Macmillan and Co., 1934, pp. 243–247.

[3] Leo W. Simmons, *The Role of the Aged in Primitive Society*, New Haven, Yale University Press, 1945, p. 18.

[4] John Koty, *Die Behandlung der Alten und Kranken bei den Naturvölkern* (Forschungen zur Völkerpsychologie und Soziologie, Band XIII), Stuttgart, C. L. Hirschfeld, 1934, pp. 22–23, 68, 101, 143, 156.

harmed. Several similar cases are also reported. Among the Ainu of Japan the aged are held in high regard. The mentally ill are kept in separate huts, but are regularly provided with food by their relatives. The Basonga of West Africa are reported to take good care of the old, particularly those who are wealthy, even when sick or in their dotage. They are respected and even feared. In the Southern Sudan, the Bongo treat the mentally ill relatively well, but the fate of the elderly is harsher. How mentally ill old people are treated is not reported. The Amerindian tribes of the Middle Atlantic area—the Iroquois, the Mohicans, the Hurons and others—respected the old and treated them well. The mentally ill were not mistreated nor abandoned. Among the Pima of southern California, on the other hand, the young people threw stones at the aged in order to see them behave like children.

Despite the fact that ethnographers have not been too careful in reporting all the desirable information on the condition and treatment of the aged, or in arranging the available information in categories convenient for our purpose, one may venture a few general statements. On the basis of the data gathered by Koty and Simmons, it seems that the old have fared worst among peoples whose resources have been limited and for whom dependents are inevitably a burden. This applies to wandering tribes or to those that live under severe climatic conditions. However, one must hasten to add that even this generalization must be qualified. A comparative view indicates the existence of a wide range of attitudes towards old age and mental illness dependent not alone on biological conditions but even more on social and cultural factors. Among certain peoples, the fate of an old person does not depend so much on his physical or mental state as it does on his social status. It makes a considerable difference whether an old person is a member of a wealthy, powerful family or a person of no consequence with few or no relatives and friends. Where the mentally ill are considered the bearers of supernatural forces, the treatment accorded to the elderly may be influenced by such attitudes. The social position of women in the tribe may be still another factor. In short, mentally ill old people are found in primitive groups, and the treatment they receive varies within a wide range, depending on the social organization and culture of the group.

Intimations of the troubles of old people can be found in the literary remains of the ancient Near East, and many of these bear comparison with the later Ecclesiastes.[5] A more solid documentation for the psychopathology of old age is provided by the literature of ancient Greece. Among the ills of life, the *Keres*, two waited

[5] James B. Pritchard, ed., *Ancient Near Eastern Texts Relating to the Old Testament*, ed. 2, Princeton, Princeton University Press, 1955, pp. 522–523.

relentlessly and could not be averted. These were old age and death. For the poets these two evils overshadowed the warming glow of life.[6] Mimnermus laments that "when dolorous age comes, it makes a man both foul without and evil within, ill cares do wear and wear his heart, he has no more the joy of looking on the sunlight, to children he is hateful, to women contemptible, so grievous has God made age."[7] Equally pathetic is the state of senility which Oedipus endures at Colonus, where "in the end he comes to strengthless age, abhorred by all men, without company, unfriended in that uttermost twilight where he must live with every bitter thing."[8] Socrates hesitates to prolong his life lest he "be forced to pay the old man's forfeit—to become sand-blind and deaf and dull of wit, slower to learn, quicker to forget," outstripped by those who were behind him.[9]

The inevitability of old age is a recurring theme in Greek literature, and often the last years of life appear as a punishment.[10] There are numerous realistic portrayals of old men, and the picture of the physical shortcomings of old age is on the whole a gruesome one. This does not mean that the Greeks had no idea of a hale, vigorous old age. In the *Wasps*, Aristophanes mentions Ephudion, who fought bravely in the pancration, a brutal sport combining boxing with wrestling, and describes him as a game old man with "ample sides, strong hands, firm flanks, an iron chest."[11] Other comments on the virtues and happier aspects of old age can be found without difficulty. One of the most charming is the discourse on the advantages of old age by Cephalus in the opening pages of Plato's *Republic*.[12] The wisdom of old age is mentioned and extolled by numerous Greek writers, and yet one cannot avoid the conclusion that the Greeks were more impressed by the unfavourable aspects of the closing years. Browning's optimistic philosophy

> Grow old along with me,
> The Best is yet to be

[6] Jane Harrison, *Prolegomena to the Study of Greek Religion*, New York, Meridian Books, 1955, pp. 172–175.

[7] J. M. Edmonds, ed., *Elegy and Iambus* (Loeb Classical Library), London, Wm. Heinemann, 1931, vol. 1, pp. 88–93.

[8] Sophocles: *Three Tragedies: Oedipus the King: Oedipus at Colonus; Antigone*, Chicago, University of Chicago Press, 1954, p. 134.

[9] Xenophon: *Memorabilia and Oeconomicus* (Loeb Classical Library), London, Wm. Heinemann, 1923, p. 357.

[10] Bessie Ellen Richardson, *Old Age among the Greeks*, Baltimore, Johns Hopkins Press, 1933, pp. 2–8; 10–11.

[11] Aristophanes: *Five Comedies of Aristophanes*, Benjamin Bickley Rogers, trans., Garden City, Doubleday and Company, 1955, p. 265.

[12] Plato: *The Republic*, Paul Shorey, trans. (Loeb Classical Library), London, Wm. Heinemann, 1937, vol. I, pp. 9–13.

was not shared by the Hellenes. They tended to see the mental and emotional sides of old age in objective but pessimistic terms.

The Greeks in common with many other peoples held that certain qualities of intellect and feeling represented the gains of old age. Among these were prudence, discretion, wisdom and mature judgement. However, superior mental endowments were not necessarily attributes of old age *per se*. While certain individuals possess such qualities to a high degree, others show a mental and emotional decline with age. According to Plato, robbing the gods and subversion of the state are excusable crimes when committed under the influence of extreme old age.[13] In several instances, Sophocles and Euripides present old age as deprived of reason, and Aristophanes does so frequently. Old age is morose and sullen-eyed to Euripides.[14] The time-honoured wisdom of the aged does not impress Aristophanes, and the decline of senescence appears often in his plays. In the *Plutus*, he describes Chremylus and Blepsidemus as "men bearded and old, yet companions enrolled in the order of zanies and fools."[15] Demos in the *Knights* is a sour old man, quick-tempered and deaf. Appropriately enough the chorus of the *Wasps* is a group of irascible old men. Lysimachus in one of the Platonic dialogues has a poor memory, and therefore leaves the discussion concerning the education of his son to others.[16] Aristotle sums up this trend of Greek opinion on the aged in his description of elderly men as distrustful, uncertain, selfish and cynical.

While one cannot expect the products of literary creation to be devoid of imaginative colouring, it is clear that the Greek poets, playwrights, and philosophers worked from a firm basis of realism. Some, but not all old people might attain that state where health, temper, and intellect combined to give a calm, peaceful and perhaps happy old age. More often, less admirable qualities and traits, moroseness, sullenness, loss of memory and reason, were characteristic of old people and one had to accept them. Nonetheless, the quality of inevitability did not derive alone from the process of senescence. Other factors were likewise involved. As Cephalus says of the miseries for which men blame old age, it is "not old age" that is the cause, "but the character of the man. For if men were temperate and cheerful even old age is only moderately burdensome."[17]

[13] Plato, *The Dialogues of Plato*, (2 vols.), B. Jowett, trans., New York, Random House, 1937, vol. 2, p. 610.

[14] Euripides, with an English translation by Arthur S. Way (Loeb Classical Library), London, Wm. Heinemann, 1912, vol. 3, p. 107.

[15] Aristophanes, with an English translation by Benjamin Bickley Rogers (Loeb Classical Library), 3 vols., London, Wm. Heinemann, 1931, vol. 3, p. 409.

[16] Laches, 189c *Platonis Opera*, Oxford, Clarendon Press, 1946, vol. 3.

[17] Plato, *The Republic, op. cit.*

The same thought is echoed by Cicero in his essay on old age. According to the critics, he says, "old men are morose, troubled, fretful, and hard to please; and, if we inquire, we shall find that some of them are misers, too. However, these are faults of character, not of age."[18] "For old men of self-control, who are neither churlish nor ungracious, find old age endurable; while on the other hand perversity and an unkindly disposition render irksome every period of life."[19] Cicero points out furthermore that the characteristics attributed to the aged are based not only on character, but arise to a significant degree from the social situation in which they find themselves. "Yet," he says, "moroseness and the other fault mentioned have some excuse, not a really sufficient one, but such as it may seem possible to allow, in that old men imagine themselves ignored, despised, and mocked at; and besides, when the body is weak, the lightest blow gives pain."[20]

Cicero's work is significant not alone for its contribution to the psychology of old age, but it may also serve as a symbol of the process by which Greek culture was adopted in Rome, and developed to create the Graeco-Roman culture. Within this context one may cite two references to ageing by Roman authors which recall earlier Greek comments.

Lucretius in his analysis of the mind points out that when

the body is shattered by the stern strength of time, and the frame has shrunk with its force dulled, then the reason is maimed, the tongue raves, the mind stumbles, all things give way and fail at once. And so it is natural that all the nature of the mind should also be dissolved, even as is smoke, into the high breezes of the air; inasmuch as we see that it is born with the body, grows with it, and, as I have shown, at the same time becomes weary and worn with age.[21]

The pessimistic view of old age is presented in its harshest form in Juvenal's tenth satire. He has not a single good word to offer in this denunciation of the vanity of human wishes. In this powerful treatment of the tragedy of human hopes, old age is described as ugly, deaf, blind, forgetful, crippled by disease and deprived of reason. Men pray to Jupiter for long life, and do not realize they are asking for "a long old age . . . full of continual evils . . . But worse than all bodily failings is the weakening mind which presently cannot remember names of slaves, nor the face of a friend he dined with last

---

[18] Cicero, *De Senectute; De Amicitia; De Divinatione*, trans. by W. A. Falconer, London, Wm. Heinemann, 1930, p. 17.

[19] *Ibid.*

[20] *Op. cit.*, p. 31.

[21] Titus Lucretius Carus, *De Rerum Natura Libri Sex*, ed. by Cyril Bailey, Oxford, Clarendon Press, 1950, vol. I, p. 325.

evening, cannot remember the names of offspring begotten and reared . . ."[22] If one must pray for something, ask for this: a sound mind in a sound body.

Within the context of interest in old age and its psychological manifestations exhibited by Greek and Roman writers, the medical literature on the subject is comparatively scanty. Celsus in his encyclopedia mentions in passing that paralysis and insomnias occur in old age. In his discussion of insanity, however, there is no reference to old people.[23] Aretaeus the Cappadocian in the second century A.D. commented on the mental decay of old age in discussing the differential diagnosis of mania. He remarked that it bears no resemblance to "the dotage which is the calamity of old age . . . dotage commencing with old age never intermits, but accompanies the patient until death; while mania intermits, and with care ceases altogether."[24] Caelius Aurelianus, who probably lived in the fifth century A.D., wrote two treatises on acute and chronic disease based on the works of Soranus of Ephesus who practised at Rome in the time of Trajan and Hadrian. Caelius also has several references to old age and mental illness. In a discussion of an acute disease called lethargy, characterized by fever and stupor, he says that according to Soranus "it is more common in old people, for impairment of the senses and depression are more characteristic of old age."[25] In the chapter on mania, Caelius states that this condition rarely occurs in old men. Finally, under paralysis he remarks that it is most common among old men. Oribasius, physician to the Emperor Julian, lived in the fourth century and wrote a digest of medicine and surgery. In this *Synopsis* he described what he called *meiosis encephalon* or cerebral atrophy. This disease, he said was accompanied frequently by baldness and manifested itself in a loss of intellectual capacity and in weakness of movement. He connected the condition with the ageing process, explaining that the brain atrophies and the nerve roots become dry. Finally, mention should be made of Paul of Aegina, a Byzantine physician of the seventh century. In his *Epitome* a chapter deals with the loss of memory and reason. The discussion is obscure and one cannot say whether the author is discussing senile

[22] Juvenal, *The Satires of Juvenal*, trans. by Rolfe Humphries, Bloomington, Indiana University Press, 1958, pp. 128–130; Gilbert Highet, *Juvenal the Satirist. A Study*, Oxford, Clarendon Press, 1954, pp. 125–129.

[23] Celsus, *De Medicina*, Cambridge, Mass., Harvard University Press, 1935, vol. I, p. 97.

[24] Aretaeus, *The Extant Works of Aretaeus, the Cappadocian*, ed. and trans. by Francis Adams, London, Sydenham Society, 1856, p. 103.

[25] Caelius Aurelianus, *On Acute Diseases and On Chronic Diseases*, ed. and trans, by I. E. Drabkin, Chicago, University of Chicago Press, 1950, pp. 125, 537, 565.

dementia, feeblemindedness or aphasia. These conditions remained poorly differentiated for a long time and were often confused with other states.

With regard to treatment or prevention, the ancient authors have little to offer. All mental illnesses were considered to be physical in origin, and the therapy combined isolation, bleeding, diet, physical therapy and some psychotherapy. While Galen wrote a book of hygiene, and devoted several chapters to the hygiene of old age, he gave no attention to mental hygiene. Of much greater interest on this subject is Cicero's essay on old age. It is our duty, he wrote,

> to resist old age; to compensate for its defects by a watchful care; to fight against it as we would fight against disease; to adopt a regimen of health; to practise moderate exercise; and to take just enough of food and drink to restore our strength and not to overburden it. Nor, indeed, are we to give our attention solely to the body; much greater care is due to the mind and soul; for they, too, like lamps, grow dim with time, unless we keep them supplied with oil. Moreover, exercise causes the body to become heavy with fatigue, but intellectual activity gives buoyance to the mind.[26]

Senile debility, in his view, is a characteristic, not of all old men, but only of those who are weak in mind and will. To prevent impairment of mind, exercise is necessary. "Old men," wrote Cicero, "retain their mental faculties, provided their interest and application continue; and this is true, not only of men in exalted public station, but likewise of those in the quiet of private life . . . the aged remember everything that interests them . . ."[27]

For centuries after the decline of the ancient world, the views on ageing and old people that had been developed by the Greeks and the Romans continued to prevail on one way or another. Old age was regarded as a period of deterioration, and certain morbid conditions and forms of disability were looked upon as the special province of this time of life. Rhazes, the Persian physician of the ninth century, mentions melancholy as an inevitable condition in the lives of old and decrepit persons.[28] The Moslem writers of the Middle Ages took over the hygienic regimes of the Graeco-Roman culture and had similar ideas on the nature of old age.[29]

[26] Cicero, *op. cit.*, p. 45.

[27] Cicero, *op. cit.*, 77.

[28] Robert Burton, *The Anatomy of Melancholy*, London, G. Bell & Sons, 1926, vol. I, pp. 228.

[29] O. Cameron Gruner, *A Treatise on the Canon of Medicine of Avicenna Incorporating a Translation of the First Book*, London, Luzac & Co., 1930, pp. 381, 432–436.

The inevitable decrepitude and melancholic character of old age were commonplace ideas during the Renaissance and Baroque periods, and even well into the nineteenth century. This should surprise no one as respect for authority remained widespread and profound, and the principal sources remained the ancient authors or medieval writers indebted to classical thought. The downward path of old age finds its classic description in Shakespeare's

> ... lean and slippered pantaloon,
> With spectacles on nose and pouch on side,
> His youthful hose, well saved, a world too wide
> For his shrunk shank; and his big manly voice,
> Turning again toward childish treble, pipes
> And whistles in his sound. Last scene of all,
>
>         \*   \*   \*
>
> Is second childishness and mere oblivion,
> Sans teeth, sans eyes, sans taste, sans everything.[30]

The learned counterpart is Robert Burton's statement that a condition

> natural to all, and which no man living can avoid, is old age, which being cold and dry, and of the same quality as Melancholy is, must needs cause it, by diminution of spirits and substance, and increasing of adust humours. Therefore, Melancthon avers out of Aristotle, as an undoubted truth, *semes plerumque delirasse in senecta*, that old men familiarly dote, *ob atram bilem* for black choler, which is then superabundant in them.[31]

Burton's treatise is not noteworthy because it deals with aspects of old age. The hygiene of senescence is an ancient theme. From antiquity onward there was a general assumption that if physicians knew enough, and men paid attention to hygienic modes of life, human beings could achieve longevity. Galen's work has been mentioned. During the medieval period, works on personal hygiene concerned themselves with such matters, and increasingly with the Renaissance books appeared under the title, *De vita longa*.[32] The classical example of this trend is the work of Luigi Cornaro, *Discorsi della Vita Sobria*, first published in 1627 and then reprinted many times. Throughout

---

[30] For a discussion of the ideas concerning successive periods in human life, see Franz Boll, "Die Lebensalter" *Neue Jahrbücher für das klassische Altertum, Ges. & Deutsche Lit.* 31: 89–145, 1913.

[31] Robert Burton, *op. cit.*, p. 240.

[32] H. E. Sigerist, *Landmarks in the History of Hygiene*, London, Oxford University Press, 1956, pp. 36–46.

this period and later, physicians and other writers showed deep concern for the hard lot of the aged, and offered advice on how to mitigate the burdens of senility. Thomas Newton's *The Old Mans Dietarie* appeared in 1586; *A Discourse of the Preservation of the Sight: of Melancholike Diseases; of Rheumes, and of Old Age*, by André DuLaurens, appeared in 1599;[33] and there were others.

Robert Burton's rambling but highly readable encyclopedia of practically everything that had been written on insanity up to his time is worthy of attention just because it is an entertaining *omnium gatherum* of anecdote, citation and knowledge. For one, it clearly reveals the roots of the Renaissance theory of mental pathology. This theory had its direct origins in the humoral speculations of Hippocrates and his successors. The mixture of the humours and elements influenced the occurrence of physical disease and was also responsible for peculiarities of behaviour. Among these is the morbid condition called melancholy, produced ultimately by the presence of black bile, the melancholic humour, in abnormal quantity or quality. Secondly, in his analysis of the causes of melancholy, Burton touches on another facet of his time which throws a light, even though a baleful one, on the psychopathology of old people, as well as on their social situation in the sixteenth and seventeenth century.

Melancholy men, Burton asserts, are easy prey for the Devil, who "moves the phantasy by mediation of the humours"[34] Furthermore, evil spirits "take all opportunities of humours decayed, or otherwise, to pervert the soul of man; and besides, the humour itself is *Balneum Diaboli*, the Devil's Bath, and, as *Agrippa* proves doth entice him to seize upon them."[35] This may lead to insanity through diabolical possession. Another possibility is that such persons will enter into a compact with the Devil and exercise infernal powers. This belief in the Prince of Darkness and in the existence of witches provides the context within which physicians and others frequently dealt with the mental pathology of old people, and especially of old women.

It is not my intention here to examine at length the complex evolution of the witchcraft delusion which reached its acme in the sixteenth and seventeenth centuries.[36] There can be no doubt that the

[33] Republished as Shakespeare Association Facsimile no. 15, 1938. This work first appeared in French in 1597.

[34] Robert Burton, *op. cit.*

[35] Robert Burton, *op. cit.*, p. 493.

[36] The literature on witchcraft and related matters is tremendous; interested readers may consult the following: J. Hansen, *Zauberwahn, Inquisition und Hexenprozess im Mittelalter*, Munich and Leipzig, R. Oldenbourg, 1900; H. C. Lea, *Materials towards a History of Witchcraft*, 3 vols., Philadelphia, University of Pennsylvania Press, 1939. See above Chapter I.

witchcraft delusion was created in the later Middle Ages by the Catholic Church. Little by little, the Church in its struggle against heresy equated it with sorcery and witchcraft. In 1484, Innocent VIII declared open war on witches with the promulgation of his bull "Summis desiderantes." Five years later, Krämer and Sprenger, the two chief Inquisitors for Germany produced the notorious *Malleus Maleficarum,,* the Hammer of Witches, a textbook of procedure for witchcraft trials. Thenceforth, torture and mythology operating on the basis of hallucination and suggestion, sexual antagonisms, family stresses, social struggles and mental disorder created an empire of darkness which then acquired a momentum of its own. How could it be stopped? Not by the Reformation. Protestant clergymen and lay officials could be as bigoted as those in Catholic circles.[37] Gradually the return to reality was brought about by the voice of reason in some areas, and by the Inquisition itself in others. For example in Spain the Inquisition as early as 1537 recognized that alleged witches might be insane, and there are several cases on record where such individuals were transferred to hospitals.[38] Meanwhile, thousands of people had been tried as witches and many had been executed. From the records of these cases and from the writings on witchcraft we derive our knowledge of the psychopathology of old age in this period.

Most of the people accused of being witches were women. Furthermore, in the light of the official doctrine that the witches were an organized sect bent on subverting the social order, it is worth noting that many of the accused were old women, ignorant peasants, who could not possibly have performed the evil deeds ascribed to them. As early as 1550, Girolamo Cardano in his treatise *De subtilitate* described those called *lamiae* or vulgarly *strigae* as miserable, beggarly old women who subsisted on chestnuts, herbs and a little milk. Pale, emaciated, deformed, taciturn and stupid were the epithets he applied to them, and he felt that they differed little from those whom he termed demoniacs.

More important in considering such old women accused of witchcraft as mentally ill is Johann Weyer. In his book, *De praestigiis daemonum et incantantionibus ac veneficiis*, first published in 1563, while maintaining his belief in witchcraft, he insisted that the accused witches were only melancholy old women misled by the Devil. The alleged witches are "well on in years, naturally melancholy,

[37] Oskar Pfister, *Calvins Eingreifen in die Hexer- und Hexenprozesse von Peney 1545 nach seiner Bedeutung für Geschichte und Gegenwart*, Zürich, Artemis Verlag, 1947.
[38] H. C. Lea, *A History of the Inquisition of Spain*, New York, Macmillan Company, 1907, vol. 3, pp. 58–63.

feeble of intellect, inclined to despondency, and weak in their faith in God."

Similar ideas were expressed in England by Reginald Scot in his work, *The Discoveries of Witchcraft* (1584). The supposed witches, he said, are

> commonly old, lame, bleare-eied, fowle, and full of wrinkles . . . in whose drousie minds the divell hath goten a fine seat; so as, what mischeefe, mischance, calamitie, or slaughter is brought to passe, they are easily persuaded the same is doone by themselves; imprinting in their minds an earnest and constant imagination hereof. They are leane and deformed, shewing melancholie in their faces . . . They are doting, scolds, mad, divelish . . .[39]

Scot's description reminds one of Cardano, but like Weyer he too conceives of witchcraft as a supernatural work.

Of the two chief accused witches in the Lancaster trials, one was a very old woman, "about the age of fourscore years" and blind. The other was "a very old withered and decrepit creature, her sight almost gone."[40] Thomas Potts who acted as clerk to the court in this case describes old Mother Chattox with "her lippes ever chattering and talking; but no man knew what." In some instances there are more precise descriptions of senile psychotic behaviour.[41]

Furthermore, one must keep in mind that the accusation of witchcraft frequently arose because the person was odd. Insanity is not enough of an explanation. Ackerknecht has pointed out that the psychopathology of the queer and awkward people in society is due "much more to their ambiguous position than to their organic structure."[42] For a long time, women, and especially old women, were undoubtedly among the awkward ones of the social group and occupied an equivocal position. Christopher Fry caught the point well in his play, *The Lady's Not for Burning*, when the accused girl asks:

> Why do they call me a witch?
> Remember my father was an alchemist.
> I live alone, preferring loneliness
> To the companionable suffocation of an aunt,

[39] Reginald Scot, *The Discovery of Witchcraft* (*1584*) London, 1886, p. 5.

[40] Thomas Potts, *The Wonderful Discoverie of Witches in the Countie of Lancaster, 1613*, ed. with introduction by G. B. Harrison, London, Peter Davies, 1929, pp. 16, 33.

[41] C. Rogers, *Scotland, Social and Domestic*, London, 1869, p. 301.

[42] E. H. Ackerknecht, "Psychopathology, primitive medicine and primitive culture," *Bull. Hist. Med.* 14: 30, 1943.

I still amuse myself with simple experiments
In my father's laboratory. Also I speak
French to my poodle. Then you must know
I have a peacock which on Sundays
Dines with me indoors.

Reginald Scot went to the heart of the matter in terms of cause and effect when he pointed out:

> that lawful favour and Christian compassion be rather used towards these poore soules, rather than rigour and extremitie. Because they, which are commonlie accused of witchcraft, are the least sufficient of all others to speak for themselves; as having the most base and simple education of all others; the extremitie of their age giving them leave to dote, their povertie to beg, their wrongs to chide and threaten (as being void of any other waie of revenge), their humor melancholicall to be full of imaginations, from whence cheefely proceedeth the vanities of their confessions . . .

Furthermore, from this point of view it is not surprising that children brought up in the environment where witchcraft was identified with such old women should have selected them for accusation.[43]

By the later seventeenth century the new scientific attitude had penetrated the study of witchcraft and demonology. Physicians collected detailed case histories of demoniacs, and began to use the terms physiology and pathology in this connection. These data were also used by deists and rationalists to explain such beliefs and observations in terms of mental illness.[44] Christian Thomasius led the fight in Germany against the witchcraft persecutions, and Frederick II of Prussia said of him that he "vindicated the right of women to grow old in safety."[45]

During this period, the gradual emergence of modern medicine based on clinico-pathological correlation began to lay the foundation for a deeper understanding of ageing and old age. Physicians whose names are better known in other connections, such as Philippe Pinel, were concerned with old people as patients. It is not often remembered that a large part of his medical life was passed in an institution

[43] E. Caulfield, "Pediatric aspects of the Salem witchcraft tragedy: a lesson in mental health," *American Journal of Diseases of Children* 65: 788, 1943; M. Tramer, "Kinder im Hexenglauben und Hexenprozess des Mittelalters. Kind und Aberglaube," *Zeitschrift für Kinderpsychiatrie* 11: 140–149, 180–187, 1945.

[44] Frank E. Manuel, *The Eighteenth Century Confronts the Gods*, Cambridge, Mass., Harvard University Press, 1959, pp. 70–81.

[45] H. Luden, *Christian Thomasius nach seinen Schicksalen und Schriften* Berlin, 1805, pp. 270, 283.

concerned with the aged.[46] During the first half of the nineteenth century a growing number of books and articles appeared dealing with the diseases and health problems of the aged, so that, by 1868, Charcot could say: "the importance of a special study of the diseases of the aged can today no longer be opposed."[47]

It is within this context that we must see the more recent observations and descriptions of the mental pathology of the aged. Many of the older somatic ideas on the causation of insanity were simply applied to old people. Carlisle, in 1818, believed that keeping the digestive system in proper order is important for the mental health of the aged. Many diseases, he said, are caused by disturbances of digestion and poor dietetic habits, and this extends to insanity. "May not some kinds of mania be attributable to continued disturbances of the stomach and bowels ..."[48]

Similar ideas were offered in a Berlin medical dissertation of 1835.[49] Due to increasingly inadequate digestion in old age, waste products accumulate and are carried by the blood to the distal parts including the head. There they cause headache, dizziness and apoplexy. Furthermore, in old age the senses decline, there is atrophy of the brain, and loss of memory.

The most comprehensive account of the psychopathology of old age in this period is found in two works, the treatise on geriatrics by Canstatt published in 1839, and the treatise on mental illness by Esquirol which appeared a year earlier.[50]

Canstatt pointed out that the old person suffers a decline of sensory perception and this leads to false judgements and ideas concerning his environment. Only his experience can help him correct these misconceptions. Furthermore, the old person easily becomes egoistic, suspicious, superstitious, and stingy. Some old people, he remarks, are marked by moroseness, irascibility, intolerance, and as a result become a burden and nuisance to their environment. Other old people develop a kind of mental apathy which can lead to suicide.

[46] P. Pinel, *Traité de médecine clinique*, Paris, 1815, p. XIII; Louis Boucher *La Salpêtrière. Son Histoire de 1656 à 1790. Ses origines et son fonctionnement au XVIIIe siècle*, Paris, 1883.

[47] J.-M. Charcot, *Leçons sur les maladies des vieillards et les maladies chroniques*, Paris, Adrien Delahaye, 1868, p. 3.

[48] Anthony Carlisle, *An Essay on the Disorders of Old Age and on the Means for Prolonging Human Life*, London, 1818, p. 65.

[49] Michael Josephus Nettekoven, *De morbis senii nonnulla*, Berlin, 1835, pp. 10, 13.

[50] Carl Friedrich Canstatt, *Die Krankheiten des höheren Alters und ihre Heilung*, 2 vols., Erlangen, Ferdinand Enke, 1839; J. E.D. Esquirol, *Des Maladies mentales considérées sous les rapports médical, hygiénique et médico-legal*, 2 vols., Paris, 1838.

Old people suffer from insomnia, vertigo, somnolence, and attacks of fainting. The most common form of insanity in the aged is senile dementia.

Esquirol gave the first good description of the mental changes of old age under the heading, senile dementia. He described the condition as follows:

> Senile dementia results from the progress of age. Man, passing insensibly into old age, loses his sensibility along with the free use of the faculties of understanding, before arriving at an extreme state of decrepitude. Senile dementia is established slowly. It commences with feebleness of memory, particularly the memory of recent impressions. The sensations are feeble; the attention, at first fatiguing, at length becomes impossible; the will is uncertain and without impulsion; the movements are slow and impracticable. Senile dementia begins rather often, however, by a general excitation which persists for a very long time, and which is revealed first by one function and then by another. This function is exercised with a new and unaccustomed energy which deceives the old man and inspires with awe those about him. Thus, there are some who, before becoming demented, experience a great sensitiveness, are irritated by the least thing; some are very active, wishing to undertake all sorts of things. Others experience sexual desires which have been dormant for a long time and which lead to acts contrary to their habits of continence. Some others, very sober, have an unrestrained appetite for highly spiced food, for wine and for liquors. Dementia follows closely after this hyperexcitation. These symptoms of general excitation are the first signs of senile dementia. The passing from excitation to dementia is abrupt, especially when old people are contrary and unreasonable in their desires, or placed in a position in which it is impossible to satisfy them.[51]

To this clinical picture, Prichard added several years later that "senile decay is occasionally the consequence of various disorders affecting the brain, such as long continued mania, or melancholia, or attack of apoplexy, or paralysis, or severe and often repeated attacks of epilepsy or typhoid fevers in which the brain has been much affected."[52]

The following decades added little. General advice on ageing continued to be offered, and this included some mental hygiene.[53]

[51] J. E. D. Esquirol, *op. cit.*, p. 261.

[52] J. C. Prichard, *On the Different Forms of Insanity in Relation to Jurisprudence*, London, 1842, p. 228.

[53] J. H. Reveillé-Parise, *Traité de la Vieillesse Hygienique, médical et philosophique*, Paris, J.-B. Baillère, 1853; George E. Day, *A Practical Treatise on the Domestic Management and Most Important Diseases of Advanced Life*, London, 1849.

Increasing attention began to be given to the pathological anatomy of old age, but histopathology was still in its beginnings.[54] Geist in his treatise on the diseases of the aged, published in 1860, presented the best general compilation of knowledge at this time, but added little definite to the earlier descriptions of Canstatt, Esquirol and Prichard.[55]

A significant contribution to the mental pathology of old age was provided by Wille in 1873–74.[56] He endeavoured to clarify the etiological, pathogenetic, and pathological-anatomical aspects of this area of investigation. The major point of the paper is the differential diagnosis of senile dementia from general paralysis. Wille also points out the importance of apparently mild depressive reactions in old people and that these may end in suicide.

Legrand du Saulle, Beard, Maudsley, and others concerned themselves with the legal aspects of senile dementia.[57] It was not until the close of the nineteenth century that histopathological studies finally began to clarify some aspects of this condition. In 1898, Redlich reported miliary plaques in the brain in cases of senile cerebral atrophy associated with memory defects and mental confusion.[58] Gradually, histological and clinical studies differentiated arteriosclerotic vascular disease from neurosyphilis on the one hand and from senile psychoses on the other. Kraepelin's textbook in its seventh edition has a well-defined clinicopathologic differentiation between senile dementia and psychoses with cerebral arteriosclerosis. In 1910, Simchowicz produced a thorough anatomic study of senile dementia, a work which is still useful.[59]

The pathological and clinical studies were made possible by the collection of increasing numbers of older people in public institutions

---

[54] C. L. M. Durand-Fardel, *Traité clinique et pratique des maladies des vieillards*, Paris, Baillière, 1854, pp. 1–334.

[55] L. Geist, *Klinik der Greisenkrankheiten*, Erlangen, Ferdinand Enke, 1860, pp. 162–169, 512–638.

[56] Wille, "Die Psychosen des Greisenalters," *Allg. Ztschr. Psychiat.* 30: 269–294, 1873–74.

[57] H. Legrand du Saulle, *La Folie devant les Tribunaux*, Paris, F. Savy, 1864, pp. 124–125, 146–148; idem, *Le Délire des Persecutions*, Paris, Henri Plon, 1871, pp. 104–107, 279–289; George M. Beard, *Legal Responsibility in Old Age, Based on Researches into the Relation of Age to Work*, New York, 1874; Henry Maudsley, *Responsibility in Mental Disease*, New York, D. Appleton & Co., 1900, pp. 273–287.

[58] Redlich, "Über eigenartige Krankheitsfälle des späteren Alters," *Ztschr. für ges. Neurol. und Psychiat.* 4: 365, 1898.

[59] T. Simchowicz, "Histologische Studien über die senile Demenz," *Histologische und histopathologische Arbeiten über die Grosshirnrinde mit besonderer Berücksichtigung der pathologischen Anatomie der Geisteskrankheiten* 4: 268, 1910.

—hospitals, workhouses, asylums for the insane.[60] This tendency to accumulate large numbers of old people in institutions which has continued to the present is due not alone to the increasing age of the general population, but even more importantly to a number of social factors which have profoundly affected the health status of older people. These include industrialization, urbanization, the consequent changes in the family, the attitudes of the community to poverty and the indigent aged, the philosophy of economy and centralization in administration, as well as the availability of various facilities such as hospitals and asylums. In large measure, many of these factors have tended to thrust aside the aged individual and to leave him socially isolated and alienated. Furthermore, ours is a work culture. Work gives a person a way of spending his days usefully; it also enables him to develop social relations with fellow workers. All these elements have a definite bearing on the mental health or ill health of the older person.

It often appears that the problems of old people, including mental ill health, are a special characteristic of modern Western civilization. While this survey is by no means exhaustive, it has shown I believe that in all ages men have cried out,

> What shall I do with this absurdity—
> O heart, O troubled heart—this caricature,
> Decrepit age that has been tied to me
> As to a dog's tail?[61]

Yet there are differences between the present and the past. Within the past hundred years, and especially in the last four decades, the ancient view that old age is necessarily a period of deterioration has been replaced, at least on a conceptual level, by the idea that ageing and disease are not synonymous. Ageing is conceived as an evolutionary process characteristic of all living matter. This process, which represents the shifting balance over a period of time between evolution or growth and involution or atrophy, leads to a fundamental biological alteration which is part of the condition designated in human beings as old age. At the same time, evidence increasingly indicates that disease is the outcome of interaction between aetiologic factors in the environment and the hereditary character and structure of the individual, no matter whether the individual is twenty

[60] Wille, "Die Psychosen des Greisenalters," *op. cit.*; W. K. Jordan, *Philanthropy in England 1480–1660*, London, George Allen & Unwin, 1959; George Crabbe, *Poems*, Cambridge, Cambridge University Press, 1905, vol. 1, pp. 417–447; Charles Booth, *Old Age Pensions and the Aged Poor. A Proposal*, London, Macmillan & Co., 1899, p. 14.

[61] W. B. Yeats, *Collected Poems*, New York, Macmillan, 1951, p. 192.

or sixty years old. These ideas are directly relevant to the mental health problems and needs of the aged. While it is difficult indeed to separate the role of inherited constitution from the influence of environmental elements, the fact remains that environment is generally more easily modifiable than constitution. When a belief in witchcraft was accepted in a disordered society looking for scapegoats who could be blamed for its terrors, senile women were burnt or hanged as witches. In the nineteenth century, if they were indigent they were relegated to the almshouse or the workhouse infirmary. Society had changed, not the women.

Thus the key to prevention, control, and therapy of mental pathology in old people lies not alone in the impaired individual, but also and even more significantly in understanding the perceptual and social environment in which he exists. Obviously our goal is not to produce Swiftian Stuldbruggs, and as more is learned about the effects of various stresses, strains and insults of living, it should be possible to influence favourably the course and future of an ageing population.[62] Whittenberger has clearly and succinctly formulated this viewpoint. "The impairment with age is real," he points out,

> but the results are not necessarily serious, as long as internal and external stresses are reduced in proportion to diminished adaptive capacities of the aged. Compensatory mechanisms and experience minimize the results of physiologic limitations, but more and more of these factors are called into play as the organism ages. Much could be done in preservation of function of the elderly, if attention were paid to maintenance of high levels of mental and physical activity. The organism will eventually "run down" as physiologic reserves are exhausted but meanwhile everything possible will have been done to make life not only longer but more satisfying.[63]

[62] Jonathan Swift, *Gulliver's Travels and Selected Writings in Prose and Verse*, New York, Random House, 1949, pp. 206–210.

[63] J. L. Whittenberger, "The nature and response to stress with aging," *Bull. New York Acad. Med.* 32: 336, 1956.

246

CHAPTER NINE

# PATTERNS OF DISCOVERY AND CONTROL IN MENTAL ILLNESS

As possible factors in the aetiology of general paresis, Krafft-Ebing in 1877, listed such diverse elements as heredity, the menopause, trauma to the head, excessive heat and cold, fright, alcoholism, excessive venery, exhaustion as a result of earning a living, and the smoking of from ten to twenty Virginia cigars daily.[1] While sexual dissipation is included, there is no specific mention of syphilis. Indeed as late as 1898, the pathologist, Virchow, vigorously denied the syphilitic origin of general paresis.[2] Yet, twenty years before Krafft-Ebing's discussion, in 1857, Esmarch and Jessen had already postulated a causal relationship between syphilis and mental disorder,[3] and fifteen years after Virchow's dogmatic denial, Noguchi and Moore demonstrated Treponema pallidum in the brain of paretic patients.[4]

Throughout most of this period, however, despite accumulating evidence in favour of an infectious origin, causal explanations of general paresis in psychologic and social terms continued to enjoy credit. Indeed, the situation was not unlike that which characterizes current efforts to unravel and to achieve an understanding of the aetiology of the functional psychoses. No single view on the causation and pathogenesis of these disorders is currently regarded as generally acceptable. Rather a multiplicity of diverse viewpoints prevails.[5] Schizophrenia may be taken as an example. Bowman and Rose point out that "A great many explanations of what goes on in schizophrenia have been proposed and attempts made to account for the clinical data by relating them to one theoretical framework or

---

[1] R. von Krafft-Ebing, "Zur Kenntniss des paralytischen Irreseins beim weiblichen Geschlecht," *Archiv für Psychiatrie und Nervenkrankheiten* 7: 182–188, 1876–1877.

[2] R. Virchow in the session of the Berliner medizinische Gesellschaft, 6 July 1898, *Berliner klinische Wochenschrift* 35: 691–692, 1898.

[3] F. Esmarch and W. Jessen, "Syphilis und Geistesstörung," *Allg. Ztschr. Psychiat.* 14: 20–36, 1857.

[4] H. Noguchi and J. W. Moore, "A Demonstration of Treponema pallidum in the Brain in Cases of General Paralysis," *Journal of Experimental Medicine* 17: 232–238, 1913.

[5] For example, see H. D. Kruse, ed., *Integrating the Approaches to Mental Disease*, New York, Hoeber-Harper, 1957.

another. There are explanations which are largely psychodynamic, cultural or sociological, psychosomatic, biological (including hereditary), and biochemical."[6]

This situation has in part created and in part been affected by a concept of aetiology which is as inchoate as it is all-embracing. The most succinct expression of this standpoint was offered in 1955 by the National Advisory Mental Health Council. "The concept of aetiology as embraced by modern psychiatry," it said, "differs from the simple cause and effect system of traditional medicine. It subscribes to a 'field theory' hypothesis in which the interactions and transactions of multiple factors eventuate in degrees of health or sickness."[7] From this idea it is not far to the recent statement by Menninger and his co-workers that "There are no natural mental disease entities," or to the logical corollary of this retreat into resignation—a unitary concept of mental illness and health.[8]

In the face of the confusion and obscurity, not to say obscurantism, which mark numerous current endeavours to understand and to control mental illness, a retrospective analysis of the ways in which certain earlier problems of mental disease have been untangled and controlled may perhaps shed light on the nature of current difficulties. Do these earlier instances exhibit some pattern of development, or of discovery? Can certain types of data emerge, or be understood only at certain levels in such a pattern? Are we at present, perhaps, expecting too much from too little? Is the concept of aetiology in terms of "anything goes" hindering the most effective ordering of the available data? Are there cultural biases that predispose clinicians and research investigators to lend credence more readily to some reports than to others, or to seek in one direction rather than in another? With such questions in mind, the history of general paresis, cretinism, and the psychosis of pellagra will now be examined.

### General Paresis

Appearing in Europe towards the end of the fifteenth century as an acute epidemic disease, syphilis spread rapidly through the population. Following the outbreak of the disease, however, there was no definite mention for almost two hundred years of any clinical

[6] Alfred Auerback, ed., *Schizophrenia. An Integrated Approach*, New York, Ronald Press, 1959, p. 7.

[7] National Advisory Mental Health Council, National Institute of Mental Health, *Evaluation in Mental Health, A Review of the Problem of Evaluating Mental Health Activities*, Public Health Service Publ. No. 413, Washington, D.C., Govt. Printing Office, 1955, p. 11.

[8] K. Menninger, H. Ellenberger, P. Pruyser and M. Mayman, "The Unitary Concept of Mental Illness", *Bulletin of the Menninger Clinic* 22: 4–12, 1958.

manifestations that can with certainty be attributed to general paresis.[9] Indeed, it was not until the early decades of the nineteenth century that general paresis was identified as a separate disease entity. How can we explain this striking fact? Were there no cases of paralysis? Did the disease appear but was not recognized? While it is doubtful whether these questions can ever be answered with any finality, a plausible explanation may be advanced.

Account must be taken first of changes in concepts of disease. Ancient and medieval physicians did not generally distinguish different specific diseases, but were concerned rather with various groups of symptoms exhibited by sick people. A new and important approach to the problem of the nature of disease was made, however, in the seventeenth century by Thomas Sydenham. Not primarily concerned with the ultimate nature of disease, he directed his attention to the phenomena observed at the bedside. Furthermore, he thought in terms of diseases rather than of disease as a general condition, and was firmly convinced that it was possible to draw up a complete picture of each disease, much as one described a plant or animal. By abstracting the signs and symptoms which he saw repeatedly in sick people, and arranging them in a co-ordinated manner Sydenham arrived at a concept of a disease as an entity, an objective thing in itself.

This idea of disease description and differentiation was taken up and developed during the eighteenth century. However, these efforts to describe and classify morbid conditions had great shortcomings. Symptoms furnished the only basis upon which diseases could be distinguished, with the result that symptoms exhibiting a superficial similarity, but differing widely in pathogenesis and significance were often grouped together. There was as yet no clear-cut idea of the intimate relationship between organ lesion and clinical observation. This situation is reflected in the earliest reports relating to general paralysis.

Beginning with Willis in 1672, a number of writers—Haslam (1798), Cox (1804), Esquirol (1805, 1814), Georget (1820), Delaye (1824), Calmeil (1826)—described a kind of paralysis associated with mental illness.[10] The clinical features of the condition were

[9] Mönkemöller, "Zur Geschichte der progressiven Paralyse," *Ztschr. ges. Neurol. und Psychiat.* 5: 499–589, 1911; T. H. Kirchhoff, "Ist die Paralyse eine moderne Krankheit? Eine historischkritische Studie," *Allg. Ztschr. Psychiat.* 68: 125–152, 1911.

[10] Lunier, "Recherches sur la paralysie générale progressive pour servir à l'histoire de cette maladie," *Annales médico-psychologiques* 1849, 183; Baillarger, "De la découverte de la paralysie générale et des doctrines émises par les premiers auteurs," *ibid.* 28: 509–526, 1859, 29: 1–14, 1860; Krafft-Ebing, "Zur Geschichte und Literatur der Dementia paralytica," *Allg. Ztschr. Psychiat.* 23: 627, 1866.

described quite accurately by these authors, but they were not aware that they were dealing with a separate and distinct disease entity. Some considered the paralysis an illness causally independent of the associated dementia, or as a complication of various forms of mental disorder. Clinical observation was not enough to establish general paresis as a disease entity, particularly in view of its chronic development, its variegated manifestations and unknown aetiology.

Furthermore, a number of other factors must be taken into account. In the first place, syphilis was originally an acute disease which killed a number of its victims before tertiary manifestations could develop or become apparent. Second, the mortality in earlier periods was so high because of epidemics, famines, wars, and diseases due to insanitary conditions that many possible candidates for tertiary lues died much earlier in life. In seventeenth-century France, for example, of 1,000 live births, only 475 individuals attained the age of 20, 318 the age of 40, and 130 the age of 60.[11] Third, not all syphilitics develop general paresis. Obviously, in order to arrive at the concept of a distinct disease entity, something more than mere clinical observation was necessary.

The clinical approach to the study of disease was paralleled by an anatomical one. Anatomical investigation had been sedulously cultivated for centuries, and in the course of innumerable dissections and autopsies, a mass of pathological observations was collected. Gradually the view gained ground that the reactions observed in human beings under the stress of disease are related to the organ lesions found after death. This idea was first given effective expression by Morgagni in his work *De sedibus et causis morborum* which appeared in 1761 at Venice. In this famous book, Morgagni showed conclusively that disease has a definite seat in the organs and that pathological changes in organs are responsible for most symptoms. By firmly linking the symptoms which constitute the clinical picture of a disease to an anatomical base which explained them, Morgagni opened up the possibility of observing the mechanism of disease and indicated the path to be followed by future research. The fusion of the clinical and anatomical approaches and their systematic application was the great contribution of the Paris school of clinical pathologists from 1800 to 1850. As a result of their labours there emerged from the earlier uncertainties and confusion relatively clear and critical pictures of diseases based upon the idea that there was a definite connection between the clinical findings and the lesions observed in various organs at autopsy.

Application of this method to the problem of dementia and

[11] Jean Fourastié, "De la vie traditionelle à la vie tertiaire," *Population* 14: 416–432, 1959.

paralysis led eventually by the middle of the nineteenth century to the delineation of a disease characterized by disturbances of motility, mental derangement, and pathological changes in the nervous system underlying these phenomena. This contribution was essentially the work of the French school. In 1822, Bayle offered a concept of general paralysis as a disease entity marked by several distinct stages. The patients exhibited at first a variety of grandiose ideas and excitement; then further disturbances of intellectual function, agitation, and paresis; and finally a greater or lesser obliteration of ideas, extensive paralysis, and sometimes paroxysms of agitation. Bayle felt that the symptoms did not occur as part of any other mental illness.[12]

This important view was not immediately accepted. After all there were cases of progressive general paralysis without mental symptoms. Most of the early studies dealt with asylum populations, and it was felt that the findings did not apply to other groups. Furthermore, there was a considerable lack of clarity as to the sequence and relationships of the mental and physical aspects of the condition. Today it is clear that the widely divergent views were based on the study of different facts.

Some considered the disease as a complication and consequence of various disorders, for example, Esquirol (1838). Others regarded it as a progressive disease with or without mental derangement. Baillarger, in 1847, stressed the division of general paralysis into two categories with or without mental symptoms, and indicated the great importance of differential diagnosis. Since he considered the disturbance of motility primary, Baillarger attempted in the same year to test patients by means of a galvanic current.

By the fifties and sixties, however, the clinical and pathological alterations had been quite accurately delineated. Falret, in 1853, established the nature of the disease in terms which, broadly speaking, are still valid. He described it as a specific mental illness with characteristic paralyses, a typical course and typical psychotic manifestations.[13] Meanwhile other investigators had been making studies of the pathological findings in the nervous system. Parchappe in 1838 reported inflammatory softening of the cerebral cortex in cases of general paralysis, and by 1858 he had autopsied 322 cases confirming his earlier findings.

With the general outlines of the condition fairly well established, attention shifted to the differentiation of the various forms of

[12] A.-L. Bayle, *Traité des maladies du cerveau et de ses membranes*, Paris, 1826, pp. 498–513.

[13] Jules Falret, *Recherches sur la folie paralytique et les diverses paralysies générales*, Paris, 1853, pp. 12–13, 128–131.

paralysis and to the question of aetiology. At the same time, German contributions to these problems became increasingly prominent and significant. Hoffmann reported in 1848 that one-sixth of the patients at Leubus were paralytics, and in 1851 Stolz published similar figures for the asylum at Hall in the Tyrol.[14] The first important German-language clinical description of general paresis, a paper by Duchek of Prague, in which he depicted the four phases of the disease, also appeared in 1851. Attention was turned to the differentiation of general paresis from tabes dorsalis, and in 1871 a means was found to do this. Westphal observed that the patellar tendon reflex was absent in tabes dorsalis, and when it was shown that this reflex was present in general paresis it became possible to separate cases of the two diseases. By the eighties, the clinical phenomena had been quite well defined, and to them were added the results of histopathological studies. While opinions as to the nature of the histopathological changes remained divided for a number of decades, they did establish the physical causation of general paresis. These studies found their culmination in Alzheimer's description in 1904 of the microscopic changes in the brain of general paretics.[15]

The histopathological studies not only provided more precise knowledge of the pathogenesis of general paralysis, but they reflect another shift in the study of the disease, a shift to the laboratory. And it was ultimately through the laboratory that the aetiology of general paralysis was clarified and established. While the early writers on this subject considered the question of aetiology, their views were quite diffuse. Bayle discussed causation in two broad categories, moral and physical. Social and psychological factors which comprised the former group were considered as potent aetiologically as the physical causes. The more frequent occurrence of the disease among former officers and soldiers of the Napoleonic armies was explained in terms of the privations experienced by these men, the terrors of war, their excessive drinking, and the disappointment resulting from the defeat of Napoleon. Emotional causes such as violent love or profound jealousy seemed to be involved in some cases. In others, excessive intellectual activity, grief, sorrow, and similar factors predisposed to the disease. Syphilis was considered a possible aetiological factor, but only one of several. Hereditary tendencies

---

[14] H. Damerow, Review of Hoffmann (Dr. Fr.), *Ursachen der allgemeinen Paresis, Allg. Ztschr. Psychiat.* 7: 155–158, 1850; Stolz, "Zur fortschreitenden allgemeinen Parese," *ibid.*, 8: 517–559, 1851 (see pp. 525–529).

[15] A. Alzheimer, "Histologische Studien zur Differenzialdiagnose der progressiven Paralyse." *Histologische und histopathologische Arbeiten ueber die Grosshirnrinde mit besonderer Berücksichtigung der pathologischen Anatomie der Geisteskrankheiten*, Jean, Gustav Fischer, 1904, vol. 1.

seemed to be more important in some instances, and the pre-
ponderance of the male sex among the patients was considered
significant. The role assigned to syphilis is characteristically summed
up by Bayle.

> About one-fifth of the patients whom I observed indulged in venereal
> excesses and often contracted syphilitic ailments. However, excesses of
> this kind and the illness which follows them are so frequent that I would
> not venture to include them among the predisposing causes of chronic
> meningitis. In addition, a physician, M. Cullerier, whose opinion has
> great weight in this matter, thinks that syphilis has no influence what-
> ever upon the development of mental alienation.[16]

Throughout the first half of the nineteenth century and well into
its second half, French clinicians and those who took their cues from
them, tended to stress sociopsychological and hereditary factors in
the aetiology of general paralysis. For example, Esquirol mentions
that one-twentieth of those admitted to the Salpêtrière were formerly
prostitutes. After indulging in all kinds of excesses, they succumb to a
form of dementia complicated by paralysis. Yet he did not associate
the occupational hazard of these women—syphilitic infection—with
their mental illness. Other examples might be cited. Indeed the
situation is all the more striking because it was during this period
that the French school gained one of its greatest distinctions by
re-establishing clarity in the understanding of clinical syphilis. John
Hunter had thrown the subject into confusion by denying the duality
of syphilis and gonorrhea. Beginning with Ricord in 1837, the French
school developed the clinical knowledge of syphilis as far as could
be done before the discovery of the organism in the twentieth
century. Why then was syphilis not more closely associated with
general paralysis in terms of aetiology?

An answer to this question must take account of the climate of
opinion in which these studies were carried on, and of the elements
in it by which they were affected. Since the eighteenth century the
view was widely held that civilization was an important factor in the
causation of mental illness.[17] Furthermore, during the nineteenth
century many psychiatrists believed that insanity must be increasing
because society was becoming more complex. Edward Jarvis, an
American physician, concluded in 1851 that insanity is "a part of
the price we pay for civilization. The causes of the one increase with
the developments and results of the other."[18] This belief in the rising

[16] Bayle, *op. cit.*, p. 412.
[17] Chapter 6 above.
[18] Edward Jarvis, "On the Supposed Increase of Insanity," *American Journal
of Insanity* 8: 333–364, 1851–1852 (see pp. 363–364).

tide of madness is a theme that is played with numerous variations throughout the century.

Not all investigators subscribed to this view. Esquirol, for example, believed the rise in mental illness was more apparent than real. Nevertheless, the very fact that the problem received so much attention and was so hotly debated meant that special areas of interest like general paralysis were more likely to be affected. Thus, it is not surprising to find the question raised: Is general paralysis a modern disease, and is it increasing?

Lunier, the first historian of the disease, commented in 1849 that while paresis had probably occurred in earlier periods, there was no doubt of its increase with the advance of civilization.[19] Moreau, in 1850, saw the progress of civilization as the cause of the increasing frequency of general paralysis, and Baillarger begins his account of the early history of the disease with the statement: "The occurrence of this terrible disease seems to increase daily."[20] Even at the end of the nineteenth century and in the early years of the twentieth century, at a time when the role of syphilitic infection in the aetiology of general paresis was becoming increasingly clear, attention was still focused on the rise in the number of cases and the possible social causes of this development. Krafft-Ebing, in 1895, attributed this increase to changes in social conditions which had brought about a physical, and even more specifically neurological deterioration of large segments of the population.[21] Kraepelin,[22] Rüdin,[23] and others[24] expressed similar views more than a decade later. According to Kraepelin the civilized peoples had lost certain protective mechanisms, which are still present among primitives and which make it difficult among them for paralysis to develop from lues.

This approach was further reinforced by the introduction of Morel's degeneration hypothesis in 1857.[25] He defined degenerations as pathological deviations from the normal type, which are trans-

---

[19] Lunier, *op. cit.*, p. 205.

[20] Baillarger, *op. cit.*, p. 509.

[21] R. von Krafft-Ebing, "Ueber die Zunahme der progressiven Paralyse, im Hinblick auf die sociologischen Factoren," *Jahrbücher für Psychiatrie und Neurologie*, 13: 127–143, 1894.

[22] E. Kraepelin, "Zur Entartungsfrage," *Zentralblatt für Nervenheilkunde und Psychiatrie* 31: 745–751, 1908.

[23] Rüdin, "Ueber den Zusammenhang zwischen Zivilisation und Geisteskrankheit," Bericht des IV. Internationalen Kongresses der Fürsorge für Geisteskranke, Berlin, 1910.

[24] E.g. Kirchhoff (see note 9), who raises the question of whether the statistics indicate an actual increase in the number of cases or an increased ability on the part of physicians to make a correct diagnosis.

[25] G. Genil-Perrin, *Histoire des origines et de l'évolution de l'idée de dégénérescence en médecine mentale*, Paris, 1913, pp. 39–47.

missible through heredity and which develop progressively to death. Degeneration was due to intoxication, social milieu, pathological temperament, heredity, and acquired or congenital insults of various kinds. Once acquired, the various generations of a family went inexorably to their doom. Mental illness was the degenerative condition par excellence, and for many general paralysis became a degenerative disease. This theory of predestination in terms of an original biological sin exerted a powerful attraction on many psychiatrists, and directed their attention away from any concept of specific aetiology. This was a comfortable position to occupy at a time when specific aetiology in general was largely out of favour, and epidemiological theories were framed in vague environmental terms.[26]

Under such circumstances, it becomes clearer why syphilis seemed to be no more significant in the aetiology of general paralysis than other factors. Nevertheless, it was in the very year in which Morel brought out his degeneration hypothesis that Esmarch and Jessen proposed a specific aetiology for the disease with syphilis as the essential cause.[27] Interestingly enough, Griesinger, who insisted that mental diseases are illnesses of the brain, rejected this hypothesis as improbable. Nonetheless, the evidence in support of this assumption accumulated slowly but surely. In a statistical study, Jaspersen, a Dane, showed in 1874 that 90 per cent of all paralytics had previously had syphilis.[28] By 1894, Fournier was able to cite a number of statistical studies which showed that syphilitic infection was far more common in the history of general paretics than in the past of other mental patients. It was found in 65 per cent of the former and only in 10 per cent of the latter. "Such being the case," Fournier concluded, "how in any logical sense is it possible for syphilis to have no connection with the causation of general paralysis?"[29]

The answer of course became increasingly evident. From a variety of sources evidence accumulated and made it more and more difficult to dispute that the close correlation between syphilis and general paresis was an aetiological one. A striking piece of evidence was provided by Krafft-Ebing in 1897. Nine paretics with no history of syphilitic infection were inoculated with luetic material. None of the experimental subjects developed secondary symptoms, and the inference was drawn that they had previously been infected.[30] This

[26] C. J. Salomonsen, *Epidemiologiske theorier i den første halvdel af det nittende aarhundrede*, Kjøbenhaven, 1910.

[27] Esmarch and Jessen, *op. cit.*

[28] J. Bodamer, "Zur Entstehung der Psychiatrie als Wissenschaft im 19 Jahrhundert. Eine geistesgeschichtliche Untersuchung," *Fortschritte der Neurologie, Psychiatrie und ihrer Grenzgebiete* 21: 511–535, 1953 (see p. 534).

[29] A. Fournier, *Les affections parasyphilitiques*, Paris, 1894, pp. 176–177.

[30] R. von Krafft-Ebing, *Die Aetiologie der progressiven Paralyse*, 1897, vol. II, p. 12.

I*

observation is obviously similar to those upon which Colles based his dictum of 1837 that a woman who gave birth to a syphilitic child was herself immune to syphilis.

Further important support came from the laboratory. Under the influence of Virchow's cellular pathology, a number of investigators undertook to study the pathological changes in tissues and cells. With the creation of the conceptual and technical bases of microbiology, others began to study the immunological properties of blood and other body fluids. In 1890, Quincke showed that cerebrospinal fluid could be obtained by direct lumbar puncture, and investigations of this material were soon turned to diagnostic purposes. Study of the chemical and cytological components of the cerebrospinal fluid revealed a combination of findings charcteristic of general paresis. In 1906, Wassermann and his co-workers evolved the complement-fixation test known by his name, and other tests were developed later. The serological tests not only confirmed the syphilitic nature of active lesions, but also showed that a latent syphilis could be present in an individual, even though there were no active lesions. Lange introduced the colloidal gold test in 1912.

By this time, the syphilitic aetiology of general paresis was quite generally accepted. As Mönkemöller put it in 1911, "the opponents of this causal connection are almost completely silenced."[31] Finally, in 1913, all remaining doubts were set aside by the demonstration of the syphilitic organism in paretic brains. More than two hundred years after the problem of general paresis first appeared dimly on the medical horizon, this discovery finally brought clarity into a perplexing aetiological problem and made possible an approach to rational methods of control. Obviously, if syphilis was the ultimate cause, prevention of paresis meant prevention of syphilis. Where this could not be achieved, early detection and treatment of syphilitic infection were in order. And it was now possible to endeavour to develop a rational therapy directed at the cause. As is well known, the steady decline in the incidence of general paresis has been due to the measures of control instituted in the last forty years on the basis I have just described.

I have devoted a large part of this discussion to general paresis because it illustrates clearly a number of important points. One is the problem of conceptualization. Whether one or more clinical observations represent a single disease entity or a group of phenomenologically similar, but basically unrelated disorders is a matter of fundamental importance. In order to establish aetiology, whether single or multiple, one has to have some reasonably clear notion of the entity to which aetiological factors are related. This problem is not

[31] Mönkemöller, *op. cit.*, p. 500.

unique to mental illness but applies as well to other diseases. For a long time this was a problem in pulmonary tuberculosis, where a number of conditions with common clinical symptoms were subsumed under the common label "consumption." Eventually, consumption was separated into several distinct entities with differing aetiologies. Very probably the understanding of schizophrenia is at a similar level today.

In short, conceptualization at a clinical level is the first stage in understanding a disease. Where a disease occurs in acute form and with striking manifestations, the observations upon which clinical conceptualization is based enable the structuring which results in the discovery of a disease entity. However, where diseases are of long duration and the clinical observations cannot be as sharply delineated or controlled, clinical conceptualization is much more difficult. As a result, the search for aetiologic factors may very possibly lead into blind alleys. The search for meaningful associations of pathogenetic factors must take off from a clinical base, but the clinical data must also be related to observations and data derived from other levels of investigation. This is the second stage in the pattern of discovery. But if the clinical data or variables are not well defined, the significance of information derived from other levels, for example, the chemical or the psychological, may be highly dubious. Horwitt has clearly shown how much research in schizophrenia is vitiated by environmental artifacts based on inadequate recognition or delineation of the involved variables.[32] This does not mean that one should wait until the mental disorders are classified and recognized in pure phenomenological form before beginning the quest for causation, but it does emphasize the need for critical evaluation and understanding of the level at which the problem is being studied.

Levels of investigation may also be considered as frames of reference within which investigators carry on their work. As a reflection of the level of knowledge, the frame of reference tends to focus the investigator's perception of the problem. Where the level of knowledge is essentially clinical and observational, with few correlates on other levels, there is wide latitude for the postulation of putative aetiological factors and processes. A recent article by Kubie on the possibility of a preventive psychiatry is pertinent here.[33] By postulating an almost ubiquitous neurotic process very early in life, and by relating it directly to some of the most complex social institutions, Kubie predetermines his basically negative answer to

[32] M. K. Horwitt, "Fact and Artifact in the Biology of Schizophrenia," *Science* 124: 429, 1956

[33] L. S. Kubie, "Is Preventive Psychiatry Possible?" *Daedalus*, Fall, 1959, 646–668.

the possibility of a preventive psychiatry. Furthermore, by operating within a psychoanalytic frame of reference, and by insisting on the independence of the psychological variables, the postulated neurotic process becomes part of a closed system. In these terms, it can neither be accepted nor rejected out of hand. Ultimate acceptance or rejection would depend on the extent to which data can be obtained outside this framework to support the postulated aetiologic factor or process. Here too the case of general paresis is instructive. Data to support the syphilitic aetiology came not alone from the clinical association of syphilis and general paralysis, but in addition from pathological studies, statistics, microbiology, and immunology. Within this constellation the social and psychological elements then found their appropriate places. In a sense, one can think of linked open conceptual systems where what happens in one system can have an effect on the others.

### Pellagra and Cretinism

The latter point may be usefully examined in the histories of pellagra and cretinism. Pellagra was first observed and described in Spain by Gaspar Casal, a physician of Oviedo.[34] He saw the first cases of the disease, which he called mal de la rosa, in 1735, but his findings were not published until 1762, three years after his death.[35] Thirty-six years after Casal saw the first cases, Francesco Frapolli reported the existence of the disease in Lombardy, and named it pellagra (rough skin), the term by which it is still designated.[36] Thereafter pellagra was observed in France, Rumania, the United States, and in a number of other countries. There is no need here to delve deeply into the history of pellagra. Those who are interested may consult the works of Roussel (1866) and Hirsch (1883–1886).[37]

Significant for this discussion, however, is that pellagra appeared in comparatively recent times as a disease hitherto unknown. The clinical picture was described quite accurately from the very outset— the skin manifestations which gave the disease its name, the general weakness and the systemic complaints, and finally the psychotic manifestations associated with the disease. Clinically, the disease was

[34] For the history of pellagra from the eighteenth century to the middle of the nineteenth century see Théophile Roussel, *Traité de la pellagre et des pseudo-pellagres*, Paris, Baillère, 1866.

[35] Gaspar Casal, *Historia natural y medica de el Principado de Asturias*, Madrid, 1762.

[36] F. Frapolli, *Animadversiones in morbum, vulgo Pelagram*, Milan, 1771.

[37] For Roussel see note 34 above; A. Hirsch, *Handbook of Geographical and Historical Pathology*, 3 vols., London, New Sydenham Society, 1883–1886, vol. II, pp. 217–247.

conceived initially as a distinct entity. Also practically from the outset it was observed that pellagra occurred almost exclusively among the poorest of the rural population. Furthermore, in the search for the aetiology of pellagra attention turned very early to the use of maize as food. While some attempts were made to explain the aetiology of pellagra in terms of contagion or heredity, such explanations were not taken very seriously except for a short period early in the twentieth century.

In contradistinction to general paresis, the story of pellagra is one where the major phenomenological aspects of the disease were established early. However, the essential cause of pellagra was not discovered until two hundred years after it was first observed, and some two decades after a method for controlling the disease had been determined. The latter point is, of course, not unusual. Diabetes mellitus is a good example of an extremely complex metabolic disease in which the accumulation of knowledge and the elucidation of one major link in the causal chain has led to a life-saving form of treatment even though the actual cause of the condition is unknown. How then can we understand the pattern of discovery in pellagra? To answer this question, a brief review of the aetiologic theories current in the nineteenth century will be useful.

There were two basic explanations. One derived from the imputed affinity of pellagra to ergotism. Spoiled grain was known to cause ergotism, and by analogy it was suggested that pellagra was due to damaged maize. Pellagra was thus conceived as the consequence of a toxic process produced by a poison arising out of decomposition changes in maize. The function of the level of knowledge as a perceptual frame is clearly evident in this theory.

The second theory explained pellagra in terms of a protein deficiency. It had been observed that the disease occurred in epidemic form, particulary when there were extreme shortages of food among peasant populations. Yet it was also known that the disease appeared in people who were not among the poorest, but who lived very largely on maize. According to this theory, pellagra was due to the low nutritive value of a maize diet. It appeared where maize formed an exclusive or at least a preponderant part of the diet, and was due specifically to the small amount of nitrogen in it. In short, pellagra was a nitrogen, or protein deficiency disease.

These theories were based on biologic knowledge available in the nineteenth century. The bacteriologic discoveries at the end of that period tended to reinforce the view that disease was due to a pathogenic agent introduced into the organism. This biologically plausible explanation was not consistent with the idea that a disease such as pellagra could be caused by a deficiency of a metabolic constituent, especially a constituent of an unknown kind. And here lies the crucial significance of Goldberger's classic epidemiologic studies, in the irrefutable establishment of a biologically implausible situation, thus creating a whole new area for further study. At the same time, his investigations indicated the means for control of pellagra and its associated psychosis. But the precise biochemical factor, called PP (pellagra preventive) by Goldberger, was not identified with nicotinic acid until 1937.[38]

The history of cretinism is in some respects similar to that of pellagra. Cretinism has been recognized as a clinical entity in Europe since the sixteenth century. The first published descriptions were those of Felix Platter (1602) and Paracelsus (1603). The former's account covers the salient features: disproportion of the body, deaf-mutism and mental retardation. Platter also observed that some cretins had goitres while others did not, and he noted the distribution of cretinism throughout the Alpine lands, particularly Switzerland and Carinthia. Since then good descriptions of cretinism have been given by numerous investigators, and it has been possible to classify this condition into five types: endemic cretinism, congenital thyroid aplasia, familial congenital goitrous cretinism, acquired athyroidism, and acquired hypothyroidism.[39] This classification based on current knowledge derives from the fact that absence or dysfunction of the thyroid gland are central to the production of the cretinous state. There is no doubt that in the eighteenth and nineteenth centuries idiots and other mental defectives were sometimes classed as cretins. However, this did not basically hinder the identification of cretinism and hypothyroidism by Gull in 1873.[40] Furthermore, thyroid medication was a logical sequence of the recognition of the unity of myxoedema and cretinism, and of the role of the thyroid in their aetiology.

Nevertheless, the causation of endemic cretinism has been marked by controversy since the condition was first described. For example, the relationship of endemic goitre to endemic cretinism is still in dispute. More recently the role of genetic factors, especially as an aspect of intermarriage in relatively isolated cretinous districts, has been emphasized in this connection. Suggestive also is Clement's comment that "the discoveries in respect of inherited deafness and congenital deafness, the sequel of maternal rubella, have clearly

[38] G. Rosen, *A History of Public Health*, New York, MD Publications, 1958, pp. 413–414.

[39] F. W. Clements, "Endemic Goitre: Scope of the Health Problem and Related Conditions," *Bulletin of the World Health Organization* 18: 175–300, 1958 (see p. 186). See also Paul F. Cranefield, The Discovery of Cretinism, *Bull. Hist. Med.* 36: 489–511, 1962.

[40] For the history of cretinism see H. D. Rolleston, *The Endocrine Organs in Health and Disease*, London, Oxford University Press, 1936, pp. 157–172.

revealed the need for making careful inquiries into the family history of persons with deaf mutism alone in goitrous areas before labelling them the victims of endemic goitre."[41] Clearly, the problem of cretinism in terms of pathogenesis is still far from solved, even though the condition has been well defined clinically, and much is known about thyroid function in relation to the severity of clinical phenomena.

## *What Does it Mean?*

What inferences, if any, can be drawn from the examples discussed above. I believe they may be set forth as follows: There is a pattern of discovery in the sense that the problem must first be defined in clinical terms. This is more easily accomplished in certain cases; it is more difficult in others. Clinical conceptualization depends to a considerable degree on the acuteness of the morbid process and on the striking character of the presenting signs and symptoms. Pellagra and cretinism are illustrative on this point. Furthermore, diseases have a history not only in the sense that they appear at a given point in time, e.g. pellagra, but also in the sense that some diseases change their character over time, from acute to chronic, from virulent to mild. Account must be taken of such aspects in any endeavour to conceptualize diseases, especially mental illnesses which in so many instances are long-term in character.

Clinical conceptualization, however, is only one aspect of the pattern of discovery. The second is the relation of clinical data to other kinds of data—statistical, biochemical, sociologic, or psychologic. As has been pointed out, these types may be considered as levels, and the pattern of discovery for a given problem is established in terms of the relations between the various levels involved. If to this relationship is added the dimension of time, the pattern of discovery may be conceived as a process, or as a pattern of interactions out of which under given conditions there can emerge a whole or partial answer to the initial disease problem.

What then are the implications for mental illness? In the first place, the history of mental illness may yield clues that are not otherwise apparent. For example, as cultures change in history, new styles of mental illness arise; and in the same culture psychopathologies differ at different periods. In Europe, the various outbreaks of the dancing frenzy in the thirteenth and fourteenth centuries gave way to epidemics of possession by demons from the fifteenth to the eighteenth centuries. These activities of the Devil were in turn displaced by the hysterical convulsions and twitchings of the eighteenth and nineteenth

[41] Clements, op. cit., p. 198.

centuries, and in our day the psychosomatic disorders seem to have pride of place.

Second, there is available considerable knowledge relevant to mental illness or organ physiology, psychodynamics, and the functioning of small and large social systems. Nonetheless, still more knowledge is needed, for instance, on the functioning of the nervous system in biochemical and biophysical terms. Even more significant, however, would be endeavours to take knowledge already available in the various areas that have been mentioned, and to design studies which would explore patterns of relations among them. This is the direction in which history points. This is what happened in the past, and what will have to happen in the future if the mental diseases are to be understood sufficiently so as to be amenable to control.

# CHAPTER TEN

# PUBLIC HEALTH
# AND MENTAL HEALTH
## CONVERGING TRENDS AND
## EMERGING ISSUES

For the past several years, schools of public health have been developing curricula designed to instruct public health personnel in the concepts of mental health and illness. Their experience along these lines, a growing eagerness among public health personnel to assume greater responsibility for community problems involving mental illness, and developments in the area of mental health itself, make it desirable, at this time, to review the factors which typically contribute to the development of sound educational programmes and which, in this instance, will enable public health personnel to deal appropriately with mental illness in a community setting.

The present account derives from this overall objective. As such, it deals with the historical origins, functions, philosophies, and trends in public health and in psychiatry which have led us to our present concern with mental health teaching in the schools of public health. Insofar as they have contributed to this concern, developments in social welfare and in the social sciences are also considered.

Our general frame of reference is the community and those actions within the community which have been designed to improve the health of its population. This orientation may not coincide with the popular concept of organized public health. However, as is evident throughout this account, a great many so-called health-oriented activities originally occurred outside of the limits of the conventional, organized health agency. Ultimately, the reverberations of many of these developments in a variety of fields reached the schools of public health.

The material contained herein is not intended to be exhaustive. Rather, it constitutes an attempt to describe general developments and trends in various areas, through the use of appropriate illustrations. Essentially, we have focused on advances in the professional or scientific areas—for example, public health, in its broad sense; maternal and child health and welfare; nursing; social work; the social sciences; and psychiatry. Without exception, these advances stemmed from attempts to fill current community needs. In other words, each phase in the development of these areas represented an expression of the efforts of the community to cope with the problems with which it was confronted at the time, to devise effective procedures towards this end, and to provide theoretical concepts or simple rationales for these procedures. The procedures and the concepts changed from time to time because the understandings and the rationales, which emanated from very specific situations, had changed. Thus, it becomes pertinent to ask why certain events occurred, and under what circumstances.

Organized public health was created to deal with a specific type of community problem, namely, mass outbreaks of communicable diseases. It developed during the middle and the latter part of the nineteenth century—under the title of sanitary reform (in essence) —to reduce the mortality caused by mass epidemics of such diseases as cholera, yellow fever, and typhus fever. And it had certain bodies of knowledge available to it for this purpose.

One might say that, in a sense, modern public health went from a diastolic to a systolic phase in the latter part of the nineteenth century. This systolic phase increased in intensity when the sanitary reform movement gave way to the era of bacteriology in the last decades of the nineteenth century and the early decades of the twentieth century. In addition to sanitary reform, specific attention was given to "dealing" with various diseases through immunization or laboratory diagnosis. Public health administration and organization were conceived as instrumentalities of the community for this purpose. And these were the origins of the school of public health. Training focused on these problems and on methods for the control of disease.

However, communities had to cope with other problems as well; and, at various times, different groups and agencies dealt with these problems. The poor—the waif, the orphan, the disabled, the aged— had always been with the community. Community responsibility for dependent groups—for those individuals who could not care for themselves and whose families could not care for them—has existed throughout history. In our society, the care of dependent groups fell to those in the community who were concerned with poor relief, and here we find the origins of social work, of child welfare, and, in a large measure, of the care of the mentally ill. We must look to poor relief for an understanding of the philosophies and the modes of action by which the community attempted to deal with this problem through such instrumentalities.

Among the mentally ill, the psychotics, rather than the neurotics or the psychosomatics, came to the attention of the community, inasmuch as these individuals were considered to represent a threat to society. Therefore, at first, they were relegated to institutions whose primary function was to isolate them from the community. However, over a period of time, this concept of exclusion gave way to a variety of approaches: moral treatment; early institutionalization, based on the "cult of curability;" and then, once again, treatment methods which were based on a pessimistic prognosis for mental illness. The mental hospital reflected each of these trends in turn.

Similarly, in the organization of facilities to care for the mentally ill, the community fluctuated between providing centralized care and responsibility and more decentralized and local responsibility. The care of the mentally ill was centralized within mental institutions for a variety of reasons. For one, the rule of economy was a fundamental precept of public administration and, presumably, public authorities would spend as little as possible to "get the job done." Secondly, public administrators could best cope with the task of disposing of patients who did not improve, and who could not be allowed to accumulate in hospitals. Frequently, such individuals were merely sent back home, which proved a rather unsatisfactory solution to this problem. Other solutions were proposed subsequently —the colony system, the boarding out plan, the foster family plan, and the open door policy. Thirdly, the community wanted to get rid of its mentally ill, so that they would not overburden their families, and so that other citizens would not be taxed excessively for their support.

These are some of the factors which gave rise to the mental hygiene movement. There have been several on-going developments. Each of these stemmed from a particular kind of problem; and, to a large extent, all of these developments operated independently of one another at various times. Ultimately, however, they all fit together within the same general framework, and towards the end of the nineteenth century, and particularly during the early part of the twentieth century, they began to converge, slowly but surely. By this time, social work had become an organized and recognized profession; we find that child health and welfare movements were beginning to develop, partly on their own and partly on the basis of concepts regarding the relationship between the individual and his environment, between parents and children, etc., which they had adopted from other disciplines, e.g. certain branches of psychiatry. We find that the social scientist (the sociologist, the social psychologist, the cultural anthropologist), who until this time had been interested in other kinds of problems, was searching for a theoretical rationale on which he might base his efforts.

265

These developments occurred for specific reasons: For the most part, earlier community efforts had been conceived of in terms of social reform. Theoretical advances in the behavioural sciences led community thinking to move away from the large area of social reform, back to the individual. Thus, in the twenties, when this "convergence" began to emerge on a relatively large scale, it was also reflected in schools of public health, which began to appear at this time. Originally, the schools were developed to train personnel to carry out these programmes, that is, to provide health officers; this was their immediate, practical goal, although their basic educational concepts were somewhat broader. They focused on public health administration, with its attendant ancillary subjects—epidemiology, statistics, tropical parasitic diseases, and the like.

However, the school of public health is a reflection of its environment, and gradually its curriculum was expanded to incorporate those pioneer developments which had proven workable outside of the realm of organized public health. To date, too few of the concepts of the mental hygiene movement have found their way into the teaching programmes of the schools of public health. It is hoped that, by providing a historical perspective of developments in the field of mental health and of trends in public health education, this analysis will facilitate and expedite this process.

## Public Health: An Overview

Community health in a rural environment received minimal attention in the American colonies. However, as was true of Europe, with the creation and growth of urban communities, it became a matter of public concern. Epidemics were prominent among the situations which precipitated this interest in community health, but attention was also given to water supply, sewage disposal and the location of privies, and the provision of medical care for indigents and other dependent groups, including the insane. The colonials were imitators in their approach to these matters. Their actions were based on European, and, more specifically, on British practices and experiences and their efforts were hampered by the same conditions that existed at the time in England and other countries. When we evaluate the attempts of local authorities to solve the problems that confronted them, it is well to remember that they had to operate within the narrow framework of town or county government. Local officials had practically no control over the external factors which affected the welfare and health of the community. Moreover, there was no permanent health organization in municipal government. Indeed, one of the basic problems involved in the genesis and development of organized public health activity in the United States and elsewhere was the lack of effective administrative machinery.

During the first three decades of the nineteenth century, American urban communities grew steadily, if not spectacularly. On the whole, social conditions were favourable, and it might be said that public health administration reflected this situation, insofar as it was simple in organization and limited in scope. Between 1800 and 1830, only a few major cities established boards of health; even as late as 1857, many large urban centres had no health departments. To illustrate, a permanent health agency did not come into existence in New York City until 1804, when John Pintard was appointed city inspector of health.[1] From 1810 to 1838, the health agency was considered a branch of the police department. While some inspectors were qualified to deal with such problems as environmental sanitation and the collection of vital statistics, at least by the standards then current, on the whole, the administrative organization was inefficient. Because such positions were much sought after, to a considerable extent, official appointments were the result of political machinations. Consequently, official decisions and actions were subject to external influences.[2] The situation was further aggravated by the division of authority among several individuals and agencies.

Conditions in other cities were similar in general, if not in detail. These inefficiences were tolerated while social conditions were favourable, but the prolonged intrusion during the 1830s of profoundly disturbing elements threw into sharp focus the basic inadequacy of existing arrangements. At that time, political, economic, and social changes in various European communities set in motion a stream of migration to the United States that was to upset with violent impact the social calm that had obtained previously. The shock produced by the influx of swarms of impoverished immigrants was felt in the seaboard cities of Boston, New York, and Philadelphia, where inadequate provision for housing, water supply, and sewage disposal and drainage soon brought into being a whole brood of evils which found their most characteristic expression in the urban slum.[3]

At first, the new arrivals found shelter in the older sections of the cities, in private houses, old warehouses, breweries—in fact, in any building with four walls and a roof. The tenement, which was

[1] G. Rosen, "Politics and Public Health in New York City (1838–1842)," *Bull. Hist. Med.* 22: 441–61, 1950.

[2] *Idem*, "Public Health Problems in New York City during the Nineteenth Century," *New York State Journal of Medicine* 50: 73–78, 1950.

[3] J. H. Griscom, *The Sanitary Condition of the Laboring Population of New York with Suggestions for Its Improvement*, New York, Harper & Bros., 1845.

originally conceived of as a multiple dwelling, designed to provide cheap housing for workers, soon became synonymous with a slum dwelling. Throughout the nineteenth century, there was perpetual overcrowding. Such toilet facilities as existed were highly inadequate; apart from the saloon, recreational arrangements were virtually non-existent. As might be expected, these conditions gave rise to disease, crime, and immorality. City life was unhealthy and sordid for a large number of people, and the significance of such conditions for the community as a whole could not be overlooked.

Catastrophe often brings into sharp focus the need for social change and precedes the accomplishment of such change. In nineteenth-century America, particularly during the period under consideration, this catalyst was provided in the form of recurrent epidemics of yellow fever, cholera, smallpox, typhoid, and typhus fever. The fact that dire poverty, inadequate housing, and unsanitary surroundings took their toll in sickness and human lives had been generally recognized. This knowledge was dramatically impressed on the public mind by each new outbreak of epidemic disease, and the need for effective public health administration became a matter of terrifying urgency.[4] Because they had to cope with similar conditions, Americans were influenced by points of view and methods which had been applied in Great Britain and on the Continent. The sanitary survey proved a most useful tool, as it had in Great Britain and France. The pioneer studies of Villermé in France, and the striking reports of Chadwick, Smith and other reformers in England, were paralleled in the United States between 1830 and 1870 by a series of equally significant inquiries.

Both in Europe and in America, the early public health movement was permeated by a spirit of social reform, and was broadly conceptualized. These characteristics are evident in the Shattuck *Report*, issued in 1850,[5] which outlined a basis for sound public health organization and made specific recommendations, most of which were realized in the next hundred years. The most important proposal contained in the *Report* was Shattuck's suggestion that a state health department be established, but he also considered communicable disease control, vital statistics, environmental sanitation, smoke control, health education, and periodic health examinations. Shattuck also recommended that the board of health be designated as the proper agency to determine whether a mentally ill person

---

[4] W. G. Smillie, *Public Health, Its Promise for the Future. A Chronicle of the Development of Public Health in the United States, 1607-1914*, New York, Macmillan & Co., 1955.

[5] L. Shattuck, *Report of a General Plan for the Promotion of Public and Personal Health . . . Relating to a Sanitary Survey of the State*, Boston, 1850.

should be committed to an institution. Despite its obvious merits Shattuck's plan was not adopted, and the task of effectively organizing public health efforts was left to others.

In any event, it was now apparent that the same process that had created the market economy, the factory, and the modern urban community, had also brought into being health problems which required new methods of health protection and disease prevention.[6] As indicated above, these efforts were hampered primarily by the lack of adequate administrative machinery. During most of the nineteenth century, civil servants were few in number, limited in function, and recruited almost wholly by patronage. A change from haphazard to efficient administration was as essential to the development of a complicated urban society as was the provision of new scientific knowledge. In fact, only a stable administrative foundation would enable the incorporation of new scientific knowledge into public health practice.

Such a foundation was established for the first time in the United States in 1866, when the New York State Legislature enacted a bill which created the Metropolitan Board of Health.[7] This led to the establishment of new and effective health departments in a number of states and municipalities. In 1869, Massachusetts finally adopted the ideas of Lemuel Shattuck, and organized a suitable state health department. Other states followed in rapid succession. A national health agency seemed to be the logical next step. In 1879, Congress created the National Board of Health, which existed only until 1883, however. Politically this action was premature, and it was not until 1953 that a national health department came into being in the United States. Nevertheless, by the last quarter of the nineteenth century, a sound basis had been created for the further development of public health in this country. Much still remained to be done, but the extensive cultivation of community health programmes and the rewards that have been garnered during this century were possible because basic organizational problems had already been solved.

Concurrently, the future content and direction of community health action were being determined abroad, in France and Germany.[8] Without question, the major task of public health was the prevention and control of communicable diseases. But there was lack of agreement on the nature and causes of these conditions. Most

[6] G. Rosen, "Economic and Social Policy in the Development of Public Health," *Journal of the History of Medicine and Allied Sciences* 8: 406–30, 1953.

[7] *Report of the Council of Hygiene and Public Health of the Citizens' Association of New York upon the Sanitary Condition of the City,* New York, Appleton, 1865.

[8] G. Rosen, *A History of Public Health,* New York, MD Publications, 1958, p. 194 ff.

early sanitary reformers accepted the miasmatic theory of disease. Indeed, it is noteworthy that their programme was effective, despite the fact that it was based, to a considerable extent, on an erroneous theory; that is, they hit upon the right solution, but mostly for the wrong reasons. During the nineteenth century, however, knowledge was accumulating that pointed to an animate contagion as the cause of infectious disease. Between 1856 and 1865, Pasteur established the germ theory of fermentation, the doctrine of biogenesis, and applied his findings to the prevention of communicable diseases. A period characterized by solid advances in technique—and, consequently, by further knowledge—began in the seventies. Koch's incontrovertible demonstration in 1876 of the microbial origin of anthrax, and his elucidation of its natural history, marked the beginning of the golden age of bacteriology. During the next two decades, important discoveries occurred with almost explosive rapidity. By the end of the nineteenth century, some of the pertinent questions concerning contagious diseases and their prevention had been answered by demonstrating specific causative organisms in numerous instances. However, certain factors remained unexplained. These obscurities in the germ theory of disease were clarified during the closing decade of the nineteenth century and the first decade of the twentieth century by a number of brilliant investigations, which elucidated the role played by vectors, or intermediaries, in the transmission of communicable diseases.

While Americans contributed in only a limited degree to the growth of microbiological knowledge, they were more alert than were their European confrères to its practical implications. Out of this awareness developed the public health diagnostic laboratory, a community institution for the application of bacteriological knowledge.[9] These laboratories enabled health departments to take over the diagnosis of communicable diseases to a considerable extent, and to control these diseases by providing free biological products to physicians in private practice, as well as public health officers.

Thus, by the first decade of the twentieth century, a solid basis had been established for the control of a number of infectious diseases, and throughout succeeding decades, up to the present, advances along this line have continued with increasing tempo. To illustrate, by 1900, diphtheria could be diagnosed by precise bacteriological methods, patients were treated with diptheria antitoxin, and carriers could be detected, thus making possible effective control. Prevention of the disease was achieved eventually by active mass immunization

[9] W. M. Oliver, *The Man Who Lived for Tomorrow. A Biography of William Hallock Park, M.D.*, New York, Dutton, 1941; C.-E. A. Winslow, *The Life of Hermann M. Biggs*, Philadelphia, Lea and Febiger, 1929.

through the use of diphtheria toxoid as an active immunizing agent.

As a result of community action, arising from the sanitary reform movement and the bacteriological discoveries, and also because of an improvement in general living conditions, the crude death rate had declined markedly by the first decade of the twentieth century. However, during this period, new developments vastly broadened the horizons of public health workers and turned their attention to new frontiers. Inevitably, the transformation of the United States from a rural, agricultural nation into one which was predominantly urban and industrial had a profound effect on its civil institutions. The expansion of governmental functions had been evident during the latter part of the nineteenth century, but the full impact of government participation in matters relating to public health was not felt until well into the twentieth century.

This participation took place in an economic setting of advancing industrialization, accompanied by urban expansion. When America laid down its arms after Appomatox and turned to the pursuit of peace, it stood on the threshold of unparalleled industrial development. The following fifty years saw a tremendous, unrestrained growth of industry and a phenomenal expansion of congested cities. Slums were not new to American cities; they had first appeared on the scene in the 1830s. But at the end of the nineteenth century, this problem became extremely acute once again. Industrial development, urban growth, and a new flood of immigration coincided to produce areas where thousands of people huddled in unbelievably inadequate housing, deprived of the most elementary requirements of civilized life. In the sprawling cities, the impact of poverty and unemployment threw into sharp relief the wastage of human life and health. Malnutrition, vice, and disease were widespread. Jacob Riis' accounts of slum conditions in New York beggar description. At the turn of the century, Americans were confronted by the inescapable fact that poverty, disease, vice, and suffering were large-scale urban phenomena; and there was a growing feeling that these were symptoms of a more deep-seated social malaise. The discontent and disorder that plagued England, America, Germany, and other countries gave rise to a stream of dissenting opinion, which was manifested concretely in various programmes of reform and even revolution.

The orientation of the reform movement in the United States was largely empirical and pragmatic; above all, it expressed confidence in the effectiveness of conscious social action. Nor were the participants in such action obliged to accept a rigid system of ideas. This was a broad movement, concerned with broad problems of social welfare. Within such a framework, one could attempt to deal with a variety of problems: poverty and dependency, infant mortality, sweatshops, tenements, prostitution, and tuberculosis prevention. In the homes of the poor, Edward T. Devine pointed out, "we find the dire consequences of death and disease, of unemployment and underemployment, of overwork and nervous strain, of dark and ill-ventilated and overcrowded rooms, of undernourishment and exposure and poisoned food, of ignorance and maladjustment." These conditions inspired responsible citizens, physicians, clergymen, social workers, and government officials to join in a united effort to prevent tuberculosis, to provide clean milk, to reduce health hazards in factories, to lower infant mortality, and the like. Community action for health was conceived and implemented largely by middle-class people, and was directed chiefly at conditions which involved members of lower-class social groups. Labour unions did take action to improve working and health conditions, but they were not a major influence in the welfare and health movement during the first decade of this century.

The earliest forms of such action were aimed at removing noxious influences from the environment. These activities, which included chlorination of the water supply, to name one, were widespread, impersonal, and specific. But as health authorities became aware of other noxious influences, they became increasingly concerned with individuals and small groups. For example, an interest in all of the phases of child development was characteristic of public health work during the early decades of this century, and has continued to be prominent up to the present. At first, this concern focused on attempts to reduce the high infant maternal mortality. It was recognized that theoretically, at least, infant mortality could be prevented; that, to a large extent, it was caused by malnutrition, contaminated food, parental ignorance, and other factors which could be attributed entirely—or in part—to poverty. Some of these factors could be eliminated completely, the effects of others might be greatly lessened. Because of its many ramifications, the problem was attacked along a number of different lines: through the provision of clean milk; by instructing mothers in the proper feeding and care of the child; through legislation which regulated the work of expectant mothers; and by providing facilities where babies of working mothers could be cared for.

The beginnings of child welfare in European and American communities at the turn of the century followed similar lines. At first, milk stations were set up; later, these became baby clinics, where workers supervised the health of infants and young children and instructed mothers in the care of the child at home. By the end of the first decade of the twentieth century, a number of private and governmental agencies in various countries had demonstrated what might be accomplished along those lines in promoting child health. In 1908, with the establishment of a Division of Child Hygiene as part of the New York City Health Department, there was official recognition of the fact that the execution of these activities as a total programme was a community responsibility, and that this responsibility properly belonged to the agency officially concerned with the health of the community.[10] The creation of the Division of Child Hygiene set a pattern for other health departments, both in this country and abroad. Federal recognition was accorded child health in 1912, when President Taft established the Children's Bureau to investigate and report on all matters relating to child welfare.[11] During this period, the protection of mothers also began to receive attention in the United States, and these actions on behalf of mothers and infants were paralleled by the development of health services for school children.

Education was a basic tool in these efforts to deal with the health problems of mothers and children. It was hoped that desired goals might be attained by spreading knowledge, by stimulating action, and, finally, by achieving changes in individual and group behaviour. With increased emphasis on this concept, techniques, personnel and organizations were developed to reach the community as a whole. Moreover, it became evident that problems which involved small groups or individuals demanded the services of health workers who could help and teach people in a manner adapted to the level of their particular needs. Over the past fifty years, a number of such health workers have been trained to fill these requirements. The first of these to appear, and the most significant, was the public health nurse, who today is a core member of the progressive health department. The nutritionist, the health educator, and the dental hygienist may be included in this category.

It is manifestly impossible to deal with all the phases in the development of the public health movement. For example, in the years from 1910 to 1920, occupational health was established as a significant form of community health action. Another important element has been the increasing professionalization of workers in the field. In general, advances since the turn of the century have produced an unprecedented improvement in over-all community health. The diseases of infancy, youth, and early adulthood have been reduced substantially; more and more people live longer. In 1900, only 13,000,000 persons in the United States, or 18 per cent of the

[10] S. J. Baker, *Fighting for Life*, New York, Macmillan, 1939.
[11] D. E. Bradbury, *Four Decades of Action for Children. A Short History of the Children's Bureau*, Washington, D.C., Government Printing Office, 1956.

population, were over 45. Fifty years later, this group comprised 43,000,000 persons, or 30 per cent of the population. Consequently, our major problems today involve the control and prevention, if possible, of the less remediable, chronic, noncommunicable diseases of a maturing population. At the same time, health programmes have been broadened, whenever feasible, to include other elements and situations which may adversely affect the well-being of the community. Thus, in recent years the widening horizons of American public health have come to encompass such problems as accident prevention and the prevention or control of mental illness, as well as renewed emphasis on the control of the physical environment, in the face of new factors which have been introduced by our expanding industrial technology.

Public health practice has moved away from its "police" activities, which, of course, were essential to the control of the pestilential diseases and to the protection of the vulnerable members of the community. As a result, the psychological dimension in community health work has become increasingly prominent and significant. Convergent contributions to this orientation have derived from concern with the health and welfare of the poor, the unemployed, the handicapped, and the ill members of the community, including the mentally ill. In consequence, the concepts of mental health and illness which public health workers are currently endeavouring to implement have their origins in various fields of community concern and professional endeavour—e.g. mental illness, juvenile delinquency, immigration, medicine, nursing, social work, the social sciences, and still others.

## The Field of Mental Illness

'Man is born free, and everywhere he is in chains!' Rousseau's angry cry did not refer to the mentally ill; yet, to no other group of his time could it be applied with greater accuracy. In the eighteenth century, madmen were locked up in jails, workhouses, and madhouses; insanity was attributed to sin and the activities of the devil, as well as to a variety of other causes, such as the retention of bodily excretions, poor diet, and lack of sleep. Ignorance, superstition, and moral condemnation dominated the treatment of the insane.

In every society there are individuals whose feelings, thoughts, judgement, and behaviour differ markedly from accepted norms. In most cultures, the criterion of severe mental disturbance or psychosis is the individual's inability to apprehend reality, as conceptualized by that society. While there may be agreement as to the presence of mental disorder, the explanations for such disorders and the methods

274

employed to deal with such individuals vary considerably, and will depend on prevailing views of causality and on the structure of the society in question.

Although physicians attempted to understand mental illness in naturalistic terms,[12] explanations in terms of evil spirits, demonic possession, or magical influence also prevailed throughout antiquity as well as the medieval and early modern periods.[13] In the sixteenth century, faint voices were raised in an effort to penetrate the dense pall of ignorance and fear that shrouded mental illness in mystery. However, concrete evidence of change did not appear until the latter part of the eighteenth century, when forces which were to alter radically the care and treatment of the insane were set in motion.

Lunacy reform was not an isolated movement. It was part of the larger concern with the rights and conditions of man, and is thus connected to other reform movements of this period: concern for the care of children, penal reform, the need for better working conditions, and the desire for a general improvement in public health.[14] The ideas of the Enlightenment and the new spirit of humanity had influenced thinking throughout the civilized world. It is not surprising, therefore, that proposals and action appeared almost simultaneously in various European countries, although they were particularly effective in France and England.

In 1774, after having investigated conditions in the madhouse at Pforzheim, G. F. Jaegerschmid proposed that less disturbed patients be given more freedom, and that restraints be employed only for violent patients. He also suggested that mentally ill patients be assigned to the care of properly trained nursing personnel, and that the staff report regularly to a supervising physician. These proposals were ultimately realized in 1788, when Vincenzo Chiarugi instituted such reforms in the Hospital of St. Bonifacio in Florence.

More profound and far-reaching was the influence of the Retreat, founded in York, England, by the Society of Friends. The Retreat, which opened its doors to accommodate thirty patients in 1796, was

---

[12] Caelius Aurelianus, *On Acute Diseases and on Chronic Diseases*, ed. and trans. by I. E. Drabkin, Chicago, University of Chicago Press, 1950, pp. 3–119; J. R. Whitwell, *Historical Notes on Psychiatry*, Philadelphia, Blakiston, 1937, pp. 178–82.

[13] A. Fischer, "Bilder zur mittelalterlichen Kulturhygiene im Bodenseegebiet," *Sozialhygienische Abhandlungen*, Nr. 7, Karlsruhe, 1923; H. Haeser, *Lehrbuch der Geschichte der Medizin und der epidemischen Krankheiten*, 1876, vol. I, p. 806; G. Bossert, "Die Liebesthätigkeit der evangelischen Kirche Württembergs von der Zeit des Herzogs Christoph bis 1650," *Württembergische Jahrbücher für Statistik und Landeskunde*, 1905, p. 15.

[14] G. Rosen, *A History of Public Health*, pp. 131–191; D. H. Tuke, *Chapters in the History of the Insane in the British Isles*, London, 1882, pp. 92–146.

the "brain child" of William Tuke, who conceived of the project in 1792. Tuke introduced a regimen based on common sense and Christianity; every effort was made to provide a "family environment" for the patients. Good food, fresh air, exercise, and occupation replaced brutality, chains, and semi-starvation; and kindness proved to be a more effective therapy than rigorous confinement. In the United States, the Friend's Asylum, established at Frankford, Pennsylvania, in 1817, and the Bloomingdale Asylum, established in New York in 1821, were modelled after the Retreat.

One year after William Tuke had conceived his project, a similar step was taken in Paris by Philippe Pinel, who had been appointed physician to the Bicêtre (for male patients) in 1793. Convinced that kindness, sympathy, and a minimum of mechanical restraint would be more effective in the treatment of the insane than the brutal methods prevalent at the time, Pinel removed the chains from fifty-three "lunatics." The results were encouraging. Three years later, Pinel introduced a similar regimen for incurably insane women at the Salpêtrière, the second largest asylum in Paris, and demonstrated conclusively the value of humane treatment for the mentally ill. Pinel's system of "moral treatment" exerted great influence, not only in France and elsewhere on the Continent, but in Great Britain and the United States as well.[15]

One of the more significant results of the movement to reform the treatment of the insane was the establishment of asylums.[16] In England, the first county asylum was opened at Nottingham in 1811. By 1815, three county asylums were in operation; and by 1842, there was a total of sixteen. In general, these institutions exhibited progress in the application of humane methods and in the development of a more professional approach to the care of the mentally ill. This movement for the creation of special institutions for the insane during the first three decades of the nineteenth century extended to the United States as well. Private institutions led the way, but by the thirties it had become increasingly obvious that systematic provision for the mentally ill must come from governmental sources. As a result, many private asylums were replaced by state hospitals in the years from 1800 to 1825. The clinical experience obtained at these hospitals provided one of the sources for psychiatric practice.

In addition to the influences noted above, impetus for the establishment of asylums derived from the belief held by many physicians that mental illness was curable. It had been demonstrated that moral treatment, combined with early hospitalization, yielded excellent

---

[15] P. Pinel, *Traité Médico-philosophique sur l'aliéntation mentale*, Paris, 1801.

[16] K. Jones, *Lunacy, Law, and Conscience 1744–1845*, London, Routledge and Kegan Paul, 1955, pp. 66–78.

therapeutic results. The reports of private institutions encouraged this view. Certainly, the effects of treatment in small institutions, where interpersonal relations could be established, were more beneficial than brutal treatment—or no treatment at all. Finally, this optimism was characteristic of the early nineteenth century. Drastic changes were occurring in politics, as well as medicine, and for some people the millennium appeared close at hand.[17]

Nevertheless, as late as the forties of the nineteenth century, no institutional provisions had yet been made for the mentally ill in many parts of the United States. In 1843, there were only about 24 hospitals, public and private, with a total bed capacity of 2,561, which were devoted entirely to the care of the mentally ill.[18] These facilities were clearly inadequate. Many such patients were cared for in general hospitals; those patients who created no social problem might be kept at home, but a much greater number were still confined in jails, poor-houses, and similar facilities.

Dorothea Dix undertook the task of providing proper facilities for the mentally ill in 1841, and ultimately her influence extended throughout the United States, as well as overseas. The work of Dorothea Dix derived from a basic humanitarianism, fused with the recognition that the mentally ill were not criminals, but sick people who needed treatment. According to J. C. Flügel, her efforts were followed by a

> wide-spread realization of the fact that insanity, feeblemindedness and criminality are conditions between which it is well to make a clear distinction, and the practical approach to which should be governed by separate and distinct principles. The mere segregation of these three main groups of persons made the problems peculiar to each group stand out in such a way as to demand attention. The treatment of the insane, the mentally defective and the criminal thus each became the subject of special study, with its own methods.[19]

In any event, the number of institutions for the mentally ill grew. These institutions were designed primarily to accommodate the most disturbed individuals in the community. Most superintendents endeavoured to apply some degree of moral treatment, and a few actually approached this ideal. The concept of moral treatment was perhaps best defined by Amariah Brigham in 1847:

---

[17] Condorcet, *Tableau historique des progrès de l'esprit humain*, Paris, Steinheid, 1900, pp. 186–88; K. F. H. Marx and R. Willis, *Decrease of Disease Effected by Civilization*, London, Longmans, Green, 1844.

[18] *American Journal of Insanity*, 1: 82, 1844.

[19] J. C. Flügel, *A Hundred Years of Psychology, 1833–1933*, London, Duckworth, 1948, p. 110.

The removal of the insane from home and former associations, with respectful and kind treatment under all circumstances, and in most cases manual labour, attendance on religious worship on Sunday, the establishment of regular habits and of self-control, diversion of the mind from morbid trains of thought, are now generally considered as essential in the Moral treatment of the Insane.[20]

However, in all probability, the majority of physicians did not fully accept these views, and they were applied to an even lesser extent. Diagnostic procedures were less than perfect, and it was not easy to predict whether a depressed or agitated patient would recover or remain chronically ill. Some patients did get well, but the chronic cases accumulated. Because the capacity of institutions was not equal to the public demand for accommodation, officials were urged to remove chronic cases to separate facilities. As a result, chronically ill patients were sent to almshouses, jails, and asylums which were established specifically for the care of long-term patients. The first of these, the Willard Asylum, was built in New York in 1869, and could accommodate up to fifteen hundred patients.[21] Later, similar institutions were established in other parts of the country. These institutions proved to be unsatisfactory, however, and ultimately they were converted into mental hospitals. Finally, a wave of criticism arose against the "cult of curability," and during the decades from 1850 to 1890, this optimistic belief was gradually eroded and undermined. In 1887, with the publication of his statistical study, Pliny Earle definitely disposed of the curability myth.[22] And as belief in the idea of curability lessened, emphasis on the role of social and psychological factors in the genesis and treatment of mental illness diminished.

A period of reaction set in,[23] the effects of which have not yet disappeared. Mental institutions became political footballs and, to a large extent, a haven for sinecurists.[24] As a result, the care of the mentally ill became increasingly insulated from developments in biology and medicine. Most physicians in mental hospitals did not devote their efforts to scientific research. Psychiatry, as that branch of medicine concerned with the diagnosis, treatment, and care of the mentally ill, became an enormous vacuum to be filled by any vagrant

[20] "Moral Treatment of Insanity," *American Journal of Insanity* 4: 1, 1847.

[21] H. M. Hurd, ed., *The Institutional Care of the Insane in the United States and Canada*, Baltimore, Johns Hopkins Press, 1916–17, vol III, pp. 160–62.

[22] P. Earle, *The Curability of Insanity*, Utica, E. H. Roberts, 1887.

[23] A. Deutsch, *The Mentally Ill in America. A History of Their Care and Treatment from Colonial Times*, Garden City, Doubleday, 1938, p. 155.

[24] E. L. Dewey, ed., *Recollections of Richard Dewey, Pioneer in American Psychiatry*, Chicago, University of Chicago Press, 1936, pp. 130–32.

doctrine. It is against this background that we must view the other developments that produced the theories of mental illness and health which now concern us.

In general, the treatment and care in custodial institutions at the turn of the century followed the medical fashions of the time. Treatment methods included the use of counter-irritants, elimination of focal infection, water treatment, spa therapy, surgery, and the like. This was also true of aetiological thought, much of which has been cyclical in nature. For example, the idea that mental illness was due primarily to psychological or social causes has alternated with the concept that it is essentially physical in origin. In the early nineteenth century, the former concept was emphasized; in the second half of the century, the latter concept was stressed, and this, in turn, was followed by a period dominated by psychoanalysis. Similarly, treatment orientation, i.e. activity versus inactivity, has also moved in cycles. Weir Mitchell's total rest programme gave way to the "total push" programme a few decades later. At present, both are advocated, as evidenced by Soviet psychiatrists, who employ prolonged sleep therapy and also urge rehabilitation through work.

On the whole, the gap that separated the care of patients with mental disorders from the general body of medicine has narrowed substantially as the result of developments over the last fifty years. These developments have come from several different directions; some were a result of the evolution of science and medicine; others stemmed from the need to deal with social problems in rapidly changing communities. The first trend is evidenced in the treatment of general paresis. During the nineteenth century and the first decades of the twentieth century, this syphilitic disease was one of the most common conditions among patients in mental hospitals. Forty years ago, the incidence of general paresis was probably at its height; since then, however, there has been a consistent decline, due to efforts to control syphilis; the introduction of malaria or fever therapy; and last, and most significant, the use of penicillin therapy.

In fact, the control of general paresis may be attributed to the confluence of a number of disciplines and specialties. Data to support the syphilitic aetiology came not only from the clinical association of syphilis and general paresis, but from pathological, statistical, microbiological, and immunological studies as well. Moreover, within this constellation, social and psychological elements were assigned their appropriate aetiological roles. Histopathological and other laboratory approaches now seemed to offer a sure path to the solution of the riddle of mental disorder. Huntington's chorea, Alzheimer's disease, senile psychoses, and mental deficiency were all viewed as abnormalities of behaviour due to impairment of brain

K                                      279

function. While it has become evident that, by itself, anatomical study of the brain cannot unravel the problem of the functional psychoses, organic psychiatry has continued to advance towards an objective understanding of brain functions and the nervous system.[25]

At the turn of the century, new and crucial discoveries were made with regard to the nature of emotional responses: Cannon began his studies of gastrointestinal motility in response to the presence or absence of adrenalin,[26] and the significance of his findings far exceeded his expectations—or the area of his initial concern. Emotion appeared to be a physiological process, linked with psychological phenomena, controlled by chemical factors, and related to the individual's response to the world around him. Demonstration of the hypothalamus as the co-ordinating centre for emotional expression, and a series of observations in comparative anatomy, enumerated by Cobb more recently,[27] have served to place reasonably definitive knowledge concerning the physiological components of emotional reactions at the disposal of the psychiatrist.

Pavlov's discovery that emotional reactions and concomitant visceral activity were related to the pressure of specific stimuli, and that these responses could be conditioned by the proper timing of stimuli,[28] constituted an outstanding contribution to our understanding of learning in man. In the United States, Pavlov's ideas were elaborated by Watson, and developed by Clark Hull in the

---

[25] K. Beringer, *Der Meskalinrausch. Seine Geschichte und Erscheinungsweise*, Berlin, Springer, 1927; E. Lindemann, *The WHO Report of the Study Group on Ataractic and Hallucinogenic Agents*, Geneva, November 4–9, 1957; L. von Meduna, "Die Konvulsionstherapie der Schizophrenie," *Psychiatrisch—neurologische Wochenschrift* 37: 317–19, 1935; A. S. Loevenhart, W. F. Lorenz, H. F. Martin, and J. Y. Malone, "Stimulation of Respiration by Sodium Cyanide and Its Clinical Application," *Archives of Internal Medicine* 21: 109–29, 1918; A. S. Loevenhart, W. F. Lorenz, and R. M. Waters, "Cerebral Stimulation," *Journal of the American Medical Association* 92: 880–93, 1929; H. C. Solomon, M. R. Kaufman, and F. D'Elseaux, "Some Effects of Inhalation of Carbon Dioxide and Oxygen and of Intravenous Sodium Amytal on Certain Neuropsychiatric Conditions," *American Journal of Psychiatry* 10: 761–69, 1931; W. Sargant and E. Slater, *Introduction to the Physical Methods of Treatment in Psychiatry*, Edinburgh, Livingston, 1944.

[26] W. B. Cannon, *Bodily Changes in Pain, Hunger, Fear and Rage*, New York, Appleton, 1929, Harper Torchbooks edition, 1963; *idem, The Wisdom of the Body*, New York, Norton, 1932.

[27] S. Cobb, "One Hundred Years of Progress in Neurology, Psychiatry and Neurosurgery," *Archives of Neurology and Psychiatry* 59: 63–98, 1948; *idem, Emotions and Clinical Medicine*, New York, W. W. Norton, 1950.

[28] I. P. Pavlov, *The Work of the Digestive Glands*, London, Griffin, 1902; *idem, Conditional Reflexes*, London, Oxford University Press, 1927; *idem, Lectures on Conditioned Reflexes*, New York, International Publishers, 1928; *idem, Conditioned Reflexes and Psychiatry*, New York, International Publishers, 1941.

form of a systematic learning theory;[29] more recently efforts have been made to apply these concepts to the neuroses, based on the contention that such phenomena are the results of faulty learning. During the past ten years, laboratory methods have been applied more intensively and rigorously to the investigation of the relationship between feeling and emotions and changing visceral activity. Finally, many early observers and investigators had studied the relationship between mental stress and the development of disorders in various parts of the body.[30]

The elucidation of the effect of past experience on subsequent behaviour has derived from the systematic investigations of Pierre Janet in France and, particularly, from the discoveries of Sigmund Freud in Vienna. During the last five decades, this work has been elaborated into impressive theoretical structures, accompanied by a large body of clinical data. Unfortunately, well-organized experimental and laboratory studies along these lines are still largely absent. However, Freud's work has been instrumental in setting the stage for efforts to describe the organism as a whole, in terms of its organization, behaviour, and adaptation to its environment. The psychological movement in American psychiatry is linked to Adolf Meyer's concept of psychobiology.[31] Meyer conceived of the individual as the total product of his life experience, and thus denied the concept of body-mind duality. He was concerned with the "functions of the total person" in his environment; thus, he was one of the pioneers of the current culture-personality approach.

As a direct result of Meyer's efforts, and due to the indirect, but even greater, influence of Freud, psychiatry is no longer considered solely within the framework of the insane asylum. Today, the psychoneurotic, the mental defective, the emotionally disturbed child, the psychopath—all are regarded as the legitimate concerns of psychiatry. However, this is a relatively recent development. Formerly, patients who suffered from "nervous disorders" and functional complaints were not to be found in asylums; such patients sought

[29] J. B. Watson, *Behaviourism*, New York, Peoples Institute, 1941; C. L. Hull "Functional Interpretation of the Conditioned Reflex," *Psychology Review* 36: 498–511, 1929.

[30] E. L. Margetts, "Historical Notes on Psychosomatic Medicine," in E. D. Wittkower and R. A. Cleghorn, eds., *Recent Developments in Psychosomatic Medicine*, Philadelphia, Lippincott, n. d. pp. 41–68; H. Wolff, ed., *Life Stress and Bodily Disease*, Baltimore, Williams and Wilkins, 1950.

[31] A. Meyer, "Objective Psychology or Psychobiology with Subordination of the Medically Useless Contrast of Mental and Physical," *Journal of the American Medical Association* 65: 860, 1915; Reprinted in A. Lief, ed., *The Commonsense Psychiatry of Dr. Adolf Meyer*, New York, McGraw-Hill, 1948, pp. 397–405. In this volume, see also "The Psychobiological Point of View," pp. 590–606.

help elsewhere—from physicians, who treated them for organic complaints; from mesmerists, Christian Scientists, and other faith healers. In general, it was the neurologists—Charcot, Janet, and Freud among them—who first recognized that such patients were mentally ill. Neurologists in the United States, were drawing similar conclusions. In 1869, George M. Beard described a clinical picture which he called neurasthenia. S. Weir Mitchell became internationally famous in 1877 through his prescription of a rest cure for certain nervous states.[32] J. J. Putnam, with G. Stanley Hall, invited Freud to lecture on psychoanalysis at Clark University in 1909, and thus indicated his interest in psychoanalytic concepts. Slowly, during these decades, medical thought was being prepared for a reorientation towards greater emphasis on the patient's personality. In the United States, and perhaps also in other countries, the turning point in this reorientation came during and after the First World War.

Before we discuss this change and its consequences, it is necessary to examine one other aspect of the situation. Throughout a large part of the nineteenth century, psychiatric theory had been a tangle of confusion. During the later part of this period, as somatic trends grew stronger, it was felt that an organic basis could be found for mental diseases. This conviction was further strengthened through the elucidation of paresis; indeed, this discovery may be said to have been the *leitmotif* for the development of psychiatric nosology. It stimulated Kahlbaum to define the morbid category of catatonia as a state opposite in character to paresis with its paralytic phenomena. Furthermore, the investigation of paresis provided one of the sources for the development of neurology, once workers began to differentiate "straightforward" neurological paralyses from the confused mass that was labelled "general paresis" and "dementia with paralysis." In 1877, Hecker pointed out that investigation of general paresis, considered an "ideal type," had shown that it was possible to set up nosologic entities that took account of the course of the disease, and to demonstrate the derivation of symptoms from the natural history of the condition.[33] Catatonia and hebephrenia were natural nosologic forms which even permitted prognostic conclusions. The terms, melancholia, mania, and the like were used simply to designate symptomatic conditions. Kahlbaum had made a first attempt in this direction in 1863. In 1898, Kraepelin presented a system for the classification of mental diseases.[34] This system was essentially

[32] S. Weir Mitchell, *Fat and Blood*, Philadelphia, Lippincott, 1877.
[33] E. Hecker, "Zur klinischen Diagnostik und Prognostik der psychischen krankheiten," *Allg. Ztschr. Psychiat.* 33, 1877.
[34] W. De Boor, *Psychiatrische Systematik, Ihre Entwicklung in Deutschland seit Kahlbaum*, Berlin, Springer, 1954.

descriptive, and was based on the concept that mental disease was organic in origin. Thus, no account was taken of psychological dynamics. Although Kraepelin's system provided a useful frame of reference for purposes of prognosis and treatment, those workers who were interested in their patient's emotional reactions to their individual needs and their social environment found such a system unsatisfactory.

The Kraepelinian system of classification and the search for an organic basis for mental disorder continued to be prominent in the early part of this century. However, under the direction of Stanley Hall, William James, and, to an even greater extent, Boris Sidis, current psychological theories began to exercise an important influence on psychiatry. The work of William A. White and Sidis on motivation focused on the search for underlying psychological and emotional factors in the genesis of abnormal reactions. Later, White was influenced by psychoanalysis, but he also emphasized the need for thorough study of social factors. This trend towards emphasis on the patient's personality and the dynamics of his life history led to a reorientation of the psychiatric approach and point of view.

After the First World War, when cases of psychoneuroses (shell shock) were widespread, the inadequacy of physical explanations for mental phenomena became particularly evident. As a result, physicians were obliged to accept these conditions as objects of investigation, and to direct their attention to the importance of psychic dynamics. To quote Macfie Campbell,

> The problem of the psychiatrist was no longer to identify a clinical picture but to get to grips with the actual dynamic situation, to reconstruct in detail the life history, with attention to the sensitizing or conditioning influence of environmental factors, and with due appreciation of the nature of emotional disturbances, of substitutes and evasive reactions, of symbolic expressions, of the various modes of getting satisfaction for the complicated needs of the individual.[35]

Thus oriented, it was relatively simple for the psychiatrist to move into the community and other settings, apart from the clinic and hospital, to "survey the field of human relations in general."[36] And the community was prepared to welcome psychiatry. This tendency found expression in the convergence of social work and psychiatry; in the mental hygiene movement; in the development of child psychiatry; in the relationship which was established between psychiatry and various social sciences; and in the influence of

[35] C. Macfie Campbell, *Destiny and Disease in Mental Disorders*, New York W. W. Norton, 1935, pp. 33–34.
[36] *Ibid.*, p. 37.

psychiatric approaches and methods on industry and public affairs, on the home, the school, and the church.

Concurrently, in studies of the assets and liabilities of psychotic and neurotic individuals, as revealed in their methods of coping with their social environment, psychiatrists recognized the need to study their patients' intellectual equipment, motor and social skills, and handicaps due to organic defects. Such investigations required the services of the psychological laboratory. At the turn of the century, Kraepelin had become interested in testing intellectual abilities, according to the methods developed in Wundt's laboratory.[37] Previously, Ebbinghaus had tried to formulate standard reading and memory tests; Binet[38] and Simon had developed standard procedures for the assessment of intellectual equipment at different age levels and the evaluation of intellectual deterioration in acquired mental disease. Clinical psychology grew out of the efforts of these workers and others; in the last decade, it has reached the status of a separate profession, working hand in hand with psychiatry, and contributing to the measurement of mental functions and the assessment of changes in emotional attitudes through projective techniques; since the Second World War, clinical psychologists have participated in the development of psychotherapeutic techniques as well.

However, neither the clinical psychologist nor the psychiatrist can provide all of the data required to understand the individual. A human being cannot be fully understood unless he is considered in his social and cultural context, as a member of a specific group, of a social system, and of institutions. The individual must fill a complex variety of roles (child, parent, worker, friend, citizen), and function within a social structure, in terms of a given culture. These constitute the matrix within which the individual acts and is acted upon in turn. These considerations, as well as others which stem from the social sciences themselves, have led to collaboration between psychiatrists and anthropologists, sociologists, social psychologists, and political scientists.

A significant phase of this development, and one most characteristic of American psychiatry, is the child guidance movement and its offspring, child psychiatry. In this area, the emphasis has shifted to a study of the child's instinctive and emotional life, of "his gropings for satisfaction and for a grasp of the outside world, and his urge towards self-expression."[39] This interest in the study of

---

[37] E. Kraepelin, "Die Erscheinungsformen des Irreseins," *Zeitschrift für die gesamte Neurologie und Psychiatrie* 62: 1–29, 1902.

[38] A. Binet, *Étude expérimentale de l'intelligence*, Paris, Schleicher Frères, 1903.

[39] C. Macfie Campbell, *op. cit.*, p. 38.

children derived, in part, from work undertaken in the last quarter of the nineteenth century. Under the influence of Preyer, a German physiologist, and Hall, the American psychologist, a series of investigations was conducted on the development of individual children from birth onward. The first of these was published by Shinn in 1893; Moore's study followed in 1896.[40] The continuing work of Jean Piaget has demonstrated the effectiveness of this method. Concurrently, a number of sociologists, psychologists, and philosophers were studying processes of socialization and personality development.[41]

At the same time, systematic studies were conducted on maladjustment in childhood. In 1896, Lightner Witmer organized a psychological clinic at the University of Pennsylvania for children with emotional or behavioural problems, who were mentally sub-normal, or had other social handicaps. The children were examined medically and psychologically, and out of these case reports Witmer established criteria for differential diagnosis between mental defect and childhood psychosis. In 1909, William Healy founded the Chicago Juvenile Psychopathic Institute, where a psychiatric perspective was brought to bear on the juvenile delinquent.[42] The out-patient department of the Boston Psychopathic Hospital began to study children in 1912; the Allentown State Hospital in Pennsylvania followed suit in 1915. The child guidance clinic grew out of these beginnings.[43] Originally focused on the prevention of juvenile delinquency, such clinics eventually directed their efforts towards more subtle behaviour problems. By 1932, 27 of the 50 largest cities in the United States has full-time clinic services, and 232 full- and part-time clinics for child guidance were registered with the National Committee for Mental Hygiene. The American Orthopsychiatric Association is a formal expression of this movement.

From the outset, the problems presented by the patients in these clinics were handled by a team, comprising a psychiatrist, a psychiatric social worker, and a psychologist. Another characteristic of child guidance work was its concept of the patient's problem as sympto-

---

[40] M. W. Shinn, "Notes on the Development of a Child," *University of California Studies*, 1893; K. C. Moore, "The Mental Development of a Child," *Psychology Review Monographs*, Supplement 1, 1896.

[41] J. M. Baldwin, *Social and Ethical Interpretations in Mental Development*, New York, Macmillan, 1897; C. H. Cooley, *Human Nature and the Social Order*, New York, Scribner's, 1902; G. H. Mead, *Mind, Self and Society*, Chicago, University of Chicago Press, 1934.

[42] F. G. Ebaugh and C. A. Rymer, *Psychiatry in Medical Education*, New York, Commonwealth Fund, 1942, p. 7.

[43] G. S. Stevenson and G. Smith, *Child Guidance Clinics: A Quarter Century of Development*, New York, Commonwealth Fund, 1934.

matic of a family and social situation. Psychoanalytic theory played an important role in this approach. As a result of this orientation, the total life situation of the child, and the need for change in the child's environment were emphasized.

The child guidance movement was also an expression of the mental hygiene movement in the United States at the turn of the century. The concept of preventing mental illness was not new; the phrase "mental hygiene" had been used by William Sweetser, an American physician, as early as 1843.[44] In 1857, an English physician proposed a programme "to promote mental sanitary reform."[45] Two years later, George Cook, the superintendent of a private mental hospital in New York, wrote two articles on the promotion of mental health and the prevention of mental illness.[46] However, the greatest impetus for the present mental hygiene movement stemmed from the publication of Clifford Beers' courageous autobiography in 1908[47] and the organization of the National Committee for Mental Hygiene[48] in 1909 by Beers, Adolf Meyer, and William James, among others.

Historically and chronologically, the National Committee for Mental Hygiene belongs to the voluntary health movement in the United States. Industrialization, accompanied by the expansion of urban communities, provided the seeds within which this movement rose and flourished. Others before Beers had engaged in similar activities, and he proposed that his Committee be "modelled after the very efficient 'National Child Labor Committee'."[49] As its first practical concern, the National Committee undertook the improvement of institutional care of the mentally ill. Accordingly, the appalling conditions in psychiatric asylums were uncovered, pressure was brought to bear on legislative and administrative bodies, and conspicuous improvements were achieved. The intervening years saw an increasing expansion in the variety of activities and facilities loosely ranged under the overarching rubric, mental hygiene. The term "mental health movement" has replaced "mental hygiene," and interest and attention have shifted from the care of the mentally ill, to the prevention of mental illness and the promotion of mental health.

This shift in emphasis resulted from a number of factors. In the

[44] W. Sweetser, *Mental Hygiene*, New York, J. and H. G. Langley, 1843.
[45] J. Hawkes, "On the Increase of Insanity," *Journal of Psychological Medicine and Mental Pathology* 10: 508–21, 1857.
[46] G. Cook, "Mental Hygiene," *American Journal of Insanity* 15: 272–82, 353–65, 1859.
[47] C. W. Beers, *A Mind that Found Itself*, New York, Longmans, Green, 1908.
[48] Now the National Association for Mental Health.
[49] C. W. Beers, *op. cit.*, pp. 295–96.

first place, the term "mental hygiene" was never a clear-cut concept, and meant different things to different people.[50] Consequently, it was possible for several disciplines to live together, so to speak, until a number of influences led to the development of a specific working hypothesis, namely, that mental illness in adults arises out of harmful experiences in childhood. The idea that children must be raised properly to achieve mental health, was the product of a number of trends and developments discussed previously, namely, psychoanalytic theory, the formulation of the concept of the psychoneurosis, and a growing interest in early behaviour disorders. The current activities and propaganda efforts of the mental health movement have developed on the basis of these theories.

As mentioned earlier, until a little over a decade ago, most mental hygiene activities were conducted by voluntary agencies; only recently has the federal government entered the picture on a large scale. The passage of the National Mental Health Act in 1946 provided great stimulus to mental health programmes throughout the country, by providing grants-in-aid for research, the training of personnel, and for the establishment and development of community mental health programmes. Emphasis on community mental health programmes has become increasingly prominent. Symptomatic is the pattern pioneered by New York in 1954, and adopted in somewhat modified form by California three years later.

In the past one hundred years, American psychiatry has shifted its field of activity from a primary concern with the custodial care of the insane, to an emphasis on the treatment of ambulatory patients with mental disorders, and, in our time, to a concern with the family, the home, the school, the factory, with marriage, juvenile delinquency, and narcotic addiction. Concomitantly, there has been a vast expansion of the psychiatrist's sphere of activity.

At the same time, institutional patterns of psychiatric care have undergone a gradual change, leading to an open door policy in many hospitals.[51] This has meant a reduction in the number of patients through home visits, greater influx into hospitals of relatives and volunteers, and a slow shift of emphasis from the custodial aspects of patient care to organized rehabilitation programmes. These innovations have necessitated further education of families and agencies in the rehabilitation of former mental patients in a community setting. Consequently, psychiatrists in mental hospitals have had to contend with community issues to an increasing extent.

[50] This is true of mental health, as well, of course.
[51] Interestingly, workers were interested in the benefits to be derived from the open door policy in the seventies and eighties; see, for example, *Journal of Mental Science*, 29: 290–91, 304, 310–11, 378, 456.

A number of medical schools have begun to emphasize family and community welfare in the training of future physicians, and a few residency programmes for psychiatric training include explicit provision for special work in community psychiatry. However, there is no agreement as yet as to the best time for the inclusion of such training in psychiatric education. For most students, the first three years of psychiatric training lead to an intensive preoccupation with the subtle psychodynamics of psychotherapy. Community issues may appear to them to be "superficial" and extraneous, and represent less valid types of psychiatric activity. Fortunately, a number of young psychiatrists visualize the unmet needs in the community as a tremendous challenge, and realize early in their career that these problems require the development of new methods, applicable on a population-wide basis. However, to the small group of interns who are attracted to psychiatry, public health offers little in the way of a challenging and respected professional identity. Nor is this confined to the recruitment of psychiatric residents. Schools of public health have not yet reached a consensus on the question of mental health as a community problem or with regard to its place in the curriculum.

## Child Health and Welfare

In the first half of the nineteenth century, physicians who were interested in children's diseases dealt as well with the "management" of infancy and childhood, in order that disturbances of adult disposition and character might be prevented. For example, in 1844, David Francis Condie, a leading Philadelphia physician, included a discussion of "moral treatment" in his treatise on the diseases of childhood.[52] Parents were advised to choose their child's nurse carefully; on how to handle fear in children; and were warned against unkindness, harshness, or impatience in dealing with an infant. However, prior to the publication of Dr. Condie's "treatise," many writers had expressed similar views with regard to the development of "moral character," the influence on children of those who cared for them, the effect of fear, and related matters.[53]

During this period, other individuals who were concerned with child welfare were also noting the effect of childhood experiences and impressions on future conduct. In 1819, the Society for the Prevention of Pauperism, in New York City, recommended the separation of young offenders in penal institutions from older criminals and

[52] D. F. Condie. *A Practical Treatise on the Diseases of Children*, Philadelphia, Blanchard and Lea, 1844, pp. 57–66.

[53] See, for example, A. Clarke, *The Young Mother's Assistant*, London, Henry Colburn, 1822.

reprobates.[54] The Society also recommended that younger convicts (from ten to eighteen years of age) be provided with "moral, religious, and elementary" instruction. A final recommendation concerned the establishment of a "House of Refuge," where boys who were vagrants, homeless, or charged with petty crimes would be "put to work at such employments as will tend to encourage industry and ingenuity, taught reading, writing, and arithmetic and most carefully instructed in the nature of their moral and religious obligations, while at the same time, they are subjected to a course of treatment that will hold out . . . every possible inducement to reformation and good conduct. . . ."[55]

From 1850 to 1880, observations which focused on the psychological dimension of child welfare came largely from those who had been entrusted with the responsibility of providing care for neglected, dependent, and delinquent children. In most instances, these observations were the by-products of practical and empirical endeavours to meet the problems which arose in the course of these duties. By the 1850s, it had been noted that large groups were not the ideal setting for the rehabilitation of the young delinquent, even if he were given adequate physical care and separated from adult paupers and criminals. In his discussion of the reform of delinquents in 1859, Charles Loring Brace, founder of the New York Children's Aid Society, stated: "Nature seems especially to indicate small groups of parents and children, or old and young, as the best forming-institution for young minds. Children in large numbers together, in constant intercourse, appear never to exert a healthful influence on each other. . . ."[56] On the basis of Brace's experience, private societies began to place children in foster homes instead of institutions. The Worcester Children's Friend Society began to make such placements in 1850;[57] the Children's Aid Society for New York followed suit in 1853.[58] The latter organization found that placing children in homes in the country, largely in the expanding Middle West, was particularly beneficial.[59] This system "saved" vagrants and criminals, lessened court and prison expenses, and removed "poisonous" influences from the city.[60]

[54] G. Abbott, *The Child and the State*, Chicago, University of Chicago Press, 1938, pp. 345–47 (extract from the *Second Annual Report of the Managers of the Society for the Prevention of Pauperism in the City of New York*, 1819).

[55] *Ibid.*, pp. 347–48 (abstract of the *Report of the Committee*, Society for the Prevention of Pauperism).

[56] *Ibid.*, p. 362.

[57] *Annual Report of the Worcester Children's Friend Society*, 1851, p. 6.

[58] *Annual Report of the Children's Aid Society*, New York, 1854, p. 9.

[59] *Annual Report of the Children's Aid Society*, New York, 1882, p. 19.

[60] *First Annual Report of the Children's Aid Society*, New York, 1854.

The states, too, were beginning to take action to improve conditions for the infants and children in their charge. In 1866, Massachusetts established a primary school at the state almshouse at Monson where children could be educated, although only "until they can be placed in the better school of a good Massachusetts family, where they can learn thrift and self-respect, and manifold lessons that are seldom taught in great public establishments. . . ."[61] In 1875, the New York State Legislature outlawed the commitment of children over three and under sixteen to county poorhouses (unless the child was rendered "unfit for family care").[62] Admittedly, in most of these early placements, foster parents were primarily interested in the potential usefulness of these children at home or on the farm. However, when this motivation was brought to light attempts were made to place children with families whose sole purpose was to provide a good environment for the development of the child. This view is reflected in a statement issued in 1867 by the Worcester Children's Friend Society: "We wish more families were ready to receive such children by adoption, rather than as helpers, or hired servants, liable at any time to be dismissed when not needed in such a capacity."[63] Interestingly, although the Society emphasized the fact that a foster child should be accepted as a son or daughter, rather than as a servant, there was no mention of a warm loving mother-child relationship as a missing factor in the indenture system. But this is hardly surprising, if one takes into account the views on family organization which prevailed at the time. Parental authority and the obedience of children were stressed. The impact of religious and economic doctrines, with their emphasis on industry and frugality as the basis for sound character, contributed to this orientation.

Concurrently, there was a growing conviction that children ought to be given the privileges of family life at an early age, long before they could be of service. The rationale for this view was discussed by Clara T. Leonard in her report to the National Conference of Charities and Correction in 1879:

> The younger the child when it enters the family, the more hopeful will be its future in life. The longer the child remains in the institution, the greater will be the prospect that it will be a public burden always. In order to bring dependent children at an early age into family life it will

---

[61] G. Abbott, *op. cit.*, pp. 38–39 (extract from the *Fifth Annual Report of the Board of State Charities of Massachusetts*, January, 1869, Public Document No. 17).

[62] *Ibid.*, pp. 71–72 (extract from An Act to Provide for the Better Care of Pauper and Destitute Children, Laws of the State of New York, 1875, Chapter 172).

[63] *Annual Report of the Worcester Children's Friend Society*, 1867, p. 8.

be necessary to pay a small sum for their maintenance for a time, in many cases. ... Their failure (i.e. institutional children becoming paupers and criminals) is not so much from inherited defects, as from the fact that moral stamina has been destroyed by a machine—life, which creates a spirit of dependence, and stultifies the affections and moral qualities.[64]

In summary, in their efforts to enable a "dependent" child to develop into a happy and self-sufficient adult, concerned individuals instituted various changes in the methods of care of such children. Starting with almshouses, emphasis shifted to institutions which catered only to children; then to foster homes (where the focus was on apprenticeship or indenture); to boarding homes where children were to enjoy the privileges of family life as a member of the family, rather than an employee; and eventually to the placement of very young children (even those under the age of three) with foster families in the sole interest of the child's development. Moreover, although, for the most part, these efforts were devoted to the care of dependents and delinquents who were removed from their own homes, there was a movement afoot to avoid commitment or foster home placement of the delinquent whenever possible, and instead to place him on probation under the watchful eye of a visiting agent. A law enacted in 1869 in Massachusetts constituted one of the earliest attempts to rehabilitate the delinquent by working with him in his own home.[65] The further development of preventive services to deal with behavioural disturbances is exemplified by the establishment of the first juvenile court in Chicago in 1899.[66] The purpose of the court was to separate juvenile from adult offenders, and to allow the judge to deal with such juvenile offenders in a "fatherly" fashion. It is noteworthy that these efforts were actively supported by Adolf Meyer, a pioneer in American psychiatry and mental hygiene,[67] and Julia Lathrop, a social worker, who later became the first director of the Children's Bureau.

During the latter part of the nineteenth century, there was a growing interest in the mental disorders exhibited by children. Under the impact of Darwinism, the theory of degeneration proposed by Morel, and subsequent studies of heredity, aetiological emphasis was placed on physical and congenital factors which were thought to account in large measure for mental illness in childhood. Thus,

[64] C. T. Leonard, "Report on Family Homes for Pauper and Dependent Children," *Proceedings of the National Conference of Charities and Correction*, 1879, pp. 170–77.

[65] G. Abbott, *op. cit.*, pp. 368–70.

[66] *Ibid.*, pp. 330–32.

[67] See p. 286 ff.

Abraham Jacobi, first president of the American Pediatric Society, considered heredity, inebriety, psychical aberrations, nervous disorders, epilepsy, and diabetes to be aetiological factors in mental illness in children.[68] Consequently, in his presidential address to the American Pediatric Society in 1889, he conceived of preventive efforts in terms of eugenics and the prevention of prenatal, birth, and childhood infections and injuries.[69] However, it should be noted that Dr. Jacobi also mentioned fear, masturbation, and poor training and education as contributing factors in mental disturbance, and suggested improvements in the physical aspects of the school environment, better school scheduling, and increased attention to the individual child by school personnel as possible remedies.

As a result of these diverse activities, child welfare workers were becoming increasingly aware that their efforts must be directed towards the very young child, if they were to prevent pauperism and delinquency.[70] This awareness led, in turn, to an increased interest in the pre-school child. Kindergartens, and day nurseries in particular, have been in existence in the United States since the middle of the nineteenth century. Ostensibly, day nurseries were established to help care for the children of mothers who had to work, but the constructive influences such institutions might exert on the impressionable child were considered as well.[71]

At this time, the emphasis was on training children to think and on teaching them self-control, rather than on establishing affectionate and stable interpersonal relations for the child within the environment of the day nursery. However, the "influence" or "spirit" of the home was not overlooked. In her report to the National Conference of Charities and Correction in 1892, M. H. Burgess urged that even at the risk of inefficiency, day nurseries ought to be kept small, so that a "home spirit" might be preserved.[72] In comparing the advantages of a home with the disadvantages of institutional life, the parent-child relationship was pinpointed quite clearly. As early as 1885, Clara T. Leonard urged preservation of the parental relationship, or that arrangement be made for a substitute mother for the

[68] A. Jacobi, *Therapeutics of Infancy and Childhood*, Philadelphia, Lippincott, 1896, p. 415.

[69] *Idem*, "President's Address," *Transactions of the American Pediatric Society*, 1899, pp. 12–16.

[70] H. Folks, "Report on the Child and the Family," *Proceedings of the National Conference of Charities and Correction*, 1892, p. 419.

[71] S. B. Cooper, "Section on Free Kindergartens. Practical Results of Ten Years' Work," *Proceedings of the National Conference of Charities and Correction*, 1889, pp. 186–92.

[72] M. H. Burgess, "Day Nursery Work," *Proceedings of the National Conference of Charities and Corrrection*, 1892, pp. 424–25.

child, if necessary. She also recognized the fact that physical cleanliness was not the most important factor in child development: "We know that very dirty, ill-managed babies do generally live and are healthy when they get the motherly brooding and tending which even a hen knows her chick needs."[73]

At the end of the nineteenth century, two other noteworthy contributions were made by this group of workers. First, in 1899, in an attempt to settle the controversy over institutional versus foster home care for dependent children, the Committee on the Care of Destitute and Neglected Children of the National Conference of Charities and Correction unanimously endorsed a report which stated that the "home is the natural place to properly develop a child." Second, because poverty was still considered almost a crime at this time, and because almost as much effort was expanded to prevent the abuse of philanthropy as to direct help to those who needed it, the report further stated:

> If, instead of turning over such families to relief societies or the public charge, charitable men and women would take a personal interest in such cases, and each would take under (his) care such a family, help them materially, give them also the "alms of good advice," ... giving them assistance in a way that will not degrade the beneficiary, much will have been done to advance the great question of the care of the dependent children.[74]

The need for professional training for social workers was still being debated during this period. Although academic courses in philanthropy, charities, social questions, and sociology were offered by many universities,[75] not until 1904 were schools with a full-time curriculum established for social workers.[76] Prior to the twentieth century, the activities of child health and welfare workers were based on the empirical observation of the kind of care that appeared to be most successful in the development of children. At the turn of the century, more complex theories of behaviour and emotions were developed which attempted to correlate and explain the relationship between early childhood experiences and later development. In many

[73] C. T. Leonard, "Saving the Children," *Proceedings of the National Conference of Charities and Correction*, 1895, pp. 192–97.

[74] H. H. Hart, "Common Sense and Co-operation in Child Saving," *Proceedings of the National Conference of Charities and Correction*, 1903, p. 180.

[75] J. R. Brackett, *Supervision and Education in Charity*, New York, Macmillan, 1903, pp. 156–202.

[76] A. Channing, "The Early Years of a Pioneer School," *The Social Service Review* 28: 430, 1954; E. G. Meier, "Highlights in Brief from 'A History of the New York School of Social Work'," *Bulletin of the New York School of Social Work* 47: 3, 1954.

cases, these theories served to reinforce the earlier concepts of far-sighted welfare workers, particularly with regard to the importance of stable family and parent-child relationships.

The early years of the twentieth century were also characterized by a growing trend among pediatricians to assume responsibility for the mental health of the child. In the first reports of the American Association for the Study and Prevention of Infant Mortality (organized in 1909), the prevention of mental disorders was discussed frequently in terms of eugenics, for some physicians still believed that crime, insanity, degeneracy, and pauperism were inherited. But, at the same time, other physicians were commenting on a phenomenon which had been observed by social workers in the latter half of the nineteenth century, namely, the increased infant mortality and retarded personality development of institutionalized children. However, because their approach differed from that of the social worker, physicians emphasized new aspects of child development. For example, infant mortality in institutions was studied in terms of artificial versus breast feeding and good versus poor physical conditions. Several observers commented that, although they were fed artificially and physical conditions were poor, children who lived in their own homes still fared better than did babies in institutions, no matter how meticulously their milk was prepared and how clean their surroundings. On the basis of these observations it was concluded that mothering and a home atmosphere were essential to healthy development.[77]

Similar observations were formulated with regard to chronically ill babies in hospitals. In 1909, Emelyn Lincoln Coolidge described a condition he termed "hospitalism," which had been observed in infants who had been hospitalized, and thus separated from their mothers for prolonged periods. These infants ultimately developed a blank facial expression and a decreasing ability to fight their disease.[78] However, when they were mothered by nurses or other hospital personnel, they responded; and Coolidge contended that their recovery was expedited as a result.

Apart from the focus on the survival and development of institu-

---

[77] T. Darlington, "Reduction of Infant Mortality in New York City," *Papers and Discussions of the American Academy of Medicine Conference on Prevention of Infant Mortality*, 1909, p. 228; W. Hutchinson, "Results of Philanthropic Experiments in Increasing and Decreasing Infant Mortality," *Papers and Discussions of the American Academy of Medicine Conference on Prevention of Infant Mortality*, 1909, p. 162.

[78] E. Lincoln Coolidge, "Care of Infants Who Must be Separated from Their Mothers Because of Some Especial Need on the Part of the Child," *Papers and Discussions of the American Academy of Medicine Conference on Prevention of Infant Mortality*, 1909, pp. 199–206.

tionalized and hospitalized infants, physicians were becoming interested in the behaviour problems of children. In 1909, William Healy founded the Chicago Juvenile Psychopathic Institute to serve the Chicago Juvenile Court, for it had become evident that judges had neither the background nor the time to study thoroughly the problem children brought before them. The Psychopathic Institute investigated these children medically, psychologically, and sociologically, in an attempt to find the causes for their delinquency and to prevent them from becoming adult criminals.[79] However, inasmuch as these children were not seen until they had committed a primary offence, emphasis was on rehabilitation rather than prevention.

The concern with all the phases of child development which characterized the early twentieth century had various repercussions. The federal government now began to take cognizance of such problems, and the White House Conference on the Care of Dependent Children, in 1909, marked the first federal recognition of the importance of the home. In his summary of the conclusions of the Conference, President Roosevelt stated: "The keynote of the conference was expressed in these words: Home life is the highest and finest product of civilization. Children should not be deprived of it except for urgent and compelling reasons."[80] In 1912, a federal act to establish a Children's Bureau (which had been proposed annually for six years) was passed.[81] The Bureau was charged with the investigation of "infant mortality, the birth rate, orphanages, juvenile courts, desertion, dangerous occupations, accidents and disease of children, employment, and legislation affecting children. . . ."[82] In keeping with this goal, the Children's Bureau proceeded to make available to parents current knowledge and ideas regarding child rearing, mortality, and delinquency. The first issue, in 1914, of its pamphlet on Infant Care included a discussion of the lasting impression of early experiences and of the desirability of establishing good habits early (the first and most essential being regularity).[83] Although the basic need for mothering was mentioned, problem behaviour continued to be attributed chiefly to physical causes. Subsequent revisions of the publication, which reflected the feeling of the times, are of particular interest. The importance of infancy and childhood for future development is emphasized throughout, but in 1914 and

[79] G. S. Stevenson and G. Smith, *op. cit.*, p. 15.
[80] T. Roosevelt, "Special Message to Congress," *Proceedings of the White House Conference on the Care of Dependent Children*, 1909, p. 5.
[81] See p. 273.
[82] D. E. Bradbury, *op. cit., p.* 87.
[83] U.S. Department of Labour, Infant Care, Children's Bureau Publication No. 8, Washington, D.C., Government Printing Office, 1914, p. 63.

in the twenties, early good habit formation was considered of paramount importance. However, by the 1940s, emphasis had shifted to the importance of early experiences in determining future ways of acting and feeling, to the importance of easy adaptation and the fulfilment of the infant's emotional needs.[84] Finally, in 1942, the mother was told that "A baby needs to be loved; he needs to be picked up and cuddled occasionally; he needs to snuggle down in the warmth and comfort of his mother's arms."[85]

The decade from 1918 to 1928 was particularly noteworthy for the increased interest evidenced among child health and welfare workers in all children, whether sick or well, dependent or not, delinquent or well behaved. A Children's Year, sponsored by the Children's Bureau in 1918, and a series of Children's Bureau Conferences in 1919, initiated by the White House Conference of that year, reflected this trend. The Conferences were attended by specialists in many fields—physicians, social workers, educators, members of the Public Health Service, the Children's Bureau, and the state departments of health, as well as experts from a number of European countries—all of whom were united by their common concern for the welfare of children. The participants considered health protection, the economic and social bases for child welfare standards, and minimum standards for children in need of special care. Children in need of special care were, first and foremost, entitled to a normal home life and, second, to "opportunities for education, recreation, vocational preparation for life, and moral, religious, and physical development."[86] The discussions concerning mental hygiene, which are of particular interest in this context, were summarized in the following statement:

> The value of the first 7 years of childhood from the point of view of health, education and morals, and formative habits cannot be overestimated. Throughout childhood attention should be given to the mental hygiene of the child—the care of the instincts, emotions, and general personality, and of environmental conditions. Special attention should be given to the need for training teachers and social workers in mental hygiene principles.[87]

Obviously, neither the Children's Year nor the Children's Bureau Conferences gave rise to new concepts. The value of these programmes stemmed from the fact that existing concepts concerning

[84] *Ibid.*, 1942, pp. 29–31.
[85] *Ibid.*, p. 31.
[86] *Annual Reports of the Chiefs of the Children's Bureau to the Secretary of Labor*, Washington, D.C., Government Printing Office, 1915.
[87] *Ibid.*, p. 19.

the home and the parent-child relationships were brought to the attention of the entire country, and were, in effect, officially endorsed and recommended by established leaders in the field of child health and welfare. As might be expected, this "endorsement" provided additional impetus to put these concepts into effect.

During these years from 1918 to 1928, child welfare workers and educators continued to concern themselves with the pre-school child, as they had in the latter part of the nineteenth century. Because they now recognized this period as crucial to the future development of the child, they actively participated in the movement to establish nursery schools (as opposed to day nurseries, which offered custodial care primarily). The goals of these organizations were many and varied, including provision of a suitable environment for the development of the pre-school child, research on developmental phenomena, and the education of teachers and parents.

In 1929, the National Society for the Study of Education conducted a survey of the goals and activities of "typical" nursery schools, in order to assess the status of pre-school and parental education.[88] The schools appeared to emphasize the child's physical health, his social adaptation, and his education—primarily the formation of good habits. No specific mention was made of the effect on the child of diminished mother-child contact, or of the need to provide an affectionate substitute mother. However, the importance of giving each child individual attention and of the positive reinforcement of good habits were stressed, and both of these procedures would necessarily have entailed some mothering on the part of school personnel.

To a great extent, this concern with the pre-school child on the part of child health workers stemmed from their emerging interest in the prevention, as well as the treatment, of disease—both physical and mental. To prevent behaviour disturbances, they had to direct their attention to the pre-school child, for it had become evident that many such problems were well established by the time a child started school. These views were stated succinctly by Richard Smith in an address before the American Child Hygiene Association in 1922: "Mental development takes place most rapidly at this age period. Habits become fixed which influence future character and health. ... It is essential that good habits be established. This is the age for mental hygiene."[89] Conceivably, the well-run kindergarten or nursery

---

[88] *The Twenty-Eighth Yearbook of the National Society for the Study of Education, Pre-School and Parental Education*, Bloomington, Illinois, Public School Publishing Company, 1929, pp. 26–38.

[89] R. M. Smith, "What Needs to be Done for the Pre-School Child," *Transactions of the American Child Hygiene Association*, 1922, p. 59.

school might exert a major influence on the early training and habit formation of the pre-school child.

The child in his home (as opposed to the child who was cared for away from home) also began to receive more vigorous attention from child health and welfare workers at this time (1918–1928). Instruction on child care was being made more available to parents, and this instruction now covered both the physical and mental aspects of the child's development. The pamphlet on *Child Care*, published by the Children's Bureau in 1918, defined the mother's role as follows: "It is believed that the chief duty of parents after providing food, shelter, warmth, and clothing for their future children is to understand them and to surround them with loving and sympathetic guidance while their development proceeds as nature intended. It is from the mother, especially, that this guidance will come."[90]

Mothers were becoming increasingly aware of their responsibility to their children and of the importance of mental, as well as physical, health. Some mothers, and even a few fathers, sought guidance in their duties. As early as 1886, a group of women in New York City had organized the Society for the Study of Child Nature, and met for reading and discussion. Their idea spread to other communities, and, eventually, these groups united to form the Federation for Child Study, which became the Child Study Association of America in 1924. This organization has had an important influence on child health in the United States. Similarly, popular writers and "semi-professionals" had a considerable impact on parents' child rearing practices. Increasing literacy and the concomitant growth of mass media of communication made it possible for such writers to reach a large proportion of the population.

A demonstration clinic was also set up by child health and welfare workers in the early 1920s to help parents to fulfill their role in the healthy mental development of their children. In 1921, the Baby Hygiene Association of Boston,[91] which was then responsible for the baby and child clinics in that city, sought the help of Douglas Thom, a psychiatrist, in an attempt to improve their preventive programme.[92] When Thom agreed to participate, the Children's Bureau co-operated with the newly formed Community Health Service of Boston to

[90] *U.S. Department of Labor, Child Care*, Care of Children Series No. 3, Children's Bureau Publication No. 30, Washington, D.C., Government Printing Office, 1918, p. 45.

[91] In the following year, the Baby Hygiene Association combined with the Instructive District Nursing Association, to form the Community Health Service of Boston.

[92] D. Thom, "Habit Clinics for Children of Pre-School Age," Read at the Annual Meeting of the American Psychiatric Association, Quebec, Canada, June 6–9, 1922.

establish what was called a "habit clinic" as "an integral part of a general health service for pre-school children."[93]

The Children's Bureau conceived of this project as providing

> the kind of help and service which mothers need to enable them to guide their children in habit formation or to change asocial habits that have been formed [and which] has not been given in most pre-school centres or clinics. As a result, habits, fears, and inhibitions—frequently easy to change—which prevent the correction of serious physical disorders, make impossible happy family and community relationships, and influence profoundly adult personality, are ignored or punished because the possibilities of other treatment are not understood.[94]

Under Thom's direction, the Habit Clinic enlisted the services of a psychiatrist, a psychologist, and a social worker to help children between two and five who employed undesirable methods to cope with their problems. Initially, attention was focused primarily on symptomatology, although the aetiology of these undesirable habits was also investigated. Ultimately, the Clinic's efforts were directed towards prevention rather than cure.

The 1920s were characterized by a greater emphasis on study and research in the fields of child development, on the part of both physicians and psychologists, than ever before. A number of child welfare institutes or stations were organized for this purpose. At first, workers were concerned with observing and recording the details of physical and mental growth, determining developmental norms, and developing testing devices. Subsequently, however, their interest turned to social behaviour.[95] At this time, Arnold Gesell worked on a survey of normal behaviour in infancy and early childhood at the Yale Psycho-Clinic. In its report to the American Child Hygiene Association in 1921, the Iowa Child Welfare Research Station stated that its goal was to develop "practical methods of child rearing, modified to suit the varied needs of child life and to give parenthood dependable counsel to ensure the continuous improvement of every child to maximum ability, consistent with his native endowment and special abilities."[96] The Institute of Child Welfare at Minnesota, under the direction of John E. Anderson, initiated a correspondence course on child care and training which

---

[93] *Annual Reports of the Chiefs of the Children's Bureau to the Secretary of Labor*, Washington, D.C., Government Printing Office, 1923, p. 8.

[94] *Ibid.*, p. 8.

[95] J. E. Anderson, "Child Development: An Historical Perspective," *Child Development* 27: 193, 1956.

[96] "Report of Child Welfare Research Station, State University, Iowa City," *Transactions of the American Child Hygiene Association*, 1921, p. 320.

included a lesson on the importance of family relationships in the development of the child. The fact that emotional and social attitudes are acquired during the early years of life was emphasized as well: "Although he will forget to a large degree the experience of his early years he cannot discard the attitudes and impressions which are being built into his character at this time. As a matter of fact . . . such traits are in large part due to the manner in which the child is treated by adults and other children, rather than to inheritance."[97]

The child guidance clinic also had its origin during this decade. In this instance, attention was focused on problem children; therefore, these workers were concerned with treatment and rehabilitation rather than the prevention of mental illness. It was their hope that the principles which governed their treatment of individual children would reach the general community, affect current standards of child care, and thus help to prevent disturbances in other children.[98]

The White House Conference on Child Health and Protection in 1930 made major contributions to child health and welfare. Once again, the family was designated as constituting the most important factor in the healthy mental development of the child. However, the specific characteristics which contributed to this development were spelled out in greater detail than was true previously. Interpersonal relations, affection, security, and encouragement within the family were emphasized.[99]

> . . . The family should provide for the child a friendly and hospitable environment for the development of his emotions and abilities, a secure relationship in a group of definite social status wherein he is loved, protected and encouraged. The child wants to belong to a family. . . . He needs the affection, the security, the encouragement of the family to fortify him for successful contacts in the outside world. He needs parents who are happy in their adjustments to each other, who are working hopefully towards the fulfillment of an ideal of living, who love their children with a sincere and unselfish love, in short, who are well-balanced individuals, gifted with a certain amount of insight, who are able to provide the child with a wholesome emotional background which will contribute more to his development than material advantages.[100]

Since these characteristics were not considered inherent in the family structure, education in mental health principles was recom-

[97] Institute of Child Welfare, University of Minnesota, *Child Care and Training, A Reading Course for Parents*, Minneapolis, University of Minnesota Press, 1928, p. 2.

[98] G. S. Stevenson and G. Smith, *op. cit.*, p. 54.

[99] White House Conference of 1930, *Addresses and Abstracts of Committee Reports*, New York, 1931, p. 135.

[100] *Ibid.*, p. 136.

mended both for the parents and professionals who dealt with children (e.g. teachers, doctors, nurses, and social workers). Current research, designed to increase basic knowledge of mental health was described. This included fact-finding studies of delinquency and behaviour problems; research on the prevalence of fears; and comparative studies of well-adjusted and maladjusted children to determine intangible family influences.[101] Finally, the 1930 White House Conference led to the formation, in 1931, of the American Academy of Pediatrics ". . . to foster and stimulate interest in, pediatrics and correlate all aspects of the work for the welfare of children which properly come within the scope of pediatrics."[102] The Academy has contributed greatly to the understanding and the acceptance by pediatricians of concepts of mental development in children. Moreover, it has played a leading role in interpreting mental health concepts to other physicians and their patients.

To illustrate, the committees formed initially by the Academy included one on mental hygiene. In an early report of this committee, Bart I. Beverly stated:

> If this attitude [that pediatricians should supervise all that pertains to physical and mental health and growth during the age period between birth and the end of adolescence] is to be carried out in practice, mental hygiene must be made a more important part of pediatrics. Such a possibility makes necessary a greater knowledge of psychiatry and mental hygiene by pediatricians. The education of doctors is, I believe, one of the accepted functions of the Society. In the case of mental hygiene it means the education of ourselves.[103]

In 1935, the Academy emphasized the need for co-operation between health and welfare workers in dealing with the mental health of children:

> Doctors should be very careful about claiming control of "the whole child" and should welcome discussions with psychiatrists, social workers and teachers. . . . The pediatricians will, in the opinion of this committee, be fulfilling their obligations whenever they organize their training and their practice so that the children under their care receive prompt and intelligent attention to the intellectual and emotional difficulties which arise. It is not at all certain that the practicing physician can provide all this care himself, but he should use his influence to see that adequate care is made available and that parents use it wisely.

[101] *Ibid.*, pp. 135–36.
[102] T. B. Cooley, "The American Academy of Pediatrics, Its Purpose and Its Scope," *Transactions of the American Academy of Pediatrics* 1: 27, 1931.
[103] "Report of Mental Hygiene Committee, June 13, 1933, Third Annual Meeting of the American Academy of Pediatrics," *Journal of Pediatrics* 3: 402, 1933.

The New York City Health Department has played an equally important role in introducing mental health concepts to professional health workers, especially those involved in public health programmes. In 1937, a training programme, financed initially by the Public Health Service and the Children's Bureau, was set up at the Kips Bay Centre for public health physicians, nurses, and dentists. There is little question that the continuing activities of the Department have left a real mark on public health practice both in this country and abroad. Similarly, child welfare organizations, notably the Child Welfare League of America, other social organizations, and educational institutions have made major contributions in disseminating and developing the mental health concepts advanced at the 1930 White House Conference.

Increased opportunity for the implementation of current mental health concepts came with the passage of the Social Security Act in 1935, partly through the nature of the child welfare provisions and partly through the extension of maternal and child health services by public health nurses in prenatal and child health clinics. With the aid of federal grants, the states, too, were able to develop and expand their child welfare programme, and services were initiated which were designed to help children who were reared in their own homes, as well as those children who were cared for away from home. The prevention of situations in the home which would hinder the healthy physical, social, and mental development of the child was emphasized. For example, the services of child welfare workers in rural areas, homemaker services, day care, and foster family day care services were sponsored to help keep the family unit intact whenever possible, and to provide continuing supportive counsel to parents, which would indirectly benefit the child. Group discussions with parents, with foster parents, and with disturbed children were initiated in some communities, in order that these problems might be resolved before they reached crippling proportions.[104]

To further illustrate, new concepts were applied to adoption procedures. It was essential to protect the child, the natural mother, and the adoptive parents; to have a single mother substitute care for the infant in the first months of life; to place infants with adoptive parents as early as possible; to increase the range of adoptable children; to carefully investigate adoptive applicants and children; to continue to supervise their care after the children have been placed.[105] The underlying motivation in all these concepts was to

[104] U.S. Department of Labor, *Child Welfare Services—How They Help Children and Their Parents*, Children's Bureau Publication No. 359, Washington, D.C., Government Printing Office, 1957.

[105] *Ibid.*, pp. 62–70.

create the best possible chance for the adopted child to develop a healthy personality.

The period from 1940 to 1950 was outstanding from the point of view of child health and welfare workers because of their increasing interest in, and application of, mental health concepts and because of their increasing attempts to undertake research in this area.

Research conducted at this time included studies on home and family atmosphere, the effects of maternal deprivation and institutionalization, and the relationship between early handling of the child and his subsequent development.[106]

The greatest single concerted effort to study and investigate personality development in children was initiated in 1950 at the White House Conference on Children and Youth. Participants included representatives of a large variety of disciplines, who were concerned primarily with the multiple factors which might influence personality development, e.g. congenital characteristics, physical limitation, parent–child relationships, economic factors, prejudice and discrimination, and religion.[107] The Conference emphasized those factors which contribute to the development of a healthy personality, and which involve the efforts of parents, as well as health and welfare workers, educators, and others who work with children. The importance of a mental health programme as an integral part of health services for pre-school, school, and adolescent children was pointed out once again. The need to include courses on personality development in the educational programmes of physicians, nurses, social workers, teachers, and other professional workers was strongly underscored.

The effect of the 1950 White House Conference has reverberated throughout the past decade. Gradually, mental health concepts, as well as concepts of normal physical growth, are becoming part of the professional equipment of many workers who are concerned with the welfare of children and their families.

## Nursing

Florence Nightingale, founder of the first training school for nurses at St. Thomas' Hospital, London in 1860, was quick to observe that the influence of nurses upon their patients went beyond the actual

---

[106] J. E. Anderson, "Child Development: An Historical Perspective," *Child Development* 27: 194, 1956.

[107] H. L. Witmer and R. Kotinsky, eds., *Personality in the Making, The Fact-Finding Report of the Mid-Century White House Conference on Children and Youth*, New York, Harper & Bros., 1952.

physical care they provided.[108] In this country, Linda Richards, a graduate of the first class of the first permanent hospital nursing school (The New England Hospital for Women in Boston) made a similar observation: "Many a poor woman dates her changed life from a short stay in some hospital ward, where trained nurses ministered to her physical needs and by helpful words strengthened her moral nature. In the nurse she found a true friend. She made her an example, and, in trying to become like her, she grew into a self-respecting and respected woman."[109]

This observation may have been overly optimistic, yet it reflected the realization that, conceivably, nurses might influence the habits of their patients, and that the potential impact of the nurse-patient relationship could not be overlooked.

In statements defining the goals of the first visiting or district nurses and in reports of their early activities, there is evidence that the task of the visiting nurse was envisioned, not only as involving physical care, but in broader terms as well. For example, the first visiting nurse in the United States, employed by the City Mission and Tract Society in New York City in 1877 to offer nursing service to the poor, taught thrift, economy, and the "importance of observing the proprieties and simple courtesies of life, in addition to fulfilling her characteristic duties."[110] As the idea of visiting nursing spread, associations to provide this service were formed in many cities.

At the end of the nineteenth century, a visiting nurse carried this concept one step further. Using Toynbee Hall and Hull House as models, Lillian D. Wald conceived of a "settlement" where nurses would live in the community with their patients, and thus improve their health and character.[111] Miss Wald, with the collaboration of Mary Brewster, founded the first nurses' settlement in New York City in 1893.

Although their work was not specifically labelled as such, by the early part of the twentieth century, nurses were functioning in a number of areas which today would be considered within the field of mental health. Nurses were concerned with child manage-

---

[108] L. Richards, "The Moral Influence of Trained Nurses in Hospitals," *Proceedings of the National Conference of Charities and Correction*, 1895, p. 256.

[109] *Ibid.*, p. 257.

[110] Mrs. A. Heermance Smith, "Trained Nurses among the Sick Poor in New York," *Proceedings of the National Conference of Charities and Correction*, 1890, p. 110.

[111] J. E. Hitchcock, "Report of the Sub-Committee on Visiting Nursing," *Proceedings of the National Conference of Charities and Correction*, 1905, p. 257.

ment, with the preservation of the home, with crime prevention, and with the relationship between mind and body. During this period, nurses, as well as doctors and social workers, once again conceived of health in broad terms; and problems of child rearing were considered important aspects of overall health management.

Nurses were also observing their influence on the patient's attitude towards his illness. Susan Tracy, superintendent of the Training School at Adams Nervine Asylum in Jamaica Plain, Massachusetts, observed that a patient's bitterness about his illness could be lessened if the nurse provided some useful or constructive occupation for him during his convalescence.[112] Nurses were writing articles for the *American Journal of Nursing*, describing the value of the intuitive use of tact, sympathy, understanding, patience, and humour in making illness a less unpleasant experience. As a result of these developments, graduate nurses in homes and hospitals became increasingly aware that social and physical problems were inextricably entangled; that without further knowledge about social ills, they were not prepared to cope with the great variety of problems they encountered in their patients. By 1910, in answer to this need, the Boston School for Social Work was offering eight lectures and conferences designed for working nurses.[113]

In the next ten years, nurses increased the scope of their activities to include new areas which allowed them to develop and apply mental health concepts: nurses began to work in public schools and in children's institutions. This increased range of activities was accompanied by changes in the educational curricula of nurses to include training for these varied tasks.

Initially, public school nurses had directed their efforts towards detecting the symptoms of disease, preventing the spread of contagious disease, and teaching hygiene. By 1913, however, some nurses were beginning to look for early symptoms of mental illness as well.[114] Nurses were also beginning to use the information they gained during home visits to alert teachers to individual problems which might not have come to light otherwise. Further efforts to prevent emotional disturbance were made by nurses who worked with infants and children in institutions. There was no question that institutionalized babies showed diminished emotional response, as compared to babies who lived at home.[115] Accordingly, nurses in

[112] S. E. Tracy, "Some Profitable Occupations for Invalids," *American Journal of Nursing*, December 1907, p. 172.

[113] *Annual Report of the Instructive District Nursing Association of Boston*, 1910.

[114] K. Manley, "Mental Hygiene in the School," *American Journal of Nursing*, November 1913, pp. 99–100.

[115] See p. 294 ff.

such institutions were urged to try to fill the mother's place, and to give genuine love to the children in their charge.[116]

Nurses had always considered teaching a vital part of their job, but during the decade from 1910 to 1920, they extended their task to include providing mothers and teachers with sex education within the setting of the classroom, lecture hall, and home.[117] Their scope of activity extended to family problems as well:

> The nurse is taught to consider the welfare of the family as a whole, and although her immediate duty lies with the patient, yet there is also great opportunity for advising about the family problems, at which time experience is needed to judge whether the help of other associations should be sought.[118]

As their contact with families continued, advanced courses of instruction were made available to prepare them for this work. In 1914, the Boston School of Social Workers and the Boston Instructive District Nursing Association jointly offered two courses to nurses who were interested in public health training. Among the topics included in these courses were "The Family;" "Housing;" "Recreation;" "Community Relations;" and "Neighbourly Relations."[119] By 1916, the Department of Nursing Education of the American Nurses' Association included in its list of suggested programmes "The Meaning of Personality; How It Can Be Conserved and Developed," and "Mental Hygiene," particularly in relation to infancy and childhood.[120]

Nurses began to concern themselves increasingly with the emotional response of the hospitalized child in the 1920s. Nurses had observed that children who had been hospitalized, even for short periods, were frightened by the experience and by their separation from their families. As early as 1923, Annette Fisk urged that nurses' training schools promote programmes to allow frequent hospital visiting by parents, so as to provide children with parental love and attention.[121]

[116] J. E. Lester, "The Psychic Principle in Nursing Infants," *American Journal of Nursing*, November 1915, p. 111.

[117] Editorial Comment, "The Nurse's Place in the Moral Education of the Child," *American Journal of Nursing*, March 1911, pp. 415–16.

[118] "Report of Training School for Boston District Nurses," *Annual Report of the Instructive District Nursing Association of Boston*, 1910, p. 35.

[119] *Annual Report of the Instructive District Nursing Association of Boston*, 1914, p. 39.

[120] "Programs for Nurses' Meetings," *American Journal of Nursing*, November 1916, p. 138.

[121] A. Fisk, "Psychology," *American Journal of Nursing*, September 1923, p. 1013.

During this decade, nurses also showed increasing interest in teaching parents the principles of child training—the formation of healthy habits, and understanding and influencing the child's behaviour and emotions.[122] In 1926, Effie Taylor, Associate Superintendent of Nurses, Johns Hopkins Hospital, set forth no small task for nurses in this area:

> Next to the mother, the nurse is the most potent factor in the early life and development of the young child. She is with the child and mother in the pre-school period and often in the adolescent period as well. . . . She must therefore know the proper reaction to sleep, nutrition, elimination, talking, walking, and all bodily wants. She should know the normal reactions to play, recreation, and the interests and associations of childhood. She must know when changes in emotions and moods are the results of physical or environmental conditions or acquired habits, desirable or undesirable, and she should know what habits and tendencies to encourage or inhibit.[123]

Of necessity, early efforts to deal with emotional problems and behavioural disturbances were based on intuition and observation for the most part. However, there was a strong feeling among nurses that formal teaching was needed, if they were to deal with these problems effectively. In fact, perhaps the nurses' major contribution to the progress of mental health during the twenties was their realization that, as nurses, they were not equipped to understand and help with all of the complex emotional and behavioural problems with which they were confronted. When this became clear, in addition to their attempts to obtain a more adequate educational background in this area, they proceeded to enlist the help and co-operation of other professions, e.g. doctors, social workers, and nurses with specialized training.

The history of the visiting nurse associations aptly illustrates these efforts towards interprofessional co-operation. The District Nursing Association in Providence, Rhode Island, hired a nurse with training in public health nursing, social work, and psychiatric nursing to advise on mental hygiene problems.[124] In 1926, for the first time in this country, the Community Health Association of Boston hired a psychiatric social worker as a mental health consultant.[125]

[122] V. M. Macdonald, "Mental Health of Children," *American Journal of Nursing*, October 1921, pp. 6–8; *Idem*, "The Public Health Nurse as a Health Teacher," *American Journal of Nursing*, February 1925, pp. 106–107.

[123] E. J. Taylor, "Psychiatry and the Nurse. Discussion of a paper by A. H. Ruggles, M.D.," *American Journal of Nursing*, August 1926, pp. 633–34.

[124] L. F. Coe, "A Mental Hygiene Program as Part of a Public Health Nursing Service," *Public Health Nursing* 18: 114–16, 1926.

[125] *Annual Report of the Community Health Association of Boston*, 1926, p. 5.

At the same time, the Committee on Education of the National League of Nursing Education attempted to improve nurses' qualifications in the area of mental health by revising the recommended standard curriculum for nurses' training in 1925.[126] These recommendations stated that pediatric nursing should include an understanding of normal physical and mental development, of child psychology, child hygiene, and child management. Mental health nursing should emphasize the importance of identifying those conditions which were likely to produce tension and fatigue; of understanding the formation of "mental habits" and the effects of early training on future development.

During the years from 1930 to 1940, nurses began to realize the full importance of their position. That is, they were able, potentially, to provide broad guidance and assistance to parents in problems of child development and child management, by virtue of the confidence placed in them. As a result, much of the opportunity for the practical application of current knowledge about mental health was falling into their hands. Glee Hastings, Mental Hygiene Supervisor at the New Haven Visiting Nurse Association, pointed out, in this connection, that public health nurses see children's problems in the early stages, and are thus in a position to redirect their activities, help build desirable habits, and prevent delinquency.[127] And Ruth Gilbert, Assistant Director of the National Organization, of Public Health Nursing, extended the nurses' responsibility a step further when she stressed the fact that nurses should attempt to recognize problem situations before symptoms had a chance to develop.[128]

However, the task of helping parents with child management and training was not as simple a procedure as it had appeared at first glance. Unless the mother understood the reason for an action, and unless such advice was congruent with her beliefs, she was inclined to disregard the nurse's suggestions. In a discussion of advice, as opposed to education, Winifred Rand pointed out that, if the nurse were to function effectively, it was necessary to educate parents with regard to the development and management of children, rather than *advise* them on these problems.[129] Parents had to participate actively in this learning process, and thus acquire an understanding of the

[126] "Revision of the Standard Curriculum," *American Journal of Nursing*, November 1925, p. 935; "Revision of the Standard Curriculum," *American Journal of Nursing*, September 1925, p. 778.

[127] G. L. Hastings, "The Nurse in the Prevention of Delinquency," *Public Health Nursing* 29: 512–16, 1937.

[128] R. Gilbert, "Mental Hygiene Activities in Public Health Nursing Organizations," *Public Health Nursing* 23: 470–74, 1931.

[129] W. Rand, "The Nurse's Opportunity to Teach Parents," *Public Health Nursing* 27: 570–74, 1935.

rationale behind a procedure, if they were to benefit from their contact with the public health nurse.

The mental health goals of nurses have remained the same during the last two decades, i.e. to prevent mental illness and to help each individual to develop to his greatest potential. However, the methods through which these goals are achieved have changed considerably. Nurses are no longer satisfied with abstract knowledge concerning emotional development; they have become aware that the patient's attitudes, their own attitudes, and the interaction of the two must be taken into consideration as well.[130]

Methods of conveying help or information to the patient have also been altered. Earlier, we described the transition from "advising" parents on the prevention of emotional or behavioural problems, to an emphasis on the need to "educate" them. In the last two decades, the emphasis has shifted once more from "education" to "counselling." This implies that the nurse must first gain an understanding of the specific individual needs and feelings of her patient, and then adapt her teaching to the individual.[131]

Other changes in methods of mental health nursing concern the nurse's approach to infant and child care. The emphasis is no longer on detailed procedures, but rather on satisfying the infant's needs, as well as those of his parents.[132] In 1943, in her capacity as mental health consultant for the Visiting Nursing Association of Scranton, Pennsylvania, Katherine B. Oettinger commented on the shift from rigid to flexible programmes of child management, and on the changes in the nurse's approach to the mother. The nurse was now encouraged to support the mother in her need to feel that she was doing a good job, and would eventually be able to function effectively without help.[133]

Finally, in the past two decades, nurses have demonstrated the applicability of mental health concepts to all ages and at all stages of human development. They have concerned themselves with the emotional needs of the pregnant mother,[134] of infants and

---

[130] R. Gilbert, *The Public Health Nurse and Her Patient*, New York, Commonwealth Fund, 1940, p. 4.

[131] E. Hildebrand, "Listening Is Part of the Job," *Public Health Nursing* 43: 436–39, 1951; N. Cline, "How the Public Health Nurse Uses Mental Health Concepts," *Public Health Nursing* 44: 83–87, 1952; P. McIver, "Trends in Public Health," *Nursing Outlook*, July 1954, p. 354.

[132] R. Chisholm, "Parents' Classes—A Fertile Field for Mental Health Concepts," *Public Health Nursing* 44: 273–75, 1952.

[133] K. B. Oettinger, "Mental Hygiene and the Nurse," *American Journal of Nursing*, December 1943, pp. 1091–94.

[134] E. Baumann, "The Visiting Nurse Views Rooming-In," *Public Health Nursing* 42: 263–66, 1950; A. Harris, "A Public Health Nurse Views Rooming-In," *Public Health Nursing* 44: 580–84, 1952.

children,[135] of adolescents, of adults in stressful situations,[136] and of the dying patient.[137]

## Social Work

Early efforts in social work focused on poverty. As stated previously, a major objective at the time was to eliminate waste in charity, and thus protect the charitable person from being imposed upon by "frauds."[138] The techniques of investigation developed by workers in the field were intended to achieve these objectives and, in the case of the sick poor, to prevent abuse of hospital and clinic facilities. The social worker's function, then, was to distribute alms, so as to encourage thrift, self-help, and independence. The English Poor Law Amendment Act of 1834, and its underlying aim to deter requests for assistance, was the basis for this attitude. Accordingly, early social workers tried to "improve" the poor, and to develop more scientific philanthropic practices. At the same time, there was a widespread assumption that indifference to prevailing social standards and criminality were characteristics of the lower classes, and that these were the dangerous classes of the community.[139]

During the early decades of the twentieth century, without giving up their interest in developing better methods of philanthropy, many social workers became crusaders for social justice and the improvement of living and working conditions; they ceased to function exclusively as advisers to the wealthy on how to dispense charity, and as preceptors of the poor on how to live virtuously. We described this general movement above, in connection with the

[135] F. G. Black, *The Child, His Parents and the Nurse*, Philadelphia, Lippincott, 1954.

[136] F. A. Beasley, "A Public Health Nursing Service for the Families of the Mentally Ill," *Nursing Outlook*, September 1954, pp. 482–84; M. E. Kincade, "A Training Program in Mental Health Nursing for Public Health Nurses," *Nursing Outlook*, December 1958, pp. 683–85.

[137] V. Barckley, "What Can I say to the Cancer Patient," *Nursing Outlook* June 1958, pp. 316–18.

[138] R. H. Bremner, *From the Depths. The Discovery of Poverty in the United States*, New York, New York University Press, 1956; A. F. Young and E. T. Ashton, *British Social Work in the Nineteenth Century*, London, Routledge and Kegan Paul, 1956.

[139] H. A. Frégier, *Des classes dangereuses de la population dans les grandes villes, et des moyens de les rendre meilleures*, 2 vols., Paris, Baillière, 1840; H. Mayhew, *London Labor and the London Poor: The Condition and Earnings of Those That will Work, Cannot Work, and Will Not Work*, 3 vols., London, Charles Griffin, 1864; C. Loring Brace, *The Dangerous Classes of New York and Twenty Years Work among Them*, New York, Wynkoop and Hallenbeck, 1872; L. Chevalier, *Classes laborieuses et classes dangéreuses pendant la première moitié du XIXᵉ siècle*, Paris, Plon, 1958.

evolution of public health in the United States. The leaders in this development, including Jane Addams, Edward T. Devine, Josephine Shaw Lowell, and Robert Hunter, maintained a pragmatic liberalism, which concentrated on problems of public health and welfare, e.g. long working hours, unsatisfactory working conditions, child labour, and the prevention of destitution.[140] However, former attitudes did not vanish overnight. Social workers were members of the middle or upper class, and while they might work for the poor, they were incapable of accepting them fully as their peers. For example, Joseph Lee, a philanthropist who worked for the well-being of immigrants in Boston, was amazed that this "human rubbish" had produced a "number of physically, mentally and morally efficient citizens."[141]

Despite these reservations, social workers continued their attempts to change societal conditions and institutions. Since they recognized the fact that they could not undertake any fundamental reform in social organization, they tended to deal with piecemeal reforms. By temperament, experience, and tradition, social workers were inclined to use education and persuasion to achieve their ends; and by the nature of their work, each family or individual constituted a unique problem. They might be aware of the social context and causes of these problems, but their immediate job was to provide help now; the elimination of the social causes was a long-term project. Out of this orientation, as well as the earlier investigations to determine the "worthiness" of the poor, grew the "case method" or case work.[142]

Case work became the dominant facet of social work, and social work, in turn, was focused on the individual, on his personal strengths and weaknesses, and on individual psychological mechanisms. It is not surprising, therefore, that social workers sought a theoretical rationale and interpretation of their work. As early as 1919, "psychiatry swept the National Conference of Social Work."[143] Eleven years later, in her presidential address to the American Association of Psychiatric Social Workers, Mildred Scoville emphasized the "realization in the social work field that all social case work has a psychological or mental hygiene aspect."[144] Indeed, according to Miles, by 1940, any deviation from Freudian psychology

---

[140] See, for example, E. T. Devine, *Misery and Its Causes*, New York, Macmillan Co., 1910.

[141] B. M. Solomon, *Ancestors and Immigrants. A Changing New England Tradition*, Cambridge, Mass., Harvard University Press, 1956, p. 140.

[142] H. L. Witmer, *Social Work: An Analysis of a Social Institution*, New York, Farrar and Rinehart, 1942, p. 127.

[143] V. P. Robinson, *A Changing Psychology in Social Case Work*, Chapel Hill, University of North Carolina Press, 1930, p. 32.

[144] M. C. Scoville, "An Inquiry into the Status of Psychiatric Social Work," *American Journal of Orthopsychiatry*, 1931, pp. 147–48.

L

in social work theory "was looked upon by some with the same horror as a true Stalinist appraising a Trotskyite."[145] Case work had been conceived by Mary Richmond in terms of diagnosis and therapy; psychoanalysis, with a relatively coherent and systematic theory of personality, provided the rationale for diagnosis and treatment that had been lacking. Furthermore, as Waller so trenchantly pointed out, the shift from economics to psychiatry probably represented an unconscious attempt to escape from the social worker's dilemma, the conflict between humanitarian and organizational mores.[146]

In part, psychiatric social work developed from the same roots as social work in general, and in part from the needs of psychiatrists. In the course of providing assistance to the poor, social workers had come into contact with mental illness, especially when they had to deal with families which were rendered indigent because a parent had become mentally ill. As noted above, about the turn of the century, psychiatrists became increasingly aware of the value of obtaining social data regarding their patients. In 1905, mental hospitals began to use trained social workers for this purpose. The earliest ideas along this line had come from Adolf Meyer, but effective action was first taken by Southard at the Boston Psychopathic Hospital, when he appointed Mary C. Jarrett Director of Social Work in 1913.[147] Southard and Jarrett planned a systematic programme, including the training of psychiatric social workers. Moreover, Mary Jarrett is responsible for the title, psychiatric social worker.

In keeping with the aftercare movement in vogue at this time, social workers were also called upon to help patients who had been discharged from mental institutions to adjust to community life.[148]

The First World War, with its aftermath of returning shell-shocked soldiers, provided impetus for the recruitment of psychiatric social workers, and led to the establishment of academic training facilities for such workers. Southard conceived of the first school of psychiatric social work at Smith College in 1918. Similar training was given in New York and Philadelphia in 1919.

Meanwhile, social work in general had not been standing still. The Association of Training Schools for Professional Social Work was formed in 1919 with seventeen charter members, and the develop-

[145] A. P. Miles, *American Social Work Theory*, New York, Harper & Bros., 1954, p. 9.
[146] W. Waller, "Social Problems and the Mores," *American Sociological Review* 1: 922–33, 1936.
[147] F. P. Gay, *The Open Mind: Elmer Ernest Southard, 1876–1920*, Chicago, Normandie House, 1938, Chaps. 10, 11.
[148] W. L. Russell, "The Widening Field of Practical Psychiatry," *American Journal of Insanity* 70: 459, 1913–14.

ment of uniform and responsible standards in education began to move forward. From the outset, the curricula of these schools were shaped by the practical and pressing demands of many agencies. Thus, there was a major emphasis on case work and on the preparation of practitioners to work in child welfare, family welfare, and medical and psychiatric social work. By 1930, there were four separate associations of practitioners—the American Association of Social Workers, the American Association of Medical Social Workers, the Visiting Teachers Association, and the American Association of Psychiatric Social Workers. In 1944, a new type of curriculum was adopted by the parent association when its curriculum committee recommended that "content in each of the following areas of subject matter be considered basic in the practice of social work in any area ... public welfare, social casework, social group work, community organization, medical information, social research (statistics and research method), psychiatry (human behaviour and psychopathology), and social welfare administration."[149]

This approach reflects considerable expansion, in both the range of function and the number of social workers. In fact, social workers were among the leaders in the mental health movement which began in the early 1920s, and subsequently many psychiatric social workers assumed administrative and consultative positions as executive secretaries or staff members of mental health associations on local, state, and national levels. During the Second World War, psychiatric social workers were called upon to function as consultants in various wartime services. Since the end of the Second World War, perhaps the strongest impetus for psychiatric social work has been provided by the development of state mental health programmes, following the passage of the National Mental Health Act in 1946.

Today, mental illness is recognized as one of the major public health problems of the country. Consequently, there has been a tendency to expand the functions of the psychiatric social worker. There has been a significant movement away from an exclusive concern with individual patients and their immediate families, towards a concern for developing methods to prevent mental illness and maintain mental health. Concepts and programmes have moved away from total preoccupation with psychoses and hospital treatment of the mentally ill, towards a concern for the health of the community. Early in their development, in addition to their work in hospitals and clinics, psychiatric social workers served as supervisors and consultants in social case work agencies in the family and child

[149] E. V. Hollis and A. L. Taylor, *Abridgement of Social Work Education in the United States*, Published for the Council on Social Work Education, New York, American Association of Social Workers, 1952, pp. 7–8,

welfare fields. As mentioned earlier, the field of public health nursing was one of the first to use psychiatric social workers as consultants. Today, the mental health nurse consultant has almost completely replaced the psychiatric social worker in nursing organizations. In a few cases, psychiatric social workers are employed in health departments. However, these assignments involve administration, education, and consultation primarily; the psychiatric social worker is not expected to provide clinical service.

In short, social work converged with psychiatry, absorbed psychiatric theory (particularly psychoanalytic concepts), and acted as a transmission channel for the implementation of these ideas in a variety of fields. While this has had some influence in bringing about an understanding of social situations involving individuals and groups, workers have also called attention to the severe limitations of such ideas. In 1942, Esther Lucile Brown regretfully observed that "so unwholesome is the environment in which vast numbers of persons live that the case-work method—time consuming and expensive—is, of necessity, limited to a mere fraction of those in need of treatment.[150] Miles' statement was even more incisive: "It seems futile to spend professional energy in attempts to adjust people who are living in slums."[151] Furthermore, one must recognize that the social agency is an element of our culture, and in its work may carry concealed moral judgements, clothed in an apparently neutral language derived from medicine. After all, there is no generally accepted state of social health on which all people agree. In this field, as in others that concern themselves with mental health and illness, it is imperative to examine and define the norms involved.

### The Social Sciences

Consideration of the social sciences, as they relate to the concepts and practices which influence mental health and illness, must begin with the realization that these disciplines comprise several diverse bodies of organized knowledge, each of which is concerned with a particular aspect of man's relationship to society. History, economics, and political science are the older members of the group; sociology, social psychology, and cultural anthropology are relative newcomers, although their roots reach back into the distant past. More recently, the latter three have been designated as the "behavioural sciences," implying that only these disciplines are concerned with human behaviour. Actually, all the social sciences are concerned with the

[150] E. L. Brown, *Social Work as a Profession*, New York, Russell Sage Foundation, 1942.
[151] A. P. Miles, *op. cit.*, p. 128.

hows and whys of human behaviour, but the point of departure differs in each case. We shall concern ourselves here chiefly with sociology, social psychology, and cultural anthropology, but attention will be drawn to such aspects of the other social sciences as are relevant.

Sociology, social psychology, and anthropology have traversed distinct and somewhat isolated routes of development. In over-simplified terms, sociology grew out of various currents of social reform and from theories intended to explain growth and change in society; social psychology resulted from early investigations of individual and group psychology; anthropology was based on the observations of geographers, travellers and explorers fructified by the theories of armchair evolutionists. Although these disciplines have travelled far since their beginnings, each bears characteristic ancestral features, and their relationship to public health and mental health is inherent in these characteristics. In recent decades, there has developed a distinct interest in applying the social sciences to community health problems. Actually, this is not as new as it sounds; in considerable measure, the social sciences have their roots in the health field. In a number of instances, areas which are of interest to social scientists today were developed initially by those concerned with public health, and this applies as well to methods of research. Political arithmetic, medical topography, and sanitary reform are some of the sources of the present-day social sciences, and Petty, Villermé, and Chadwick belong no less to the history of social science than to the history of public health.

Increasing maturation and knowledge led to a separation of the health sciences and the social sciences. Only recently have public health workers and social scientists become aware that their respective problems coincided in the same population, or that some piece of empirical research conducted by one group threw light on the problems of other groups. To date, the major contributions of social scientists to public health have been predominantly in research and, to a lesser degree, in teaching, consultation, and training. While any classification is manifestly arbitrary, in some measure, in general, social science research in the field of public health has tended to focus on three areas: the structure and cultural patterns of the community, as they affect the health practices and values of its members; institutions concerned with health; and the social dimensions of health and disease. Because of the obvious connections between mental illness and social, cultural, and psychological factors, and because social science investigations have been encouraged by mental health workers, there has probably been more research in this area than in any other.

315

Before 1920, anthropologists were not particularly concerned with either mental illness or psychiatry. While ethnographic accounts frequently contained some information on health and disease, data on the incidence, aetiology, and types of mental disorder among primitive peoples were very meagre. For the most part, anthropologists were concerned with culture in an abstract sense; their efforts were directed towards cultural traits and their distribution and the reconstruction of historical evolution, rather than current life situations. The individual either remained completely submerged or was of interest only insofar as he represented the locus of cultural concepts.

From the twenties on, however, rising recognition of the significance of the individual in the transmission of culture led to the study of personality theories. A new generation of anthropologists was concerned with the processes through which the individual came to embody his culture.[152] Accordingly, some anthropologists began to look for a body of psychological theory which might help them to solve the question of personality formation. Psychoanalytic theory exerted a considerable influence on anthropological thought. As a result of this influence, an interest arose in the deviants and abnormal members of our culture, as compared with the population of other cultures. Actually, psychiatrists had been much quicker to perceive the possible relevance of anthropological data for their investigations. A superficial glimpse at the writings of Freud and his colleagues will reveal the extent to which they drew an ethnological literature. A spate of articles was published which dealt with mental illness among non-literate groups.[153] Out of these tendencies grew an approach, combining studies of culture and personality, which has given an important stimulus to the anthropological study of mental illness, mental health, and related matters.

This trend was further strengthened by the employment of anthropologists as technical aides in administration. John Collier, as Commissioner of Indian Affairs, and the British, in their African

[152] E. Sapir, "The Unconscious Patterning of Behavior in Society," in *The Unconscious: A Symposium*, New York, Knopf, 1929, pp. 114–42; *idem*, "Cultural Anthropology and Psychiatry," *Journal of Abnormal and Social Psychiatry*, 27: 234–35, 1932; M. Mead, *An Anthropologist at Work. Writings of Ruth Benedict*, Boston, Houghton Mifflin, 1959; *Idem, Coming of Age in Samoa*, New York, Morrow, 1928; *idem, Growing Up in New Guinea*, New York, Morrow, 1930; *idem, Sex and Temperament in Three Primitive Societies*, New York, Morrow, 1935.

[153] E.g. E. Kraepelin, "Vergleichende Psychiatrie," *Zentralblatt für Nervenheilkunde und Psychiatrie* 27: 433–39, 1904; A. A. Brill, "Publokto or Hysteria among Peary's Eskimos," *Journal of Nervous and Mental Diseases* 40: 514–26, 1913; I. H. Coriat, "Psychoneurosis among Primitive Tribes," *Journal of Abnormal Psychology* 10: 201–208, 1915–16.

colonies, endeavoured to aid administrators by analysing communities and groups, and by gathering data which would help to resolve practical problems. Such problems as morale, psychological stress, social integration, and the like were dealt with from this viewpoint. The study by Alexander Leighton of a Japanese relocation centre reflected this orientation.[154] In the past fifteen years, there has been an intensified collaboration between anthropologists and psychiatrists, as evidenced by the research efforts of the Leightons with Kluckhohn, Bateson with Ruesch, Rennie with Leighton and Opler, Kardiner with Linton, and others.[155]

What has the anthropologist contributed to mental health concepts? First, he has provided data on the kinds of emotional and mental disturbances manifested in different cultural groups. Second, he has developed concepts which enable a better understanding of human interaction. Third, the concept of normality has been clarified in some respects (and made more complicated in others) on the basis of comparative cultural studies. Finally, anthropological studies can be used to test psychiatric concepts and hypotheses.

The sociologist's contribution stems from other interests. Early sociologists were concerned, in large measure, with social problems —poverty, crime, illegitimacy, immigration, insanity. They postulated a connection between these problems and particular aspects of the social environment; for example, the relationship between occupation and tuberculosis was emphasized. Out of these concerns emerged an impulse towards social reform which had a considerable impact on the early public health movement and on the beginnings of social work.

It was felt, as it had been for a long time, that social instability and maladjustment were related to mental disorder. And within this broad framework, attention was focused on the element of rapid social change as an important causal factor. Consequently, thought was given to the elaboration of methods to investigate these phenomena, so as to throw further light on the causation of mental disorder. Such studies began to make their appearance in the United States and England towards the end of the nineteenth century,[156] and

[154] A. H. Leighton, *The Governing of Men*, Princeton, Princeton University Press, 1945.

[155] For a fuller account of the interaction of anthropology and psychiatry up to 1944, see C. Kluckhohn, "The Influence of Psychiatry on Anthropology in America during the Past One Hundred Years," in J. K. Hall, G. Zilboorg, and H. A. Bunker, eds., *One Hundred Years of American Psychiatry*, New York, Columbia University Press, 1944, pp. 589–617.

[156] J. B. Andrews, "The Distribution and Care of the Insane in the United States," *Transactions of the International Medical Congress, Ninth Session*, V., 1887, pp. 226–37.

became more sophisticated in the twentieth century.[157] Concurrently, other sociologists were concerned with the laws which governed social organization and social change. This concern eventually led to the empirical study of community life. The work of the Chicago school, under the direction of Robert E. Park, and the efforts of W. I. Thomas and of Florian Znaniecki are pertinent in this connection. Thomas' famous "methodological note" introduced the situational theory of action and motive, the effect of social strains on personal integration, in terms of delinquency, mental illness, and other problems. In this context, Faris and Dunham later conducted their study on the spatial distribution of mental disorders in Chicago.[158] In a broad sense, this and various other epidemiological studies which followed have focused on the consequences of social disorganization. This problem and its relation to mental illness has been studied along a number of lines—in terms of age, sex, social class, occupation, social mobility, and social isolation.[159]

Throughout most of this period, a large number of sociologists were influenced by psychoanalytic theory. Similarly, some analytical psychiatrists were beginning to recognize the importance of cultural or situational factors in the neuroses and psychoses. In fact, from about 1915 to 1940. the preponderant theoretical currents were psychoanalysis and sociology. To this degree, sociology is not unlike anthropology, social work, and child health and welfare. This was part of a general trend, which resulted from various changes in Western society. Economic crises, institutional malfunctioning, and social disorder served to emphasize the fragility of civilized values, a fragility which had become evident after the First World War. It is said that today sociologists and social workers are concerned primarily with psychological maladjustment, and that this is symptomatic of a sick society.[160] Recently, however, sociological analysis has been directed to mental hygiene and its axioms as social phenomena; Kingsley Davis, for example, has traced these axioms to norms absorbed from the ethos of middle-class Protestant culture.[161]

Since the Second World War, a number of sociologists have also undertaken to test some of the hypotheses formulated on the rela-

[157] W. A. White, "The Geographic Distribution of Insanity in the United States," *Journal of Nervous and Mental Diseases* 30: 257–79, 1903.

[158] R. E. L. Faris, and H. W. Dunham, *Mental Disorder in Urban Areas*, Chicago, University of Chicago Press, 1939.

[159] A. M. Rose, ed., *Mental Health and Mental Disorder. A Sociological Approach*, New York, W. W. Norton, 1955.

[160] M. P. Hall, *The Social Services of Modern England*, London, Routledge and Kegan Paul, 1952, p. 8.

[161] K. Davis, "Mental Hygiene and the Class Structure," *Psychiatry* 1: 55–65, 1938.

tionship between child rearing and personality development.[162] Doubts have been raised concerning the importance of early experiences in determining adult personality, particularly as conceptualized in psychoanalytic theory.[163]

Social psychologists have concerned themselves with communication, perception, and attitudes, among other areas, as reflected in the work of Kurt Lewin, Gordon Allport, J. L. Moreno, and Muzafer Sherif. The studies by these workers on group dynamics and the application of sociometric methods have provided valuable knowledge to psychiatrists.

During this period, political scientists have also turned to psychopathological theory to shed light on problems of interest to them. Charles E. Merriam, of the University of Chicago, had sensed the potential importance of this area; his student Harold D. Lasswell, undertook to examine the topic in detail. Lasswell, as well as others, turned to psychoanalysis for this purpose. Since psychoanalysts had already invaded this area, especially in Europe, there was a meeting of interests. Attention has focused on propaganda, "brain washing," and so-called pathography, that is, psychological analysis of historical figures.[164]

Finally, mention might be made of the development by social scientists of methods for the collection and analysis of empirical data. These include field observation, interviewing, and surveys. These methods vary with the particular discipline. For example, social psychologists are inclined to employ data secured under conditions of controlled research design. Anthropologists rely heavily on field notes, based on their own observation of individual and group behaviour and on repeated, extensive interviews with small numbers of informants.

Efforts are currently under way to develop interdisciplinary research, under the auspices of such groups as the Institute of Human Relations at Yale, the Commission of Human Development at the University of Chicago, and the Department of Social Relations at Harvard. Obviously, interdisciplinary research presents certain

[162] W. H. Sewell, "Infant Training and the Personality of the Child," *American Journal of Sociology* 58: 150–59, 1952; W. H. Sewell, P. H. Mussen and C. W. Harris, "Relationships among Child Training Practices," *American Sociological Review* 20: 137–48, 1955; J. R. Thurston and P. H. Mussen, "Infant Feeding Gratification and Adult Personality," *Journal of Personality* 19: 449-58, 1957; J. W. M. Whiting and I. L. Child, *Child Training and Personality Development*, New Haven, Yale University Press, 1953.

[163] H. Orlansky, "Infant Care and Personality," *Psychological Bulletin* 46: 1–48, 1949.

[164] H. D. Lasswell, *Psychopathology and Politics*, Chicago, University of Chicago Press, 1930.

problems, but few of the problems that arise from collaboration between community health and the social sciences are unique to this specific area. They are, in fact, generic to all teamwork, whether it occurs within a single discipline or between two or more disciplines.[165]

Finally, the social sciences do not offer any panaceas for public health or mental health work. They have called attention to certain important areas which have a bearing on health and disease, and have contributed both knowledge and tools to enable our understanding of these areas. In some cases, these contributions require further exploration; others can be applied without question. Most important, we have yet to determine all of the areas of mental health to which social scientists can make an effective contribution.

## Schools of Public Health

The emergence of the public health movement in the United States did not immediately bring into being the school of public health. The earliest teaching in the field was carried on in medical schools, where public health was identified with, and was subsidiary to, bacteriology. Nor was this unreasonable in view of the fact that environmental sanitation and communicable disease control were the chief public health responsibilities, and effective action in these areas was based on a sound knowledge of bacteriology. As early as 1897, Hermann Biggs urged that physicians be trained for careers in public health and advocated the establishment of an organized school of public health.[166] In 1913, the Harvard Medical School and the Massachusetts Institute of Technology jointly organized the first graduate school of public health in the United States, under the sponsorship of W. T. Sedgwick, M. J. Rosenau, and G. C. Whipple. This joint effort was discontinued in 1922 for legal reasons, and each institution then maintained its own school.

In the decade from 1910 to 1920, according to returns from a nation-wide survey conducted late in 1918, twelve institutions, all of them medical schools with one exception (M.I.T.), offered formal instruction in public health, leading to some academic degree, usually the Dr. P.H. The first degree was awarded by Harvard in 1911; the University of Pennsylvania followed in 1912. Altogether, no more

---

[165] V. Bronfenbrenner, and E. C. Devereux, "Interdisciplinary Planning for Team Research on Constructive Community Behaviour," *Human Relations* 5: 187–203, 1952; J. W. Eaton, "Social Processes of Professional Teamwork," *American Sociological Review* 16: 707–13, 1951; W. Caudill, and G. H. Roberts, "Pitfalls in the Organization of Interdisciplinary Research," *Human Relations* 10: 12–15, 1951; M. G. Luszki, *Interdisciplinary Team Research, Methods and Problems,* New York, New York University Press, 1958.

[166] W. G. Smillie, *op. cit.,* p. 446.

than one hundred degrees (C.P.H., M.S., Diplomas, M.P.H., Dr. P.H.) had been awarded up to 1920, and the great bulk of these were from the University of Pennsylvania, Harvard University and the Massachusetts Institute of Technology. Moreover, during these first ten years of their existence, public health students from other countries, notably Europe and Asia, outnumbered those from the United States.

Until the twenties, training needs were conceived of in modest terms because the objectives of public health were themselves relatively modest, in that they focused chiefly on communicable disease control, environmental sanitation, and malnutrition. These problems were considered relatively simple aetiologically, and amenable to straightforward, technical, and authoritarian methods of control. As described earlier, seventy-five years ago, society turned to the physical sciences and engineering for the knowledge needed to deal with its health problems. It had little confidence in biology and medicine as protectors of community health. With the advent of the bacteriological discoveries, society placed the same faith in the biological sciences that it had related to the physical sciences earlier.

In those years, the physician and the engineer dominated the field of public health in more or less coordinate rank. Such special training as they received for their tasks was highly practical, and was secured chiefly through very short periods of apprenticeship, followed by long and tedious experience. Furthermore, no institution in the United States had fully adequate facilities for teaching public health.[167] Out of these needs, the School of Hygiene and Public Health was established at Johns Hopkins in 1918, to train public health officers. The curriculum comprised physiology, epidemiology, bacteriology and immunology, chemistry, medical zoology and protozoology, virus diseases, and vital statistics. Instruction in public health administration was included somewhat later.

However, during this period, the mental hygiene movement and activities on behalf of mothers and children were also expanding. One is not surprised to find, therefore, that mental illness was considered a public health problem from the outset. Indeed, as early as 1882, Henry Putnam Stearns urged all state boards of health to appoint one or more physicians "whose duty it would be to ascertain and make public reports upon the prevalence of such conditions as conduce to the production of mental disease."[168] Forty years later, James V. May, Superintendent of the Boston State Hospital, emphasized the fact that mental illness was a community problem, and

---

[167] S. Flexner and F. T. Flexner, *William Henry Welch and the Heroic Age of American Medicine,* New York, Viking, 1941, p. 353.

[168] H. P. Stearns, *Insanity; Its Causes and Prevention,* New York, 1882, p. 248.

that data were needed on the incidence and prevalence of the various mental diseases. He also pointed out that

> the New York plan of holding the health officer responsible for providing proper hospital care and treatment for mental cases not coming directly under the legal jurisdiction of other persons or officials is well worthy of serious consideration. There would appear to be no reason why the health officer should not be responsible for mental conditions in somewhat the same way that he is for communicable diseases. Nor is there any public official to whom the supervision of the insane pending commitment can more logically be delegated.[169]

In the years from 1915 to 1935, public health agencies were dealing with certain aspects of mental hygiene, chiefly in relation to maternal and child health, especially the period of infancy and early childhood. These activities reflect the developments sketched above. Moreover, there were intimations that public health officials would do well to broaden their concern with mental health. A number of schools of public health acted on this proposal.[170] From 1922, when the Harvard School of Public Health became independent, until 1938, the school offered courses in mental hygiene,[171] under the direction of C. Macfie Campbell, Professor of Psychiatry at the Harvard Medical School. The content of these courses dealt with the types of mental defect, delinquency, and child guidance. Opportunities were available for clinical instruction, for research, and for advanced work.

Similar courses were provided at the Institute of Public Health, London, Western Ontario, Canada, which had been established initially in 1912 by the Provincial Government. From 1922 to 1945, this school offered instruction in mental hygiene, as a required course for the D.P.H. In 1922–1923, B. T. McGhie gave a five-hour course, consisting of lectures at the Institute, and demonstrations at the clinics of the Westminster Psychopathic Hospital, where McGhie was Superintendent. In 1924–1925, the course was described as covering "the acquired types of mental disorder met with in the community; methods of examining and investigating mental cases; survey of the problem of primary mental defect and its relation to public health." In 1931, a course, entitled "Mental Health Clinics," was added. This consisted of seven hours of lectures and demonstrations, instruction on the operation of clinics, mental testing and

[169] J. V. May, *Mental Diseases. A Public Health Problem*, Boston, Badger, 1922, p. 62.

[170] The data which follow are based on the catalogues of the schools discussed. Data for Johns Hopkins were kindly made available by Dr. Paul V. Lemkau.

[171] Thereafter, instruction in mental hygiene disappeared from the catalogues and was not resumed on any appreciable scale until the late forties.

related matters. In the following year (1932), the catalogue of the Institute listed a new course—"Mental Hygiene"—comprising fifteen hours of lectures and demonstrations.

The curriculum content listed in the first prospectus for the Johns Hopkins School of Hygiene and Public Health, as formulated by William H. Welch, who had long been interested and active in the mental hygiene movement, and Wickliffe Rose, included mental hygiene. The first faculty appointment was not made until April 29, 1926, however, when Esther Loring Richards was appointed lecturer in mental hygiene.

In 1932, the Eastern Health District of the City of Baltimore was established as a research and practice area, to work with the Johns Hopkins School of Hygiene. While gathering statistical data on the District, Harry S. Mustard, the health officer, initiated the first epidemiological study of mental health in the area. Formal research on mental hygiene began at the School in 1934, with the establishment of the Mental Hygiene Study Group, comprising a psychiatrist (Ruth Fairbanks), a biostatistician (Bernard M. Cohen), and a psychiatric social worker (Elizabeth Green). Research conducted by the Group was the urban counterpart of investigations in rural Williamson County, Tennessee. Accordingly, the Eastern Health District was surveyed for cases of mental disorder, illness, or retardation, and the data accumulated was analysed with regard to age, sex, socio-economic status, and other variables. This original team was later replaced by Lemkau, Tietze, and Cooper, who continued these investigations.[172] The initial studies on the epidemiology of mental disorders in the Eastern Health District were followed by investigations of specific conditions. This work, chiefly under the guidance of Benjamin Pasamanick, Associate Professor in the Division of Mental Hygiene, focused on the relationship of maternal gestational history to the outcome of pregnancy and injury to the child's nervous system.

The mental hygiene teaching programme of the School of Hygiene became better organized after 1940. The first course relating knowledge of personality development to public health practice was given in 1941. Later, courses in the organization of community mental health services were added, as were clinical opportunities to work in the Eastern Health District and in community agencies. The Division of Mental Hygiene presented its first degree of Doctor of Public Health in 1941, and the first students to specialize in mental hygiene received their degrees in 1942. A course in military mental hygiene was initiated in 1946. In retrospect, it would appear that the establish-

[172] A Mother's Advisory Service, established by Fairbanks, has continued to the present.

323

ment of the Mental Hygiene Study Group marked a turning point in the recognition of mental health as an important area of research and instruction.

As early as 1930, C.-E. A. Winslow included mental health content in the public health course at Yale. Furthermore, during this period, students had some exposure to the work conducted at the Institute of Human Relations, through people like Brock Chisholm, E. F. Gildea, and others who had branched out from the field of psychiatry. However, formal teaching in mental hygiene did not begin at Department of Public Health of the Yale University School of Medicine until 1938, with the introduction of a required course in that academic year. Entitled "Psychiatry in Relation to Public Health," and taught by E. F. Gildea, Associate Professor of Psychiatry and Mental Hygiene at the School of Medicine, the content of the course was described as including "Lectures and discussion on psychiatry, its relation to medicine, to psychology, and in particular to problems underlying the development of various types of personality. The origins of health fads and of various healing cults are discussed." Ten hours in the winter and spring terms were devoted to these topics. In addition to the required course, the following electives were listed: "Seminar in Paediatric Psychiatry;" "Treatment in Psychiatry;" "Social and Cultural Problems in Relation to Psychiatry;" "Psychiatry in Relation to Public Health;" "Problems in Late Adolescence, with Special Consideration of Psychotherapy;" "Seminar in Legal Psychiatry;" "Biological Approach to Personality;" "Research;" "Psychiatric Dispensary."

From 1953 to 1959, the catalogues of the Graduate School of Public Health of the University of Pittsburgh listed various courses in mental health. In 1953–1954, courses in "Social Psychiatry," "Mental Health Problems," "Mental Health Conference," and "Industrial Psychiatry" were given by Dr. Taylor. The same courses were offered in 1955–1956, with the exception of "Mental Health Conference." In addition, there are "Field Work in Mental Health," and "Mental Health Seminar in Nursing."

In summary, then, the teaching of mental hygiene to students of public health began early in the 1920s at several universities. Since most schools of public health are less than twenty years old, one cannot expect to find many such programmes during the twenties and thirties. Moreover, the general impression is that the institution of these early programmes depended on the initiative of individuals. All of the early teaching in this area was done by psychiatrists, who had their academic base in a medical school. As far as one can determine from various catalogues, the content of the courses offered reflected the prevalent interests and emphases of the particular period when they were initiated. But some of the topics dealt with are certainly as current and pertinent today as they were twenty or thirty years ago. In general, teaching emphasized (a) consideration of the types of mental disorders, i.e. their prevalence, aetiology, and management; and (b) clinic organization and administration. In addition, some elective courses or seminars were available. Apparently, there was no organized mental health teaching unit; teaching was more or less an isolated effort, and was not truly integrated in the curriculum. The time setting is interesting in relating teaching developments to outside interests and pressures. Historically, these may be classified in three phases: the period up to the First World War, the period between the two world wars, and the period after the Second World War. The pressures from the community on psychiatry increased considerably following each world war. Perhaps the first teaching programmes can be seen in part as a reaction to these pressures.

## Conclusions

At present, schools of public health are contributing relatively little to the field of mental health, at least in comparison with other graduate schools (social work, medicine, nursing). In part, this may be due to the purposes which originally motivated the establishment of schools of public health; moreover, in all probability, the conditions which govern their financing have deterred their expansion into newer areas. In any event, we would do well to identify more precisely the major obstacles which have impeded the adequate development of educational programmes to enable students of public health to deal effectively with the community aspects of mental illness and health. Are they essentially ideological? Do they reflect a cultural lag on the part of the schools of public health? Or do these obstacles stem primarily from the fact that the content to be taught is vague and inapplicable?

The mental health movement and the concepts within which it has operated are diffuse and vague. Kingsley Davis' thorough analysis of definitions of mental health, as expressed in the literature, has shown that much of the work in this field "hides its adherence behind a scientific façade, but the ethical premises reveal themselves on every hand, partly through a blindness to scientifically relevant facts.[173] Eaton and Weil contend that "the concept of mental health is not a scientific but a value judgement."[174]

[173] K. Davis, *op. cit.*
[174] J. W. Eaton and R. J. Weil, *Culture and Mental Disorders*, Glencoe, The Free Press, 1955, p. 189.

Moreover, the goals of the mental health movement have tended to range all the way from the aetiology of disease to consideration of the causes of unhappiness; from the treatment of the mentally ill and aftercare programmes to the mental hygiene of daily life; from the management of well-understood mental disorders to the promotion of mental health. Some workers have expressed the opinion that mental health efforts should be devoted largely to the improvement of care for the mentally ill; that too much emphasis is placed on prevention, in view of the fact that available knowledge in this area is meagre. They further contend that only very modest preventive efforts should be undertaken within a public health framework. Others maintain that there are sound bases for preventive programmes in the psychiatric field, and that these warrant consideration by public health administrators.

Undoubtedly, some of the confusion is due to the lack of historical perspective. In other words, one must examine what is meant by mental illness and health at a given time, in a given place. This also involves a knowledge of the major physical, biological, and social theories which have prevailed from time to time with regard to the causation of mental illness. Action programmes are usually developed in terms of current concepts and theories of causation. And, in turn, the value judgements of society will determine, to a considerable degree, the emphasis placed on aetiological theories.

The competence of the psychiatrist to fill the role of mental hygienist raises additional questions. Within the field of mental hygiene, psychiatrists face new functions and goals; occasionally, they assume or are assigned responsibilities which they are poorly equipped to fulfil. They have been trained as medical practitioners, but they are moving from their therapeutic role to invade such areas as education, social science, and community organization. Indeed, many of the weaknesses in the mental hygiene movement reflect the deficiencies that psychiatrists have brought to it.

As a result, the opinion has been expressed that psychiatrists should not assume leadership in the mental health field; that other professionals, such as social workers or psychoanalytically oriented sociologists, are better equipped for this task, which calls for a knowledge of cultural history, sociology, and educational matters. Leadership in the field must be geared to the total community effort; the psychiatrist is fully qualified only in those areas which deal with treatment.

However, there is marked disagreement with this point of view: Other workers believe that the psychiatrist is best fitted to serve as leader of the team, since he has the basic knowledge and capacity to encompass more of the variables involved than any other member.

In answer to the concern which has been expressed regarding the psychiatrist's seeming unwillingness to assume leadership of the mental hygiene movement and his reluctance to direct it towards more modest preventive goals, this faction has pointed out that however much one discipline may know about education or the community, the problem in mental hygiene is basically one of aetiology. Leadership must, therefore, rest with those individuals who have the greatest knowledge and understanding of aetiology, namely, the psychiatrists, if efforts along these lines are to develop from sound premises regarding the fundamental nature and cause of mental disorder. In fact, psychiatrists are not alone in their relative ignorance of the social and preventive aspects of medicine, although their deficiencies in this area may be more acute, since the aetiological agents in mental disorder are less well defined than they are in some of the other medical specialties. However, most physicians who enter the public health field must go through an "unlearning" process, in order that they may acquire an "appropriate" point of view and approach. No matter what their specialty, physicians in public health must be interested in the social aspects of medicine; they must understand the natural history of disease and the underlying factors. In other words, they require a broad understanding of disease processes. rather than great therapeutic skill.

Just as the total prevention and control of most health problems are beyond the competence of medical personnel alone, the mental hygiene programme is too broad to lie within the jurisdiction of any one individual or profession. The many and varied aspects involved require the contributions of many other disciplines. Invariably, as the understanding of mutli-faceted aetiologies increases, a team effort is initiated. Leadership of the team should rest with the profession which possesses fundamental knowledge of the problems involved. Traditionally medicine has assumed the leadership in such efforts, and this would seem to apply to psychiatry and the field of mental hygiene. At the same time, there can be various levels of leadership, in relation to various areas of need and various degrees of competence among team workers. For example, where the emphasis is on the treatment of the emotional disorders of the individual, the responsibility clearly belongs to the psychiatrist. If, on the other hand, the problem is clearly an educational one, someone else might assume the leadership, with the psychiatrist serving as a technical expert. When one goes beyond the limited problem of diagnosis, one may find that more complicated problems of treatment and prevention involve various social problems which are not basically medical. Obviously, the psychiatrist can make an important contribution to the resolution of such problems.

327

The development of a more intensive research programme regarding mental disorders represents another pressing need. At present, except for federal programmes, very little of this type of research is being done in public health. Moreover, almost all of these scattered attempts at research in public health, as related to mental health, have developed within the last twenty years, which means that methodology is still being developed. There are many methodological difficulties, and these extend to the formulation of hypotheses. Public health workers have been relatively unsuccessful in their attempts to adapt their conventional methodology to psychiatric concepts. It is apparent that unless psychiatry can produce more manageable data, public health will have to devise new methods.

In summary, then, public health administrators are confronted presently with two major problems with regard to their participation in mental health programmes. First, they must determine those methods which are most likely to influence the prevalence of mental disorder. Second, they must determine the knowledge and competencies needed to implement these methods. Finally, in order that such public health programmes may prove effective over the long term, students in schools of public health must have an understanding of the factors which precipitate such problems, and they must be taught skills which will enable them to appraise their efforts and measure results.

We have reached a point where a number of disciplines are beginning to converge, where various orientations, developments, and interests are meeting in an effort to achieve a common understanding of the nature of mental health and illness (although with little agreement as yet). And public health workers appear to be coming to grips with their responsibilities in this area: An increasing number of public health workers are beginning to devote their attention to the identification of data which can actually be drawn upon, in terms of more or less precise categories and bodies of knowledge, for the content of mental health teaching in schools of public health. The efforts of public health workers have also been directed towards the resolution of the many uncertainties which characterize the field, in terms of the prevalence and incidence of mental disorder and its aetiology, and the development of effective research methodologies.

# ACKNOWLEDGEMENTS

The author wishes to express his appreciation for the financial support provided by the National Institutes of Health, U.S. Public Health Service, under project grant MH–03171. All the papers in this volume except two were supported by this grant.

The author also wishes to thank the following publishers and to acknowledge permission to reprint:

"Psychopathology in the Social Process" (originally published under the title "Psychopathology in the Social Process. I. A Study of the Persecution of Witches in Europe as a Contribution to the Understanding of Mass Delusions and Psychic Epidemics") from the *Journal of Health and Human Behaviour* 1: 200–211, 1960.

"Western and Central Europe During the Late Middle Ages and the Renaissance" (originally published under the title "The Mentally Ill and the Community in Western and Central Europe during the late Middle Ages and the Renaissance") from the *Journal of the History of Medicine and Allied Sciences* 19: 377–388, 1964, and "Irrationality and Madness in Seventeenth and Eighteenth Century Europe" (originally published under the title "Social Attitudes to Irrationality and Madness in Seventeenth and Eighteenth Century Europe") from the same journal, 18:220–240, 1963.

"Some Origins of Social Psychiatry: Social Stress and Mental Disease from the Eighteenth Century to the Present" (originally published under the title "Social Stress and Mental Disease from the Eighteenth Century to the Present: Some Origins of Social Psychiatry") from the *Milbank Memorial Fund Quarterly* 37: 5–32, 1959.

"Psychic Epidemics in Europe and the United States. Dance Frenzies, Demonic Possession, Revival Movements and Related Phenomena, Fourteenth to Twentieth Centuries" (originally published under the title "Psychopathology in the Social Process. II. Dance Frenzies, Demonic Possession, Revival Movements and similar so-called Psychic Epidemics. An Interpretation") from the *Bulletin of the History of Medicine*. This article constituted the Fielding H. Garrison Lecture of the American Association for the History of Medicine, delivered at the annual meeting, Chicago, 1961.

## Acknowledgements

"Psychopathology of Ageing: Cross-Cultural and Historical Approaches" (originally published as "Cross-Cultural and Historical Approaches") from *Psychopathology of Aging*, edited by Paul H. Hoch and Joseph Zubin, New York, Grune & Stratton, 1961. By permission Grune & Stratton.

"Patterns of Discovery and Control in Mental Illness," from *American Journal of Public Health* 50: 855–866, 1960. Copyright 1960, by the American Public Health Association, Inc.

"Public Health and Mental Health: Converging Trends and Emerging Issues," from *Mental Health Teaching in Schools of Public Health*, published by School of Public Health and Administrative Medicine, Columbia University, 1961.
Drs. James A. Crabtree, Martha M. Eliot, and Benjamin Pasamanick contributed memoranda suggesting material for inclusion when this chapter was being prepared for the conference on Mental Health Teaching in Schools of Public Health held at Arden House, New York, on December 6–11, 1959. The author is solely responsible for the chapter as written.

# INDEX

Adrenalin, 280
Aetiology:
    of various diseases, 113–14
      247–58, 259–60
    of mental disorder, 179,
      247–8, 255, 279, 291, 299,
      327
Aged:
    in ancient societies, 13, 67–8,
      231–6
    mental disorder of, 14, 122,
      229, 231
    in primitive societies, 230–1
    diseases of, 235–6, 238, 245
Ageing, 67, 229, 233–8, 243,
    245–6
Agoraphobia, 96
American Academy of Paediatrics,
    301
American Child Hygiene
    Association, 297, 299
American Orthopsychiatric
    Association, 285
American Pediatric Society,
    292
Anabaptists, 173, 202, 209, 211,
    214, 224
Anxiety, 8, 12, 31, 113, 118, 121,
    154
Aristides, 110–21
Arteriosclerosis, 244
Asclepius, 110–11, 114–20
Asthma, bronchial, 83
Asylums, 129, 139, 178, 190,
    276–7, 278. *See also* Hospitals,
    Institutions
Auditions, 53, 59, 60n, 215

Bacteriology, 180, 259, 264,
    270–1, 320
Beard, George M., 282
Beers, Clifford, 286

Bible (cited), 21–30, 31–3, 35–43,
    45–7, 52–3, 58–9, 61, 68, 98–9,
    104, 154
Bile, 74, 93, 145n, 238
Binet, A., 284
Brain, 186, 235, 242–4, 247,251–2,
    255, 256, 279–80
Brain washing, 319

Camisards, 209–12, 214
Cannibalism, 6, 10, 79, 100
Catalepsy, 55
Catatonia, 282
Catholic Church, 6, 7–8, 10, 12,
    150, 154–5, 159, 161, 168, 239
Child Study Association, 298
Child welfare, 265, 272–3, 288–303,
    313–14, 322
Child Welfare League of America,
    301
Children's Aid Society, 289
Children's Bureau, 273, 291, 295,
    296, 299
Classical authors (cited), 33, 71–3,
    75–82, 84–108, 110, 127–35
Clinics, 272
    Salpêtrière, 16, 163, 164, 253
    child guidance, 284–6,
        298–300, 302
    mental health, 322–3
Condie, David F., 288
Convulsions, 2, 204, 206, 219,
    220, 261
Cretinism, 258, 260–1

Dancing, 2, 103
    effects of, 23 and n
    ceremonial, 51 and n, 213,
      216, 221–2
    *See also* Frenzy, dancing
Darwinism, 291
David, 21–2, 25–8, 30, 32, 34–6